Eastern Cherokee Stories

Eastern Cherokee Stories

A Living Oral Tradition and Its Cultural Continuance

Sandra Muse Isaacs

Foreword by Joyce Dugan

UNIVERSITY OF OKLAHOMA PRESS : NORMAN

This book is published with financial assistance from the Faculty of Arts, Humanities, and Social Sciences at the University of Windsor.

Davy Arch, "Legends of the Uktena"; Kathi Smith Littlejohn, "The Cherokee Little People" and "Nunnehi, the Gentle People"; and Freeman Owle, "The Daughter of the Sun," "The Nikwasi Mound," and "The Trail of Tears" have been reproduced from Barbara R. Duncan, ed., *Living Stories of the Cherokee*. Copyright © 1998 by the University of North Carolina Press. Used by permission of the publisher. www.uncpress.org

All stories by James Mooney are reproduced from *Myths of the Cherokee and Sacred Formulas of the Cherokees*, by James Mooney (Nashville, Tenn.: Charles and Randy Elder–Booksellers, 1982), a reprint of the 1900 and 1891 editions of Mooney's work, which were published in the 19th and 7th Annual reports, Bureau of American Ethnology.

Library of Congress Cataloging-in-Publication Data
Names: Muse Isaacs, Sandra, 1957– author.
Title: Eastern Cherokee stories : a living oral tradition and its cultural continuance / Sandra Muse Isaacs ; foreword by Joyce Dugan.
Description: Norman, OK : University of Oklahoma Press, [2019] | Includes bibliographical references and index.
Identifiers: LCCN 2018051409 | ISBN 978-0-8061-6350-5 (hardcover) ISBN 978-0-8061-9012-9 (paper) Subjects: LCSH: Cherokee Indians—North Carolina—Folklore. | Tales—North Carolina.
   | Oral tradition—North Carolina. | LCGFT: Folk tales.
Classification: LCC E99.C5 I74 2019 | DDC 398.209756—dc23
LC record available at https://lccn.loc.gov/2018051409

The paper in this book meets the guidelines for permanence and durability of the Committee on Production Guidelines for Book Longevity of the Council on Library Resources, Inc. ∞

In memory of those who have crossed over:

Lenora Sellers Muse
(*agitsi*, my mother and favorite storyteller)

Edohi, Walker Calhoun
(community chief, Raven Rock stomp grounds)

Jerry Wolfe, EBCI Beloved Man
(fluent speaker and Cherokee traditionalist)

Contents

Foreword

Joyce Dugan

Principal Chief, Eastern Band of Cherokee Indians, 1995–1999

Throughout our Cherokee history, our ancient stories have been the essence of who we are. They have taught us how to understand and appreciate the world around us, including how we respectfully interface with plant and animal life of that world. I believe most, if not all, tribes have similar stories, which is why we have a reverence for all living things and are taught to respect and protect them. Most of our stories seem geared to the minds of the young, and as a former educator, I like to imagine inquisitive Cherokee children asking why we have mountains, why the bear's tail is short, why the possum's tail has no hair, why the buzzard's head is bald, and many more, and I then imagine the elders deriving a story to explain such mysteries. Thus, we have been gifted with wonderful stories that may have been attempts to respond to those questions and, in the end, have allowed us to delve into our ancient culture, a culture that has survived for centuries.

Sandra Muse Isaacs writes that "oral teachings encourage everyone to think of the whole community first and recognize our individual responsibilities within the group." This belief that the whole tribe comes before the individual has been practiced by our people as long as our history and is no doubt why we are still here after many efforts to annihilate and assimilate us. Muse Isaacs leads the reader to recognize how our stories taught this concept. With each story she presents, she shows how the story teaches us about *Gadugi*, the practice of helping the whole community, and *Duyvkta*, the belief that individuals have the responsibility to promote harmony, peace, balance, and kindness. Many scholars and researchers have gathered and studied our culture and our stories, but none have tied those stories to Gadugi and Duyvkta concepts.

It was my blessing in 1996 to initiate the purchase of Kituwah, our sacred Mothertown. At the time, the site was known as Ferguson Fields and was not accessible to our people, so its history was buried in the hearts and minds of those who knew the history. Truly, it was because of oral history, much of which was carried to Oklahoma by our Cherokee brothers and sisters, that we learned the importance of the site. If oral teachings are discontinued, our culture will be severely impacted. Thankfully, we have storytellers like those described herein who will carry the tradition forward.

Acknowledgments

It has been a true honor to learn from those Giduwah people who shared their stories and wisdom with me, like Kathi Smith Littlejohn, Davy Arch, Freeman Owle, Lloyd Arneach, Jerry Wolfe, Butch and Louise Goings, Bear Taylor, Chief Joyce Dugan, Walker Calhoun, Amy Walker, Pat Calhoun, Tom Belt, and Robert Conley. I'm lucky to have had these Elders in my life.

I wish to acknowledge the Cherokee storytellers from the Qualla Boundary in Cherokee, North Carolina, whose oral stories and narratives are the focus of this project. I was fortunate to be able to record their public storytelling events and transcribe the materials to analyze. They are Lloyd Arneach, Freeman Owle, Kathi Smith Littlejohn, and Davy Arch. Oral history narratives by T. J. Holland are also included from events held at the New Kituwah Language Immersion School. Many thanks to T. J. Holland for the videotape and DVD of oral history narratives recorded at the Junaluska Museum in the Snowbird community. I was lucky to take Cherokee language classes with Tom Belt (UKB) and hear stories every single week for two terms, and he is a big part of this sharing. Without this archive of Cherokee stories, this book would not have been possible. *Sgi* and *Wado*.

I had a great deal of help with the Cherokee language from community members during the writing stage, so a big thanks to Tom Belt, Louise Goings, Gil Jackson, Kevin Jackson, Mike Thompson, and Alitami (Emma Taylor) for your help during the writing stage. I appreciate you all. And thank you to Dr. Ben Frey, a linguist and assistant professor of American Studies at the University of North Carolina–Chapel Hill and an enrolled Eastern Band of Cherokee Indians member, for all your work on helping me with the final manuscript. Your language knowledge and attention to detail made me realize how much I've yet to learn. *Sgi ginali* (friend)!

Thanks to my friends and colleagues who have directed and advised me over the past few years, and for all those hours in discussion about my hopes for this project—Drs. Daniel Coleman, Anne Savage, and Mary O'Connor (McMaster University), Dr. Daniel Heath Justice—Cherokee Nation citizen (University of British Columbia), Dr. Chris Teuton—Cherokee Nation citizen (University of Washington), Drs. Alexander MacLeod, Gugu Hlongwane, Renee Hulan, and Russell Perkins (Saint Mary's University), Dr. Malissa Phung (Sheridan College), and Dr. Shar Cranston-Reimer. Special thanks to Dr. Barbara Duncan of the Museum of the Cherokee Indian and Dr. Brett Riggs, Sequoyah Distinguished Professor of Cherokee Studies at Western Carolina University. I appreciate all your encouragement and support.

Finally, this project would not have happened if not for my wonderful family—my husband, Kevin (Whoodat) Isaacs (Kanienkehaka, Wolf Clan, of the Six Nations), who has been my unwavering anchor of support and love over the months and years of PhD work and book revisions; my daughter, Constable Nicole Caal Bonilla (Karonhiakwas), who was always just a text away and has always believed in me; my son, Dalton Miller (Sgigi), whose common sense helped me see my way through the fog; my beautiful grandchildren, Leighton, Jacob, and Ellie; my sisters, Judy Muse, Bear Taylor, and Louise Goings—strong Cherokee women who have been there for me and taught me so very much. A special *Welalin* to my dear friend, adopted daughter, and future teacher, Buffy MacNeil Boutilier. And thank you to my TA at Saint Mary's, Luke A. Doyle, for all your help in transcribing stories from the recordings. You all have my love and respect. *Sgi* and *Nia:weh.*

All proceeds from this book will go to the Qualla Public Library and the Snowbird Public Library on the Qualla Boundary in Cherokee, North Carolina.

Eastern Cherokee Stories

Introduction

Adalenisgv ◆ The Beginning

My mother was a storyteller. She used to regale us with tales about her child-hood in a little wooden cabin in Trion, Georgia, a cabin made with red clay jammed between rough-hewn pine boards. The clay would wear out quickly from the weather and was replaced each spring. Mom said she could often slip her little hand between the boards where the clay had chipped out, and if it snowed, she could see and feel the flakes blowing through, sometimes on her face as she slept. Not that it snowed too often in north Georgia, mind you. We always thought Mom was an only child, but it turns out she had an older sister she never knew who had died before Mom was born. I guess the girl was just six years old when she danced too close to the outdoor cookfire and her dress made of flour sacking caught a spark. My grandmother did her best to save her, but Grandma was too late. That was Mom's saddest story. We never got to know our aunt, and Momma never knew her big sister, but a beautifully framed old hand-painted portrait of that sister and aunt hung in our house in Detroit.

Mom never thought she was very smart because she had dropped out of school in the third grade when the family needed her to go to work in the cotton fields. She said she used to drag along a burlap sack that was as long as she was tall and fill it. Picking cotton is hard work because the tough bolls that hold the cotton jab and cut the fingers and make them bleed, especially the tender fingers of a child. If one of us kids wanted to stay home from school for no good reason, my mother would tell that story. Then we would be sent to school. When my sisters and I complained about washing dishes for our family of fifteen, Mom would tell how she used to have to go out back to the creek and draw a bucket of water, heat the water on the open fireplace in winter or outdoor cookfire in summer, and then wash dishes in a tin wash pan on their rough wooden table in water that was as hot as her little hands could stand. She told us we were lucky to have running water, period. My grandmother had died when my mother was only two years old, and at some point, my grandpa sent her to his sister's family to be raised with her three male cousins. It was a hard, scrabbling life filled with extreme poverty and few physical comforts, and my mother learned to subsist on little. This came in handy while raising the thirteen of us.

My mother, Lenora Sellers Muse, often told stories to teach us a lesson or to explain to us just who our people are, what she knew about where our Tsalagi (Cherokee) and white Ancestors came from, and why we had southern accents even though we lived up north.[1] She told us how her dad had always kept quiet the fact that he was a mixed-blood who had moved to Georgia from Oklahoma's Cherokee Territory as a young man;[2] she never knew that until well after his death.[3] For the most part, her stories were somewhat hard for me and my twelve siblings to relate to, considering our upbringing in a racially divided black and white neighborhood in Detroit during the 1960s and 1970s. Our childhood was nothing like hers, as ours was filled with violence and walking a racialized tightrope daily. But Mom was the storyteller of the family and took that job seriously. I understand now that those family stories grounded me and helped shape my values and work ethic. They created a profound sense of pride in who I am and from where we originated. This sense of family and origin was hard to hang onto growing up in Detroit, far from both of my parents' families—grandparents, aunts, uncles, and cousins—who all lived in northern Georgia.

Both my parents' ancestors had come from what is now North Carolina and were a mix of Cherokee, Scots, and Irish. So, my father, John Muse, tried hard to hold tight to his roots and sense of self by returning every summer to the South, mainly to Dalton, Georgia, to visit his kinfolk and also to Cherokee,

North Carolina, so he could show us where the rest of the Cherokee people lived.[4] When our family became too large for us all to fit in the car, my dad would take two or three of us with him, leaving my mother behind each summer to care for the younger children. It was then that those of us lucky enough to go with him would get to visit all the old Cherokee historical sites in Georgia such as New Echota[5] and the Chief Vann house,[6] along with Red Clay Council Grounds in nearby Tennessee.[7] My father would take us to visit the Etowah Indian Mounds in Cartersville, Georgia, and explain that the People who built those mounds were the Ancestors of the Cherokees. He always got into arguments with the archaeologists who were excavating one of the three mounds, furious with them for desecrating the dead and disturbing the Spirits in this sacred ground. As a child, I remember feeling embarrassed and then later, as an adult, realizing how angry and passionate he had been about this desecration and how frustrated he must have felt seeing this horror and not being able to stop it. Then, going across the north Georgia mountains to Cherokee, he would tell us about the Trail of Tears and the sadness of the People who were forced to leave, and how many of them died on the way—whether from sickness, cold, starvation, or a broken heart. These stories, too, stayed with me as a child, and since I loved the beauty of the mountains and the red clay earth and always hated to go back to Detroit and our lives there, I would imagine and promise myself that one day, I would live in Cherokee and always have those mountains around me to protect and hug me tight.

That sense of origins and belonging to this southern mountain home stayed with me and, coupled with my mother's stories of her upbringing and her earnest longing to return to her southern roots, became deeply ingrained in my spirit, mind, and heart. It is to honor my mother that I went on my journey of higher education, eventually to arrive at the PhD level, which was my chance to collect and examine the oral stories of the Giduwah people of North Carolina.[8] My mother's stories inspired me in writing this book and gave me its overall aim, which is to show the enduring strength of the Cherokee oral tradition and how stories that are thousands of years old continue to define the modern lifeways and culture of today's Eastern Cherokee community. Oral stories have changed somewhat, evolving and adapting to the changing world around the People, but always proving to be powerfully vital and necessary for cultural and spiritual continuance as well as being a tool for self-preservation, sovereignty, and Indigenous nationhood in resistance to the colonizer government's patriarchal oppression and dominance.

Everyone has family stories that tell us who we are and where our ancestors came from; such oral memories essentially create our identities as individual human beings. Oftentimes, the storytelling role falls to an Elder in the family because he or she would have the largest store of family knowledge; this fact cuts across all racial and ethnic lines. Cree author Neal McLeod likens such oral stories to an "echo of older voices from a long time ago" (6). Stories teach us about religious beliefs and ceremonies, what our personal responsibilities are within our family and community, and even about the good fortune and hardships our people have had to endure just to get to the present day and living situation. Not only can these narrated stories inform people of their cultural and religious heritage, they also offer a form of countermemory and alternative history, which is particularly vital for colonized people as a way of physically and verbally "talking back" to the colonizer. Maori theorist Linda Tuhiwai Smith argues that for Indigenous peoples, that kind of talk "about the colonial past is embedded in our political discourses, our humor, poetry, music, storytelling and other commonsense ways of passing on both a narrative of history and an attitude about history" (19). It is one of the best methods of correcting the biased, one-sided historical accounts offered by colonial institutions. Such stories are vital for cultural and spiritual continuity and the sharing of a common background, whether within the family or an entire community. When I think back over my mother's repertoire of stories, I can clearly see from whom I am descended and what my duties are as a mother, wife, daughter, sister, aunt, and as a Cherokee woman. My mom was told she was Ani-Tsisqua, which is the Bird clan of the Tsalagi;[9] ours is a matrilineal and matriarchal clan system. The role of the Bird clan in the olden days was that of messenger or speaker. Since our villages were scattered throughout what is now the Appalachian mountain range on lands that now make up parts of seven southern states, it was up to the Bird people to carry messages and news from town to town.[10] Bird people always seem to be the talkers who have no fear of speaking in front of a crowd; we are often teased by the other clans for "chattering" too much. The Bird clan arbor at the Raven Rock Stomp Grounds is generally the noisiest. My mother would talk to anyone and was far from shy; she was so obviously a Bird person, as am I, with our gift of gab. This may be why I worked for years as a radio journalist and public speaker, along with being a college teacher and lecturer, and now a university professor. For most of my adult life, I have made a living from my words—both written and spoken—and it is nice to get paid for what you love doing.

Oral narratives are a method of communicating the past to people in the present, keeping alive the voices, memories, and traditions of the Ancestors. Cherokee writer Robert J. Conley explains that for Native people, storytelling is much more than entertainment or education.[11] "It is vital and necessary to continued life—the life of the tribe and the life of the world itself. Creation stories are told ritually to ensure the continued existence of the world" (*The Witch of Goingsnake* xiii). For the Tsalagi, these are not just the familiar creation and origin stories that explain how our mountain homeland was made for us, or how Selu, the Corn Mother, brought corn to the People, or even how the water spider delivered Fire to the Tsalagi (these will be examined in my first chapter)—these origin stories also explain the role of the various nonhuman creatures, how a particular town or community came to exist, why a certain name was given to a particular Earth place, or how a specific ceremony was born and how it is to always be conducted and who is to have this responsibility. Cherokees have been telling stories since the beginning of their existence and will undoubtedly continue to do so as long as there are Cherokees living, in order for us to always remember our connection to Mother Earth, for without that, we could not continue to exist. Stories are not only told by individual community-recognized storytellers but are often held and known collectively by a small or larger group of people within the community or tribe who have either witnessed or participated (or have a family member who has) in certain events that have had a rippling effect and deep impact upon the entire Tsalagi nation. It is these lesser-known intergenerational stories, some originary and some explanatory, and many contemporary, that interest me. The contemporary ones share how life and land for the People have changed since the European invasion and how the Cherokees have adapted, but I prefer not to call them postcolonial for that gives too much importance to the colonizer. It is better to see how the Cherokees have indigenized many of the inventions that the Europeans brought with them, and how very different the newcomers were compared to the Indigenous peoples of this land. And I have been curious about how the old stories are kept alive and how these ancient explanations of how things came to be continue to have relevancy for today's Cherokees.

After reading collections of Cherokee stories and oral narratives from Oklahoma scholars and storytellers, I wondered what newer stories and histories were held by the Eastern Cherokees that differ from what is shared and spoken of among the western bands (known as the United Keetoowah Band [UKB] and the Cherokee Nation). The year 2018 marked 180 years since the horrific and deadly forced removal that broke the nation apart and separated the Giduwah People, and even though the western brothers and sisters have kept the origin stories from the ancient oral tradition, newer ones based on their new home, its geography, and the land's spiritual attributes—along with those of other living beings—have come about and are told.

This evolution can be witnessed and read about in books like Robert J. Conley's *The Witch of Goingsnake and Other Stories* and his *Cherokee Medicine Man*, along with *Friends of Thunder: Folktales of the Oklahoma Cherokees*, by Anna and Jack Kilpatrick, and Chris Teuton's *Cherokee Stories of the Turtle Island Liars' Club*. These excellent works feature narratives of the Oklahoma Ani-Giduwahgi, which are rich and intricately connected to the newer, diasporic settings and communities, and give testament and insight into the political, spiritual, and social environment as well as the natural ecology of eastern Oklahoma.[12]

My project is intended to offer not only an examination of several of the origin stories that are the ancient markers for Cherokee culture and society overall but also to begin a scholarly discussion about the modern and post-Removal narratives and oral stories that are unique to the Eastern Cherokees within the sacred homeland. At this time, the only collection that offers a good number of the contemporary oral works by Eastern Cherokee storytellers, along with several modern retellings of the older stories, is *Living Stories of the Cherokee*, which was collected and edited by Dr. Barbara Duncan, a folklore scholar who works for the Museum of the Cherokee Indian. Along with that collection is James Mooney's books, *Myths of the Cherokee* and *Sacred Formulas of the Cherokees*, which the ethnographer compiled in the 1880s—more will be said about Mooney later in this introduction. It is hoped that this manuscript will provide some insight and understanding into the stories—both ancient and contemporary—that are the foundation of the unique culture of the Eastern Cherokees on the Qualla Boundary and the way the oral tradition continues to be a vital component of this community. The Qualla Boundary is so named because it is not a true "reservation" in the sense that the U.S. government did not allocate the land to the Eastern Cherokee;[13] instead, it is land that was purchased over several decades by the Ancestors of the current band members. The name Qualla comes from the ancient village that sat closest to what is now the "downtown" section of the land base or boundary.[14]

Before the arrival of European colonizers, every Native nation utilized the oral tradition for passing down the intricacies of culture, such as history, ceremonies, clan/gender responsibilities, spiritual duties, war and battle, song and dance, ancient art forms, food gathering and preparation, gardening and/or hunting, and all the other facets of communal life—a life lived within an interdependent natural environment. Too often, people have the mistaken notion that, once Indigenous people learned to read and write the colonizer's language, the oral tradition fell by the wayside. Most Native people, particularly those who grow up in their home community, know this is far from the truth. Modern Indigenous writers and scholars frequently point to the continuing life and vitality of the oral tradition, and many Native writers of fiction employ these ancient stories within their contemporary works—thus regenerating and giving the traditional story new life each time their work is read. Indeed, scholars like Susan Berry Brill de Ramirez, as described in *American Indian Literary Nationalism*, choose to examine written Native literature "from an oral center [that] comes from a conviction that oral storytelling is foundational to these literatures and, in fact, all literatures" (Weaver, Womack, and Warrior 22). The coauthors of this book, Robert Warrior (Osage Nation citizen), Jace Weaver (Cherokee descent), and Craig Womack (Oklahoma Creek-Cherokee ancestry), note that "Native storytellers never disappeared or ceased their telling" (23). This is abundantly clear within the world of the Eastern Cherokees, as my final two chapters will examine the modern usage of the oral tradition and its continuing vitality and importance within the Qualla Boundary community. Jerry Blanche focuses on oral tradition in his *Native American Reader: Stories, Speeches and Poems* and addresses the endurance and continuity of Native tribes' orality, despite the "bombardments of social, political, religious, and economic forces both from within and without Indian culture and society. It is this long-term ability to stimulate thought, challenge, enlighten, and provide alternative viewpoints that make wisdom stories so valuable today" (26). He chooses to call the tribal stories he has collected "wisdom stories," arguing this "is a better reference term than 'legend, 'tale,' 'narrative,' or the simple 'story,' because wisdom stories go beyond the singular intent to recreate real or imagined events and experiences" (22). When it comes to the wide array of Cherokee oral tradition, I, too, refuse to use terms such as "myth," "legend," or "tale"—this decision will be discussed further in my first chapter.

Having worked for many years in the field of radio journalism, where news stories are spoken and news script written "for the ear," I have always been fascinated by the power of the spoken word, the art of storytelling itself, and the way so many Native people are still compelled to use their oral skills to pass on cultural ways of knowing. The oral tradition of Turtle Island has garnered more and more attention by scholars, both Native and non-Native, over the past few decades, and many recognize the continuing life of all the forms of spoken word. In examining Anishinaabe scholar and author Gerald Vizenor's employment of the spoken word within his writings, Kimberly Blaeser notes that he "acknowledges not only the primacy of the word but also its place in the relationships that constitute an oral tradition. Storytellers (and, by extension, writers) are merely vehicles or voices for the words that have always existed" (18). Vizenor, an enrolled member of the Minnesota Chippewa tribe, White Earth Reservation, believes that the way Native people understand words as origin is closely linked to the power of thought and their understanding that "thought realized in words becomes creator of our reality," which he also links to our identity (18). Blaeser points out that this belief in the power of words and thought to actually create is not uniquely a part of early tribal stories, asserting that "past and present, words and thought are believed to have a certain power, and this power is enlisted to order all manner of things in American Indian life" (20). In their introduction to *The Way: An Anthology of American Indian Literature*, coeditors Shirley Hill Witt (Akwesasne Mohawk) and Stan Steiner note that "the spoken word contains a life all its own, an endless life. The spoken word does not fall to the ground, shatter, and turn to dust, in Indian comprehension. The spoken word is born, takes flight, and lives forever—always ready to be recalled if need be. And, when words have the value of immortality, one is careful not to use them haphazardly or falsely" (xxiii–xxiv).

Penny Petrone suggests that words have the sacred power to create or cause things to occur, such as helping the hunter in a successful hunt, using a medicine plant to heal, or causing food plants to grow well—quite simply to try and influence the cosmic powers that control life (10).[15] She goes on to note, "Words do not merely represent meaning. They possessed the power to change reality itself. They were 'life, substance, reality.' The word lived before earth, sun, or moon came into existence."[16] For a people who carried their history in the spoken word and incorporated their values in story and song, it was only natural for them to invest words with power and reverence. They relied on the ability to use and manipulate language—the fluent and artful use of words—to influence not only other people but also spirits" (10).

Petrone does a commendable job of examining the oral tradition as told by various First Nations storytellers in Canada; however, her analysis is overshadowed by the fact that she writes in the past tense and speaks of it as being something of the past, as seen through her book title, *Native Literature in Canada: From the Oral Tradition to the Present*. Such a title seems not to recognize the continuing vitality and power of that tradition today. My project contradicts such a notion, even though the telling of stories and narratives has been altered because of colonization and modern technology as well as by the modern use of English (or French or Spanish) as opposed to an Indigenous language. The power of the spoken word as a means of cultural production and regeneration is still with us today, especially in those tribes or First Nations that still have enough Native speakers in their communities, giving evidence of the "sanctity and imperishability" of the oral tradition (Hill Witt and Steiner xxiii).

I must note here that there is an ongoing discussion among literary and Native scholars concerning the way language loss and translation of ancient Native stories into English has also meant misinterpretation and misunderstanding of the true words—essentially a loss of meaning and Indigenous knowledge from so many old stories and teachings due to the imposition of a foreign language; this discussion is far too complex to thoroughly address here. Suffice it to say that I do agree with Acoma Pueblo scholar Simon Ortiz, who argues that Indigenous peoples have subverted the colonizers' languages—English, Spanish, and French—and "created a body of oral literature which speaks crucially about the experience of colonization" ("Towards a National Indian Literature" 9–10). Ortiz suggests that using the new foreign language does not destroy the authenticity; "rather[,] it is the way that Indian people have creatively responded to forced colonization. And this response has been one of resistance; there is no clearer word for it than resistance. It has been this resistance—political, armed, spiritual—which has been carried out by the oral tradition. The continued use of the oral tradition today is evidence that the resistance is ongoing" (10). I most certainly learned of the beauty and true meaning of Cherokee words and names when I took the course "Tsalagi Gawonihisdi Aksasdohdi" (the language Tsalagi we are speaking) and saw how English-translated words and phrases simply do not do justice to the Indigenous concepts and teachings.[17] The reality, however, for Eastern Cherokees is that the stories are learned, spoken, and transcribed in English for the most part, and in order to inform outsiders of the perpetual Indigenous affiliation with the land, it is necessary to translate Cherokee concepts into language that non-Cherokee neighbors will understand, thus fulfilling a political purpose through the continued use of the oral tradition. Also, this book project must be written and presented in the colonizer's language, so English will be the format presented here, with explanation of various Cherokee words, names, and phrases when necessary.

The power of Native orality and orature is astounding and physically moving, particularly because stories are told to a crowd of people; each of us experiences it in a collective fashion, rather than as an individual quietly reading a book in silence with no one sitting nearby and reading/hearing the same thing. While we learn many things from books, and most certainly gain much knowledge, reading is again more of a personal, interior experience rather than a communal one. When we listen to a storyteller, we partake in a ritual of sorts that prompts the uniqueness of group emotions, because if we laugh or shed a few tears, everyone witnesses those emotions, and that sort of audience participation can even influence how our neighbor reacts to the orature. A good storyteller can hold the attention and thus the minds and hearts of her listeners and influence them in ways they may not realize she could. Cherokee elder Kathi Smith Littlejohn says she especially likes telling stories to children, because they immediately react with their creative imaginations and completely immerse themselves in the action, quickly relating to the characters and their situations. Many people can remember childhood tales that were told to them by parents, and oftentimes hearing a spoken-word story can be comforting as we revisit those nurturing moments. As adults, we can hark back to childhood and physically and emotionally feel the story and its action. Listening to stories can alter or prompt behavior, create fear and apprehension, mystify, envelop one in a sense of comfort and serenity, teach a lesson, provoke tears of sadness or longing, cause laughter, introduce wonderment, and inspire curiosity. In his book *Orality and Literacy: The Technologizing of the Word*, Walter Ong refers to Bronislaw Malinowski who points to the way spoken words have power and a type of "magical potency" because "sound cannot be sounding without the use of power. . . . In this sense, all sounds, and especially oral utterance, which comes from inside living organisms, is 'dynamic'" (Ong 32). When we allow ourselves to become fully surrounded and immersed in the story, our imagination provides the pictures and action. Emotions and thoughts take control of our very being. We can feel the sacredness of certain aspects, begin to see the interconnectedness of nature and human beings, and come to a deep understanding of our individual roles and how we affect one another and all of life around us. In his foreword to the book *The Native Stories from Keepers of the Earth*, by Joseph Bruchac and Michael Caduto, Kiowa/Cherokee writer and poet N. Scott Momaday posits that stories within the oral tradition generally "center upon one of the most important of all considerations in human experience: the relationship between man and nature. In the Native American world, this relationship is so crucial as to be definitive of the way in which man formulates his own best idea of himself" (viii). This nature-based understanding allows for "an affirmation of the human spirit" (viii). Bruchac, who is of Abenaki heritage, expresses the belief that the traditional knowledge which Native people held for thousands of years came from the living experience of seeking balance with nature and all its creatures. He notes that the oral teachings urge people to always live in a sustainable fashion upon the Earth while considering the consequences of our deeds upon the seventh generation ahead. These teachings and lessons were not taught in books or in school but instead through the oral tradition and storytelling (ix–x).

In the case of Indigenous oral teachings, hearing and experiencing the strength of those words and their cultural signifiers can provide for a sense of belonging and community. When the stories are of olden or ancient times, we marvel at the resiliency of our Ancestors and begin to consider our own lives; we often realize how little we know, despite technology and instant knowledge through the internet, and understand how we should reconnect with the land and the many other forms of life upon Earth. With some stories, we may laugh at the ineptitude of humans and the awkwardness of trying to anticipate others' behavior and our own response. We cry for the fragility of human emotions, for the passion of love, for losses, and for the sadness of death because a good storyteller will affect listeners in this way. Ong discusses Freytag's pyramid concerning written plotlines and uses it to describe speech as operating with a linear rise and fall of climactic action, which has been likened to the tying and untying of a knot.[18] I suggest this visual could be applied to Cherokee spoken word more as a weaving and tightening of threads—reaching back in time and picking up cultural threads and pulling them forward to weave into the present time, thus intricately weaving and linking our Ancestors' lives with our own.[19] Such a method allows for the Ancestors to be present with us today and establishes a communal and familial connection and continuation along with a sense of self. For the Cherokees, this brings to mind two of the numerous ancient crafts still in practice today by the Eastern Cherokee—basket weaving and yarn finger-weaving—both beautifully colorful and intricate. A good storyteller can be thought of as a word weaver.

Talking stories are meant to be listened to with spirit, intellect, and passion. Throughout my life, I recall how, when given the chance to sit and hear about various Native teachings, I felt the excitement of knowing I would learn something new and be reminded of things I may have learned long ago and had too frequently forgotten. Certain Native speakers may instruct us not to record her or his words in any way—whether by pen and paper, keyboard, or electronic recording—but instead to listen with our hearts and our minds. We are told that recording the story removes the sacredness and power of the spoken words. These Elders know that too much of our brain and thought processes would be far too busy taking notes and writing, intent on scribbling down every word so that we would not have time to actually listen and feel. What is really needed is for the audience to simply sit back, hear the words, and absorb them with every part of the body and spirit.

As we sit and listen to stories and teachings, we may tense up when there is anticipation or anxiety; sometimes we are on the edge of our seat. Our body shakes with laughter or trembles with sorrow and tears. Our gestures and body language are evidence of allowing ourselves to become fully enveloped and involved in the story, sometimes relating to and perhaps becoming one of the characters ourselves. Some of us may hark back to our youth and the pure joy and excitement of listening to our mother or father sitting and telling us a bedtime story. Simpler times. Often happier times. For the time that we are listening to a story, we can suspend reality and allow the words to pour over us, immersing us in the strangeness and unfamiliarity of it or in the shared experiences, familiarity, and commonality. Oral stories hold a unique and sometimes elusive power that can often defy explanation. We are accustomed to books with their physical text, which we can reread when we do not comprehend quickly or when we lose our train of thought. Talking stories oftentimes allow for just one chance to hear the words and grasp the meaning, and this is why we must block out all extraneous noise and activity and focus on the talking story, although with some storytellers, there is a certain amount of repetition involved in the telling so it sticks in our heads better. Phrases may be said over and over in the same way or in a paraphrased manner to bring the listener back to the action at the transitional stages of a story, and without a hard-copy text we must pay close attention. Listening to oral stories truly involves our entire being, as we react in more physical ways to an animated storyteller than when we read a book, using only our imagination and mind as we sit quietly.

Ironically, then, for the purposes of this project, it was necessary to electronically record and then transcribe the oral stories, narratives, histories, and teachings of the Eastern Cherokee storytellers as well as to work with existing collections of transcribed oral interviews and works.[20] This is indeed problematic in the fact that reading those stories is clearly not as emotionally and spiritually powerful and enjoyable as hearing them and witnessing the performance of a knowledgeable storyteller. As noted by Renee Hulan and Renate Eigenbrod in their book *Aboriginal Oral Traditions: Theory, Practice, Ethics*, "The process of writing down oral stories adds layers of meaning through recording, transcribing, translating and editing for the page, and the damage that can be done when stories are recast through this process is well known. Interpreting oral stories on the page means uncovering each of these layers" (9). This is why I have created an archive of the visual and aural recordings that I was fortunate to gather.[21] Since a book must be a written document, this is the only process that allowed me to collect and examine the oral tradition of the Eastern Cherokees, and I respectfully hope it is effective. This project relied heavily on a number of resources, such as the video recordings I made of public storytelling events; CDs and cassette tapes made by individual storytellers and gifted to me; transcriptions of interviews with community Elders; written notes from cultural and historical sharing at community meetings; lecture notes and recorded CDs from the Cherokee language classes that I attended; published collections of transcribed stories, most notably the Duncan and Mooney books; and DVDs and VHS tapes produced by the Junaluska Museum in Robbinsville, North Carolina.[22] I must admit that although this collection may sound fairly comprehensive, I feel I have barely scratched the surface of the entire set of stories that lie within the hearts and minds of so many Eastern Cherokee people, for many do not think of themselves as storytellers, simply because they do not perform and speak in a public forum but rather tell their narratives and stories at family functions and everyday community social interactions and events. I believe there is a wealth of such stories out there, and my fear is that so many will be lost when the community loses each of these Elders; indeed, that is already happening as ninety-three-year-old EBCI Beloved Man Jerry Wolfe passed over in the spring of 2018.

When considering my research topic, I wondered about how this particular Native community has held so tightly to the oral tradition, what Jay Hansford Vest calls "Native *residual orality*" (6). A number of factors would lead one to expect the members of the Eastern Cherokee community on the Qualla Boundary to lean more heavily on the written word. The scholar Sequoyah, who had no formal education and was essentially illiterate (in the English language) as well as disabled—most likely from a hunting accident—developed a writing system known as a syllabary,[23] and within two years of its introduction in 1821 (prior to Removal), the entire Cherokee nation became fully literate and able to read and write in their own language. The syllabary has eighty-five symbols to represent each sound or syllable in the Cherokee language. This invention led to the creation of a Cherokee constitution and in 1828 America's first Native bilingual newspaper, the *Cherokee Phoenix*, a remarkable achievement. His-torians Theda Perdue and Michael Green refer to the invention and adoption of the Sequoyah writing system as an "expression of Cherokee nationalism" (14), and I suggest that its usage today is a testimony to continuing Cherokee nationalism more than 190 years later.[24] Anna and Jack Kilpatrick address the fact that "Sequoyah is so highly revered by the Cherokee people that some elders even believe he will come back some day. . . . It is highly significant that the national hero of the Cherokees was an intellectual, not a warrior" (*Friends of Thunder* 180). The syllabary continues to be used today, although there has been tremendous language loss among the Cherokees as there has been among all Indigenous groups in North America and around the world, but the Cherokees were the only Native group to develop their own writing system, and this is indeed a source of pride.[25] In addition, the Cherokee syllabary was the first Native language to be adapted for use on Apple products, such as iPhones, iPads, and computers. Several language and cultural specialists from the Cherokee Nation in Oklahoma, such as Joseph Erb and Roy Boney, worked with Apple for three years to create ways for the syllabary to be made applicable for these technological devices. Language-immersion students have been able to type and use the syllabary on their Apple computers in school since 2010 (Murphy 2010). The Eastern Band, which is considerably smaller than their counterparts in Oklahoma, has fewer than three hundred language speakers on the Qualla Boundary, and most can read and write the Sequoyah syllabary; children who attend the New Kituwah Academy, which started as an immersion school in 2004, also learn to speak, read, and write in Cherokee. Since the language is being revitalized, more and more Eastern Cherokees are learning to speak their own tongue[26] and thus have varying degrees of fluency and literacy.[27] The original *Cherokee Phoenix* newspaper, which launched in 1828,[28] was printed in both Cherokee and English, and the newspaper office and press were located in New Echota, Georgia, the last capital of the nation prior to Removal. Today the *Cherokee One Feather* informs band members of the EBCI of local news as one of America's oldest Native weekly newspapers; it celebrated its fiftieth anniversary in 2015.[29]

The Qualla community is not only highly literate (in both English and some in written Cherokee),[30] with three tribally owned schools for K–12 and the New Kituwah Academy immersion school, but computer literacy is also fairly widespread and comprehensive. The tribe—its departments, agencies, and businesses like their profitable bingo and casino operations—is the biggest employer on the reservation, and all employees are required to have a high school diploma or college degree (depending on the job) and computer skills. The IT department of the tribe employs highly trained tribal members and others who ensure the reservation-wide network is kept up-to-date and maintained by mobile technicians. There are two tribally owned public libraries on the Boundary and a library in each of the three public schools. The staff and parents at New Kituwah Academy have worked to develop books and resource materials for their students in the Sequoyah syllabary, and these children also learn to read and write English, as the Cherokee school system must abide by North Carolina state educational mandates. So, there are many reasons why the Eastern Cherokee community, as a literate and technologically modern Indigenous society, should have little need or place for a thriving oral culture; however, there are a number of reasons why this society continues to rely heavily on the power of the spoken word.

The Qualla Boundary is, in a sense, geographically isolated because of the surrounding mountains, which range from 5,000 to 6,000 feet above sea level. While most Americans enjoyed radio and television for the decades following the initial introduction of these modes of communication, those Cherokee mountains prevented radio and television signals from reaching the Qualla Boundary, which stretches throughout several valleys and in and out of the coves surrounding those mountains. It was not until cable was laid across the reservation in the early 1980s that some households began to enjoy the luxury of entertainment programming and news. Satellite signals now allow for the same access to radio and TV programming that any other community gets in the country. Yet up until this point, if Cherokees wanted to find out what was happening in their community, they relied mainly on word of mouth. After all, the *Cherokee One Feather* hits the newsstands only once a week, so when news or social events happened on or near the Boundary, people got their information from others in their family or community. There is an old joke that is quite applicable in Cherokee: if you want to spread the word about something, simply "telephone, telegraph, or tell an Indian."[31] Another old phrase that many Cherokee people refer to is the so-called "moccasin telegraph," which harks back to ancient times when runners took news and information from one Cherokee village to another.

This reliance on the spoken word continues today with most Cherokee households having a police monitor so that the entire family can hear the police, ambulance, and fire calls. Some may call this gossiping or curiosity, but it is part of the reliance on orature that is simply ingrained within the Eastern Cherokee culture, along with caring about one's neighbor. This is also why weekly tribal council meetings are televised—people feel the need to know, and they prefer to hear it for themselves. Some people I know have even suggested that when something happens, they would rather call someone and find out for themselves rather than rely on the tribal newspaper, which is under complete editorial control of the chief and council, like most other tribal newspapers across the land.[32] It is also interesting to note that there are several published writers from the Eastern Cherokee community. Those who have published tend to write things like poetry, historical fiction and nonfiction, cookbooks, children's literature, and collections of the old origin stories; this includes B. Lynne Harlan, who is the public relations coordinator for the EBCI, and Annette Saunooke Clapsaddle, former director of the Cherokee Preservation Foundation.[33] Yet even though people are literate and the Eastern Cherokee community has access to the written word in all its modern media, a firm reliance on orature in all forms is very much part of the evolving Tsalagi culture and lifestyle in the ancient territory.

These long-spoken stories offer testimony of the indigeneity of the Eastern Cherokees to the mountain homeland in the South. Spoken stories about the tribe's origin, which precedes the physical creation of the Earth, give a human voice to the nonhuman beings, the elements, the Sky World, the plant creatures, as well as the Cherokees themselves and present the earthly reality of how the Ani-Yunwiyah, or Real Human Beings,[34] learned how to live and walk in a respectful and harmonious fashion with the rest of Creation. Whenever something or someone upset that delicate natural balance, it affected many in a disruptive and negative fashion until a solution was found that restored everything and everyone to a good way of living, known as *Duyvkta* or "right path." I will discuss Duyvkta as a truly unique Cherokee concept later in this introduction.[35] The oral teachings and knowledge conveyed in the stories give numerous examples of how closely connected the Kituwah culture is to the specific environment of the southern mountains known now as the Appalachian system. Hearing these stories gives the listener a sense of how important it is to the Eastern Cherokees to maintain their home in this land base, as their very lifeblood runs with the fast-running mountain springs and rivers and their hearts beat with the rhythm of the Earth seasons. Listening to these ancient words can impress listeners—Cherokee and non-Cherokee alike—with an understanding of the Cherokees' deep and abiding belief that this land was created specifically for them and the thousands of creatures who reside there.

Ethnologist James Mooney

We cannot examine the oral tradition of the Eastern Cherokees without discussing the large body of stories, historical narratives, and "sacred formulas" collected by ethnologist James Mooney in the 1880s on the Qualla Boundary. This collection, though problematic for a number of reasons, is the most extensive set of translations from Cherokee to English of the oral offerings of Cherokee storytellers from the Eastern Band to date; indeed, I agree with Bo Taylor, former archivist and now director of the Museum of the Cherokee Indian, who in a personal conversation referred to the Mooney book as the "bible" of Cherokee stories. The modern storytellers with whom I have worked have each referred to Mooney's *Cherokee History, Myths, and Sacred Formulas* at various times throughout their artistic careers for clarification or simply to compare the written version of a story with the spoken one that they have themselves learned from their mentors. Needless to say, the Eastern Cherokee community has acknowledged their collective indebtedness through former Principal Chief Michell Hicks in his foreword to the 2006 edition of Mooney's book. Hicks says, "James Mooney has preserved for the Eastern Band of Cherokee Indians an invaluable source of Cherokee knowledge, wisdom, and practices. To this day, we look back at his 1880s work and appreciate its dedication to authentic Cherokee lifestyle and language. Mooney worked closely with our people in order to better understand, with little judgment, our culture. Because of this, his complete works on the Eastern Band stand today as one of the most important documents on Cherokee history and culture ever published" (no page number).

Mooney's original manuscripts, known as *The Sacred Formulas of the Cherokees* (1891) and *Myths of the Cherokee* (1900) were originally published in the seventh and nineteenth annual reports of the Bureau of American Ethnology. For many years, the Mooney manuscript was only available through the Smithsonian, with copies held at particular university libraries,[36] and it was not until 1982 when a full version of his combined manuscripts was reproduced and published—a total of 672 pages of small print—that it was finally available for public perusal after the Museum of the Cherokee Indian worked with others on that first edition in 1982 and a second edition in 2006.[37]

James Mooney was the son of Irish immigrants and grew up hearing his mother tell stories of fairies, spirits, and little people, along with historical readings about the ancient Gaelic kings of Ireland.[38] The boy also listened to oral stories from the Irish soldiers who returned from the Indian wars and the Civil War. Hearing those stories sparked an interest in American Indian tribes that he carried into adulthood. Despite his lack of formal training of any kind, Mooney tried for several years to get a job with the Smithsonian Institution's newly formed Bureau of Ethnology,[39] hoping to impress the agency with his written work on Natives, and was finally hired in 1885.[40] He spent the next two summers on the Qualla Boundary, sitting in as interviews were conducted with Principal Chief Nimrod Jarrett Smith. These early interviews led Mooney to his fieldwork among the Eastern Cherokees from 1887 to 1889 that saw him learn the language and live with the People as he "recorded all that he could about beliefs, history, mythology, places, religion, and ritual" (Duncan, "Introduction" 4). Despite the Cherokee belief that certain sacred things should not be shared with anyone who is not of the tribe, and the strong insistence by the medicine people in the community that their personal healing knowledge was not meant for anyone other than themselves, Mooney persisted and found ways to cajole and bribe these healers with money, at times even threatening to get the formulas from a different medicine man, essentially pitting one against another in his quest for information. Barbara Duncan from the Museum of the Cherokee Indian notes, "He discovered that the traditional way of obtaining information was to either pay for it or exchange information of equal value. This led him to exchange some of his knowledge of Irish folk medicine, and at one point, presumably carried away by his enthusiasm for getting information, Mooney claimed to one shaman that he could raise the dead, and that he would share this information in exchange for Cherokee formulas. Mooney performed part of the ceremony, and then claimed that he needed water from Ireland to complete the ritual. Needless to say, such methods would be considered unethical today" (Duncan, "Introduction" 6). Many Cherokees of that time period, as well as the present, believe that sacred Indigenous knowledge should *never* be written down and should only be shared through oral teachings with those who are respectful and deserving of such learning—and such a decision can only be made by the knowledge holder. It is also believed that such medicine and healing formulas cannot be learned from a book, so "whether Mooney's published formulas are accurate or not, according to this belief, is irrelevant, because they can't be used anyway" (Duncan, "Introduction" 11). It is interesting to note that long before the term "cultural appropriation" became known, these carriers of Indigenous knowledge knew it was unwise to share sacred information with someone outside of the culture, especially one who persisted and demanded in the way in which Mooney did.

Mooney found out that the Cherokee medicine people wrote down their formulas and knowledge of medicines in books using the Sequoyah syllabary.

This was surprising to him at first, because healers of other Native tribes did not have this capability, so it was helpful that the Cherokees were literate in their own writing form. Mooney was able to convince Ayvini (Swimmer) to share his personal book, even though other medicine men tried to discourage Swimmer from doing so, because they were afraid the formulas would lose their power if written down and taken away to Washington (Duncan, "Introduction" 5). Mooney writes of how he was able to persuade Swimmer, who had shared the story of the People who became bears, to teach Mooney the songs to attract bears. Swimmer did not want to sing the songs after he told the story, but Mooney went back the next day and "Swimmer was told that if he persisted in his refusal it would be necessary to employ someone else, as it was unfair of him to furnish incomplete information when he was paid to tell all he knew" (Mooney, *Sacred Formulas of the Cherokees* 311).[41] Some would call this persuasion, others coercion, or possibly bullying and threatening. Mooney did point out to Swimmer that the purpose for copying the formulas was to preserve them for the future, when all the medicine people were dead and gone, so that the world would know just how wise the Cherokees were; this evidently persuaded Ayvini (311). The ethnologist worked with several storytellers and medicine people, but he got the most information from Swimmer. The other knowledge holders included Itagvnahi (John Ax), Tagwadihi (Catawba Killer), Suyeta (the Chosen One), Ayosta (the Spoiler),[42] Chief Nimrod Jarrett Smith, Tsesani (Jessan), David and James Blythe, and Tsuskwanvnawata (James D. Wafford). He also used Will West Long,[43] who was a teenager at the time, and James Blythe as interpreters. In later years, Mooney added a number of other storytellers and medicine people, finally completing his manuscript in 1900 and publishing it later (Duncan, "Introduction" 5–6).

While living on the Qualla Boundary for my research, I consistently heard the same sort of comments from local Cherokees about Mooney anytime the topic came up in conversation, and that was that they had always been told that the medicine people only told Mooney what they wanted him to hear in regard to medicines and healing formulas, and that those Ancestors were very selective about sharing stories as well, simply telling Mooney certain parts of a story, rather than the complete version. Along with that, as storyteller and mask-carver Davy Arch points out in discussing Mooney, "he put a spin on a lot of things" and was thought to distort what he had been told, whether intentionally or through translation mistakes (Personal interview). The more time the ethnologist spent on the Boundary, the more he became respected by and respectful of the People, and, needless to say, his views of Natives changed over the years. It is not surprising, though, that when Mooney started his ethnology work, he held the same Eurocentric perspective that his colleagues at the bureau had about Natives, viewing them as "'primitives' or 'savages' [who] reflected an earlier stage of European cultures, and these 'survivals' could shed light on the 'hidden past of present civilized society'" (Duncan, "Introduction" 11). After living with the Cherokees for several years, Mooney went west and studied the Kiowa tribe. Clearly taking a paternalistic view of them, he wrote in 1898 that "The savage is intellectually a child, and from the point of view of the civilized man his history is shaped by trivial things" (Lincoln 7). Then, concerning his examination of the Cherokee stories and storytellers, Mooney writes, "There is the usual number of anecdotes and stories of personal adventure, some of them irredeemably vulgar, but historical traditions are strangely wanting. The authentic records of unlettered peoples are short at best, seldom going back much farther than the memories of their oldest men" (*Myths of the Cherokee* 231).

Clearly, the ethnologist underestimated the endurance and depth of the Tsalagi oral traditions, because these stories and histories are handed down from generation to generation and held communally, so his statement is grossly inaccurate. In contrast, after living for just one year on the Qualla Boundary, Mooney wrote in his 1888 article on the tribe that "the Cherokees are undoubtedly the most important tribe in the United States, as well as one of the most interesting" (*Myths of the Cherokee* 97). However, Mooney's article in the *Journal of American Folklore* published in 1890 entitled "Cherokee Theory and Practice of Medicine" has him writing of how superior white doctors are to those medicine men. "A moment's reflection," he writes, "must convince any intelligent person that the skill of the Indian doctor, whose knowledge is confined to the narrow limits of a single tribe . . . is not to be compared with that of the educated physician who has devoted years to study under trained specialists, who has the whole world as a pharma-copoeia" and adds that, in truth, a common farm wife knows as much of herbal medicine as these medicine men and are far better at nursing and patient care than the Indian (44). As the years went by and his perspective changed, Mooney became an advocate for not only the Cherokees but for all tribes; in particular, he pushed for fair treatment and religious freedom, helping draft the first charter for the Native American Church.[44] He became concerned over the high death rate among Eastern Cherokees and asked the Bureau of Indian Affairs for a medical intervention; this became the first time Western medicine was formally introduced on Cherokee territory (Duncan, "Introduction" 8). His advocacy for religious rights created enemies for him among some missionaries and Indian agents, who demanded that the Bureau of Ethnology recall him to Washington; in one instance, Mooney managed to leave the Kiowa reservation before agents could arrive to arrest him (Duncan, "Introduction" 9).

Over the years, the ethnologist made many return trips to visit his Cherokee friends, who had echoed his English name in their language with the name Nvdo (Moon). Despite his early questionable ethics and methods in obtaining the oral stories and formulas, he had made lasting friends with many of his informants and began bringing his wife and family with him on these trips back to Qualla. Mooney is still recognized as having done a tremendous service for the Cherokees, and "it is obvious that his work can never be duplicated, but only revered for its contributions to ethnology and Cherokee history" (D. King, "James Mooney" 7). While spending the last few years listening to the stories and working to examine them, I have experienced conflicted feelings about James Mooney and his tactics and occasional spurts of patronizing writings, even as I compare those against the wealth of good he has done with his meticulous recording of the Cherokee oral tradition and lifeways at that time. I admit that overall, despite the lack of respect he demonstrated at times, his collection is such a remarkable and enduring contribution to the continuance of the Giduwah culture that we must all be grateful.

———

In his book *Red on Red: Native American Literary Separatism*, Craig Womack points to the need for Indigenous scholars to examine Native literature from a more tribally specific focus and thus through their own nation's lens. Just as he uses a particular Creek-Cherokee perspective in his own scholarly approach to various Indigenous works, he states his "greatest wish is that tribes, and tribal members, will have an increasingly important role in evaluating tribal literatures" (1), which would include those oral works that helped birth many written works. His suggestion takes Native literary criticism a step further than examining Native word art from a still-formulating set of theories that are uniquely Indigenous in nature but somewhat pan-tribal, as it can be difficult to create Indigenous literary theory that can cover the wide array of cultures, languages, histories, geographies, and spiritualism. Daniel Heath Justice has accomplished this tribal focus in his book *Our Fire Survives the Storm: A Cherokee Literary History*, in which he applies his own uniquely Cherokee perspective as a citizen of the Cherokee Nation of Oklahoma. Taking a cue from Womack's reading of the Red Stick Warrior Society of his Creek people, Justice reaches back in time to when many of our Giduwah villages were established as "White towns" and "Red towns," with white being the peaceful, harmonious path that avoids warfare and red being the color of war. A deeply complex system of governance and ceremonies surround this binary, with Beloved Men and Women and clan mothers deciding on matters of warfare, and chosen red chiefs implementing the strategy of battle or the white chiefs negotiating to maintain peace at all costs with neighboring tribes.[45] (It should be noted that quite often, a game of stickball was played against the enemy tribe in order to settle contentious issues.) Justice examines how various contemporary Cherokee Nation and UKB writers exhibit within their written literature their own personal red path or white path personalities and writing styles or, in some cases, a mixture of both. This is an effective critical method and one that demonstrates a unique aspect of Cherokee culture that remains a part of modern memory for the Giduwah people. He notes that his book "is a work of tribal nationalism . . . and takes for granted the primacy and centrality of Cherokee and other Native voices to the analysis" (8). Accepting the idea that some readers might think of his book as an essentialist text, Justice states that he "offers no apologies for placing Cherokees at the center" (8–9). It is important for my book that Justice has taken this nationalistic stance, because I, too, wish to employ a Cherokee-centric methodology in my examination of Cherokee orality, quite simply because our cultural perspectives, lifeways, and values have been created through the ancient spoken stories, and this is the most effective and appropriate path to follow in mapping out ways to understand and perhaps make use of those oral teachings and histories today. Employing a Tsalagi-centric approach can help us avoid filtering the stories and their interpretation through the kind of distorting comparisons and assumptions that shaped Mooney's helpful, but sometimes patronizing, views. This methodology can be viewed as an interconnected process that is self-perpetuating in that the stories have created Cherokee culture, and since each telling and retelling provides learning opportunities, the culture is strengthened and reinvigorated by my retelling and discussing them. I, too, choose to privilege, first of all, a Cherokee methodology while also making use of other Indigenous critical theories proposed by both Native and non-Native scholars alike.

In order to begin to understand these enduring oral stories from a Cherokee perspective, I will turn to concepts within the Giduwah worldview that are also ancient and enduring, as these ideologies continue to play a vital part of contemporary Eastern Cherokee life on the Qualla Boundary. These concepts, or cultural values, are known as *Gadugi* (pronounced *gah-doo-ghee*) and *Duyvkta* (*duh-yugk-tah*). Gadugi is explained as "People coming together as one and helping one another," and Duyvkta describes the "right path of walking or living"[46] in that we should strive for harmony, peace, balance, and kindness at all times;[47] the first represents a communal action while the latter is more individual. Both words and concepts are used frequently in the Qualla community, and Gadugi plays a prominent role in the springtime there, as a special day is set aside in mid-May for activities that are for the betterment of the community as a whole called "*Gadugi*—A Day of Caring." This Cherokee Day of Caring sees community members turn out in droves to perform manual labor at the homes of Elders and other vulnerable residents—chores like painting, cleaning, mowing lawns, trimming bushes and trees, tilling soil, planting and weeding vegetable gardens, building wheelchair ramps, tearing down old sheds, cutting firewood, and a wide range of other much-needed work. Cherokees, young and old, will don customized T-shirts that represent their particular workplace or community on the reservation and spend a long day working hard and getting dirty and tired, in order to improve the lives of those who cannot do such things for themselves.[48] Many of the groups will sit down and enjoy a community potluck meal prepared by the women, and it's easy to see how such activities build and strengthen that sense of community and pride in their Cherokeeness as well as re-create (in a modern form) the way things were done by our Ancestors. Such events also give those with the talent for speaking and knowledge of the spoken stories a good opportunity to share with the People gathered together, truly fulfilling the spirit of Gadugi. This example of Gadugi on a large scale on the Eastern Cherokee reservation can be seen to encompass what Jace Weaver calls "communitism" (ix) in his examination of written Native literature. This term is a combination of the words "community" and "activism," and Weaver posits that Native literature is exactly that, "to the extent that it has a proactive commitment to Native community, including what I term the 'wider community' of Creation itself" (xiii). "Communitism" is a powerful word because it projects a sense of most Native peoples' individual love of and for their tribal community and the intricate interconnections within those communities in terms of kin, nature, spirituality, medicine and health, education, etc. Weaver sees the need for this neologism because there is no other word, including the Latin *communitas,* that truly conveys the deep sense of community which Native people feel—a community that includes the natural world and all the rest of Creation (xiii). Gadugi can be thought of as a uniquely Cherokee form of communitism. Yet we must remember that Gadugi is not just a once-a-year event; rather, it is a lifelong personal and group commitment to living as good Cherokees. Gadugi is held within one's heart and spirit in order that one will always do good for all those around and also not become overwhelmed with selfishness but rather always share and help others. The oral teachings encourage everyone to think of the whole community first and recognize our individual responsibilities within the group.

Throughout the upcoming chapters of this book, I will show how the ancients, both human and nonhuman, employed their sense of Gadugi within their actions and experiences, always thinking ahead to those seven generations yet to come and preserving the harmony and balance among the Earth's creatures, respecting each other and the right to live as the Creator meant for each being to live. The word *Gadugi* may not have been used within these stories, but the behavior of each being in the stories gives evidence of this concept. Their actions created an underlying sense of community and egalitarianism and always doing what is best for everyone, rather than just what is best for one or a few. That is evident in so many of the oral narratives, beginning with the Creation. Other concepts related to Gadugi were shared while I was learning the basics of the Cherokee language on the Qualla Boundary. These include the following:

Ulisgedi detsadayelvsesdi—Treat each other's existence as being sacred or important;

Detsadaligenvdisgesdi—You all take responsibility for one another's well-being;

Detsadatlanigohisdodidegesdi—Strengthen one another with encouraging words in all that you do (a term I use for my chapter 5 title);

Detsadadohiyusesdi—You all have a strong conviction for and believe in one another; and

Nigaya'iso gadugi nitsvnesdi—In the mind and heart, always have the thought of working together (with the final expression including the word *gadugi* within it).

These ancient teachings or concepts are best understood within the Giduwah language and are reflective of the caring and harmonious Cherokee perspective of the proper way to live as Real Human Beings. A number of other concepts have been shared with me during my incredibly formative time living in Cherokee, but these are the ones most closely related to Gadugi and the Qualla community's ongoing efforts to maintain and strengthen the ideologies behind what it means to be a good Giduwah person.

I will also use the concept of Duyvkta, or the right path to walk and live, and trace how the oral tradition teaches the best way to proceed along a life path that is balanced and in harmony with all the rest of Creation. The teachings of Duyvkta encourage Cherokees, young and old, to care for themselves and to have self-respect and self-love in order that we may carry within and have love, kindness, and respect for every other creature around us. Duyvkta means to recognize how all parts of our being—body, spirit, mind, and heart—must be fed and nurtured by all that we do. This is why Cherokees are encouraged to pray and attend ceremonies (or church), to take part in sports and physical activities, to participate in community events designed to bring everyone together, to laugh, sing, and dance, and to always help others around us so that everyone and every creature can also live in harmony.

Walking the right path is necessary if one wants to be *Yvwi osda* or a good human being. There is no room for negative thoughts and behavior, because those things will make a person sick and unhealthy; when one is balanced and in harmony with all Creation, one will be healthy and happy and able to contribute to keeping the entire group happy and well. To practice Duyvkta means that we are helping ourselves and thus the group as we walk the path the Creator wishes us to walk. This concept of Duyvkta is related to the ideas laid out by well-known anthropologist Robert K. Thomas (Cherokee descent) in a 1958 thesis entitled "Cherokee Values and World View," where he describes the manner in which Eastern Cherokees conduct themselves in their inter-personal relationships.[49] Thomas explains that the more traditional-thinking folks will always avoid giving offense to another human and go out of their way to maintain friendly and harmonious relationships. This may include walking away from someone who is angry, refusing to gossip about others, avoiding anyone who is argumentative, and kindly doing what it takes to help another person correct their own bad or inharmonious behavior (1). While Thomas's theory relates to human-to-human interactions, Duyvkta is much more, as it defines relationships between humans and all other Earth beings and elemental Spirits. Duyvkta is an all-encompassing way for a person to, at all times, consider every living part of the environment and natural world around us and to make every effort to always behave appropriately so that other beings and their purpose on Earth is respected and honored.

Another core value that Thomas defines in his thesis is similar to Gadugi, as he describes how a good Cherokee is always willing to give of her/himself to others in regards to material goods or her/his time, and this also helps with interpersonal relationships, thus maintaining harmony within the community. This sense of sharing allows for every individual in a community to feel that when they or their family are going through hard times, one or more of their fellow Cherokees will be willing to help out and share so that no one goes without, and any problem can be handled with the kind help from a neighbor or friend. Gadugi, meanwhile, is a much larger community-minded effort that is intended to better the lives of many. Again, both Gadugi and Duyvkta are uniquely Cherokee concepts that have been handed down from the Ancestors through oral teachings and stories, and both concepts within the Cherokee intellectual tradition are vital and a part of contemporary life for Eastern Cherokee people as well as their kin in Oklahoma.

Along with employing Duyvkta and Gadugi principles, I'll utilize the ideas surrounding Indigenous connections with the Earth and other creatures that are presented in Gregory Cajete's book *Native Science: Natural Laws of Interdependence*. The Tewa scholar suggests that in addition to the healers and medicine people of a tribe who had intimate knowledge of plant medicines and the necessary prayers and rituals to conduct healing, "each member of the tribe in his or her own capacity was a scientist, an artist, a storyteller, and a participant in the great web of life" (2). He notes that Indigenous peoples always had that ecological knowledge which came from "a lived and storied participation with the natural landscape" (2). The entire body of Indigenous Earth knowledge can be considered as "Native science," and the Cherokees had their own ways of knowing based on their specific environment, and much of this knowledge is contained within the oral tradition. Cajete posits that "Native science is the collective heritage of human experience with the natural world; in its most essential form, it is a map of natural reality drawn from the experience of thousands of human generations" (3). Since the Cherokees have been in their homeland since the Earth was created, and indeed, we are told our homeland was created for us as a people, the Cherokees have tens of thousands of years of personal and communal relationships with all the rest of the beings living among those mountains and valleys. The ancient stories represent and explain those interdependencies and shared lives in that particular environment, and these notions of traditional ecological knowledge, or TEK (McGregor 385), will assist me in my examination of Cherokee orality and its continuance, as the stories are not human-centric but rather Earth-centric. I hope to show the wide range of spiritual and intellectual traditions within this examination.

This project is offered in five chapters to follow this *Adalenisgv* or beginning. Unlike many academic texts, there will be no conclusion, simply because this is an unending examination of a living, growing, and enduring body of orality. I suggest there can be no conclusion or end point because each time a story is told and shared, the learning, words, and images come alive again, thus there will *always* be more to say about Cherokee oral tradition. Instead, I'll share what I have learned at the end of my writing in a chapter entitled "*Uninetsv oni* / Last Words." Each of the five chapters has a Cherokee name, followed by the best translation to English that I can find, thanks to those many language speakers on the Qualla Boundary who have kindly helped me.

Chapter 1, "*Kituwah* / 'The place from which we came,'" will offer readings of a number of the earliest origin stories of events and experiences that took place following the Creation. We will witness how the Cherokee homeland was formed and the creative role that many four-legged and winged beings played in the formation of not only the physical realm but also of Giduwah culture. Chapters 2 and 3 are each named "*Dusgaseti Tsalagi Kanoheda*," with the second chapter being part 1 and the third chapter being part 2 of these "Cherokee stories of those creatures who are dreadful and are to be avoided, and also fill us with wonder and awe." The word *Dusgaseti* has that double meaning, and the conflicted role that each of them plays within Cherokee culture seems to require that I separate the stories of these various beings. By so doing, I hope to demonstrate how even the more dreadful Dusgaseti are vitally important for the People for the ultimate goodness these beings produce(d), while the awe-inspiring Dusgaseti always appear to have the intention of helping the Cherokees in a good way but may be misunderstood and thus dreaded by the People.

Chapter 4 is entitled *"Nudele yvwi dideyohdi* / 'To teach other people, to make them strong': Sharing Tsalagi Oral Teachings with Others." Here I introduce contemporary scenes of storytelling and examine how the stories are shared by Eastern Cherokees on the Qualla Boundary with visitors and tourists, in order to educate these outsiders about Native culture and to present the Cherokee side of history in comparison to the colonizer-written form. The writings and perspectives of Bob Thomas will provide a framework to explain how the Eastern Band community uses their oral tradition to welcome and embrace those non-Native visitors in a harmonious way. I'll present the more contemporary, post-Removal stories along with modern retellings of some of the older ones that Eastern Cherokee storytellers share and revitalize with their live performances. The fifth and final chapter is *"Detsadatlanigohisdodidegesdi* / 'Strengthen one another with encouraging words in all that you do': Tsalagi Stories Told for Tsalagi," which is one of the Gadugi-related concepts mentioned above. Today's Eastern Cherokees remain an orality-centered Native community and use the spoken word in everyday life in order to teach and promote the culture. In this chapter, I will present and examine the ways that the tribe is utilizing the ancient oral stories and historical narratives to express sovereignty, create new community leaders, reclaim land in a friendly (toward nearby settler-descendants) manner, offer paths of healing from historical trauma for enrolled members, educate the young about culture and language, promote the use of traditional foods and medicines, and a wealth of other usages. This final chapter will bring us full circle, as it shows a repurposing of the ancient origin stories that give evidence of the continuing belief that the Cherokee homeland has been created for the Giduwah People and that the Eastern Band members will continue to do all in their power to maintain that sacred homeland for generations of young to come, while continuously regenerating culture in the Qualla community.

1

Kituwah

◆ The place from which we came ◆

Creation and Origin Stories of the Tsalagi Ancestors

One cannot talk about a people or their culture until one learns where they came from and thus how their environment has shaped their society. This is most necessary in the case of North American Native groups and their acknowledged indigeneity to the land. The best way to learn of this sense of origins is through a tribe's collection of stories within their oral tradition because "stories involve place, usually homelands with deep human attachments. Homelands . . . can never be taken away as long as the Indian mind wants to recall such places" (Fixico 30). While the Eastern Band of Cherokees continue to live in their original territory, this spiritually and emotionally charged recalling of homelands is vital today for the two bands of Cherokees in Oklahoma, as will be discussed in greater detail in my final chapter; we will also hear how the true Mothertown of all Giduwah people has been reclaimed in that chapter. The story of how the Earth came to be and how Cherokee territory was created is vitally important in understanding the deep physical and spiritual connection the Tsalagi have to their land, mountains, valleys, rivers, and streams and, of course, to all the thousands of nonhumans living there. Indeed, when the Eastern Cherokees speak about land, we can equate it to these southern mountains because they are the most predominant Earth beings one sees when looking at this Indigenous nation's territory; these living mountains, often referred to as Grandfathers for the wisdom each holds, are essentially the Cherokee homeland. All these mountains and every other being residing there—be it the red clay, rivers, birds, reptiles, boulders, plants, wind, fog, animals, or insects—are alive with their own spirits, behaviors, methods of communication, and responsibilities. The Creation story gives an account of the existence of Giduwah culture and the original people long before the physical Earth was made. One modern retelling[1] is given by Eastern Band storyteller and mask-carver Davy Arch.[2]

Well, / they claim that in the beginning / that everything lived / all in the same place / in heaven / under the sky arch. / And I use heaven a lot of times / because people are familiar with that term / which is / where the Creator / lived and that's where everything existed / in the beginning. / And the earth was completely covered with water / and it was getting crowded / and the people and the animals and everybody wanted / another place to live / and so they sent messengers down to find a place to live. / Everything that was sent searched / and found nothing but water / until the Water Beetle / dayunisi / was sent / and it was able to dive down into the water / and found the mud at the bottom / and brought it to the surface / and it started to grow into the continents / and I think this was after the first / dry land when the first ice age happened / and the polar caps / probably froze / and the land dried up you know / in the beginning basically. / And the earth was cold and covered with mud / and that's when the great Buzzard came / and created these mountains / by striking its wings / they said it was so tired / by the time it had flown all the way around the world / that when it got here / it started hitting the ground with its / wings. / Beat the valleys down into the ground / and pulled the mountains up out of the mud / when it pulled its wings up / and Suli / the great Buzzard / Suli egwa is how we say / great Buzzard. / It's really / buzzard great / in the literal translation / egwa is great or big. / And that's why it has such significance in the culture / I think. / That it was involved in the Creation / and then / everything came down / you know / the Sky Arch or heaven cleared out. (Arch, DVD, June 2012)

We hear how the insect, bird, and animal beings worked hard to physically form the Cherokee homeland when time began, presenting the earliest example of Gadugi—the first concept that, I posit, defines Cherokee culture—which is the People coming together as one to help one another and benefit the entire community. In this story of Creation, it is the nonhuman creatures who come together, with everyone thinking of and working toward a situation that was best for the entire Sky Island community. The various creatures volunteered and did so at the risk of possible death or injury, but their Gadugi, their communitist mode of thought and actions, helped them use their particular talents and abilities to help all beings, thus making them co-creators of this land. *Dayunisi* (water beetle) and *Suli egwa* (great buzzard) were vitally important in the creation of this land of soft mountains and lush valleys for the Ani-Yunwiyah and their fellow beings whom the Creator chose to place first upon the eastern sky home, and then upon Mother Earth where they were to coexist in harmonious relations and to walk the path of kindness and balance known as Duyvkta. Petrone notes that such Creation stories "explain so much concerning the local geography and topography of each Native community's homeland, linking it inextricably to that Creator-given land base" (16).

Cherokee Nation scholar Chris Teuton has written extensively about the story of the Creation of *Elohi*, Earth, and shares with readers how often he reflects on the deep meaning of the planet as well as the beauty of such cooperation for the good of all. He writes that "it is both a story and a constant source of reflection on the responsibilities of being. These two aspects of its reality are inextricable" ("Applying Oral Concepts" 194). And with the frequent telling and retelling of this story in both the eastern and western territories, along with all the many written versions of it by various scholars, this Cherokee philosophy of Gadugi is reinforced for all. Teuton notes that the Ancestors were very practical in their growing realization that they were running out of room on Sky Island, and something had to be done, so they chose to begin by holding council and giving everyone a chance to speak their mind, a practice that became instituted within Cherokee society as a means of communal resolution and problem-solving. He posits that "in council, the animals communicated with each other as equals. In the end, the council of animals relied upon an apparently weak creature, little Dayunisi, who alone could search the great expanse of water and dive deep enough to find earth. Elohi is created as a world of self-sustaining harmonious relationships in which every creature is necessary to the survival of all" (194). Teuton notes that this is so much more than just a story of a beetle diving into water and looking for mud, but rather that it is theoretical, much like Plato's story of the cave and the deeper meaning behind that much-studied allegory (194).

The most thorough accounting of this oldest of all Cherokee stories is that presented by James Mooney, first told to him in the late 1880s by the Elders Ayvini, or Swimmer, and Itagunuhi, or John Ax, who were "the two most competent authorities of the eastern band" when the Irish American ethnographer was doing his fieldwork in Eastern Cherokee Territory for the Smithsonian Institution (*Myths of the Cherokee* 430). There are many abbreviated versions of the story told orally and in print today, with the Swimmer/ Ax version accepted by many Cherokees as the most comprehensive and accurate. Ayvini and Itagunuhi only spoke Cherokee, so Mooney's English translation is somewhat problematic for the obvious difficulties he must have had in trying to translate and explain Cherokee concepts and worldviews while filtering these important matters through his non-Cherokee, Euro-Christian perspectives; however, the story is told as closely as possible to the original Swimmer telling and is considered complete by most modern Cherokee storytellers. I present it here, in the paragraph form it takes in Mooney's book.

HOW THE WORLD WAS MADE

The earth is a great island floating in a sea of water, and suspended at each of the four cardinal points by a cord hanging down from the sky vault, which is of solid rock. When the world grows old and worn out, the people will die and the cords will break and let the earth sink down into the ocean, and all will be water again. The Indians are afraid of this. When all was water, the animals were above in Galun'lati, beyond the arch; but it was very much crowded, and they were wanting more room. They wondered what was below the water, and at last Dayu-ni'si, "Beaver's Grandchild," the little Water-beetle, offered to go and see if it could learn. It darted in every direction over the surface of the water, but could find no firm place to rest. Then it dived to the bottom and came up with some soft mud, which began to grow and spread on every side until it became the island which we call the earth. It was afterward fastened to the sky with four cords, but no one remembers who did this.

At first the earth was flat and very soft and wet. The animals were anxious to get down, and sent out different birds to see if it was yet dry, but they found no place to alight and came back again to Galun'lati. At last it seemed to be time, and they sent out the Buzzard and told him to go and make ready for them. This was the Great Buzzard, the father of all the buzzards we see now. He flew all over the earth, low down near the ground, and it was still soft. When he reached the

Cherokee country, he was very tired, and his wings began to flap and strike the ground, and wherever they struck the earth there was a valley, and where they turned up again there was a mountain. When the animals above saw this, they were afraid that the whole world would be mountains, so they called him back, but the Cherokee country remains full of mountains to this day.

When the earth was dry and the animals came down, it was still dark, so they got the sun and set it in a track to go every day across the island from east to west, just overhead. It was too hot this way, and Tsiska'gili, the Red Crawfish, had his shell scorched a bright red, so that his meat was spoiled; and the Cherokee do not eat it. The conjurers put the sun another handbreadth higher in the air, but it was still too hot. They raised it another time, and another, until it was seven handbreadths high and just under the sky arch. Then it was right, and they left it so. This is why the conjurers call the highest place Gulkwa'gine Digalun'latiyun', "the seventh height," because it is seven handbreadths above the earth. Every day the sun goes along under this arch, and returns at night on the upper side to the starting place.

There is another world under this, and it is like ours in everything—animals, plants, and people—save that the seasons are different. The streams that come down from the mountains are the trails by which we reach this underworld, and the springs at their heads are the doorways by which we enter it, but to do this one must fast and go to water and have one of the underground people for a guide. We know that the seasons in the underworld are different from ours, because the water in the springs is always warmer in winter and cooler in summer than the outer air. (239–40)

Today, the Museum of the Cherokee Indian offers an audio exhibit that tells the Creation story and shows computer-generated graphics of the many stages of the remarkable and vibrant Creation epic while contemporary storytellers offer up their own interpretation of this ancient origin story; the story can also be found in many other books and websites of Native "legends." B. Lynne Harlan, former director of cultural resources for the Eastern Band of Cherokee Indians, explains that the Creation story continues to have deep meaning for modern Cherokees "not as a single story but as a complex of ideas and knowledge woven into our history and life-ways" (G. K. Parker 37). She adds that every individual interprets this origin story in his or her own way, but ultimately each of us hears what is most important for us when we listen to it (37). Paul Zolbrod concurs with Harlan's analysis, as he argues that a community's oral tradition "expresses a shared morality and shapes activity according to a common outlook" (Zolbrod 22).

In his book *Reading the Voice: Native American Oral Poetry on the Page*, Zolbrod posits that Creation stories are the essential key to understanding a culture and defines "creation narratives" in this way: "Along with the complex of poetic works they engender, these narratives are fundamental to what emerges in a poetic tradition of a People and its greater-than-human belief system. They often verbalize what lies at the heart of all that emerges as that People's culture" (126). Zolbrod suggests that such tribal Creation stories are as powerful for North America's Indigenous peoples as the Genesis story is for the Western world (3), a thought that I strongly concur with and now share with students in my Indigenous literature courses at the University of Windsor (Ontario, Canada), as a prelude to studying particular works of literature in connection to each Indigenous writer's ancestral land base.

The Tsalagi story of Creation is one of cooperation, perseverance, fortitude, and harmonious sensibility among the animals, insects, and birds;[3] the story shows the intelligence and bravery of the nonhuman creatures when it comes to doing what is best for the entire group—something that is emphasized throughout Cherokee culture in regard to human relations with one another and with the rest of Creation in the concept of Gadugi. As Teuton notes, "Crucially, the existence of all those relationships depends upon discussion and one individual risking his life for the good of the whole. Dayunisi dives into the water not because it is his duty but because he can; he has the specific tools needed to help others, and his sacrifice is an act of altruism . . . upon which the world depends" ("Applying Oral Concepts" 198). This oldest Tsalagi story tells how a homeland was created for them during troubled times and with an overwhelming need to relocate from the heavens, as it were. It also establishes that the Cherokees existed *prior* to the actual forming of the Earth and that their culture, therefore, is older even than the land itself.[4] Their mountains, now known as the Smoky Mountains that are part of the modern-day, colonizer-labeled Appalachian range, immediately became the home of all beings, including the Cherokees, as soon as those hills and valleys were created. It is a sacred belief that most Cherokees, regardless of where they grew up and have lived, carry within their hearts—that the Creator made the southern mountains to be the home for the Cherokees *forever*. They have always been there and always will be, despite all efforts by the colonizer to relocate them, kill them off, weaken their bloodline through miscegenation, erase their Indigenous culture, or even to appropriate that culture.

The Creation story also shows how the animal beings were more adept at survival than the Cherokees, because it was the nonhuman creatures who ultimately took control and assisted in the Creation; the human beings came later and were, more or less, invited guests to the new Creation. Cherokee Nation elder Tom Belt of Oklahoma, who has lived on the Qualla Boundary for over twenty years, has explained that the Real Human Beings were the last to be allowed to come down to Earth following the Creation. He states that if any one individual animal or plant life were to become extinct tomorrow, there would be repercussions throughout the natural world because of the interdependency of all creatures for food and, thus, survival. On the other hand, if humans were to become extinct, the rest of Creation would continue with no real impact because we humans do not contribute anything essential to nature's ecosystem. He stipulates that we humans are invited guests and need to learn how to be more respectful like our Ancestors (Belt, Lecture). G. Keith Parker suggests that "as one experiences the Cherokee creation story, one can get a sense of their inner world, the deeper awareness of their place not only in the mountains of Appalachia and in the world itself, but also of their rightful individual existence" (37).

The Earth has shaped and created Cherokee culture since the beginning of time, and the Cherokee people have imprinted their lifeways upon the land in a symbiotic relationship. The people depend on the nonhuman creatures of the land—plant and animals, fish and birds, rain and sun—for sustenance, and they recognize that their very existence is tied to maintaining harmonious relations, only taking what is necessary and being aware of the sacrifices made by those nonhuman beings. Cherokee culture is deeply connected to the cycles and rhythms of the growing seasons and movement of the birds, animals, and fish. The ancient stories reflect those lifeways and all that the People received and learned from their fellow beings within Creation. This is all a part of the Native science of which Tewa scholar Gregory Cajete writes, when he compares it to the modern fields of study known as environmental or earth science. He suggests that "while Native people don't have a particular word for either of those Western terms, they certainly have an understanding of the practice of those disciplines of Western science at the individual and communal levels. And so this understanding that Indigenous people have is a very particular and very profound relationship to the natural world. This relationship is predicated on the fact that all Indigenous tribes—their philosophies, cultural ways of life, customs, language, all aspects of their cultural being in one way or another—are ultimately tied to the relationships that they have established and applied during their history with regard to certain places and to the earth as a whole" (4). Davy Arch knows of the power of these interspecies relationships and how Cherokee culture and spirituality wouldn't be what it is were it not for the entire ecology and its interconnected residents. He notes, "I think we modeled a lot of what we live as a culture today from observing nature and animals and how they interacted and reacted with one another in the environment" (personal interview).

Most of Cherokee oral tradition is closely and geographically connected to what the Real or Original People consider their holy land, and it reflects stories that present the harmony and natural balance among all the human and nonhuman beings who live there. Each and every story describes and defines particular flora and fauna of the Cherokee homeland, including all the animals, birds, insects, and fish, along with the many plant foods and medicines that can be gathered in the forests of those southern mountains, allowing for "nourishing relationships with [their] ecosystems" (Battiste and Henderson 9). The Eastern Cherokees continue today to gather and hunt the same foods their Ancestors enjoyed, and newer oral stories have been added to the ancient ones to pass on the knowledge about the land; indeed, every family seems to have their own stories to share about the seasonal process of gathering wild foods from the surrounding environment and for the preparation and feasting. For example, many Eastern Cherokees today go out in the spring to pick wild ramps, a plant that is a member of the leek or wild onion family; ramps have an intensely strong garlic-like odor and leave one with very bad breath and often stomach gas—needless to say, there is much joking and many humorous stories shared during ramp season. The conscientious gatherer is careful not to pull the plant out by the root so that more will grow from the plant the following spring.[5] An entire day is dedicated to the celebration of the wild ramp on the Qualla Boundary to mark the start of spring,[6] and this annual event is now linked with a trout festival, since the Oconaluftee River is kept well stocked with rainbow trout for the tourists and visiting fishermen by the Cherokee Fisheries and Wildlife department.[7] A special luncheon is provided on this day for the Elders, and it is a chance for these seniors to gather together to laugh and tell those humorous family and community stories and to celebrate in a communal fashion the harvesting of the rare and uniquely Cherokee food. Along with ramps, Cherokees continue to go out into the woods, hills, and creek beds to pick sochan, poke salad, kale, and other wild greens as a part of everyday dinners. Dozens of wild mushrooms are unique to Cherokee Territory and are picked and enjoyed fresh during their annual growing season, along with huckleberries, blackberries, blueberries, and wild strawberries. Today, Cherokee women spend time in the spring and summer picking, canning, drying, and freezing many of these wild foods to preserve them for the winter months, and their daily work and home schedules are made to coincide with these gathering and preserving activities. They know the cycles and seasons and work with urgency when particular plants and wild foods are available. It is not unusual to see an entire family working alongside a reservation road in the hot sun, gathering many of these delicacies for the day's supper. My adopted sisters, Louise Goings and Bear Taylor, taught me a great deal about gathering greens as to where to find them, what they look like, and how to wash and cook them, all the while sharing stories from their childhood about their mother, Miss Emma Taylor, a well-known basket-maker, who had passed down her traditional Earth knowledge. This experience gave me a deep sense of the respectful relationship that Cherokee women have always had with the plant beings for all they offer in terms of nutrients, sustenance, healing, and delicious taste.

In her book *Our Knowledge Is Not Primitive: Decolonizing Botanical Anishinaabe Teachings*,[8] Wendy Makoons Geniusz (Ojibway heritage) presents the Anishinaabeg concept of their relationships with all of Creation, describing the four levels of Creation according to Elder storyteller Basil Johnston. Those teachings hold that the first beings gifted by the Creator were the elemental forces, the rocks, and the Spirits who carried the teachings, stories, songs, and ceremonies. The next group of beings were the plants and the trees, and the third set of beings were all the various nonhuman creatures (birds, animals, etc.). The people, in this case the Anishinaabeg, were the last to be created. All these beings then made the promise to the Creator that they would live and work together cooperatively, helping and supporting one another to survive. Geniusz clearly defines how vital the promise was in maintaining that symbiotic, cooperative, interdependent set of relationships among all of Earth's creatures when she posits, "Without the plants, the animals would not be able to eat or breathe. Without the animals, the plants would not be able to move to new locations, and they would not have what we now call carbon dioxide. Without the plants and the animals, the Anishinaabeg would have no food or resources for their survival. Without the first level, including the sun, rain, and teachings, to guide them, all three of the other levels would perish. The only level of Creation that could survive without the other three is the first level, for they were here long before the other levels of Creation" (57). The Anishinaabeg philosophy of cooperation for survival parallels that of the Cherokees with the belief that each and every creature or being of the Earth has the agency and consciousness to accept their individual responsibilities in maintaining healthy and harmonious relationships with all those around them.

It is this interconnectedness with the natural seasons and offerings of the Earth that the Acoma Pueblo scholar Simon Ortiz posits is the heart of all Native stories, be they spoken or written. He points out how tribal oral narratives have always reiterated each group's origin and their attachment to the land. This is why the elder Cherokees frequently remind the young that their home—the rivers, mountains, forests, and lands—are a part of their very being, just as the Native person is a part of the Earth. We can see here that reciprocal relationship between the people and the land and the animals of which Cajete and Geniusz speaks. The Cherokee Creation story shows how all creatures, human and nonhuman, lived harmoniously in the Sky World and worked together in the way of Gadugi to create and move below into a new home that would allow for a continuing sacred and mutually respectful coexistence. Likewise, Ortiz explains that "the tradition of the oral narrative, expressed by the many different Native languages of the indigenous Americas, is at the core of this philosophy of interdependence" ("Introduction" xiii). The old traditional stories present and confirm the origin of the Earth, of a tribe's particular land base, and assert the emergence of Native people from the Mystery and the "boundless creative energy of the universe" ("Introduction" xiii). The term "Mystery" represents the Indigenous belief that a supernatural and all-powerful being has this ultimate power to create or build and to cause the intricate parts of the natural world to behave in certain ways, and that human beings are probably the weakest and least

41

important part of that universe while animals and plants operate through a much greater knowledge and awareness of what is best for all of Creation around them. Indeed, as storyteller Davy Arch notes, the Cherokees learned all about Gadugi from the behavior of the nonhumans, and since it has always worked well for those wiser beings, it does and will continue to be the most beneficial form of society for the Giduwah people. These beliefs are emphasized through the ancient stories, as Marie Battiste (Potlotek Mi'kmaq First Nation) and Sakej Henderson (enrolled, Chickasaw Nation, Oklahoma) point out in *Protecting Indigenous Knowledge and Heritage*, explaining that "we carry the mysteries of our ecologies and their diversity in our oral traditions, in our ceremonies, and in our art; we unite these mysteries in the structure of our languages and our ways of knowing" (9).

Cherokee ways of knowing include Indigenous names for the particular beings involved in the Creation of their mountain homeland as well as names for various features of the land. This ancient original naming (as opposed to colonizer renaming) of important Earth sites and creatures provides testimony of the truth of the very first origin story within Cherokee oral tradition. Such linguistic evidence cannot be ignored and counters Western theory that suggests Native groups of this continent are migrants from Asia and Siberia, which disavows indigeneity and lumps Natives in with newcomers. The "Earth-Diver" form of Creation story—where a single creature swims to the bottom of a great flood of water and comes up with a chunk of mud that grows into a land mass—is common among various tribal groups in particular regions of North America, while other First Nations offer an "Emergence from the Lower Earth" story of Creation.[9]

Jay Hansford Vest, an enrolled citizen of the Monacan Nation, is quite critical of Western scholars who disregard Indigenous wisdom-centered intellectual traditions. In his *Native American Oralcy: Interpretations of Indigenous Thought,* he suggests there is great ecological wisdom held within Native philosophies and oral narratives that is drastically different from Western ideologies and written metanarratives that are born in the mind rather than from nature. This causes such scholars to have a problem in grasping and thus interpreting Earth-based knowledge and oral traditions and, too often, to view oral cultures as primitive while literacy is deemed as civilized—an age-old problem, indeed. This problem originated with early contact. "When the first adventurers, conquistadors, and colonialists first arrived in the Americas, they encountered a people wholly immersed within an oral paradigm of reason and epistemology. It was indeed a *primary orality* free of literary based abstractions and hence centered upon the organic concrete world of nature. As such, reason was grounded in the organic realities and beholding to a harmony with the natural world. Conversely European invaders were steeped in abstract ideology as a product of literary evolution. Their abstractions governed their value axioms, so much so, that they had come to question the very nature of organic existence with mind over matter fantasies" (5).

Hansford Vest goes on to posit that the abstract, literate, and rational mind continues to be in direct contrast with those who hold organic-centered and oral-based realities. He makes reference to David Abram, a cultural ecologist and philosopher, who has studied how Western literacy has negatively impacted such Indigenous societies that had always been primary oral cultures. Abram's study "warns of a divorce through literacy from the natural world. It is a thorny problem wherein we have become lost in our literate based abstractions and thereby fail in our misplaced reason removed from a sustained ecological wisdom" (4). In essence, the literate mind is far removed from nature and any Earth-based knowledge because of dwelling within written narratives that "invok[e] an abstract reality over the organic world. Conversely Native *residual orality* offers an ecological salvation if we learn to recognize this oral paradigm" (6). I suggest that the strong emphasis on spoken-word stories is evidence of the enduring reality of such residual orality within the Eastern Cherokee community. Throughout this book, I will try to provide a Cherokee-centered framework with which to examine the oral tradition in hopes of opening cultural doors for a deeper understanding of this ancient traditional ecological knowledge.

The insistence by many Western scholars on using their literary theory concerning Indigenous people and their orature, rather than offering support and acceptance of those groups' ancient stories of origin, is most certainly a bone of contention for Native scholars who understand the world otherwise. Simon Ortiz feels that too often, non-Indians will try to belittle Creation stories because they are living proof of the indigeneity of the various Native groups to their particular homeland, and many non-Natives do not want to accept this, preferring instead that this was once a land empty of people; this is why some Western scholars continue to dispute those origin stories and replace them with their own theories that "demean and denigrate their indigenous identity by implying that their origin was elsewhere and away from their Native American world" ("Introduction" xiii). Ortiz emphasizes that modern Native writers and storytellers are fully aware of their individual tribe's origin, and that "speaking for the sake of the land and the People means speaking for the inextricable relationship and interconnection between them" (xiii). Cajete posits that "all the basic components of scientific thought and application are metaphorically represented in most Native stories of creation and origin," as each "relates central ideas of interdependence and respect for plants, animals, places, even tools, and for those behaviors that have assisted human survival in the natural world" (13). Vizenor promotes the realization of the validity and power of the ancient stories and personally employs the oral tradition in his own modern works of written literature. He believes that Native literature is what it is today because of those early oral stories, as he recognizes that his Ojibway language is as ancient as the Earth herself (Blaeser 18).

This notion of a "forever" language that has always existed is an intriguing one and ties in closely with the Creation story for the Cherokees. Since the language was given to the Cherokees by Unelanvhi, the Creator or the Great Mystery, and Unelanvhi has always existed as a living power or Spirit who has complete control of all living things, these words have indeed always existed. One Cherokee oral story (known as "The Origin of Disease and Medicine," which I'll discuss later in this chapter) relates that all the nonhuman creatures once spoke the same language as the people, and it was only after the Earth was created, and the humans began to hunt and kill animals, fish, and birds, that the creatures decided to speak a different language so the Cherokees could no longer understand the words of their animal and plant siblings. That is why the sounds and songs of the four-footeds, winged, and gilled creatures seem strange to us humans; it is one way these creatures have of protecting themselves. Storyteller Davy Arch suggests that it was not a verbal type of communication between all creatures but rather one of body language and nonverbal communicating that went on. Of course, he says, there are many animals and birds that do communicate with their own spoken sound, but everyone was so aware and respectful of each other that they could communicate by reading the other's movement.[10] Meanwhile, the Cherokee language is so very ancient that no one knows how old the words actually are, even though new words for things that did not exist in the old days are added all the time; these new words describe, define, and explain things that have come about since the colonizer came to this land.[11]

It seems necessary here for our thinking about the meanings of Cherokee origin stories and the forever language in which they are told to consider some of what Wahinkpe Topa (Cherokee/Creek ancestry) suggests is "ancestral Indigenous thinking" (19), beliefs, and assumptions concerning life. He offers this list in his introduction to a collection of essays by Native scholars entitled *Unlearning the Language of Conquest: Scholars Expose Anti-Indianism in America*. Many of these values and beliefs are clearly evident within the Cherokee oral tradition. Indigenous beliefs include but are not limited to the following:

- The natural world is ultimately more about cooperation than it is about competition.
- The concept of reciprocity can guide living systems toward balance.
- Humans are entwined in and with Nature, and the idea of "conquering" or "being in charge" of it rather than honoring the relationship is considered an aberration.
- A Great Mysterious Spirit is within all its creations.
- Diversity gives strength and balance to the world.
- Material possessions are less important than generosity, and generosity is the highest expression of courage.
- Resolution of conflict should be about restoring harmony rather than enacting vengeance or punishment (19).

The final concept above of "restoring harmony" is what Duyvkta is all about, while the next-to-last is one way of describing Gadugi. These defining Indigenous beliefs are reflected in many of the origin stories from Tsalagi culture, along with many other cultural intricacies that define the uniqueness of the Cherokee worldview, based on the ancient experiences and, most certainly, the mountainous natural world and particular creatures and spirits who reside there.

After the Earth's Creation, the old Cherokee stories tell of another example of the nonhuman beings working together, in some cases becoming scarred and injured, just to give warmth and light to all living beings, including humans. The "How the Animals Got Fire" story,[12] for example, exhibits the harmonious system of mutual cooperation within which the four-footed, winged, and creeping creatures function. Even though the modern tellings are a bit shorter than Mooney's (see the appendix), each version demonstrates how the various birds and reptiles who make the dangerous journey and are forever marked by their action were practicing the concept of Gadugi—as each individual did what they could for the betterment of everyone.

Elder Lloyd Arneach shares this story on the banks of the Oconaluftee River, during the summertime bonfires for tourists who visit Cherokee.

HOW THE ANIMALS GOT FIRE
Lloyd Arneach

This is how we / first got the fire. / Long ago / it was cold and dark / and the animals were / freezing / and they asked for help. / So the Creator sent a bolt of lightning down / and it hit a hollow tree. / It was out on an island / and it started blazing / and the animals saw the blaze out on the island / and they started asking for animals to go out / [to] bring the fire back so / at least they could be warm. / Now the screech owl went out / he landed on the edge of the stump / and when he looked down / there was a gust of wind / that brought some of the hot coals up and they / singed the / the feathers around his eyes / and he still has great big circles round his eyes to this day. / And then they sent / the black racer out / and the racer went out / and he found a hole in the bottom of the stump / and he went in / but he couldn't get a coal / it was so hot / he was dashing around real quick / back and forth on hisself / and finally found the hole / and came out. / But he's burned black / and today / whenever you see a black racer running / it's like he turned back on himself / never going in a straight direction. / And then they send / the great / black snake out / and the great black snake went out / and he found another hole in the bottom of the stump / and he started going around / again it was too hot for him / and he came out but / he's burned black all over. / And none of the other animals wanted to go out. / The birds had been burned / snakes been burned. / Then the little water spider says / I will go. / They all agreed / she / wove a little basket / and put it on her back / and she went across the water. / This was the one / that could walk on top of the water. / Went out to the island. / She went into the hole and got a small coal and / put it in her basket / and brought it back across the water. / And so the animals finally got fire. / And as a reward / they let the little water spider keep / the small bowl on her back. / And that's the story of how the animals got fire. (Arneach, DVD, 30 June 2013)

Like so many Indigenous stories, it is often the smallest or ugliest creatures who risk their lives to accomplish what needs to be done for the good of others, and the fire story shows how even a bug that many people too often simply step on and kill is thoughtful, resourceful, and brave. Kanane'ski Amai'yehi (Mooney's spelling), the water spider,[13] still weaves and carries her *tutsti* bowl on her back to forever remind others of her connection to the life-giving fire—the Fire that is the centerpiece of Cherokee culture and spirituality. Davy Arch connects the act of getting the Fire to the Sky Island emptying out, with all beings moving down to the Earth. His version flows from his telling of the Creation, but I've separated them for this book.

FIRST FIRE
Davy Arch

Everything came to Earth / but it was cold and dark / and that's when the first fire / was sent by / they say it was sent by the Thunders / and the Lightning / and I always heard that / it was sent by the Creator himself / and set a tree on fire / to provide light and warmth for the world / and everything tried to get the fire / and bring it back so it could be used. / Everything failed / but a lot of things got / their characteristics from that first fire. / They claim the black snake / was a white snake in the beginning / and he swam across / and was able to swim on top of the water / and thought he could bring the fire back. / But when he got to the tree and went / into the tree it scorched him. / He couldn't stand the heat / and when he turned / he came back out that same hole he went into / his body turned black from being scorched / he's been black ever since. / You can scare a black snake sometimes and / he'll go out and come right back to you. / The Raven was a white bird and he got / scorched black. / They claim the hoot owl rubs circles round his eyes 'cause / the smoke burned his eyes. / Everything tried and failed / until the Water Spider / was able to walk across the water / and / she brought back an ember / back from the burning tree / and from that time forward / everybody shared the warmth and the light. / First fire. / The Creation story of the first fire at Giduwah / our Mother Town / was that a group of Elders had gone / to the Mulberry Place / where Clingman's Dome is at / and lightning struck a tree back there / set it on fire / and they brought that fire / to Giduwah / and built the first council house fire / with that fire off the mountain. / And that fire still burns. / The eternal flame at the theater was lit / from that fire / and when the removal took place / they took fire from Giduwah / and took it to Oklahoma / and it still burns out there. / So that / fire has burned continuously / for probably eleven thousand years / since the last ice age. (Arch, DVD, June 2012)

Arch's telling of the story connects the gift of Fire directly to the Cherokee Mothertown of Kituwah, which I'll discuss at length in chapter 5.

Another modern retelling of the Fire story by Kathi Smith Littlejohn says the little spider uses a clump of red clay mud to fashion a bowl and place it on her back to hold the hot coal, again showing original intelligence and thought. She explains to the audience that once the coal was in the clay bowl, it baked the mud; this also prefigures how Cherokee women learned to use fire to harden and set their clay pottery to make it waterproof (Duncan, *Living Stories* 53–55). Yet perhaps this telling is not as modern as it seems at first glance. An alternative version (as opposed to the Mooney one) is confirmed by ethnologists Jack and Ana Gritts Kilpatrick in their 1964 manuscript "Eastern Cherokee Folktales: Reconstructed from the Field Notes of Frans M. Olbrechts."[14] Olbrechts had collected stories from the same Will West Long whom Mooney had worked with in the 1880s, along with Long's half-brother Morgan Calhoun in early 1927. The Kilpatricks note that Olbrechts never wrote these stories down in full text, and they were working with his collection of stenographic notes—which included English, Cherokee words, and Flemish phrases—in order to create a more readable text. The couple note that this was a difficult task, as the Flemish anthropologist/linguist used a complex system of phonetics, mixed with marginal notes scribbled in haste, along with embedding Cherokee words, all contained in eight small lined notebooks along with several loose sheets; this forced them to retranslate many of the Cherokee words and phrases, but ultimately several previously unrecorded stories were simply lost because of the difficulty in reading Olbrechts' handwritten notes (385). There are also eighteen stories told to Olbrechts that were not published anywhere else, according to the Kilpatricks; it is clear to them that the anthropologist had intended to publish them, as he had made rough drafts of sixteen of the stories (386). What is most remarkable about the stories Olbrechts had collected, they note, is how old the stories told by Long and Calhoun were. The couple write, "One gets some concept of the extent of backward reach of many of these stories when one considers that Calhoun learned them from a certain *Tsi:sghwana:i* ('birds, going, they') who was born about 1836, and who in turn doubtlessly learned them from individuals born about the time of the founding of the United States" (386). It is also interesting to note that in this Calhoun version recorded by Olbrechts the spider is referred to as "he" rather than a female water spider. This spider threw the clay bowl into the fire and then used "spinrags" (thought to be spun rags) to pull it back out again before attaching the bowl on his back with silken web and carrying it over to the other creatures. This version also included animals that are not named in the Mooney version, such as the bear, skunk, and black fox (387).

This story of selfless bravery by the various creatures to capture the fire shows their personal traits—courage, intellect, resourcefulness, and inventiveness—that, too often, narcissistic humans assume are limited to human behavior. It also contradicts the now-outdated Western anthropological notion that most animals lack the mental capacity to use tools of any sort to assist them in normal activities, and that humanity's ability to create and use tools makes humans superior to the nonhuman creatures, a belief that most Native people scoff at. Cajete notes that such oral stories "reflect a kind of 'natural democracy,' in that rather than presenting humans as the gifted and favored species of the world, the special traits of plants and animals are regularly depicted again and again with mention of human dependency upon them" (33–35). Many of the ancient oral Cherokee stories hold the nonhumans in high esteem and describe the moral codes and kinship system of the animals, birds, and water creatures that have been emulated by the Ani-Yunwiyah. Humans are presented as lacking natural instinct and as operating on learned behavior, while other creatures have been given their own set of instincts by the Creator, which helps them to instinctively know how to find food and prepare it, how to birth and raise their young, how to defend themselves from stronger creatures, and simply how to survive and thrive. We humans are weak in comparison.

Humans do take front and center, however, in another major ancient story, that of Kanati (the Great or Lucky Hunter) and Selu, the Corn Mother. Selu, pronounced *shay-loo*, is the Tsalagi word for corn. James Mooney does not tell specifically which of his Cherokee friends tells the story, but this lengthy version is the most complete, and I offer it in its entirety here, in the same format Mooney used.

KANA'TI AND SELU: THE ORIGIN OF GAME AND CORN

When I was a boy this is what the old men told me they had heard when they were boys. Long years ago, soon after the world was made, a hunter and his wife lived at Pilot knob with their only child, a little boy. The father's name was Kana'ti (The Lucky Hunter), and his wife was called Selu (Corn). No matter when Kana'ti went into the wood, he never failed to bring back a load of game, which his wife would cut up and prepare, washing off the blood from the meat in the river near the house. The little boy used to play down by the river every day, and one morning the old people thought they heard laughing and talking in the bushes as though there were two children there. When the boy came home at night his parents asked him who had been playing with him all day. "He comes out of the water," said the boy, "and he calls himself my elder brother. He says his mother was cruel to him and threw him into the river." Then they knew that the strange boy had sprung from the blood of the game which Selu had washed off at the river's edge.

Every day when the little boy went out to play the other would join him, but as he always went back again into the water the old people never had a chance to see him. At last one evening Kana'ti said to his son, "Tomorrow, when the other boy comes to play, get him to wrestle with you, and when you have your arms around him hold on to him and call for us." The boy promised to do as he was told, so the next day as soon as his playmate appeared he challenged him to a wrestling match. The other agreed at once, but as soon as they had their arms around each other, Kana'ti's boy began to scream for his father. The old folks at once came running down, and as soon as the Wild Boy saw them he struggled to free himself and cried out, "Let me go; you threw me away!" but his brother held on until the parents reached the spot, when they seized the Wild Boy and took him home with them. They kept him in the house until they had tamed him, but he was always wild and artful in his disposition, and was the leader of his brother in every mischief. It was not long until the old people discovered that he had magic powers, and they called him I'nage-utasun'hi (He-who-grew-up-wild).

Whenever Kana'ti went into the mountains he always brought back a fat buck or doe, or maybe a couple of turkeys. One day the Wild Boy said to his brother, "I wonder where our father gets all that game; let's follow him next time and find out." A few days afterward Kana'ti took a bow and some feathers in his hand and started off toward the west. The boys waited a little while and then went after him, keeping out of sight until they saw him go into a swamp where there were a great many of the small reeds that hunters use to make arrowshafts. Then the Wild Boy changed himself into a puff of bird's down, which the wind took up and carried until it alighted upon Kana'ti's shoulder just as he entered the swamp, but Kana'ti knew nothing about it. The old man cut reeds, fitted the feathers to them and made some arrows, and the Wild Boy—in his other shape—thought, "I wonder what those things are for?" When Kana'ti had his arrows finished he came out of the swamp and went on again. The wind blew the down from his shoulder, and it fell in the woods, when the Wild Boy took his right shape again and went back and told his brother what he had seen. Keeping out of sight of their father, they followed him up the mountain until he stopped at a certain place and lifted a large rock. At once there ran out a buck, which Kana'ti shot, and then lifting it upon his back he started for home again. "Oho!" exclaimed the boys, "he keeps all the deer shut up in that hole, and whenever he wants meat he just lets one out and kills it with those things he made in the swamp." They hurried and reached home before their father, who had the heavy deer to carry, and he never knew that they had followed.

A few days later the boys went back to the swamp, cut some reeds, and made seven arrows, and then started up the mountain to where their father kept the game. When they got to the place, they raised the rock and a deer came running out. Just as they drew back to shoot it, another came out, and then another and another, until the boys got confused and forgot what they were about. In those days all the deer had their tails hanging down like other animals, but as a buck was running past the Wild Boy struck its tail with his arrow so that it pointed upward. The boys thought this good sport, and when the next one ran past the Wild Boy struck its tail so that it stood straight up, and his brother struck the next one so hard with his arrow that the deer's tail was almost curled over his back. The deer carries his tail this way ever since. The deer came running past until the last one had come out of the hole and escaped into the forest. Then came droves of raccoons, rabbits, and all the other four-footed animals—all but the bear, because there was no bear then. Last came great flocks of turkeys, pigeons, and partridges that darkened the air like a cloud and made such a noise with their wings that Kana'ti, sitting at home, heard the sound like distant thunder on the mountains and said to himself, "My bad boys have got into trouble; I must go and see what they are doing."

So he went up the mountain, and when he came to the place where he kept the game he found the two boys standing by the rock, and all the birds and animals were gone. Kana'ti was furious, but without saying a word he went down into the cave and kicked the covers off four jars in one corner, when out swarmed bedbugs, fleas, lice, and gnats, and got all over the boys. They screamed with pain and fright and tried to beat off the insects, but the thousands of vermin crawled over them and bit and stung them until both dropped down nearly dead. Kana'ti stood looking on until he thought they had been punished enough, when he knocked off the vermin and made the boys talk. "Now, you rascals," said he, "you have always had plenty to eat and never had to work for it. Whenever you were hungry all I had to do was to come up here and get a deer or a turkey and bring it home for your mother to cook; but now you have let out all the animals, and after this when you want a deer to eat you will have to hunt all over the woods for it, and then maybe not find one. Go home now to your mother, while I see if I can find something to eat for supper."

When the boys got home again they were very tired and hungry and asked their mother for something to eat. "There is no meat," said Selu, "but wait a little while and I'll get you something." So she took a basket and started out to the store-house. This storehouse was built upon poles high up from the ground, to keep it out of the reach of animals, and there was a ladder to climb up by, and one door, but no other opening. Every day when Selu got ready to cook the dinner she would go out to the storehouse with a basket and bring it back full of corn and beans. The boys had never been inside the storehouse, so wondered where all the corn and beans could come from, as the house was not a very large one; so as soon as Selu went out of the door the Wild Boy said to his brother, "Let's go and see what she does." They ran around and climbed up at the back of the storehouse and pulled out a piece of clay from between the logs, so that they could look in. There they saw Selu standing in the middle of the room with the basket in front of her on the floor. Leaning over the basket, she rubbed her stomach—so—and the basket was half full of corn. Then she rubbed under her armpits—so—and the basket was full to the top with beans. The boys looked at each other and said, "This will never do; our mother is a witch. If we eat any of that it will poison us. We must kill her."

When the boys came back into the house, she knew their thoughts before they spoke. "So you are going to kill me?" said Selu. "Yes," said the boys, "you are a witch." "Well," said their mother, "when you have killed me, clear a large piece of ground in front of the house and drag my body seven times around the circle. Then drag me seven times over the ground inside the circle and stay up all night and watch, and in the morning you will have plenty of corn." The boys killed her with their clubs, and cut off her head and put it up on the roof of the house with her face turned to the west, and told her to look for her husband. Then they set to work to clear the ground in front of the house, but instead of clearing the whole piece they cleared only seven little spots. This is why corn now grows only in a few places instead of over the whole world. They dragged the body of Selu around the circle, and wherever her blood fell on the ground the corn sprang up. But instead of dragging her body seven times across the ground they dragged it over only twice, which is the reason the Indians still work their crop but twice. The two brothers sat up and watched their corn all night, and in the morning it was full grown and ripe.

When Kana'ti came home at last, he looked around, but could not see Selu anywhere, and asked the boys where was their mother. "She was a witch, and we killed her," said the boys; "there is her head up there on top of the house." When he saw his wife's head on the roof, he was very angry, and said, "I won't stay with you any longer; I am going to the Wolf people." So he started off, but before he had gone far the Wild Boy changed himself again to a tuft of down, which fell on Kana'ti's shoulder. When Kana'ti reached the settlement of the Wolf people, they were holding a council in the townhouse. He went in and sat down with the tuft of bird's down on his shoulder, but he never notice[d] it. When the Wolf chief asked him his business, he said: "I have two bad boys at home, and I want you to go in seven days from now and play ball against them." Although Kana'ti spoke as though he wanted them to play a game of ball, the Wolves knew that he meant for them to go and kill the two boys. They promised to go. Then the bird's down blew off from Kana'ti's shoulder, and the smoke carried it up through the hole in the roof of the townhouse. When it came down on the ground outside, the Wild Boy took his right shape again and went home and told his brother all that he had heard in the townhouse. But when Kana'ti left the Wolf people, he did not return home, but went on farther.

The boys then began to get ready for the Wolves, and the Wild Boy—the magician—told his brother what to do. They ran around the house in a wide circle until they had made a trail all around it excepting on the side from which the Wolves would come, where they left a small open space. Then they made four large bundles of arrows and placed them at four different points on the outside of the circle, after which they hid themselves in the woods and waited for the Wolves. In a day or two a whole pack of Wolves came and surrounded the house to kill the boys. The Wolves did not notice the trail around the house, because they came in where the boys had left the opening, but the moment they went inside the circle the trail changed to a high brush fence and shut them in. Then the boys on the outside took their arrows and began shooting them down, and as the Wolves could not jump over the fence they were all killed, excepting a few that escaped through the opening into a great swamp close by. The boys ran around the swamp, and a circle of fire sprang up in their tracks and set fire to the grass and bushes and burned up nearly all the other Wolves. Only two or three got away, and from these have come all the wolves that are now in the world.

Soon afterward some strangers from a distance, who had heard that the brothers had a wonderful grain from which they made bread, came to ask for some, for none but Selu and her family had ever known corn before. The boys gave them seven grains of corn, which they told them to plant the next night on their way home, sitting up all night to watch the corn, which would have seven ripe ears in the morning. These they were to plant the next night and watch in the same way, and so on every night until they reached home, when they would have corn enough to supply the whole people. The strangers lived seven days' journey away. They took the seven grains and watched all through the darkness until morning, when they saw seven tall stalks, each stalk bearing a ripened ear. They gathered the ears and went on their way. They next night they planted all their corn, and guarded it as before until daybreak, when they found an abundant increase. But the way was long and the sun was hot, and the people grew tired. On the last night before reaching home they fell asleep, and in the morning the corn they had planted had not even sprouted. They brought with them to their settlement what corn they had left and planted it, and with care and attention were able to raise a crop. But ever since the corn must be watched and tended through half the year, which before would grow and ripen in a night.

As Kana'ti did not return, the boys at last concluded to go and find him. The Wild Boy took a gaming wheel and rolled it toward the Darkening land. In a little while the wheel came rolling back, and the boys knew their father was not there. He rolled it to the south and to the north, and each time the wheel came back to him, and they knew their father was not there. Then he rolled it toward the Sunland, and it did not return. "Our father is there," said the Wild Boy, "let us go and find him." So the two brothers set off toward the east, and after traveling a long time they came upon Kana'ti walking along with a little dog by his side. "You bad boys," said their father, "have you come here?" "Yes," they answered, "we always accomplish what we start out to do—we are men." "This dog overtook me four days ago," then said Kana'ti, but the boys knew that the dog was the wheel which they had sent after him to find him. "Well," said Kana'ti, "as you have found me, we may as well travel together, but I shall take the lead."

Soon they came to a swamp, and Kana'ti told them there was something dangerous there and they must keep away from it. He went on ahead, but as soon as he was out of sight the Wild Boy said to his brother, "Come and let us see what is in the swamp." They went in together, and in the middle of the swamp they found a large panther asleep. The Wild Boy got out an arrow and shot the panther in the side of the head. The panther turned his head and the other boy shot him on that side. He turned his head away again and the two brothers shot together—*tust, tust, tust!* But the panther was not hurt by the arrows and paid no more attention to the boys. They came out of the swamp and soon overtook Kana'ti, waiting for them. "Did you find it?" asked Kana'ti. "Yes," said the boys, "we found it, but it never hurt us. We are men." Kana'ti was surprised, but said nothing, and they went on again.

After a while he turned to them and said, "Now you must be careful. We are coming to a tribe called the Anada'duntaski ('Roaster,' i.e., cannibals), and if they get you they will put you into a pot and feast on you." Then he went on ahead. Soon the boys came to a tree which had been struck by lightning, and the Wild Boy directed his brother to gather some of the splinters from the tree and told him what to do with them. In a little while they came to the settlement of the cannibals, who, as soon as they saw the boys, came running out, crying, "Good, here are two nice fat strangers. Now we'll have a grand feast!" They caught the boys and dragged them into the townhouse, and sent word to all the people of the settlement to come to the feast. They made up a great fire, put water into a large pot and set it to boiling, and then seized the Wild Boy and put him down into it. His brother was not in the least frightened and made no attempt to escape but quietly knelt down and began putting the splinters into the fire, as if to make it burn better. When the cannibals thought the meat was about ready they lifted the pot from the fire, and that instant a blinding light filled the townhouse, and the lightning began to dart from one side to the other, striking down the cannibals until not one of them was left alive. Then the lightning went up through the smokehole, and the next moment there were the two boys standing outside the townhouse as though nothing had happened. They went on and soon met Kana'ti, who seemed much surprised to see them, and said, "What! are you here again?" "O, yes, we never give up. We are great men!" "What did the cannibals do to you?"

"We met them and they brought us to their townhouse, but they never hurt us." Kana'ti said nothing more, and they went on.

He soon got out of sight of the boys, but they kept on until they came to the end of the world, where the sun comes out. The sky was just coming down when they got there, but they waited until it went up again, and then they went through and climbed up on the other side. There they found Kana'ti and Selu sitting together. The old folk received them kindly and were glad to see them, telling them they might stay there a while, but then they must go to live where the sun goes down. The boys stayed with their parents seven days and then went on toward the Darkening land, where they are now. We call them Anisga'ya Tsunsdi (The Little Men), and when they talk to each other we hear low rolling thunder in the west.

After Kana'ti's boys had let the deer out from the cave where their father used to keep them, the hunters tramped about in the woods for a long time without finding any game, so that the people were very hungry. At last they heard that the Thunder Boys were now living in the far west, beyond the sun door, and that if they were sent for they could bring back the game. So they sent messengers for them, and the boys came and sat down in the middle of the townhouse and began to sing. At the first song there was a roaring sound like a strong wind in the northwest, and it grew louder and nearer as the boys sang on, until at the seventh song a whole herd of deer, led by a large buck, came out from the woods. The boys had told the people to be ready with their bows and arrows, and when the song was ended and all the deer were close around the townhouse, the hunters shot into them and killed as many as they needed before the herd could get back into the timber.

Then the Thunder Boys went back to the Darkening land, but before they left they taught the people the seven songs with which to call up the deer. It all happened so long ago that the songs are now forgotten—all but two, which the hunters still sing whenever they go after deer. (242–48)

To place this story in contemporary times, we should note that the couple lived in the area now known as Pilot Knob or Pilot Mountain, which is in a modern North Carolina state park, a clear example of the colonizer overwriting traditional Indigenous place-names and theft of what were once sacred pieces of land that held historic and spiritual significance; this issue will be discussed further in chapter 3. The original name for this area is Tsuwatelda, which means "where he/she swung, or was hanging."[15] (There is another oral story besides this one of Kanati and Selu that explains how a secret lush and beautiful Cherokee village is hidden within this mountain and is only to be viewed by chosen people.) This particular mountain has a solitary quartzite rock-faced peak that rises 1,400 feet straight above the rolling piedmont surrounding it. The top peak, known as Big Pinnacle, has bare walls of rock with a rounded top that is covered with vegetation. The sheer rock face makes the mountain stand out at a distance for its starkness; the state park service proudly boasts that "this iconic peak is the most recognizable mountain in North Carolina" ("Pilot Mountain"). Pilot Mountain was also designated a National Natural Landmark in 1976 for its geological uniqueness. Cherokee Territory, like the rest of Indigenous North America, is overflowing with such examples of colonizer place-renaming in order to erase the Indigenous subject; by claiming sacred sites and turning them into state or federal designated sites, protected by law, Euro-Americans relegate each site's Native connection firmly to the past along with the "vanishing" American Indian of long ago.[16] There will be more on this issue of renaming in chapter 3.

Elder Freeman Owle recounts a shortened version of the Kanati side of this very long story that he calls "Ganadi,[17] the Great Hunter, and the Wild Boy" (Duncan, *Living Stories* 231–36), while other storytellers refer to Selu as the Corn Mother within their oral performances, most probably because a modern audience may not sit through such a long session of the most complex story from the oral tradition. James Mooney refers to it as the "Origin of Game and Corn," interestingly placing the male procurement of game in a predominant place over that of corn, which became the main staple of the Cherokee diet; however, over time, the story of how the Cherokees received the gift of Selu is better known, while Kanati and his role as First Man and the Great Hunter has decreased in importance in the oral tradition, perhaps due to the fact that the new American government through its Indian policies forced the Cherokee men to abandon hunting and learn the European form of agriculture. The colonizers imposed their beliefs and even mandated in legal policies that only men should work the fields and grow crops for profit, while the women should rule over the domestic sphere inside the home with cooking, cleaning, and childrearing, all the while remaining subservient to the male. This patriarchal view turned upside-down the ancient Cherokee lifestyle of the women doing the farming while the men hunted and went to war, and it had a far-reaching impact on all of Cherokee society, helping bring about the destruction of the matrilineal clan system and disrupting the delicate balance and harmony that had long been established. This inversion of responsibilities effectively ended the traditional importance and power of women as clan mothers and decision-makers, and it thwarted their role in the economy and political life within their own village and household.[18] The story of Kanati and Selu also establishes the responsibilities of men and women within Cherokee society. It explains much about the important environmentally sustainable method of subsistence hunting and farming, which is also a large part of Duyvkta and living a balanced life that does not allow for greed and waste, as well as Gadugi, as the couple showed their Giduwah descendants how to conserve and grow enough to help feed others.

In her book *Cherokee Women*, historian Theda Perdue points out that Selu and Kanati were indeed the examples for all Cherokees when it came to creating and maintaining a harmonious balance (*Cherokee Women* 13). Cherokee men and women divided labor according to gender: women farmed and tended corn because that is what Selu did, and men hunted because Kanati, the first man, did so to provide his family with meat. When women went with their men on the winter hunt, the women took care of their usual duties while the men hunted. In summer, after the men broke and turned the soil, they rested while women worked in the gardens. Then in winter, women stayed indoors in warm houses while men braved the cold to hunt. The Green Corn ceremony, which is the most important ritual on the ancient Cherokee calendar of thirteen moons and thirteen ceremonies, is meant to honor Selu—both the corn and the Spirit of Corn or the Corn Mother—and women in general. It "marked the social and spiritual regeneration of the community, and the role of women in the ceremony symbolized that which they played in Cherokee society" (26). This "new year" or harvest ceremony "connected corn to the community and women to rebirth and reconciliation" (27), as Green Corn was the time to forgive anyone who had harmed or hurt another individual, family, or village (with the exception of murder),[19] and "unhappy spouses could be released from their marital bonds" (25). Ceremonies started with a vigorous cleaning of each entire town. The women swept out their houses, disposed of any old ashes from the cook fires, washed or broke old pottery and replaced it with new, and, finally, got rid of any food left over from the previous year's harvest. Meanwhile, the men swept the council house (which each village had built upon an earthen mound), cleaned the ashes from the hearth, whitewashed all public buildings, built brush arbors, wove new seating mats, and brought in new dirt to cover the council house floor (26).[20] There were also personal purification rites to be done, as many fasted for two days. "During the fast, the beloved women brewed and served warriors sacred medicine that acted as an emetic, purging their bodies of spiritual as well as physical pollution," and everyone went to water to perform their individual cleansing, which was also a daily morning event for the entire village (26). There was, and still is, a great deal of ritual associated with the corn crop during this four-day harvest ceremony, such as offering symbolic ears to the fire as purification of and thanksgiving for the crop. This presentation was and is the central act of the Green Corn ceremony,[21] and this corn, just like Selu, "linked the present to the past and bound Cherokees to one another" (27). Then, and only then, could the new corn be eaten.

Selu is a powerful role model for the Cherokees because of the way that she offered her body and her very life so that the People could forever after have food—and as corn is such a main staple then and now, her life and death means that she literally gave life to the People as a whole—we would not be here were it not for Selu, the first *Agehya* (Woman) and the perpetual Spirit of the Corn. To actually give up her own life so that the People would live is probably the highest form of Gadugi—sacrificing and doing what is best for everyone. First, we see that Selu would rub her body in the storehouse in order to produce the corn that fell into her basket—so the corn literally came from her physical body—and where her blood drops fell (after her death), corn sprang up.[22] The boys' murder of Selu may seem horrific to non-Cherokees, but the sacrifice of the Corn Mother is far from that when we view it through the Cherokee perspective.[23] After all, the death of the physical body is simply that, and the spirit enters a different realm, and as we know today, the Corn Mother and her Spirit are very much present in Cherokee life today. Selu fully expected her sons would kill her because they suspected her of being a *Tskili* (witch), and such creatures were known to steal the life from others in order to live longer themselves (more about this in chapter 2) and were often killed for the good of the entire village or community. Selu's death as the Corn Mother also seemed to be necessary, and she accepted what was about to happen, knowing that she would live on in the form of a plant food that would continue to be vital for her people's continued existence upon this Creation. We can view this as the self-sacrifice that accompanies motherhood, which Selu selflessly gives without argument, as she was clearly focused on her tribe's ultimate survival. Many modern Eastern Cherokee women walk the balanced path of being a mother and pursuing education and/or employment, oftentimes working for the tribe in jobs that allow them to use their college and university degrees or life knowledge. In this way, the *Anigehya* (women) are taking care of their responsibilities as mothers of their own children and taking care of the enrolled members of the EBCI through the jobs they perform within tribal service agencies. There have long been female tribal councillors and, to date, one female principal chief, Chief Joyce Dugan, whom we will hear more about in my final chapter.

The Corn Mother also told the boys how to treat her corpse so that there would forever be corn, but their laziness and inattention to detail mean that corn does not easily grow even after proper tilling and sowing; it must be tended to and protected from hungry birds and bugs, and sometimes it simply will not grow if there is drought or too much rain. These are hard lessons that can mean the difference between feast and famine, and the boys' behavior has forever established the dependency the People have on the natural world for survival when it comes to planting and caring for food crops. In olden times, the People were forbidden to eat the new corn of the season until the proper rituals, meaning the Green Corn four-day ceremony, had been conducted. In fact, there was some sort of punishment for anyone violating this taboo, as everyone was to always think first of the entire community and not their own wants and needs. It is easy to see how such a law was vital, when we consider the precariousness of rain and a good growing season and the possible need for rationing of food. This is why the women were given the responsibility of caring for the food storehouse of each village.

One note about James Mooney's version of the story. He tells us that the second, or new, son is called I'nage-utasun'hi or "He who grew up wild," and that the parents thought he had "magical powers" (*Myths of the Cherokee* 242). This is a specific example of the problems in translation from Cherokee to English, along with a distorted Euro-American perspective (thus Mooney's interpretation) of what the Cherokees would have called the special abilities that some Yunwiyah have who have been blessed or given those gifts by the Creator. The term "magic" has a number of connotations within the

Christian worldview, most of which would be negative or thought to be mere trickery or hocus-pocus. It is simply an accepted Indigenous belief that certain chosen people have strong personal medicine or abilities, which everyone hopes will always be used for good things and in good ways. And, indeed, the two brothers became the Anisgaya Tsunsdi' or the Little Men who are essentially the Thunder Boys, and we know that Thunder and Lightning have an important positive and yet harmful dual purpose, so these brothers have been given necessary responsibilities that are meant for the good of everyone in Creation.

Tsalagi teachings, much like those of other Native groups in North America, are meant to remind us to always think ahead to our children, grandchildren, and so forth so that the Earth and all its resources will be preserved for those future generations, and this is clearly what Selu was doing. Her single life was unimportant, and her body produced a bounty that fed and preserved life while ensuring there would be sustenance for those future generations of Tsalagi people. Most Eastern Cherokee adults and many of the children within that community today have heard the Selu and Kanati story and the lessons behind it at some point in their lives.[24] The fact that Selu and Kanati were happy to see their sons at the end of the journey and welcomed them and allowed them to spend a few days with them in peaceful family relations also reflects the reconciliation and forgiving part of the Green Corn ceremonies, which continue up until the present day. It is not clear if this was in the Spirit World, since Selu was dead while Kanati and their sons were still in the physical world, but since she is thought to be ever-present even today, perhaps she is one of those Spirits who can pass easily back and forth between realms. It is also interesting to note that the couple were in the East—the land of sunrise, new life, and rebirth—so we may feel the two are forever living. After the family reunion, the sons were sent on to fulfill their role as the Thunder Boys, so they also went through a transformation. Fixico suggests that such stories continue to come alive in their telling, even in these contemporary hi-tech times, because "[s]tory is the vehicle for sharing traditional knowledge and passing it from one generation to the next. Its purpose includes sharing information, providing lessons in morality, confirming identity, and telling experiences of people. Stories sometimes tell us about the future. Powerful and vivid, each account is an entity of power. When the story is told effectively, it transcends times, as traditional knowledge lives on with each new listener, becoming a part of them and a part of the next generation" (21–22). Such continuing stories, as Marie Battiste and Sa'ke'j Youngblood Henderson point out, are a "manifestation of caring that extends for at least seven generations. . . . These choices and the responsibilities that follow from them are the defining characteristics of our collective order and wisdom" (11). The choices the two brothers made may seem drastic and uncalled for, but many may realize that there was a purpose to their actions, and the two ultimately were given important responsibilities that not just anyone could fulfill. Their new job as Anisgaya Tsunsdi' suited their personalities in that Lightning and Thunder are life-giving and rejuvenating for the Earth but can also be deadly and destructive.

In presenting the ancient story of Selu and Kanati,[25] Virginia Moore Carney notes that many white Americans find the tale quite violent and disturbing,[26] yet the Cherokees have used the oral story for thousands of years to "teach children the consequences of disrespect, and how they can help to restore harmony among the People" (47). Carney quotes poet Marilou Awiakta (Cherokee heritage), who describes it as a "timeless and reliable compass to right relationships with Mother Earth, with the human family and with oneself" (47). Stories such as this one may be set in the distant past, just after Creation, but transcend time and the many changes that the Giduwah people and culture have undergone, and are examples of the uniquely Cherokee worldview. As Robert J. Conley posits in one of his best-known written collections of oral tales, *The Witch of Goingsnake*, "Behind these stories are gathered a whole set of cultural referents, a different way of interpreting events, a different notion of time, a different concept of language, and, of course, a different view of the purpose and art of storytelling" (xii). He also explains that the Cherokee concept of time is more cyclical, as opposed to the European concept of time being linear, so "in a sense there is no past, no future. All things are present" (xii). The difference between the Native circular mind and the "linear" mind-set of the non-Native seems so drastic that Donald Fixico dedicated an entire book to its examination. He concurs with Conley and numerous other Indigenous scholars who point to this cyclical concept of time as being unique to the Native worldview. Fixico posits that this is most evident within the oral tradition because "[t]he past becomes the present and when common patterns are a part of the experience told about, they are lessons for the future" (25); therefore, *when* something happened is seen as less important. This is why Selu and Kanati are spoken of today as if they are still a part of everyone's family and of the community on the Qualla Boundary and among the diasporic Cherokees of Oklahoma; as for the two brothers, they continue to live as Thunder and Lightning and remind the Yunwiyah of their presence when the Earth needs to be cleansed. This role can be both positive and negative, and this dichotomy also reflects the nature of the two brothers, as it were, and may also represent the perceived internal struggle of all Yunwiyah who do not abide by the ancient teachings. It can also symbolize the balanced opposites that maintain harmony within the Cherokee world. It is not so much that the "Wild Boy" was bad and his brother good, but rather that there can be good and bad within each of us and that these opposing emotions and characteristics must be kept in balance so that one is not stronger than the other. The Thunder Boys can also be considered to be Dusgaseti—those that amaze us and fill us with wonder yet at the same time are to be feared. I'll discuss more about the stories of Dusgaseti in chapters 2 and 3.

Quite often, non-Cherokee scholars have presented the Kanati and Selu story in collections of "legends" and attempt to interpret it by linking these two Indigenous Ancestors to Adam and Eve of the Christian tradition;[27] however, it is not a comfortable or accurate connection. Karl Kroeber suggests that doing so simply does not work, even though he, too, opens his discussion of the Cherokee story with Adam and Eve, then clarifies as he writes, "The contrast of Cherokee and biblical narratives illustrates an essential difference between Native American and Judeo-Christian mythologizing: we distinguish absolutely between natural and supernatural—Indians literally fuse them" (*Native American Storytelling* 52). I do disagree with him on one point, however, and that is his suggestion that Kanati and Selu "are neither divinities nor ancestral Cherokee" but are instead "humanized manifestations of the principal foods of the Indians" (52). Considering the way modern Cherokees speak of Selu, in particular, exemplifies how she and her Great Hunter are *indeed* ancestral Cherokee who lived and breathed and had special talents that they used in a kind, loving communal Gadugi fashion, looking ahead for their descendants and continuing generations.

We must note here that Kanati could have killed his two sons when he learned what they had done at the cave, but chose instead to punish them with the unleashing of the "plague of vermin," because what they had done threatened not only that family's lives but all Cherokee families in the future, yet Kanati stopped the biting insects when the boys were close to death. Even when he discovered his sons had killed Selu, Kanati chose instead to go to the Wolf People so that they, not he, could handle the reciprocity—in this case, death. This is in keeping with the intricate clan system and its rules for blood revenge. If a life had been taken by accident or by murder, the victim's clan had the right to take a life of someone from the attacker's clan; that clan had the right to decide who they would offer up to be killed. Such action was necessary to maintain balance—Duyvkta—and life within Cherokee society focused on that consistent harmony, using balanced categories such as summer/winter, animals/plants, war/peace, farming/hunting, death/life, upper/lower world, and the like. Historian Theda Perdue notes that "[p]eace and prosperity depended on the maintenance of boundaries between these opposing categories, and blurring the lines between them threatened disaster" (*Cherokee Women* 13).

Disaster was averted in the next origin story—that of how disease and medicine came to be—again, a balanced combination of opposites. Again, James Mooney tells this lengthy story in its entirety, and it's crucial for understanding a key foundation of Cherokee culture—the power and agency of the nonhumans.

ORIGIN OF DISEASE AND MEDICINE

In the old days the beast, birds, fishes, insects, and plants could all talk, and they and the people lived together in peace and friendship. But as time went on the people increased so rapidly that their settlements spread over the whole earth, and the poor animals found themselves beginning to be cramped for room. This was bad enough, but to make it worse Man invented bows, knives, blowguns, spears, and hooks, and began to slaughter the larger animals, birds, and fishes for their flesh or their skins, while the smaller creatures, such as the frogs and worms, were crushed and trodden upon without thought, out of pure carelessness or contempt. So the animals resolved to consult upon measures for their common safety.

The Bears were the first to meet in council in their townhouse under Kuwa'hi mountain, the "Mulberry Place," and the old White Bear chief presided. After each in turn had complained of the way in which Man killed their friends, ate their flesh, and used their skins for his own purposes, it was decided to begin war at once against him. Some one asked what weapons Man used to destroy them. "Bows and arrows, of course," cried all the Bears in chorus. "And what are they made of?" was the next question. "The bow of wood, and the string of our entrails," replied one of the Bears. It was then proposed that they make a bow and some arrows and see if they could not use the same weapons against Man himself. So one Bear got a nice piece of locust wood and another sacrificed himself for the good of the rest in order to furnish a piece of his entrails for the string. But when everything was ready and the first Bear stepped up to make the trial, it was found that in letting the arrow fly after drawing back the bow, his long claws caught the string and spoiled the shot. This was annoying, but some one suggested that they might trim his claws, which was accordingly done, and on a second trial it was found that the arrow went straight to the mark. But here the chief, the old White Bear, objected, saying it was necessary that they should have long claws in order to be able to climb trees. "One of us has already died to furnish the bowstring, and if we now cut off our claws we shall all have to starve together. It is better to trust to the teeth and claws that nature gave us, for it is plain that man's weapons were not intended for us."

No one could think of any better plan, so the old chief dismissed the council and the Bears dispersed to the woods and thickets without having concerted any way to prevent the increase of the human race. Had the result of the council been otherwise, we should now be at war with the Bears, but as it is, the hunter does not even ask the Bear's pardon when he kills one.

The Deer next held a council under their chief, the Little Deer, and after some talk decided to send rheumatism to every hunter who should kill one of them unless he took care to ask their pardon for the offense. They sent notice of their decision to the nearest settlement of Indians and told them at the same time what to do when necessity forced them to kill one of the Deer tribe. Now, whenever the hunter shoots a Deer, the Little Deer, who is swift as the wind and can not be wounded, runs quickly up to the spot and, bending over the bloodstains, asks the spirit of the Deer if it has heard the prayer of the hunter for pardon. If the reply be "Yes," all is well, and the Little Deer goes on his way; but if the reply be "No," he follows on the trail of the hunter, guided by the drops of blood on the ground, until he arrives at his cabin in the settlement, when the Little Deer enters invisibly and strikes the hunter with rheumatism, so that he becomes at once a helpless cripple. No hunter who has regard for his health ever fails to ask pardon of the Deer for killing it, although some hunters who have not learned the prayer may try to turn aside the Little Deer from his pursuit by building a fire behind them in the trail.

Next came the Fishes and Reptiles, who had their own complaints against Man. They held their council together and determined to make their victims dream of snakes twining about them in slimy folds and blowing foul breath in their faces, or to make them dream of eating raw or decaying fish, so that they would lose appetite, sicken, and die. This is why people dream about snakes and fish.

Finally the Birds, Insects, and smaller animals came together for the same purpose, and the Grubworm was chief of the council. It was decided that each in turn should give an opinion, and then they would vote on the question as to whether or not Man was guilty. Seven votes should be enough to condemn him. One after another denounced Man's cruelty and injustice toward the other animals and voted in favor of his death. The Frog spoke first, saying: "We must do something to check the increase of the race, or people will become so numerous that we shall be crowded from off the earth. See how they have kicked me about because I'm ugly, as they say, until my back is covered with sores"[;] and here he showed the spots on his skin. Next came the Bird—no one remembers now which one it was—who condemned Man "because he burns my feet off," meaning the way in which the hunter barbecues birds by impaling them on a stick set over the fire, so that their feathers and tender feet are singed off. Others followed in the same strain. The Ground-squirrel alone ventured to say a good word for Man, who seldom hurt him because he was so small, but this made the others so angry that they fell upon the Ground-squirrel and tore him with their claws, and the stripes are on his back to this day.

They began then to devise and name so many new diseases, one after another, that had not their invention at last failed them, no one of the human race would have been able to survive. The Grubworm grew constantly more pleased as the name of each disease was called off, until at last they reached the end of the list, when some one proposed to make menstruation sometimes fatal to women. On this he rose up in his place and cried: *"Wadan'!"* [Thanks!] I'm glad some more of them will die, for they are getting so thick that they tread on me." The thought fairly made him shake with joy, so that he fell over backward and could not get on his feet again, but had to wriggle off on his back, as the Grubworm has done ever since.

When the Plants, who were friendly to Man, heard what had been done by the animals, they determined to defeat the latter's evil designs. Each Tree, Shrub, and Herb, down even to the Grasses and Mosses, agreed to furnish a cure for some one of the diseases named, and each said: "I shall appear to help Man when he calls upon me in his need." Thus came medicine; and the plants, every one of which has its use if we only knew it, furnish the remedy to counteract the evil wrought by the revengeful animals. Even weeds were made for some good purpose, which we must find out for ourselves. When the doctor does not know what medicine to use for a sick man the spirit of the plant tells him. (Mooney 250–52)

This is another vitally important explanatory tale, one that took place not long after the Creation, when the nonhuman creatures "could all talk, and they and the people lived together in peace and friendship" (*Myths of the Cherokee* 250), up until when humans created weapons and learned to kill for food. It is good to see the animals' perspective, as we see the arrogance, disrespect, and even cruelty with which the People began to treat their fellow creatures as they veered off or forgot to live by Duyvkta, the right path. Yet each time the animals tried to retaliate in a cruel way, something happened to interfere with the swing from the drastic behavior by humans to a matching one by the animals, thus some balance was maintained. The resolve by the Ani-Yona (Bear people) to make war on the humans was frightening but also justified, given the fact that the peace and friendship that all of Creation had been enjoying was disrupted by the slaughter perpetrated by Yunwiyah against their nonhuman relatives without permission or explanation and without respect being shown.[28] We can only imagine how things could have turned out had the bears been successful in using the humans' new inventions to not only protect themselves but, in turn, to kill the people and thus "prevent the increase of the human race" (250).[29] As humans ourselves, we can see that obtaining food is necessary, but those early Yunwiyah were self-centered and did not conduct themselves in a proper and harmonious fashion. Perhaps this is because it was in the earliest days after Creation, and the People had much to learn still about their responsibilities within the interconnected society of the Earth—but learn they did.

This story reminds us, too, of the way that the animals held councils in order to give everyone a voice, much like the way the creatures all came together on the Sky Island during Creation, and how a decision was made to go and get the Fire, despite the danger. We see what storyteller Davy Arch alluded to in the way the Cherokees observed and learned from their animal kin, basing their egalitarian governance system on the wiser nonhumans. Another note, about the place where the Yona held their council—the two-footed bear council was held "under Kuwahi mountain, the 'Mulberry Place'"

(*Myths of the Cherokee* 250), which gives a specific location within Cherokee Territory, just like the Kanati and Selu home at Pilot Knob. Kuwahi or the Mulberry Place is today called Clingman's Dome,[30] and it is the highest peak in the Great Smoky Mountains National Park; many Cherokees know it as the place where another story took place that involves a burning bush.[31] Many of the ancient stories locate the action in a spot that modern-day Cherokees know of, even if that location is now lived upon by non-Cherokees and called by an English name. It is a constant reminder of that deep connection to the land and to the knowledge that despite the intrusion and land theft by the colonizer, Cherokee culture is embedded in and imprinted upon the Earth. There will be more about sacred locations in chapter 3.

Meanwhile, the solution created by Ahwi usti (*ah-wee oos-dee*) or Little Deer not only offered balance and harmony, but it was always a reminder for the hunter to show respect to the Spirit of the deer in a prayer. There is fairness and strength in the deer council's decision to send messengers to visit the nearest Cherokee village and inform them of the expectations for prayers for the fallen deer whenever the People found the need to kill one for food. It became a part of the ritual of feeding one's family to simply ask forgiveness from the deer's Spirit, and all hunters learned to only kill when necessary for food.[32] Knowing that a violation of this harmonious act of respect and appreciation would bring the wrath of Ahwi-usti in the form of rheumatism that could mean possible starvation for a hunter's family would most certainly cause the ritual of prayer to be incorporated into the act of hunting, and this lesson would be handed down to each generation—indeed, Ahwi-usti is still mentioned today. This common concern and instance of both Gadugi and Duyvkta by the deer council may be why the Ani-Kawi became one of the ancient seven clans;[33] the deer people are "important in Cherokee society because they supplied the main source of protein to the tribe, the deer. The Deer Clan were the hunters of the deer who were known as the fastest runners with the best eyesight," and it was their responsibility to hunt and "distribute the meat among all of their Cherokee brothers and sisters so that no one was ever hungry" (McGowan 1996). As mentioned in my introduction, the fastest runners, the deer people, were often called upon as messengers to carry news from village to village. The Mooney version tells us that the fish and reptiles also retaliated and decided to cause humans to have frightening dreams about eating rotten fish and getting sick, along with dreams of slimy snakes wrapping around them and breathing bad snake breath in their face. This, however, did not stop the People from catching and eating fish, and there are Cherokees today on the Qualla boundary, and no doubt in Oklahoma as well, who know the proper songs to sing before going out into the woods to keep the snakes away from them as they walk.[34] These sacred songs tell of respect for the Inadv and of the desire to avoid crossing each other's path out of the wish to cause no harm. We will hear in the next story, "The Daughter of the Sun," of how many snakes used to be Anisgayah (men) and of how the Utsonadi (the Rattlesnake) is viewed as a kind creature.[35]

It would seem that the smallest of the creatures had the most cause for anger toward the People, as each Tsisqua (Bird), Tsvsgoyi (Insect), and other small creature denounced the humans for stepping on and kicking them. Walosi (Frog), in particular, seems to have been treated quite cruelly, getting kicked so much by humans that sores developed all over her/his back and leading the frog to insist that something should be done to stop an overpopulation of people. While the frog was kicked and insects stepped on, the bird family complained of the Natives killing them for food. It was the old Cherokee way to shoot birds with a blowgun and impale them on a skewer to roast over a fire;[36] in fact, young children were often taught to hunt first with a blowgun before being able to handle a bow and arrow, and birds and squirrels are the easiest to hit this way. It must be noted that this was not for sport or fun, since the animals and birds were eaten. This story tells us that anger over human cruelty and injustices led this mixed council of creatures to decide that disease should be created and inflicted upon the unsuspecting people with the intention of exterminating their race. Unbeknownst to the humans at the time, the plant beings took it upon themselves to offer up their bodies to provide medicine cures. Here we are told that every herb, shrub, and tree agreed to carry a cure for one or more of the many diseases, each vowing that "I shall appear to help Man when he calls upon me in his need" (*Myths of the Cherokee* 252). Whether we today recognize this selfless act of sacrifice, this ultimate Gadugi, it is exactly that—a kindhearted commitment by the green plants to give of themselves for the betterment of the entire community living within Cherokee country.[37] Of course, so much of that traditional ecological knowledge (TEK) concerning plant medicines has been lost to the Cherokees and every other Indigenous group, but it can be recovered. The old-time Native healers knew how to pray to the Spirit of the plant to find out what it was to be used for, as every disease has a natural botanical cure; today, the Elders say that if there is a disease that is reputed to be incurable, it is only because the correct plant cure for it has not yet been found or refound. Many Indigenous healers from around the world often admonish Europeans and Euro-Americans for their foolishness in believing that many wild plants are nothing more than "weeds" that are pesky and should be wiped out for their lack of beauty and their intrusiveness on immaculately manicured grassy lawns; this, of course, led to the creation of deadly pesticides and herbicides that have contaminated the soil in many areas, and of which humans have clearly lost control. It is interesting to note the recent discovery by master chefs worldwide of many wild foods that have long been ignored or denigrated as mere weeds. Dandelion greens, chicory, lamb's lettuce, mustard greens, and other such "weeds" now make up the so-called spring salad mix that several companies are packaging and making a nice profit from, yet not long ago, most of the ingredients of this salad mix were considered invasive weeds.

Native groups like the Cherokees have always collected many wild foods and enjoyed the healthy benefits of things like greens. Many Eastern Cherokees continue to have "intimate relationships with their plants" (Cajete 110). I had grown up eating greens that my mother bought in Detroit grocery stores, so many were familiar, but while living on the Qualla Boundary, I was fortunate to learn when, where, and how to gather the plants and then how to cook them or make healing teas, giving me that more profound appreciation. Cajete notes that Native people have always understood that each plant has its own energy and its own purpose and place, and this ecological knowledge "derives from intuition, feeling, and relationship, and evolves over extensive experience and participation with green nature. This close relationship also leads to the realization that plants have their own destinies separate from humans, that is, Native people traditionally believed that plants have their own volition. Therefore, Native use of plants for food, medicine, clothing, shelter, art, and transportation, and as 'spiritual partners,' was predicated upon establishing both a personal and communal covenant with plants in general and with certain plants in particular" (110). Plant life is so import-ant to the Eastern Band people that the Cherokee Reservation Cooperative Extension was established by the tribe to help its residents with sustainable agriculture and use of natural resources. This agency works with the local basket makers and other artists to ensure a good supply of the river cane, white ash, and other plants with which they create their works ("Cherokee Reservation Cooperative Extension").

Such origin stories as presented thus far demonstrate how the nonhuman creatures, along with the natural powers and forces of the Earth, offer lessons to the Cherokees as to "how to live and how to communicate with and respect other life forms. They reveal to the People how to hunt and fish, how to take medicines from the earth, and how to respect what they harvest" (Battiste and Henderson 10). It is clear that until the human beings were forced to acknowledge the deadly effects they were having on the animals and birds, they would have continued their self-centered behavior, with little to no regard for the rest of life around them. How tired the creatures must have become of the Ani-Yunwiyah, with their clumsiness and thoughtlessness! Yet the nonhumans were sensible enough that, even in their anger, they knew that humans were a part of Creation, and their desire for death and destruction to be wreaked upon the People was somehow tempered by caretakers like Ahwi-usti and the plants, while prayer and spirituality became an intricate part of the everyday natural world as humans were forced to feel and thus express gratitude for the life of the animals and plants who provided sustenance and healing.

The oral tradition shows that the four-footeds and winged creatures, as well as the plants and insects, always thought of what was best for all, and even when scared for their lives would still follow the path of Duyvkta and balanced relations. One may feel that humans, meaning Cherokees, were like little children who had to be helped along and given time and situations that would force them to mature and learn the lessons of Duyvkta. This is quite in contrast to the Eurocentric notion that humans are the rulers of the Earth and can control the forces of nature and subdue the animal kingdom over which people are deemed to be intellectually superior. Paul Zolbrod suggests we need to step away from the confines of the Judeo-Christian religions in order to witness the interfusion of the sacred within Native oral tradition, or what he calls "oral poetry," as there are "deep spiritual underpinnings of poetry shared in oral performance" among people who have a completely different concept of the cosmos and the Earth and their place within them (13). Kroeber seems to agree, as he notes that "Judeo-Christian tradition absolutely separates the natural from the supernatural; for Native Americans the natural environment is in every aspect divine in its naturalness," a concept that he calls "ecological sacredness" (*Native American Storytelling* 7).

The Cherokees found that they were at the mercy of one of the strongest beings in nature and again needed the help of animals, while they learned from their own human mistakes in the ancient story known as "The Daughter of the Sun." This innocuous-sounding name does not reflect the life-and-death battle that was waged against the destructive yet also life-giving sun force. Elder Freeman Owle offers a modern retelling of this early, origin story of life and death for all Creation, which is reproduced here from Barbara Duncan's book, *Living Stories of the Cherokee.*

THE DAUGHTER OF THE SUN
Freeman Owle

The daughter of the Sun was another legend the Cherokees told.
And this one is not told as much,
but it has a lot of very interesting meanings and value to teach,
and it's unusual that the Sun would be a woman.
The Sun and her daughter the Moon are crossing the sky.
And one day the Sun looked down and noticed
that all the people were looking at her rather squinch-eyed
and with ugly faces every time they looked at her
because of her great brightness.
So the Sun got very angry
and said that she didn't like for people to look at her like that.
And the Cherokee were making fun of her
by making faces at her.
And she got very angry,
and she began to increase her heat
coming down upon the earth.
And the people were so hot their crops began to dry up,
and they began to pray to the Great Spirit
to get the Sun to stop making it so hot.
And it continued on.
So they began to turn to their medicine people,
and they went to this old medicine man,
and he said,
"Well, we can talk to the Sun,

and we can sing to her,
and see if we can get her to calm down
and lessen her heat."
So they began to sing to the Sun.
But of course when they looked at her
their faces were still all squinched and drawn.
And she was not very happy,
and she didn't like the music,
so she made it even hotter.
And the streams began to dry up,
and the trees began to die,
and the crops they planted wouldn't even come up,
so the Cherokees had real problems.
And they decided, through their medicine people,
that they would kill the Sun.
And so the medicine man changed a person into a rattlesnake,
and he was supposed to go up into the heavens
and find his way to where the Sun crossed the sky,
and when she went in to visit her daughter the Moon,
the next morning when the Sun came out,
the rattlesnake was to bite her and kill her.
So sure enough,
he made his way into the heavens
and found the house of the Moon,
and he sat out by the doorway
and waited for the Sun to come out.
And she came out that morning,
and she came out so quickly
that he struck—
and she was so bright,
and he missed.
So he came back to the earth,
and told the medicine people what had happened.
So they were very upset with him
and told him that the next day they would send a copperhead.
So the copperhead went up and he hid by the doorway,

73

and the Sun came out,
and he struck—
and he was to try to get her before she came out—
and he struck too soon
and missed,
and the Sun went on its way.
So the next day they sent both of them up
and told them that they would *have* to kill the Sun,
that they would both strike
just before she came out,
as soon as the door was open, they would strike.
And sure enough, the door opened that morning,
and they struck,
and all of a sudden they hit something
and looked,
and it fell to the ground,
and it was the daughter of the Sun.
The Moon had come up that day.
And so they were very upset.
And when the Sun saw this,
she was very, very angry,
and she began to burn
and even set fires on the earth with her great heat.
The people were digging into the earth trying to save themselves.
And the rattlesnake came back, and the copperhead,
and they changed themselves back into people,
and they told the people what had happened.
So the medicine man said the only way they could make things
right
would be to go to the land of the dead.
Take seven sourwood sticks
and find the daughter of the Sun
dancing in the great circle of the dead,
and when she came around
they would touch her
seven times

with those sticks,
and she would fall down asleep,
and they would put her into a great basket
and carry her back to the land of the Cherokee.
But the medicine man said,
"Under no conditions should you open the basket
even just a little bit."
So they had gone to the land of the dead;
after many, many days' journey
and great problems finding their way there,
they finally made it.
And sure enough,
there was that great circle of death
where the people were dancing,
and they saw the daughter of the Sun.
She danced around to where they were,
and they touched her the first time,
and seven times they touched her
with those sourwood sticks,
and she didn't even know it.
On the seventh time she fell to the ground.
They picked her up and put her in the basket
and started their long journey back to the land of the Cherokee.
On the way back, the daughter of the Sun began to talk
in the basket.
Said she was getting very warm inside,
and would they please open it just a little bit.
But they wouldn't do that;
they remembered their instructions.
After a while she began to say she was getting thirsty,
and then they ignored that.
The she said she was hungry,
and they sort of thought,
"Well, if we let her starve to death, we'll really be in trouble,"
and they were tempted to open the basket,
but they didn't.

After a while she began to say
in a very weak voice,
"I'm hungry
and I'm smothering to death.
I need air."
So one of the people in the group decided they could open it
just a little bit
to give her some air.
When they opened it
there was a red light,
a flittering coming out of the basket,
and it went off into the forest.
And they closed it back real quickly
and said,
"Well, we can't do that.
We better follow instructions."
They carried the big basket
all the way back to the village,
and when they got there,
immediately the medicine man knew they'd opened the basket.
So when he looked inside he was very angry
because there was nothing inside at all.
They began to wail in their great sadness.
They looked outside, and the Sun was scorching the earth.
All of a sudden they noticed that it began to cool off a little bit.
They looked out, and the lady Sun was smiling.
And they listened,
and they heard this sound
of a beautiful song
coming from a bird in the bush.
They looked over to the bush,
and there was
a beautiful redbird.
And as it sang,
the Sun smiled,
and the heat decreased.

They then knew that the redbird
was the daughter of the Sun.
From that day forward,
the Sun has been good to the Cherokee people. (208–12)

Again, we see the balanced role that so many beings in Creation have—a life balance of which the early Cherokees became ever-mindful of as they found their place in the natural world during the Earth's younger days. This story explains how death of the physical body came to be while defining the boundaries of this Earth world and that of the Spirit world,[38] and it cautions how the use of bad medicine to cause harm must always be avoided while showing how human fears and frailties can jeopardize the existence of an entire group of people and all other beings who depend on the sun. There is a drastic disruption of Duyvkta in this early story, and something must be done to reestablish balance and harmony. The older telling of this story from Mooney's book is slightly different from Freeman's but necessary to read because we hear of the first time how the horned serpent from the water, *Uktena,* is explained.

THE DAUGHTER OF THE SUN

The Sun lived on the other side of the sky vault, but her daughter lived in the middle of the sky, directly above the earth, and every day as the Sun was climbing along the sky arch to the west she used to stop at her daughter's house for dinner.

Now, the Sun hated the people on the earth, because they could never look straight at her without screwing up their faces. She said to her brother, the Moon, "My grandchildren are ugly; they grin all over their faces when they look at me." But the Moon said, "I like my younger brothers; I think they are very handsome"— because they always smiled pleasantly when they saw him in the sky at night, for his rays were milder.

The Sun was jealous and planned to kill all the people, so every day when she got near her daughter's house she sent down such sultry rays that there was a great fever and the people died by hundreds, until everyone had lost some friend and there was fear that no one would be left. They went for help to the Little Men, who said the only way to save themselves was to kill the Sun.

The Little Men made medicine and changed two men to snakes, the Spreading-adder and the Copperhead, and sent them to watch near the door of the daughter of the Sun to bite the old Sun when she came next day. They went together and hid near the house until the Sun came, but when the Spreading-adder was about to spring, the bright light blinded him and he could only spit out yellow slime, as he does to this day when he tries to bite. She called him a nasty thing and went by into the house, and the Copperhead crawled off without trying to do anything.

So the people still died from the heat, and they went to the Little Men a second time for help. The Little Men made medicine again and changed one man into the great Uktena and another into the Rattlesnake and sent them to watch near the house and kill the old Sun when she came for dinner. They made the Uktena very large, with horns on his head, and everyone thought he would be sure to do the work, but the Rattlesnake was so quick and eager that he got ahead and coiled up just outside the house, and when the Sun's daughter opened the door to look out for her mother, he sprang up and bit her and she fell dead in the doorway. He forgot to wait for the old Sun, but went back to the people, and the Uktena was so very angry that he went back, too. Since then we pray to the rattlesnake and do not kill him, because he is kind and never tries to bite if we do not disturb him. The Uktena grew angrier all the time and very dangerous, so that if he even looked at a man, that man's family would die. After a long time the people held a council and decided that he was too dangerous to be with them, so they sent him up to Galun'lati, and he is there now. The Spreading-adder, the Copperhead, the Rattlesnake, and the Uktena were all men.

When the Sun found her daughter dead, she went into the house and grieved, and the people did not die any more, but now the world was dark all the time, because the Sun would not come out. They went again to the Little Men, and these told them that if they wanted the Sun to come out again they must bring back her daughter from Tsuginai, the Ghost country, in Usuhi'yi, the Darkening land in the west. They chose seven men to go, and gave each a sourwood rod a handbreadth long. The Little Men told them they must take a box with them, and when they got to Tsuginai they would find all the ghosts at a dance. They must stand outside the circle, and when the young woman passed in the dance they must strike her with the rods and she would fall to the ground. Then they must put her into the box and bring her back to her mother, but they must be very sure not to open the box, even a little way, until they were home again.

They took the rods and a box and traveled seven days to the west until they came to the Darkening land. There were a great many people there, and they were

78

having a dance just as if they were at home in the settlements. The young woman was in the outside circle, and as she swung around to where the seven men were standing, one struck her with his rod and she turned her head and saw him. As she came around the second time another touched her with his rod, and then another and another, until at the seventh round she fell out of the ring, and they put her into the box and closed the lid fast. The other ghosts seemed never to notice what had happened.

They took up the box and started home toward the east. In a little while the girl came to life again and begged to be let out of the box, but they made no answer and went on. Soon she called again and said she was hungry, but still they made no answer and went on. After another while she spoke again and called for a drink and pleaded so that it was very hard to listen to her, but the men who carried the box said nothing and still went on. When at last they were very near home, she called again and begged them to raise the lid just a little, because she was smothering. They were afraid she was really dying now, so they lifted the lid a little to give her air, but as they did so there was a fluttering sound inside and something flew past them into the thicket and they heard a redbird cry, *"kwish! kwish! kwish!"* in the bushes. They shut down the lid and went on again to the settlements, but when they got there and opened the box it was empty.

So we know the Redbird is the daughter of the Sun, and if the men had kept the box closed, as the Little Men told them to do, they would have brought her home safely, and we could bring back our other friends also from the Ghost country, but now when they die we can never bring them back.

The Sun had been glad when they started to the Ghost country, but when they came back without her daughter she grieved and cried, "My daughter, my daughter," and wept until her tears made a flood upon the earth, and the people were afraid the world would be drowned. They held another council, and sent their handsomest young men and women to amuse her so that she would stop crying. They danced before the Sun and sang their best songs, but for a long time she kept her face covered and paid no attention, until at last the drummer suddenly changed the song, when she lifted up her face, and was so pleased at the sight that she forgot her grief and smiled. (252–54)

The Mooney version is longer and more complex, while Freeman Owle's telling of it is probably more understandable to a non-Cherokee audience. One noticeable difference is that Mooney's sources say that the moon was brother to the female sun and do not actually describe the form the sun's daughter took, while Owle says the daughter is the moon. Either way, it is clear there was cruel and disharmonious behavior by nearly everyone involved, and the repercussions have had long-lasting effects upon not only the Cherokee world but for all Earth creatures and people the world over because "Indigenous peoples do not view humanity as separate from the natural world" (Battiste and Henderson 24).

It is an Indigenous belief that what is commonly called the "elements" within the natural environment are living, thinking, feeling creatures who are much like humans in that each one has a mind and a spirit; this includes beings like the sun, moon, Earth, winds, and thunders as well as mountains, waterways, trees, etc. who carry their own uniqueness and have a purpose and role in their own life and within the lives of others. Looking at the older version by Mooney, we see the female sun, who is a mother and a giver of life who also has the responsibility of deciding how she should use her "powers" of life and death. She seems a hardworking being who travels a long way across the Sky Vault to do her job, and she is a devoted and obviously loving mother who spends time and shares her midday meal with her only daughter. Yet the sun has the weaknesses or frailties of character that so many humans also have—she is jealous of her brother and wishes for everyone to love her and think that she is beautiful, so she lashes out in anger when those humanlike emotions are harmed. Fixico argues that such oral stories "have purposes and lessons for teaching about morality or the future. They are lessons in life about vanity, pride, showmanship, hidden danger, and how life can be lost—all as a part of the natural laws of the universe" (24). The sun seems to forget the responsibility that the Creator gave her, which is to warm and nurture the many creatures upon the Earth and promote their ecological interdependency—not to control or rule them. In contrast to Western society where the matter of control is of the utmost importance, most Native societies do not include such a concept but rather aim for "reciprocity, balancing, right acting and right telling in the interests of equilibrium. Power *flowed*; it was not wielded" (Swann xi–xii). When someone abuses the abilities that they have been blessed with, bad things often happen to them. This result is designed to be a reminder—sometimes a gentle nudge and other times a harsh slap; it works with the humble notion that we are all on a balanced footing within the Creator's great plan and must all work hard to live harmoniously and with all other life-forms in mind. Of course, "we" refers not only to the Yunwiyah but to all forms of life, be they animal, bird, fish, plant, rock, water, or the beings that live in the Sky World. Seeing the sun as a being capable of hurt, anger, and sorrow should make the humans understand and perhaps even sympathize with her, while at the same time respecting her for her abilities and the never-ending job she does in promoting life and renewal of the Earth's creatures.

This story is also one of contrasts, of the sun/moon, male/female, earth/sky, drought/flood, and life/death, and, as pointed out earlier, those opposing categories had to be strictly enforced in order to maintain balance and harmonious relations (*Cherokee Women* 13). Opposition, in this case, does not mean each entity is contrary or antagonistic to the other but rather that they are generally complementary in their position; it is interesting to note that some dictionaries use the example of the sun and the moon to explain the meaning of the word opposition. Kenneth Lincoln posits that many "[t]ribal stories pivot on contrasts, releasing sorrow, sparking laughter, inspiring invention, purging primal fears. They give humankind a range from the animals and the earth to the gods and the sky" (25). Lincoln, like so many other non-Native scholars, mistakenly suggests that tribal peoples are polytheistic and recognize or even worship many gods, such as a "sun god" or "rain god," while the Cherokees and other Indigenous folk see these living entities as exactly that—other living creatures who are governed by their own unique Spirits within. When they become too full of their own importance and use their talents or powers in an unkind way, as the sun did in this story, things will happen to remind them that their personal abilities are to be shared and used for the common good. Brian Swann concurs with the reality of one God for most Indigenous groups. In his introduction to the book *Smoothing the Ground: Essays on Native American Oral Literature,* Swann argues that the Native concept of the ultimate power is that of the "Great Spirit" or "Creator" who created the entire universe.[39] He argues that the Western notion of religious or supernatural awe "suggests a large element of fear in the 'holy' and potential self-abasement. This may be appropriate enough for the white mans' understanding of holiness" (xii) but differs vastly from the Native relationship to the Mystery and its Creator. Swann refers to Morris Edward Opler's work with Apache culture, which suggests that "power itself is a force for common good" (xii). Fortunately for the Earth creatures, the sun generally does use her power for the good of all, as does the Earth, yet we see in these modern times that when we humans do not respect the Earth, she is forced to fight back against the devastations and abuses heaped upon her by employing her abilities to create natural disasters, violent weather systems, and deadly chaos.

In this story, the sun began the cycle of disrespect and abuse of abilities, which the humans, in turn, respond to by attempting to misuse the healing abilities and medicine knowledge that had been given to the Little Men by Unelanvhi. It was a deadly project on both sides, and disharmony and death were the result of these abuses, as these actions led to the finality of death and the permanence of the human journey to the Spirit World in the West. It is not truly clear how death was viewed or how the spirit journey happened prior to these events, according to UKB elder and language professor Tom Belt, as this is not a well-known oral story and is not one that is often recounted by contemporary storytellers—perhaps because it is so complex and may conflict with theology brought by the colonizer. Conversion to Christianity has influenced and colored the beliefs many Cherokees hold today about death, as nearly all Cherokees, regardless of age, have been taught at church or by family the biblical teachings concerning death and heaven and hell. Belt suggests that the more traditional folks do not believe in a concept of hell or a place for what are considered "bad" people, because we are all capable of being bad or disharmonious, yet there is indeed a heaven or Seventh Heaven (Belt, Interview #2); the Cherokee word for this is the same word used for the Sky World—Galvladi or, as Mooney spells it, Galunlati. There are seven levels or planes that a Spirit proceeds along or climbs to that heaven from this Earth, and Belt states that "we are all on a journey" and that the seven levels are simply a part of that ongoing journey. He suggests that no one knows how long it takes to reach the next level from the one a person or Spirit is currently on, but that until one learns particular things, one cannot move on to the next level (Interview #2). Cherokee Nation scholar Christopher Teuton's work with storytellers from the Cherokee Nation and the United Keetoowah Band of Cherokees of Oklahoma shows that those traditional men follow this same belief. Elder Hastings Shade explains that the final step in the seven levels is "the one everybody works for. That's that last place where the Creator is. There's no end there . . . the living continues. But you're living in a different form . . . it's not this body. It's a body that doesn't hurt, a body that doesn't require food or anything like that. It's everlasting. There's no want for anything. There's no need for anything. It's just a continuation" (105). Teuton posits that the journey along those levels is "represented by our interactions with the natural world. Moving on a journey from the water world to the world of the sky and beyond, we learned things along the way and brought that knowledge with us. We also make this journey as individuals" (105). It is thought that the deceased person is not gone completely from the lives of their loved ones until they have reached that Seventh Heaven, and that the Spirit can still communicate with those who have their physical bodies or are still alive on Earth. Those Spirits can travel and journey back and forth between the Spirit World and the Earth, sometimes paying visits to those loved ones, oftentimes passing on knowledge, information, and teachings that the Spirit feels the loved one needs to hear and learn. Sometimes this is done through dreams or other psychic and spiritual events or even during prayer; however, Belt states, we, as the living, cannot call to the dead or ask them questions because it does not work that way; they communicate with us on Earth when there is a need (Interview #2). These Spirits are also known to travel with the wind, and their voices can be heard in the wind, but only if one "listen[s] with a different set of ears" (Teuton 106).

In regard to consoling the sun after the Cherokee men mistakenly open the box and release the Spirit of her daughter—never to return to Earth—we see that the real solution to the sun's displeasure and grief lies in kind, harmonious actions by the People. It is only when the most talented humans are sent to dance and make music for her that she begins to return to a friendlier state of mind. The sun may certainly bear much blame for her original meanness in trying to kill so many humans just for their grimacing at her brightness, yet the cruel and murderous actions by the humans, the Little Men,[40] and the snakes cannot be viewed as a counterbalance when they should have looked for harmonious ways to deal with the sun in the first place. The old adage of "two wrongs don't make a right" comes to mind. When the Yunwiyah finally recognize the pain and sorrow of the sun and remember that she is a living creature with agency and emotions, then the humans look for a solution that will bring harmony and balance back to the world.[41] There is cooperation among the seven Anisgayah (men) as they make the most-likely frightening journey to the Spirit World in order to save their own loved ones from further suffering, but it is a human mistake—one made out of concern for the unhappy daughter trapped in the box—that ultimately has an all-encompassing and everlasting impact upon the rest of the world's creatures. Death of the physical body becomes permanent and cannot be reversed, because "when they die we can never bring them back" (*Myths of the Cherokee* 254), and this holds true for all living beings within Creation. Comfort can be found in the notion of the seven levels of existence that progress to a heaven in the sky, which does allow for the dead to occasionally pay visits and offer advice to those less experienced kin who are bound to the Earth by a physical body. It seems fitting that Cherokee views about life and death are strongly connected to the sun, a giver of life for many creatures, and a series of steps to the Sky World. After all, she rises in the eastern sky, where the first home of Sky Island hung and from where all the nonhuman beings and the People originated. The sun is also a form of that sacred Fire that burns for the ceremonies, the stomp dances, and prayer circles and that always burns within the spirit of every Cherokee who knows the Giduwah way.

Within these origin stories from thousands of years ago, the Cherokee homeland was created, but it was not just for the Giduwah people, as this is an Earth made for every living creature. Everything in Creation has agency and spirit, from the smallest pebble or blade of grass or bug to the massive mountains and cold, racing rivers and green trees and plants within these southern lands of the Cherokee world. The animals, birds, and other nonhumans worked hard to assist in the Creation and set examples for the People to learn to practice Gadugi for the benefit of all and to live in the Duyvkta manner with harmonious and kind behavior every day in their relations with all Earth beings. The Eastern Cherokees remember that it was the snakes and birds who risked their lives to try and bring the Fire Spirit to the rest of the world, and the humble little water spider who was finally successful and forever after honored for her brave contribution. That fire has become the centerpiece of not only Cherokee life but of the set of spiritual beliefs known as the Kituwah ways. The Ani-Yunwiyah Ancestors learned how to live in harmony with the four-footed, winged, and scaled creatures and how to always say prayers of respect and gratitude to those animals and plants who give their lives so that the People can eat, be strong, and heal themselves. The ancient stories discussed so far, and so many others that I have no space to share in this project, have laid the foundation for Giduwah culture and society and ensured that as long as there are Cherokees on this Earth, the Fire will burn strong.

In ancient times, physical death seemed to be a fluid concept in the Cherokee world when it came to certain creatures. As we will see in the next chapter, Tskili and Dusgaseti seem to defy any rules about physical forms, and their decisions and actions to take the lives of others to satisfy themselves have serious reverberations throughout the natural world.[42] These upcoming stories suggest that there is always someone or something willing to upset the balance and disrupt the harmony, yet those deadly behaviors must be stopped for the good of all.

2

Dusgaseti Tsalagi Kanoheda nole Tskili • Part 1

Cherokee Stories of "Those who are to be avoided;
dreadful; wondrous things" and Witches

We have heard of how the nonhuman creatures worked together to create the world known as the Cherokee homeland, and the way those early animals, birds, reptiles and other beings established the concept of both Gadugi in giving of themselves for the benefit of everyone and Duyvkta by setting the lifeways that respect others and allow for mutual interdependence. In many ways, it seems the animals helped the less-strong humans who lacked natural instincts. According to Native science, the relationships and associations between animals and Indigenous peoples have their own "internal logic. The way Native people traditionally classified animals had an 'aptness' based on their value, their use as food, and their relative role in the reality of the natural environment that both Natives and animals inhabited" (Cajete 150). This goes hand-in-hand with the belief that each animal has its own Spirit, and this belief extends to every other living creature within the natural world (Cajete 150). The nonhumans and the People had learned to coexist in a mutually beneficial manner, and the Ani-Yunwiyah recognized that this environment offered all they needed for a comfortable life.

Yet everything in this beautiful, lush mountain world was not always pleasant and respectful. Some of the ancient stories of the Cherokees tell of a darker side of life, of beings and creatures who are not very friendly or congenial, and are far from being brave, selfless, or as cooperative as those in the stories examined thus far. The Cherokee homeland is filled with spiritual beings and nonhuman creatures who roam the ancient shrouded forests and mist-covered mountains, or slither and crawl through the icy cold mountain streams and rivers, often killing indiscriminately and creating widespread fear; these Dusgaseti populate the Cherokee oral tradition yet bring a form of balance to the land (Muse, "North America's Oldest 'Monsters'" 1). Just as many creatures kill and feed off others, allowing for that ecological give-and-take of life that maintains a natural equilibrium, there are others who kill for what may seem like pure cruelty. Many of these Dusgaseti appear in human form, while others are clearly more of an animal nature. Despite their deadly personalities, they can still unintentionally bring about good things for those Aniyvwi whom they prey upon.[1] There are also those Dusgaseti who frighten everyone around them but are simply misunderstood and try hard to be accepted, such as Tsudvkula,[2] who will be discussed in chapter 3.

Cherokee has no word for "monsters"; that is an older Middle English term (from Anglo-French) which generally has negative connotations and is defined as "an imaginary beast, usually compounded of incongruous parts" (*New Webster's Dictionary*, 1992, 647). The word "monster" today brings to mind ideas of Hollywood movies like *Dracula, Curse of the Werewolf, Creature from the Black Lagoon, Frankenstein*, or any of the assorted films that often take the legendary beasts from ancient European folklore and distort them into oversensationalized killing machines. In contrast, *Usgaseti* simply means a fierce creature or a being who should be avoided and who is generally *not* friendly, yet it can also mean "wondrous" beings (Muse, "North America's Oldest 'Monsters'" 1–2). In fact, Mooney includes many of the stories of these creatures in a section he labels "Wonder Stories" (*Myths of the Cherokee* 311). These Dusgaseti who live in the Cherokee mountains may have animal and/or human characteristics and can sometimes shape-shift, changing their appearance in order to deceive the unsuspecting people. Even though some of the Dusgaseti are dreadful and can kill people, they are a part of the Cherokee world and very real—*not* fictionalized and open to artistic interpretation like Hollywood versions of culturally relevant European monsters. These frightening creatures are not considered abnormal, simply because the Cherokee worldview holds that every creature put upon the Earth is supposed to be here and each looks the way it is meant to appear; they each have a Spirit and thus the right to exist. Each of them has a purpose because, the Cherokee believe, every living being has been given a reason for its existence, even though some are to be avoided at all costs, and each creature is a part of the natural balance of life and death (Muse, "North America's Oldest 'Monsters'" 1–2).

Needless to say, some Dusgaseti can bring chaos and oftentimes death to the world. They disrupt the harmony other Earth beings try to maintain within the natural realm, and that means it is up to others within Creation, Yvwi included, to take appropriate action to restore balance and harmony. Some of those storied creatures include beings who seem to delight in behaving badly or even killing people and eating them—yet something good usually comes out of these beings' existence, as we will see in this chapter. Despite the fact that many of these creatures can and do kill, which does not seem harmonious in any way, each Usgaseti offers its own form of Duyvkta because its negative actions can also lead to positive outcomes for the Cherokees—each one in a different manner. Along with these Dusgasetis' own unusual form of creating balance, the threat that these dreadful beings bring to the People provides opportunities for Gadugi as the Cherokees do what is best for the entire community or village, with everyone coming together in a strong united effort. In chapter 3, I will turn to the "friendlier" Dusgaseti who seem to be more wondrous but are still meant to be avoided or, at least, not sought after. First, let us establish more of the environment of the ancient Cherokee world, where such awesome and dreadful creatures live and thrive in good or bad ways.

The sacred lands of the Ani-Yunwiyah are resplendent with a haunting beauty and filled with soft, blue-green, mist-enshrouded mountains. There are days when the clouds wrap themselves around the mountaintops and fill the deep valleys with thick gray threads of foggy mist, blurring and distorting the hilly shapes and outlines, making it difficult at times to distinguish the misty mountaintops from the gray billowing clouds on the horizon. The trees and brush are so thick up and down the mountains, hills, and valleys that one can scarcely see beyond the front rows of trees, and there are often sudden movements through the woods that one catches out of the corner of the eye that startle the senses and may fill the observer with disturbing unease. There are deep ravines that are uninviting for anyone daring enough to go for a hike through the woods, as one could quickly turn an ankle and slide uncontrollably down the steep slopes. Cold, gurgling streams flow down the hills and offer instant chills to those who venture into the woods, despite the bright rays of sunshine that beam through the treetops dozens of feet above the ground. When a wet weather system moves into the mountains, it often comes as a complete surprise, leaving no time to run for shelter, and sometimes brings a wall of rain that hits quick and hard—penetrating and drenching everything within a few moments.

To say the Cherokee mountains are forbidding or even frightening for their perpetual darkness and green coolness would be an oversimplification, as these hills and woods are also naturally beautiful, amazingly wondrous for their spectacular panoramic views, and even soft and comforting for many who live there or visit. The summer temperatures often peak in the nineties (Fahrenheit), since the elevation is so high, and then drop into the crisp fifties at night. Like so many things in the natural world of the Cherokees, there seem to be many personalities and appearances to these grandfather mountains and lands of mainly red clay soil that suggest a constant back-and-forth play of a welcoming yet fiercely intimidating balance of Earth forces and life. The wintertime offers a different, stark landscape as monstrous mossy boulders and jagged, fallen, and decaying trees litter the hillsides, unseen in the summer because of the thick foliage; deep scars and gashes in the red clay skin of the mountainsides become visible through the naked trees after the autumn winds strip the leaves. It is not surprising to hear that there are many creatures who live in these forbidding areas, and it is best to avoid these beings.

As described in the story "The Daughter of the Sun," one of the most famous Usgaseti is Uktena,[3] the enormous horned serpent who is still thought to swim the many streams and creeks, both above- and belowground. Then again, some believe there are many Uktena, who are more dangerous than even the rattlesnakes, copperheads, and water moccasins that live all over the Cherokee mountains. The Mooney version is the most complete, and I offer it here.

THE UKTENA AND THE ULUNSU'TI

Long ago—*hilahi'yu*—when the Sun became angry at the people on earth and sent a sickness to destroy them, the Little Men changed a man into a monster snake, which they called Uktena, "The Keen-eyed," and sent him to kill her. He failed to do the work, and the Rattlesnake had to be sent instead, which made the Uktena so jealous and angry that the people were afraid of him and had him taken up to Galun'lati, to stay with the other dangerous things. He left others behind him, though, nearly as large and dangerous as himself, and they hide now in deep pools in the river and about lonely passes in the high mountains, the places which the Cherokee call "Where the Uktena stays."

Those who know say that the Uktena is a great snake, as large around as a tree trunk, with horns on its head, and a bright, blazing crest like a diamond upon its forehead, and scales glittering like sparks of fire. It has rings or spots of color along its whole length, and can not be wounded except by shooting in the seventh spot from the head, because under this spot are its heart and its life. The blazing diamond is called *Ulunsu'ti*, "Transparent," and he who can win it may become the greatest wonder worker of the tribe, but it is worth a man's life to attempt it, for whoever is seen by the Uktena is so dazed by the bright light that he runs toward the snake instead of trying to escape. Even to see the Uktena asleep is death, not to the hunter himself, but to *his family*.

Of all the daring warriors who have started out in search of the Ulunsu'ti only [O]gan-uni'tsi ever came back successful. The East Cherokee still keep the one which he brought. It is like a large transparent crystal, nearly the shape of a cartridge bullet, with a blood-red streak running through the center from top to bottom. The owner keeps it wrapped in a whole deerskin, inside an earthen jar hidden away in a secret cave in the mountains. Every seven days he feeds it with the blood of small game, rubbing the blood all over the crystal as soon as the animal has been killed. Twice a year it must have the blood of a deer or some other large animal. Should he forget to feed it at the proper time it would come out from its cave at night in a shape of fire and fly through the air to slake its thirst with the lifeblood of the conjurer or some one of his people. He may save himself from this danger by telling it, when he puts it away, that he will not need it again for a long time. It will then go quietly to sleep and feel no hunger until it is again brought out to be consulted. Then it must be fed again with blood before it is used.

No white man must ever see it and no person but the owner will venture near it for fear of sudden death. Even the conjurer who keeps it is afraid of it, and changes its hiding place every once in a while so that it can not learn the way out. When he dies it will be buried with him. Otherwise it will come out of its cave, like a blazing star, to search for his grave, night after night for seven years, when, if still not able to find him, it will go back to sleep forever where he has placed it. Whoever owns the Ulunsu'ti is sure of success in hunting, love, rain-making, and every other business, but its great use is in life prophecy. When it is consulted for this purpose the future is seen mirrored in the clear crystal as a tree is reflected in the quiet stream below, and the conjurer knows whether the sick man will recover, whether the warrior will return from battle, or whether the youth will live to be old. (297–98)

The storytellers that Mooney learned from told him of how the failure by the rattlesnake and Uktena to kill the sun left Uktena so angry that he hated people, and if a man even looked at the serpent, his family would die. The danger was so great to the People that the medicine men finally had to send him away to the Sky World (*Myths of the Cherokee* 253). The oral stories say that even though Uktena was taken up to Galvladi,[4] he left some of his own kind behind in the mountain streams, and this seems to be an accepted truth around the Qualla Boundary, as many Cherokees have heard in their lifetime of someone spotting one. The belief in the water snake's existence continues today, without any sensationalism or hype, but merely a calm acceptance within the community. This is evident in the way that Davy Arch tells his contemporary account, recorded by Barbara Duncan in her *Living Stories of the Cherokee.*

LEGENDS OF THE UK'TENA
Davy Arch

There's quite a few stories around about the Uk'tena.
And not long ago, maybe ten years ago,
there was a crystal found, over on Tellico Plains,
when they were doing the excavation over there,
that was a crystal like the Uk'tena was supposed to have guarded.
And they found this crystal wrapped in a full deerskin
and put away the way it was supposed to have been
when it was put away not to be used anymore.
And when they were using this crystal
they had to feed it.
Then they had a formula or a prayer to put it to sleep with

when it wasn't going to be used.
But Uk'tena was the giant snake that was supposed to have guarded this.
And there's a lot of stories about it being a horned serpent,
a serpent with horns.
So I don't know whether there were two types of snakes that large
in this part of the country
or what it was.
And there's also stories about the people who lived in the underworld
that rode giant rattlesnakes.
And the entrance to this underworld
was through the rivers and the streams.
They would go into the big pools in the rivers,
go into the passages that led into the underworld
where the snakes were large enough to ride like horses. (93–94)

In discussing Seneca oral stories and what is sacred in them, Paul Zolbrod notes that the work of Seneca historian and folklorist Arthur C. Parker, who collected his people's stories,[5] examines the connection between the natural world and the transcendent. Zolbrod states, "The 'unseen spirits' in Seneca lore that 'pervade all nature and affect man for good or evil' must be placated by the things that people actually do rather than by magic or superhuman deeds" (16). We will see how, with each of these Dusgaseti, that the Cherokee had to determine how best to deal with the often-destructive beings, and then take action collectively in the manner of Gadugi and what is ultimately best for the entire group. In the case of the Uktena, Mooney's storytellers explain how it is not the snake but rather the Ulvsuti crystal that is placated by being fed the blood of both a large and a small animal. The typical Cherokee would not go out hunting for Uktena in order to exterminate its species (as would happen in many other world cultures) but instead accept his existence and avoid him, informing others of the various locations where the Uktena may live so that even children are aware of the dangers. As we see in the Mooney story, only the medicine people sought the serpent in order to acquire the healing powers of the crystal embedded in its forehead, and it was only by tricking the serpent that these healers were able to kill him and take the Ulvsuti. This deception can be viewed as a form of Gadugi, for the medicine people needed the crystal to help with their healing rituals for their Cherokee patients and the community as a whole, and killing the Uktena was the only way to obtain the crystal.

Dusgaseti creatures like the Uktena continue to exist for the Cherokees because, as Fixico suggests, "[t]he spirituality of any entity is timeless, such that a story is reawakened and moved through linear time. In the full release of its power and its effects on the audience, the story is enlivened such that the past becomes a part of the present, and the past and present is projected into the future" (27). This is why Uktena and many other of these spiritual creatures remain a part of the Qualla community's orature even today. Fixico notes that oral stories can be highly influential on Native societies, and this is not always recognized. He disagrees with those scholars of Native American studies who often suggest there is a fair bit of twisting the truth, which is a part of what they call folklore, but he argues there is an inherent power in the oral tradition that is bigger than the storyteller or the listeners, because "[i]t is an Indian reality" (26). Brian Swann also argues against those who admonish such ancient spiritual stories, noting that today's mainstream society is lacking in authentic symbolism and balance. He suggests that those outside of Native American society are envious of Indigenous ideas, energies, and attitudes, which place great importance on maintaining harmony and good order "within what one might call a cosmic framework and reference" (xv). There is a great need to continue telling such ancient stories in order to infuse today's reality for Native people with the concepts and beliefs of their Ancestors and thus to keep the culture alive. Zolbrod recognizes the importance of stories—what he calls oral poetry—about events and beings that are outside the familiar natural world, like the Dusgaseti stories of the Cherokees. He notes that "[b]ecause they suggest alternative views of the sacred, works of oral poetry in many cases also distinguish between mythic time . . . and remembered time; and therein they designate relationships between the phenomenal and the supernatural as neither conventional history nor empirical investigation can specify" (18–19). It is vitally important for the Eastern Cherokees today to continue telling and embodying the oral stories so that the sacred lessons will stay strong within the Qualla community and work to form a cultural protection against the daily onslaught of the intruding colonizer society's ways of life and values. The Dusgaseti stories may cause discomfort and perhaps even frighten people, but these beings are a part of the spiritual reality of the Cherokee and have a purpose and role.

We must try to imagine an immensely long, horned serpent with a body as big as a tree trunk—not difficult if we consider the size of prehistoric dinosaurs—with a bright, blazing crystal in his forehead and scales that glitter and sparkle like fire all up and down his body. He is spotted all over, and—worst of all—he cannot be wounded except exactly at the seventh spot from his head, because that is where his heart and life reside. Yet this frightening *Inadv* (snake) who can kill with just a look can be viewed as a balanced creature, since the crystal in Uktena's forehead holds healing powers;[6] the crystal is called Ulvsuti, which means transparent, while the root of the word means flickering or giving off light. The old ones say that anyone who sees Uktena is so dazed by the brightness of the Ulvsuti that they run right to the serpent, rather than running for their life. In ancient times, some medicine people did acquire their own Ulvsuti, which they used for conjuring or for prophecies, and they kept it hidden or even buried to protect themselves and the People. For the purpose of Gadugi, the conjurers risked their own lives, and perhaps that of their family, in order to obtain and have those healing abilities that the deadly crystal offered for their medicine work within their village. Every seven days, the Ulvsuti has to be rubbed with the blood of a small animal and twice a year with the blood from larger game; if this is not done, the crystal will awake and fly through the air, killing the conjurer or anyone nearby (*Myths of the Cherokee* 297–98). The Uktena stories—and there are many—though relayed to Mooney in the late 1800s and still told in our modern times,[7] have much more ancient roots: as historian Charles Hudson notes in his article entitled "Uktena: A Cherokee Anomalous Monster," artifacts of stone, pottery, and even shell from prehistoric sites throughout the Southeast have been unearthed that bear "representations of serpents with horns, wings, feet, and other unsnakelike features" (65–66). Some of this artwork, including shell gorgets found of a later time period in east Tennessee (part of traditional Cherokee territory),[8] show giant serpents with rings and spots on the bodies and oftentimes a rattlesnake tail; some representations even show teeth and large circles on the head that could be eyes or the expected crystal (66–67)—ample evidence that the ancients knew of the Uktena. (I should point out that even though some drawings show wings, there is no mention in any oral story I have found of a flying Uktena. That doesn't mean a winged one didn't or doesn't exist.)

No one knows what has happened to those Ulvsuti that belonged to the medicine people and healers from those ancient times. A British army officer,

Lieutenant Henry Timberlake, describes in his memoirs how some Cherokees at that time (1756–65) told him of one healer who wrapped himself in leather hides, which deflected the bites of the deadly Uktena, and then lay in wait for the giant serpent; the Cherokee man surprised and killed Uktena and grabbed the crystal from its forehead. Timberlake relates how the story goes that the healer then kept the Ulvsuti hidden, with only two women knowing of its whereabouts. Despite numerous bribes and money offers, the healer refused to divulge where he kept the crystal, knowing that it would kill anyone who touched it—since no one was supposed to even look upon it (Williams 73–75). The stories say that those ancient healers had to use trickery and deceit to trap and kill the serpent, because the belief was that possessing this powerful crystal "insure[d] success in hunting, love, rain making, and all other undertakings, but its great use is in life divination, and when it is invoked for this purpose by the owner the future is mirrored in the transparent crystal as a tree is reflected in the quiet stream" (*Myths of the Cherokee* 460–61). In fact, Mooney was told an oral story of three Cherokee men who went to battle during the Civil War for the Confederate army who first had gone to consult a conjurer with an Ulvsuti; the crystal correctly predicted the fate of the men, with two dying in the second year of the war and the other (whose image had risen above the other two in the reflected image in the crystal) returning home at the end after enduring "great hardships and narrow escapes" (461).[9] Cherokee storytellers Ayvini and Itagunuhi shared a number of stories with Mooney about various healers who had the difficult task of taking care of an Ulvsuti. One man had a crystal as big as an egg and so bright that it kept his entire cabin lit up in winter; the stone, which the man claimed to have found near a dead snake, would even flash like lightning so brightly that his neighbors were afraid for their very lives, particularly those who were weak in body or spirit. When the conjurer died, the crystal was buried with him underneath his home because his family knew there was a chance that someone would think to dig up the grave in order to capture the Ulvsuti and take it (461). There is so much danger in possessing such a stone that stealing it could cost someone their life and even that of their family.

This two-sided ability of Uktena to offer up either death or healing is why Hudson suggests the serpent is "neither unmitigatedly evil nor straight-forwardly antithetical to man" ("Uktena"). He refers to stories from the Cherokees in Oklahoma who "sometimes invoked a spiritual Uktena in their magical formulas" (64) in these postcolonizer times. We do not hear of medicine people or conjurers today still having possession of any such healing crystals, but that doesn't mean these powerful gems do not still exist, particularly when we note that the stories of Uktena are part of contemporary life on the Qualla Boundary. We must understand that even though these stories are ancient and come from the beginning of time, they are still relevant now and the People still know them to be a truth. Fixico posits that the Native reality is one that combines the physical and metaphysical environment. He argues that "[s]tories convey this reality of spiritual beings interacting with people on a regular basis. That nature and its phenomena of metaphysics interact with people in a nonconcrete fashion that Western society usually dismisses. This metaphysical and physical combined reality is natural to Indian people, and it is much a part of their lives and the realm that their community functions within" (34). The Dusgaseti of the Cherokee homeland are a part of this combined reality of spiritual creatures who cross paths and physically interact with people, or what Zolbrod refers to as the "overlapping of the real with the supernatural" (17).

The oral tradition and belief in Uktena and other wondrous creatures is just as strong today among the People as it ever was. The serpent continues to live in the deep, cold creeks through the mountains and within the Oconaluftee River that runs through the heart of the reservation. If you swim in the river, you must watch for Uktena, and even if he does not make an appearance, his power can make someone swimming in the Oconaluftee sick with fever and chills.[10] The Uktena has not gone away, and he is believed by some to have caused the death of people in modern times, often by way of car accidents on rainy days and nights near the river or in its branches throughout the surrounding counties, as the downpour seems to help Uktena extend his watery territory. Elder Tom Belt suggests these deaths may happen because the Uktena does not know the non-Cherokees who travel through its territory; one way, he says, to prevent this is to speak your own name when driving or walking by a waterway that is reputed to be home to an Uktena in order to identify yourself (Lecture). Some stories say the great serpent is as much as three miles in length, and because he swims deep within the fast-running depths of these rivers, streams, and ponds—which are known to be connected under the land surface—no one ever knows exactly where he is since he moves about so quickly. He is spoken of as if he were a single massive snake, but again, many believe there is more than one, although everyone simply speaks of "the" Uktena.

Perhaps it is because the Uktena carries within him both the ability to kill and to heal, two balanced opposites, that the deadly serpent continues living in today's world. Then again, maybe there is no way to fully extinguish such a being because Unelanvhi (the Creator) gave him life for a reason. Since the Ulvsuti is so strong with healing powers yet dangerous at the same time, perhaps such a crystal had to be carried and protected by a serpent, making it difficult to acquire, because in the wrong hands the stone could be deadly for many people around it. It is clearly meant for the positive benefits of humankind and must be respected;[11] in fact, some may consider Uktena to be living a balanced life, or his own form of Duyvkta. Hudson notes that archaeologists and historians doubt the existence of such a massive snake because no skeletal remains have ever been found of it in the Southeast, yet many of the ancient stories tell that birds and other animals quickly devour the dead Uktena, bones and all, so that nothing remains. The only thing that is ever left are many small crystals which can be found throughout the southern mountains[12]—these crystals are believed by the Cherokees to be scales from Uktena and hold some lesser healing powers than the large one from its head. Hudson poses the question, "Why, we may ask, did the Cherokees believe in a monster which to us seems so obviously fanciful?" ("Uktena" 67). From a Western viewpoint, it may be hard to acknowledge and accept the Tsalagi perspective, one which simply sees the reality in knowing that this creature, or creatures, does indeed exist because the Cherokees, like other Indigenous peoples, "respect and appreciate the inherent value of every life force and place in the ecological order" (Battiste and Henderson 11). Noting the difference in traditional Native views of animals and the natural world and those held by Western science, Cajete argues that, for Natives, "there is a fluid and inclusive perception of animal nature that makes less of a distinction between human, animal, and spiritual realities. These realities are seen as interpenetrating one another" (150). Indeed, in discussing the Uktena, Tom Belt suggests that out in the woods, there are most likely many other Dusgaseti that are unknown to the People simply because no one has encountered them as yet, adding that when the Creator means for us to know of them, it will happen. He discards the notion that humans may know everything about the mysteries of the Earth, suggesting that many creatures avoid humans because of our destructive nature (Personal Interview #2).

In his article, Hudson discusses the writings of James Adair, a famous fur trader during the mid-1700s who closely studied many tribes in the Southeast and clearly believed in the creature. Hudson notes that the Cherokees were so firm in their beliefs of the serpent's existence that they somehow convinced Adair, who was "unusually intelligent and skeptical" and was indeed a well-educated man for his time who "did not emphasize the bizarre for its own sake" (65). As mentioned earlier, Hudson noted that there are Cherokee spiritual formulas in use in Oklahoma that invoke the metaphorical power of Uktena, which shows that even for Cherokees removed from the sacred homeland, the healing purpose of this Dusgaseti continues to exist. Having non-Cherokees believe or not believe in the Uktena is irrelevant to most Tsalagi because it is part of our lifeways and ecological knowledge, which differs greatly from that of the newcomers. In a chapter entitled "Animals in Native Myth and Reality," Cajete notes that animal characters are in over 75 percent of Indigenous oral stories, which is "evidence of the intimate relationship with animals felt by Native people" (166). Such stories carry teachings about moral and ethical behavior, and most are "elegant and complex, and contain great wisdom," which is why most stories took a long time to tell as well as to commit to memory (166). Perhaps, as Kenneth Roemer suggests, the problem is that many non-Natives have a skewed perception of the oral tradition of Native people, and "[b]ecause of the ways most non-Indians learn about Native American oral narratives, they tend to associate them with 'quaint' or 'primitive' fairy tales, folklore, or superstitions" (39).

We must remember that Uktena was first a man and was changed into the huge serpent in order to try and kill the Sun and her deadly rays, and in that regard, perhaps Uktena came to believe that certain deaths are necessary to achieve balance and harmony. For the Cherokees, he is not a fantastical, imaginary concoction that one should question as Hudson does, but rather is both physical and spiritual. He exists as a deeply embedded cultural truth and a part of the natural world of the Tsalagi. This scholarly need to make something like the Uktena serpent, which has a unique role and purpose within the Cherokee world, into an imaginary myth or legend is symptomatic of the Eurocentric belief that any of the world's cultures that are non-European are primitive and uncivilized and can only be improved upon once those cultures accept the European form of civilization. Many Western scholars reflect the Euro-American thought that their "superiority is based on some inherent characteristic of the European mind or spirit and because non-European peoples lack this characteristic, they are empty, or partly so, of ideas and proper spiritual values" (Battiste and Henderson 21). Such scholarly skepticism is part of what Wahinkpe Topa (Irish and Cherokee ancestry) refers to as the "third wave" of killing Indigenous peoples around the world. The "first wave" was the physical assault upon the land and Native inhabitants of North America by Europeans and their soldiers, explorers, and missionaries; this was conducted mainly through violence and disease. The "second wave" is still going on, and it occurs through politicians, courts, the military, and corporations who work to control traditional Native territory and their natural resources, along with their culture, language, and sovereignty. The "third wave," also ongoing, is carried out by scholars and academics with their formal scholarly publications that "erroneously attack the philosophies, worldviews, and histories of Indigenous People" (20). The dismissal of the role and validity of the Uktena within Cherokee culture is an example of the Euro-western approach that only recognizes the writings of scholars with degrees or titles and ignores the vast collective of Indigenous ways of knowing.

In his book *Smoothing the Ground: Essays on Native American Oral Literature*, Brian Swann recognizes that for many years, Native oral stories "have been treated as tales for children" (xiv) by some who study them. He posits that Native orality is much more than childish tales because the stories tell the truth, even if that truth is disturbing, frightening, or even horrific. He quotes what an old Eskimo/Inuit once told Danish anthropologist Knut Rasmussen.[13] "Our narratives deal with the experiences of man, and these experiences are not always pleasant or pretty. But it is not proper to change our stories to make them more acceptable to our ears, that is[,] if we wish to tell the truth. Words must be the echo of what has happened and cannot be made to conform to the mood and the taste of the listener" (xiv).

It is this assertion of truth that is key to the Dusgaseti and all other oral stories because even today, these stories and the teachings that come from them create and maintain the everyday reality for the Eastern Cherokees. Many of these Dusgaseti stories are not pleasant, because as Penny Petrone points out, the main function of oral literature among the North American tribes was "utilitarian and functional rather than aesthetic" (4). She argues that its purpose was not only to communicate with one another but also to effectively communicate to and with "powerful spirits" (4), for as many Cherokees or other Native persons would know, each time you tell a story of one of these Spirits or Dusgaseti, you are speaking to them and telling them how important they have been within the culture, thus promoting a ceremonial function through storytelling. It is a way of calling them back and giving them respect for what they have done for the People and acknowledging how that Spirit or being continues to belong to the community. Robert J. Conley explains in his introduction to *The Witch of Goingsnake* that "[t]he American Indian spirit world does not exist as a world apart from the real world. The world we inhabit in this life is both physical and spiritual. To Cherokees, as to other American Indians, spirit life is an everyday reality" (xiii). Paul Zolbrod concurs with this belief and emphasizes the blending of the supernatural with physical reality within much Native oral poetry (his term), adding that "[a]ccordingly, poetry acquires the power to connect the inner self and the natural with what dwells outside the self and beyond nature" (17). He goes on to suggest that "the verbalized world view of a culture has roots in a shared sacred vision of the universe" (2). Karl Kroeber adds to this discussion when he writes, "The physical world in which all humans dwell is sacred because every part of it [and this would include Dusgaseti] . . . is equally infused with divine life and equally worthy of respect for what it is in itself and as a useful contributor to the dynamism of the whole" (7). In an early work by Charles Hudson entitled *The Southeastern Indians*, he notes that such belief systems are much more than what many non-Natives would often call magical or religious. "The fact is," he argues, "the categories and beliefs of the Southeastern Indians represented the world as they believed it existed, and this included both the natural and the supernatural, the normal and the abnormal, and the sacred and the profane. The social arrangements, customary practices, and rituals of the Southeastern Indians make sense only when viewed against the ideological background of their belief system" (120).

Edward Chamberlin posits that such spiritual stories "are always more or less about the greater design of things, their universal purpose or end; but they often illustrate this by telling us about the means, the mechanisms, the particular good or evil" (210).

Perhaps the more applicable term should be "good AND evil" when we consider Uktena and his purpose, and that of another well-known Usgaseti who is simply called Stonecoat or Nunyunuwi, which means "dressed in stone" (*Myths of the Cherokee* 319).[14] He has skin of solid rock and is feared because he is known to kill and eat hunters who cross his path, most often those who are out alone. Stonecoat roams the hills looking for people, and he uses a particular walking stick made of stone to help find them. He simply points the stick in a direction and then smells the end of it for the scent of humans to steer him to potential food, and it is hard to escape or fight because of the power of the stone stick and the fact that he has rock-hard skin to protect him. Here's how Mooney recorded this important story.

NUN'YUNU'WI, THE STONE MAN

This is what the old men told me when I was a boy.

Once when all the people of the settlement were out in the mountains on a great hunt one man who had gone on ahead climbed to the top of a high ridge and found a large river on the other side. While he was looking across he saw an old man walking about on the opposite ridge, with a cane that seemed to be made of some bright, shining rock. The hunter watched and saw that every little while the old man would point his cane in a certain direction, then draw it back and smell the end of it. At last he pointed it in the direction of the hunting camp on the other side of the mountain, and this time when he drew back the staff he sniffed it several times as if it smelled very good, and then started along the ridge straight for the camp. He moved very slowly, with the help of the cane, until he reached the end of the ridge, when he threw the cane out into the air and it became a bridge of shining rock stretching across the river. After he had crossed over upon the bridge it became a cane again, and the old man picked it up and started over the mountain toward the camp.

The hunter was frightened, and felt sure that it meant mischief, so he hurried on down the mountain and took the shortest trail back to the camp to get there before the old man. When he got there and told his story the medicine-man said the old man was a wicked cannibal monster called Nun'yunu'wi, "Dressed in Stone," who lived in that part of the country, and was always going about the mountains looking for some hunter to kill and eat. It was very hard to escape from him, because his stick guided him like a dog, and it was nearly as hard to kill him, because his whole body was covered with a skin of solid rock. If he came he would kill and eat them all, and there was only one way to save themselves. He could not bear to look upon a menstrual woman, and if they could find seven menstrual women to stand in the path as he came along the sight would kill him.

So they asked among all the women, and found seven who were sick in that way, and with one of them it had just begun. By the order of the medicine-man they stripped themselves and stood along the path where the old man would come. Soon they heard Nun'yunu'wi coming through the woods, feeling his way with his stone cane. He came along the trail to where the first woman was standing, and as soon as he saw her he started and cried out: "*Yu!* my grandchild; you are in a very bad state!" He hurried past her, but in a moment he met the next woman, and cried out again: "*Yu!* my child; you are in a terrible way," and hurried past her, but now he was vomiting blood. He hurried on and met the third and the fourth and the fifth woman, but with each one that he saw his step grew weaker until when he came to the last one, with whom the sickness had just begun, the blood poured from his mouth and he fell down on the trail.

Then the medicine-man drove seven sourwood stakes through his body and pinned him to the ground, and when night came they piled great logs over him and set fire to them, and all the people gathered around to see. Nun'yunu'wi was a great ada'wehi and knew many secrets, and now as the fire came close to him he began to talk, and began to sing, and sang the hunting songs for calling up the bear and the deer and all the animals of the woods and mountain. As the blaze grew hotter his voice sank low and lower, until at last when daylight came, the logs were a heap of white ashes and the voice was still.

Then the medicine-man told them to rake off the ashes, and where the body had lain they found only a large lump of red wa'di paint and a magic u'lunsu'ti stone. He kept the stone for himself, and calling the people around him he painted them, on face and breast, with the red wa'di, and whatever each person prayed for while the painting was being done—whether for hunting success, for working skill, or for a long life—that gift was his. (319–20)

This is a complex story that further exhibits the balance of opposites within a being and the potential for both good and evil that is believed to reside in all creatures of the Earth. Mooney's Cherokee informants told him that Stonecoat was a great Adawehi—the old Cherokee word for "wise one"—because he knew secrets (320). We must imagine how those men listening to Nunyunuwi, as his oral teachings spilled forth from the depths of the deadly fire, had to work hard to listen, comprehend, and learn those sacred songs and formulas word-for-word as well as memorize the harmony and tune for each song, along with all the information about the medicines and how to treat sickness.[15] They had one night to accomplish this work—a phenomenal task and an example of the oral mind at work. Linguist Walter Ong describes the difference between the oral mind and a literate mind in that the oral person will either feel the feeling or see the thing that the word represents or its connection to other things, but when a literate person hears a word, he or she will see the word visually (12). Without any means of writing it down and instead feeling the feelings, the Cherokee men listening to the dying Nunyunuwi and his sacred knowledge of healing words and songs had to learn quickly. Ong goes on to posit that "[t]he interiorizing force of the oral word relates in a special way to the sacral, to the ultimate concerns of existence. In most religions the spoken word functions integrally in cere-monial and devotional life" (74). The songs, words, and teachings shared by Nunyunuwi are considered to have formed the basis of Cherokee spiritualism, and Stonecoat is still credited for his legacy of healing knowledge even today. This shows the Cherokee acceptance of the concept of balanced opposites or contrasts residing within a being. Stonecoat was cannibalistic, but he most certainly had a purpose that was also life-giving for the Giduwah people, because his songs and words created the Giduwah set of spiritual teachings.

Those men, those hunters, had a sacred responsibility to learn everything they could from the dying man of stone skin because "[t]he story properly told, or the song properly sung, *is* true" (Chamberlin 147), and the future of their people was literally in their hands. They had to learn those sacred words and music, and we can just imagine how the physiological process of intense, rapid learning must have embedded this oral memory within their bodies, spirits, and minds. The story does not tell who these men were, but they were clearly thinking of the generations of Cherokees to come, and what a remarkable feat they accomplished. Yet this is the way with oral societies, as Cree scholar Neal McLeod explains about oral memory among his First Nation in Canada when he says "[t]heir bodies become houses of ancient sound" (100). He suggests that those oral songs and stories must be memorized in the Native language and recounted in the language as well, for there is great power in those words and sounds. Nunyunuwi is credited with holding and sharing tremendous knowledge that was then passed down from generation to generation and is intricately woven into the songs and healing rituals that the Cherokee have long practiced, as "[i]t is these traditions that have permanence" (Chamberlin 192). Despite the fact that Nunyunuwi was a wondrous yet dreadful being to be avoided—what all Dusgaseti are known for—he ultimately is someone who should be respected for his talents and is spoken of with reverence by many modern Cherokee storytellers. Quite simply put—where would the Tsalagi be without these important cultural intricacies that Nunyunuwi was gifted with and that he in turn gifted to the People? These songs and healing formulas form a tremendous part of Kituwah spiritualism, and this is something for which all Cherokees must be grateful; it is what sets them apart from all other Indigenous peoples of the world. It is sad to think, though, that because of the genocidal colonization process, some of those hunting songs, ritual prayers, healing formulas, and the rest of this cultural repertoire that was freely given to the People by the dying Nunyunuwi may have become lost, at least for the time being, simply because when such orality is not practiced on a regular basis and when it is not handed down to the younger generation, it becomes lost to memory. Add to that the tremendous language loss that has gone on over the past five hundred years and the fact these songs and healing prayers were to be said in the Cherokee language, it is easy to see how much of the knowledge shared by Nunyunuwi has become lost to the People.

G. Keith Parker, in his examination of seven particular Cherokee stories, makes an interesting observation—one that, in a sense, contradicts Tsalagi belief. Instead of recognizing that the Stonecoat is overcome by the poison blood that naturally comes out of the women's bodies, Parker suggests the women are offering their "life-giving blood to save their people" (107). Parker employs Jungian theory and Christian perspectives in his effort to make Cherokee oral stories acceptable and understandable to non-Cherokees, a noble endeavor, but he too often misreads them or gives them an interpretation that is not consistent with that of the Cherokee worldview. It is this Christian view, most likely connected to the idea of Christ offering his blood to give eternal life to his followers, that leads Parker to think of the women's menstrual flow as life-giving, while the Indigenous view is that it is powerful and dangerous in the fact that it is toxic waste, mixed with blood, of which the female body is purging and ridding itself. In a medical sense, it is the *absence* of the menstrual blood that actually gives life, as the monthly flow ceases during pregnancy. A woman's moon-time is extremely dangerous for men because of the female powers, and Stonecoat was clearly horrified by their sight and then overcome.

Let's hark back to chapter 1 and the story of the "Origin of Disease and Medicine," where some angry animals wanted women to die from their monthly cycle; instead, the plants bargained and all agreed that having their moon-time would not kill women but would give them the ability to purge their bodies of unwanted (female reproductive) materials. Within a Cherokee village, and indeed any Indigenous community, in olden times, it was no secret as to which women were experiencing their cycle because those women were treated well and fed by their female kin while being removed from their family, especially male relatives, and spending a few days in a separate hut. Historian Theda Perdue explains that exclusive rituals were involved, as such women "had great power, and men regarded them as dangerous; consequently, they [men] kept their distance and knew nothing about the rites women performed to control and channel that power" (*Cherokee Women* 4). It was a personal time in which those women could do what they wanted in terms of hobbies, craft-making, or attention to their personal selves. Food was brought to them by their mothers, sisters, daughters, or aunts and left outside of the hut since they could not cook or otherwise touch any of the food that would be consumed by others because of the danger of poisoning and harming the boys and men (*Cherokee Women* 29). Among the Cherokee today, if a woman is having her time, she is not allowed to participate in ceremonies; this is one of the rules that are spoken of at the beginning of stomp dances. When the women prepare the feast at the stomp grounds or even at social events, those special women get to relax and stay far away from the cooking area and have food brought to them; some menstruating women will simply stay home to avoid harming others. Indigenous groups usually had and some still have special ceremonies to honor a young woman when she receives her first moon-time, as it was and still is a cause for celebration and honor. It is the big step from childhood to womanhood, as a female comes into her own power. It must be emphasized here that this belief contrasts greatly with the Western thought that a woman's menstruation makes her dirty and unclean; even today, too many young Euro-American women are often told that it is the "curse" and something to be ashamed of and embarrassed about, even to be kept a secret and hidden from all others. It was no secret to Nunyunuwi as he came upon these seven Tsalagi women because the poison hit him quickly and weakened him. Their blood was not life-giving but rather caused an agonizing death for Stonecoat. These women showed their sense of Gadugi, as they, in a sense, violated the normal rituals involved in their monthly cycle of cleansing and instead came out into the open, in full view of the medicine man and Anisgaya (men) hunters, and participated in this ritualistic killing of an Usgaseti for the benefit of the People.

One wonders how it is that such a creature who went around killing and eating humans could also hold such incredibly sacred knowledge that was meant to greatly benefit the Tsalagi people as a whole. Much like the fearsome Uktena with its ability to both kill and heal, Nunyunuwi was created exactly the way he was so that the People could understand that every being has a purpose and their life should be respected, but when that being threatens the welfare and lives of the group members, something drastic must be done. As we have seen, the Ani-Yunwiyah learned early on from the animals and plants that taking the life of another living creature, no matter what species, is a serious matter and is not to be done unless absolutely necessary for the good of the entire village or community. Yet this was also the case with another of the Dusgaseti who lived within the homeland of the Tsalagi, and this human-looking creature is still believed to wander the darkened paths through the fog-enshrouded mountains. The story of Utlvta, or the Spearfinger, is one of the scariest of the Dusgaseti stories, particularly for the children who hear of her.[16] James Mooney refers to her as an "ogress" (*Myths of the Cherokee* 316), a French term for a female monster or giant who eats humans, but this denotation erroneously links Utlvta to European fairy tales.[17] This shape-shifting Tskili often took the appearance of an old woman but could really turn into anyone she wanted; she seems to be the first Tskili mentioned in the old stories and establishes the belief that anyone who is a Tskili is capable of shape-shifting.[18] Again, Mooney's is the most detailed version I have found.

U'TLUN'TA, THE SPEAR-FINGER

Long, long ago—*hilahi'yu*—there dwelt in the mountains a terrible ogress, a woman monster, whose food was human liver. She could take on any shape or appearance to suit her purpose, but in her right form she looked very much like an old woman, excepting that her whole body was covered with a skin as hard as a rock that no weapon could wound or penetrate, and that on her right hand she had a long, stony forefinger of bone, like an awl or spearhead, with which she stabbed everyone to whom she could get near enough. On account of this fact she was called *U'tlun'ta*, "Spear-finger," and on account of her stony skin she was sometimes called *Nun'yunu'wi*, "Stone-dress." There was another stone-clothed monster that killed people, but that is a different story.

Spear-finger had such powers over stone that she could easily lift and carry immense rocks, and could cement them together by merely striking one against another. To get over the rough country more easily she undertook to build a great rock bridge through the air from Nunyu'-tlu'gunyi, the "Tree rock" when the lightning struck it and scattered the fragments along the whole ridge, where the pieces can still be seen by those who go there. She used to range all over the mountains about the heads of the streams and in the dark passes of Nantahala, always hungry and looking for victims. Her favorite haunt on the Tennessee side was about the gap on the trail where Chilhowee mountain comes down to the river.

Sometimes an old woman would approach along the trail where the children were picking strawberries or playing near the village, and would say to them coaxingly, "Come, my grandchildren, come to your granny and let granny dress your hair." When some little girl ran up and laid her head in the old woman's lap to be petted and combed the old witch would gently run her fingers through the child's hair until it went to sleep, when she would stab the little one through the heart or back of the neck with the long awl finger, which she had kept hidden under her robe. Then she would take out the liver and eat it.

She would enter a house by taking the appearance of one of the family who happened to have gone out for a short time, and would watch her chance to stab some one with her long finger and take out his liver. She could stab him without being noticed, and often the victim did not even know it himself at the time—for it left no wound and caused no pain—but went on about his own affairs, until all at once he felt weak and began gradually to pine away, and was always sure to die, because Spear-finger had taken his liver.

When the Cherokee went out in the fall, according to their custom, to burn the leaves off from the mountains in order to get the chestnuts on the ground, they were never safe, for the old witch was always on the lookout, and as soon as she saw the smoke rise she knew there were Indians there and sneaked up to try to surprise one alone. So as well as they could they tried to keep together, and were very cautious of allowing any stranger to approach the camp. But if one went down to the spring for a drink they never knew but it might be the liver eater that came back and sat with them.

Sometimes she took her proper form, and once or twice, when far out from the settlements, a solitary hunter had seen an old woman, with a queer-looking hand, going through the woods singing low to herself: *Uwe'la na'tsiku'. Su' sa' sai'*. Liver, I eat it. Su' sa' sai'. It was rather a pretty song, but it chilled his blood, for he knew it was the liver eater, and he hurried away, silently, before she might see him.

At last a great council was held to devise some means to get rid of U'tlun'ta before she should destroy everybody. The people came from all around, and after much talk it was decided that the best way would be to trap her in a pitfall where all the warriors could attack her at once. So they dug a deep pitfall across the trail and covered it over with earth and grass as if the ground had never been disturbed. Then they kindled a large fire of brush near the trail and hid themselves in the laurels, because they knew she would come as soon as she saw the smoke.

Sure enough they soon saw an old woman coming along the trail. She looked like an old woman whom they knew well in the village, and although several of the wiser men wanted to shoot at her, the others interfered, because they did not want to hurt one of their own people. The old woman came slowly along the trail, with one hand under her blanket, until she stepped upon the pitfall and tumbled through the brush top into the deep hole below. Then, at once, she showed her true nature, and instead of the feeble old woman there was the terrible U'tlun'ta with her stony skin, and her sharp awl finger reaching out in every direction for some one to stab.

The hunters rushed out from the thicket and surrounded the pit, but shoot as true and as often as they could, their arrows struck the stony mail of the witch only to be broken and fall useless at her feet, while she taunted them and tried to climb out of the pit to get at them. They kept out of her way, but were only wasting their arrows when a small bird, Utsu'gi, the titmouse, perched on a tree overhead and began to sing "*un, un, un.*" They thought it was saying *u'nahu'*, heart, meaning that they should aim at the heart of the stone witch. They directed their arrows where the heart should be, but the arrows only glanced off with the flint heads broken.

Then they caught the Utsu'gi and cut off its tongue, so that ever since its tongue is short and everybody knows it is a liar. When the hunters let it go it flew straight up into the sky until it was out of sight and never came back again. The titmouse that we know now is only an image of the other.

They kept up the fight without result until another bird, little Tsi'kilili', the chickadee, flew down from a tree and alighted upon the witch's right hand. The warriors took this as a sign that they must aim there, and they were right, for her heart was on the inside of her hand, which she kept doubled into a fist, this same awl hand with which she had stabbed so many people. Now she was frightened in earnest, and began to rush furiously at them with her long awl finger and to jump about in the pit to dodge the arrows, until at last a lucky arrow struck just where the awl joined her wrist and she fell down dead.

Ever since the tsi'kilili' is known as a truth teller, and when a man is away on a journey, if this bird comes and perches near the house and chirps its song, his friends know he will soon be safe home. (316–19)

Cherokee elder Kathi Smith Littlejohn told the story of Spearfinger to a group of children at the Cherokee Elementary school in the mid-1990s, and here's an excerpt that describes her:

> she was covered with this rock-like skin
> that no bullet, no weapon could penetrate.
> And she was bloodthirsty.
> She had one long,
> razor-sharp,
> spear-finger,
> that she would slip up behind you,
> slip it through your back,
> pull out your liver,
> and eat it in one gulp.
> She was covered with dried blood
> and snot, and gore dripped from her teeth.
> She loved to eat the flesh of young children
> more than anything.
> And to get close to the young children,
> she could change her shape.
> She could turn and look just like your sister,
> just like your granny.
> And as you were out picking blackberries
> or fishing, or playing

your friend could disappear,
and she would take his place,
and you'd never know until it was too late. (Duncan, *Living Stories* 63)

It's quite frightening to think that Spearfinger could sometimes shapeshift into a family member of a household and enter that home, and the folks living there were none the wiser. Once inside, it was just a matter of time before she stabbed and pulled out someone's liver. Neither the ancient nor the modern telling goes into detail as to why not having a liver can kill a person, because such intricate medical explanations aren't needed.

At first glance, Utlvta or Spearfinger seems quite different from Uktena or Nunyunuwi in that she did not give any special gifts to the People like the serpent's healing crystal or the powerful songs and medicines from the Stonecoat. She was devious and murderous and fed off humans; children were often her victims, and that seems quite despicable because it violates the basic Cherokee values when it comes to the protection all adults are expected to offer to those who are vulnerable. It is our job as adults to care and look out for the babies and young ones because they are the future of the Tsalagi. Spearfinger is a Tskili,[19] and her story established some of the characteristics that such Usgaseti are known for, such as the shape-shifting into another human or into an animal form, and stealing life years from people as they are dying. There is still the belief held by many in this Eastern Cherokee community, as well as those in Oklahoma, that some Tskili will take the form of a relative of a person who is dying in order to gain admittance into the home, as the extended family gathers, and use the opportunity to extract the dying person's life essence from them, hastening their death and extending their own life. That is why family members stay close by the sick or injured loved one and watch closely as to who is allowed into the home.[20]

In his collection of oral stories from among the Cherokee of Oklahoma, Robert J. Conley describes in the titular short story, "The Witch of Goingsnake," how a man becomes convinced that a local conjuring woman is causing all his bad luck; every time something bad occurs or someone in his family gets ill, the man spots a particular squirrel nearby, watching him. He knows in his heart that the *Saloli* (squirrel) is the old woman in her changed form. This story shows the extremes to which doing battle with a Tskili can lead someone, as so many bad things happen to the lead character, including his only daughter dying from illness, that he eventually goes over and kills the conjurer and burns down her house. The man goes to jail for murder, and his wife dies of sickness while he is jailed, and eventually his own death is linked to a squirrel. One other story in the collection, entitled "Moon Face," also tells of a Tskili who shape-shifts into a black cat and causes problems for a Cherokee family in Oklahoma. In this story, the husband throws a bucket of hot coals onto the cat, and the very next day he pays a visit to the nearby neighbor whom he suspects of being the Tskili cat. The old woman is in bed and suffering from burns to her arm, face, and hair, and the man knows for certain that she was indeed the black cat. Such stories are also told around the Qualla Boundary,[21] and certain people are thought to have the ability to use conjuring and bad medicine to achieve their desired goals—whether in romance, fame, or wealth. Those people both enjoy and suffer from having such a reputation, and it is generally the type of thing that is whispered and gossiped about by other Cherokees who know that reputed Tskili.

The story of Utlvta is a reminder of the importance of Gadugi and working toward Duyvkta, as those frightened members of the village met in council and agreed to work together for the good of all concerned, despite the personal danger. We can hark back to chapter 1 and the Fire story, where the various creatures bravely acted to capture and carry the Fire, as dangerous as it was, and after becoming scarred and traumatized, the bigger animals, birds, and snakes finally gave up; but it was the little water spider who ultimately managed to carry the burning coal across the water to share with everyone, including the weaker humans. We saw how those nonhumans did what they had to do at great personal sacrifice in order to benefit all creatures. In the case of Spearfinger, the People had to go against their normally peaceful and harmonious way of life, and the blood laws of the clans, and kill the Tskili because she threatened entire communities since she got stronger every time she ate a victim's liver. The village residents came together as a group, knowing that Utlvta would not stop her vile habit of spearing the liver from the bodies of her victims, and too often those victims were the small children who trusted the sweet old woman who approached them. The People decided as a group on the best course of action, which was to lure Spearfinger into the disguised pit and then kill her. The People undoubtedly knew this would not be an easy task, and the men and women all had to work together to build the pit and hide it, and then the men worked in unison to shoot arrows at the fallen Spearfinger to kill her, knowing that she had the rocklike skin and that their arrows were limited. At any point, there was the danger of more villagers being killed if she did not fall into the pit or was able to get out of it. This was the risk. Retellings of this story today, no doubt, remind the People of the bravery of the Ancestors and that Gadugi is a part of the ancient cultural teachings and a large part of what being a Cherokee is all about, thus continuing to reinforce and regenerate all that is unique about the culture.

The general set of Indigenous beliefs and assumptions listed in chapter 1 holds two particular tenets that can be connected to the story of Spearfinger as well as to the Stonecoat story. The first is that "[t]he concept of reciprocity can guide living systems toward balance" (Wahinkpe Topa 19) as the murders committed by both of the humanlike Dusgaseti had to be counterbalanced with their own murder. This tenet of reciprocity would most often refer to the gifts and kindnesses that all living beings can offer within the balanced eco-system in which they live and coexist, allowing for mutual interdependency; however, it can also refer to the way that creatures exist from the nourishment that other creatures provide from their body. The problem is that these two Dusgaseti did not routinely give anything back to anyone or anything else within Creation, and Spearfinger, in particular, was preying on the weakest. The People could not allow for this to continue, and that meant death for the two. Another tenet also can apply to the Spearfinger story, which is that "[r]esolution of conflict should be about restoring harmony rather than enacting vengeance or punishment" (Wahinkpe Topa 19). The People did not look to capture the Tskili and then punish her in some way, and they did not kill her in revenge for the lives she had taken; rather, they decided as a community that her devious murders had to be stopped, and that could only happen with her death. They did not act in anger or in haste, but decided in council—with everyone getting a chance to speak—on what was best for the community, and their actions restored Duyvkta and harmony to the People. Parents no longer had to worry about their children out playing or picking berries, and being suspicious of their neighbors and relatives was no longer necessary.

There are other Dusgaseti stories, although too many to properly and fully discuss here because each story contains its own teachings. I have chosen the best known of these beings because their life stories are still shared in public storytelling events today on the Qualla Boundary. Let us turn our discussion from the "dreadful" Dusgaseti to the "wondrous" Dusgaseti, who are also frightening for many Cherokees. The stories may be ancient, but these beings are still present within the Eastern Cherokee community; many non-Natives whose families have lived in the area for many generations are also familiar with the stories of these particular beings as these stories are freely shared by the Cherokee with visiting tourists, as we will hear about in chapter 4. These wondrous beings include the Yunwi Tsunsdi or Little People, the "slant-eyed" giant Tsutlakalv who has left his mark all over the mountains, and the Nunehi or Spirit Warriors in whom even one town's non-Native settlers came to believe.

3

Dusgaseti Tsalagi Kanoheda • Part 2

Cherokee Stories of "Those who fill us with wonder"

The "dreadful" Dusgaseti continue to be a part of the Indigenous reality within the Cherokee sacred homeland, even though encounters between them and the Ani-Yunwiyah today do not happen all that often. These beings continue to live and wander throughout the mountains, and they can still bring the occasional imbalance or instability to others in the world around them; this may be their way of ensuring their fellow creatures practice Duyvkta and strive to follow a harmonious path. The stories of "those who fill us with dread" remind the People, and especially the children, of the dangers out in the woods and dark valleys, and the lifestyle today for the Tsalagi includes living in modern housing, which means less time spent in the outdoors. Yet there are other Dusgaseti who interact with Cherokee families on a near-daily basis, even though no one sees them. The Yunwi Tsunsdi or Little People who live throughout the territory are wondrous Dusgaseti who are a part of everyday life on the Qualla Boundary and are, for the most part, accepted and even welcomed as small folks who share many of the same living spaces as the humans. The Little People are said to be one to two feet high and look like small Cherokees; they usually have very long hair almost to the ground and dress just like the humans. It is said that most adults cannot see these small people but that children and family pets can; however, this is not always the case, and some grownups have reported seeing Little People both in modern and olden times. The stories also say that if an adult does actually see any Little People, that person will soon die if they tell anyone about what they have seen, and there are cases of that coming true. There are a few older stories of these small people that Mooney wrote down, yet there seems to be no single collective oral story that explains their existence or describes their physical appearance; instead, there are countless oral narratives told throughout Cherokee territory that generally describe encounters—either from ancient times, from a handed-down family narrative that originated with long-dead or more recent Ancestors, or from personal living memories. In other words, nearly every adult living within the Eastern Cherokee community seems to have their own personal or family story about the Little People—whether it is of their own encounter or that of some friend or kin who has had an experience with one or several Little People. Kathi Smith Littlejohn offers her own storytelling about the communal role that the Little People fulfill in bringing joy and playfulness to so many Cherokees—especially those who are young at heart.

THE CHEROKEE LITTLE PEOPLE
Kathi Smith Littlejohn

There are a lot of stories and legends about the Little People.
You can see the people out in the forest.
They can talk, and they look a lot like Indian people
    except they're only about two feet high,
    sometimes they're smaller.
Now the Little People can be very helpful,
    and they can also play tricks on us, too.
And at one time there was a boy.
This boy never wanted to grow up.
In fact, he never wanted to grow up,
    and told everyone that so much
    that they called him "Forever Boy"
    because he never wanted to be grown.
When his friends would sit around and talk about:
    "Oh when I get to be a man, and when I get to be grown

I'm gonna be this and I'm gonna go here and be this,"
    he'd just go off and play by himself.
He didn't even want to hear it,
    'cause he never wanted to grow up.
Finally his father got real tired of this,
    and he said,
    "Forever Boy, I will never call you that again.
    From now on you're going to learn to be a man,
    you're going to take responsibility for yourself,
    and you're going to stop playing all day long.
    You have to learn these things.
    Starting tomorrow, you're going to go to your uncle's,
    and he's going to teach you everything that you need to know."
Forever Boy was brokenhearted at what his father told him,
    but he could not stand the thought of growing up.
He went out to the river and he cried.
He cried so hard
    that he didn't see his animal friends gather around him.
And they were trying to tell him something,
    and they were trying to make him feel better,
    and finally he thought he understood them to say,
    "Come here tomorrow. Come here early."
Well, he thought they just wanted to say goodbye to him.
And he drug his feet going home.
He couldn't even sleep, he was so upset.
The next morning he went out early, as he had promised, to meet his friends.
And he was so sad,
    he couldn't even bear the thought of telling them goodbye forever.
Finally
    he began to get a sense that they were trying to tell him something else,
    and that is to look behind him.
And as he looked behind him,
    there they were—
    all the Little People—
and they were smiling at him and laughing and running to hug him.
And they said,

"Forever Boy, you don't have to grow up.
You can stay with us forever.
You can come and be one of us and you will never have to grow up."
"I can't do that. I have . . . my uncle's waiting on me.
I can't do that. It would hurt my parents if I never came home again."
And they said,
"No, we will ask the Creator to send a vision to your parents
to let them know that you are safe and you are doing what you need to do."
Forever Boy thought about it for a long time.
But he decided that's what he needed to do.
And he went with the Little People.
And even today
when you're out in the woods and you see something,
and you look, and it's not really what you thought it was,
or if you're fishing and you feel something on the end of your line,
and you think it's the biggest trout ever,
and you pull it in,
and all it is is a stick that got tangled in your hook,
that's what the Little People are doing.
They're playing tricks on you
so you'll laugh and keep young in your heart.
Because that's the spirit of Little People, and Forever Boy,
to keep us young in our hearts. (Duncan, *Living Stories* 68–70)

Mooney's book presents his translations of several stories he has been told by those long-gone Cherokee Elders in the late 1800s. As those storytellers told the ethnographer, there are a variety of Yunwi Tsunsdi, and for the most part they are "all good-natured, but more or less tricky" (*Myths of the Cherokee* 335), which shows the Duyvkta balance of their activity and function within Cherokee society and culture in the past and continuing today. Mooney refers to the Little People as Spirits, which seems to suggest they are ethereal, rather than a tangible part of Cherokee reality. We don't know if that was Mooney's personal belief and way of explaining such small beings or if it's a matter of the cultural loss of meaning in translating Cherokee to English. Mooney's presentation begins with stories of the Nunnehi, which will be discussed later in this chapter, so I've taken the last section of his lengthy story.

THE NUNNE'HI AND OTHER SPIRIT FOLK

There is another race of spirits, the *Yunwi Tsunsdi'*, or "Little People," who live in rock caves on the mountain side. They are little fellows, hardly reaching up to a man's knee, but well shaped and handsome, with long hair falling almost to the ground. They are great wonder workers and are very fond of music, spending half their time drumming and dancing. They are helpful and kind-hearted, and often when people have been lost in the mountains, especially children who have strayed away from their parents, the Yunwi Tsunsdi' have found them and taken care of them and brought them back to their homes. Sometimes their drum is heard in lonely places in the mountains, but it is not safe to follow it, because the Little People do not like to be disturbed at home, and they throw a spell over the stranger so that he is bewildered and loses his way, and even if he does at last get back to the settlement he is like one dazed ever after. Sometimes, also, they come near a house at night and the people inside hear them talking, but they must not go out, and in the morning they find the corn gathered or the field cleared as if a whole force of men had been at work. If anyone should go out to watch, he would die. When a hunter finds anything in the woods, such as a knife or a trinket, he must say, "Little People, I want to take this," because it may belong to them, and if he does not ask their permission they will throw stones at him as he goes home.

Once a hunter in winter found tracks in the snow like the tracks of little children. He wondered how they could have come there and followed them until they led him to a cave, which was full of Little People, young and old, men, women, and children. They brought him in and were kind to him, and he was with them some time; but when he left they warned him that he must not tell or he would die. He went back to the settlement and his friends were all anxious to know where he had been. For a long time he refused to say, until at last he could not hold out any longer, but told the story, and in a few days he died. Only a few years ago two hunters from Raventown, going behind the high fall near the head of Oconaluftee on the East Cherokee reservation, found there a cave with fresh footprints of the Little People all over the floor.

During the smallpox among the East Cherokee just after the war one sick man wandered off, and his friends searched, but could not find him. After several weeks he came back and said that the Little People had found him and taken him to one of their caves and tended him until he was cured.

About twenty-five years ago a man named Tsantawu' was lost in the mountains on the head of Oconaluftee. It was winter time and very cold and his friends

thought he must be dead, but after sixteen days he came back and said that the
Little People had found him and taken him to their cave, where he had been
well treated, and given plenty of everything to eat except bread. This was in large
loaves, but when he took them in his hand to eat they seemed to shrink into
small cakes so light and crumbly that though he might eat all day he would not be
satisfied. After he was well rested they had brought him a part of the way home
until they came to a small creek, about knee deep, when they told him to wade
across to reach the main trail on the other side. He waded across and turned to
look back, but the Little People were gone and the creek was a deep river. When
he reached home his legs were frozen to the knees and he lived only a few days.

Once the Yunwi Tsunsdi' had been very kind to the people of a certain settlement, helping them at night with their work and taking good care of any lost
children, until something happened to offend them and they made up their minds
to leave the neighborhood. Those who were watching at the time saw the whole
company of Little People come down to the ford of the river and cross over and
disappear into the mouth of a large cave on the other side. They were never heard
of near the settlement again.

There are other fairies, the *Yunwi Amai'yine'hi*, or Water-dwellers, who live
in the water, and fishermen pray to them for help. Other friendly spirits live in
people's houses, although no one can see them, and so long as they are there to
protect the house no witch can come near to do mischief.

Tsawa'si and *Tsaga'si* are the names of two small fairies, who are mischievous
enough, but yet often help the hunter who prays to them. Tsawa'si, or Tsawa'si
Usdi'ga (Little Tsawa'si), is a tiny fellow, very handsome, with long hair falling
down to his feet, who lives in grassy patches on the hillsides and has great power
over the game. To the deer hunter who prays to him he gives skill to slip up on the
deer through the long grass without being seen. Tsaga'si is another of the spirits
involved by the hunter and is very helpful, but when someone trips and falls, we
know that it is Tsaga'si who had caused it. There are several other of these fairies
with names, all good-natured, but more or less tricky. (333–35)

Such community and family stories are indicative of what historian Ian
Cunnison found among the Luapula people of Africa, according to David
William Cohen, who notes that oral tradition is ever-evolving among Indigenous groups. Cohen suggests, "In everyday life, common folk produce and
maintain histories of their own little collectivities and resist the construction

of more universal historical compositions," adding, "[t]he knowledge of the 'universal' past is not simply given or handed down but is continuously and actively gathered and dissected" (10). The Little People stories of the Eastern Cherokees do indeed have their own "processual life" (Cohen 10) in the way that the narratives defy containment into a simple collection or archive that can be easily documented or recorded, but instead continue to grow and evolve with each encounter, each narration, and each retelling even today.

The largest published collection of Little People stories to date came about when an English professor at Western Carolina University, Jeannie Reed, offered her students in a compositional writing course the idea of interviewing and recording such oral stories among the Eastern Cherokee community. These stories may be uniquely and culturally Cherokee, but many non-Natives living in western North Carolina have heard of the Little People through their friends on the reservation, as had Reed. The effort by her students, both Native and non-Native, led to a small booklet that is called *Stories of the Yunwi Tsunsdi: The Cherokee Little People*,[1] published in 1991, from which this book borrows. These students were able to talk with elderly residents of the Tsali Manor nursing home on the Qualla Boundary as well as other Cherokee Elders and/or family members. There is a list of the storytellers in the booklet, but a name is not attached to each particular story, so one cannot determine who the narrator of each story is. In the introduction, Elder Al Lossiah suggested that "the Little People are here to teach lessons about living in harmony with nature and with others," a Duyvkta-centric explanation with which many would agree (n.p.). Another unnamed source points out how the stories can be used to teach children honesty, as he or she describes how his or her father would say that the Little People "are God's witnesses. They are always around, but you don't see them. They know everything you do" (n.p.). Knowing that small spiritual beings could be anywhere around you and watching your every action (much like we tell our children about Santa Claus at Christmastime) should make most people, not only children, be on their best behavior, which, again, would promote Duyvkta and walking the right path.

It is thought that the more traditional community of Snowbird has many Little People because of its being more isolated and less populated.[2] Elder Bessie Jumper of Snowbird talks about the ones who live in her area, have trails under her house, and rattle on the pipeline, adding, "I believe these are the Little People walking all over the place. They say they're good Little People.

You're not supposed to tell if you know for sure they are the Little People. They'll shorten your life if you tell" ("Fading Voices" 34). Some Cherokee families have Little People living with them inside their home at all times, simply accept that they are there, and feel that this arrangement is generally a good thing. The most common belief seems to be that if you have one (or more) in your house, no one will ever break in or rob you. A resident Little People is almost like having a good security system in this mainly rural community where houses are far apart and heavy foliage generally obstructs the view of neighbors and where, like many rural communities, people don't always lock the doors.[3] Many also say that if you go out into the woods, you may come home with a Little People on your shoulder that you didn't realize you had picked up and you can't see or feel. Then he/she will take up residence in your home.

There do indeed seem to be several types of Little People, and depending on who tells the story, the way in which it's best to handle these small beings also varies. Little People can be helpful and even life-saving; playful and oftentimes mischievous; secretive, annoying, intimidating, frightening, and even dangerous and life-threatening—character traits that fulfill the double meaning of the word *Dusgaseti*. Most stories about encounters, however, seem to be of a more positive nature in modern times, while some of the older stories of Little People who threaten approaching humans are seldom part of the contemporary narratives, though you will at times hear of a Cherokee person being very frightened to go into certain areas because of their experiences with Little People around there.[4] The more common story that Cherokee people share today is that of the Little People who attach themselves to a particular person or house. Those are usually talked about as being playful and sneaky because they delight in hiding things around the house, and they can sometimes be glimpsed out of the corner of the eye without ever fully seeing them. They will move items in the home, so that the car keys left on the kitchen table can't be found, but later appear on top of the TV set. Rather than think they're losing their mind, the Cherokees will realize the house has at least one Little People who has moved in, though there could be more than one. Often such Little People will tease and play with the family pet—be it a cat or dog—and the animal will act skittish and sit and look rapidly all around them at what seems like thin air to a human observer, leaving one to wonder just what it is our animal friend is doing. The Little People might just be playing and having fun with the pet by teasing, or it may be a mean creature who's being cruel to the four-legged household member, poking it or tugging on its fur.

While many Cherokees today do not distinguish between different types of Little People, still others suggest the differences are according to where each of the small folk comes from, and that there are three places in which the Little People reside. One unnamed source says, "They can live in rocky places, in laurel thickets, or under dogwood trees" (*Stories of the Yunwi Tsunsdi* n.p.). Al Lossiah recalls how his grandmother, who was a member of the Deer Clan, also related to him that each group had a specific purpose within the Cherokee world. "The Rock People are the mean ones who practice 'getting even,' who steal children, and the like. But they are like this because people have invaded their space and have taken wood from their designated areas. The Laurel People play tricks and are generally mischievous. For example, when you find children laughing in their sleep, it is because the Laurel People are pinching and tickling them. They are humorous and share joy with others. Finally, there are the Dogwood People who are good and take care of people" (*Stories of the Yunwi Tsunsdi* n.p.). It's interesting to hear that the Rock People retaliate against those Cherokee who have invaded their area, perhaps demonstrating the loss of intimate human knowledge of the land and respect for just where one should not tread. Lossiah's grandmother said the lessons of the Little People are clear; he relates that "the Rock People teach us that if you do things to other people out of meanness or intentionally, it will come back on you. We must always respect other people's limits and boundaries. The Laurel People teach us that we shouldn't take the world too seriously and that we must always have joy and share that joy with others. The lessons of the Dogwood People are simply—if you do something for someone, do it out of the goodness of your heart. Don't do it to have people obligated to you or for personal gain" (*Stories of the Yunwi Tsunsdi* n.p.).

That final lesson is closely connected to Gadugi and how one should always do what is best for the entire community, not just for oneself; it also reflects the Cherokee perspective that Bob Thomas speaks of regarding always giving of your time and possessions with no expectation of getting something in return. Another teaching is that if you have a Little People in your home or encounter them anywhere outside, you must be accepting that even though you cannot see them, they are there in their outdoor home and you are intruding on their space, or that they now live with you, and everyone in the family, including this small one, must get along. It is the same Cherokee value of acceptance one must have with any Spirits who are around; they have as much right to be where they are as we humans do, and we must strive to live together amicably.

In the old days, it was strictly believed that if the Little People found any small children outside by themselves, they would steal those children and raise them as their own. The old stories tell that if a toddler disappeared and the parents couldn't find them, it was the Little People who took them because it was believed the parents didn't want their young offspring. Older children often found themselves teased and tricked by Little People when playing outside. One unnamed storyteller notes that "[m]any times when we were children, our parents told us not to be out in the woods on cloudy days or in the evenings" (*Stories of the Yunwi Tsunsdi* n.p.). The narrator continues describing how every evening just before dusk, the entire family would see two small children come out of the woods and proceed to run up a big tree near the house, and then calmly walk back down it, over and over. The Cherokee children wanted to go play with these interesting tree-climbers, and the parents would tell them "[g]o ahead if you ever want to leave. Just follow them to that rock cliff" (*Stories of the Yunwi Tsunsdi* n.p.), which would make the children back out, for they feared never being able to come home again. The parents warned them that those were *not* little kids but rather were Little People. Other stories tell of older children and even adults being led by voices in the woods calling out to them and inevitably becoming lost and realizing it was Little People who had lured them away—for fun or out of meanness. Still other stories tell of people who were out in the woods or along a river—somewhere outside—and having rocks thrown at them. No matter how hard they looked, they could never find who threw the rocks. One story in this collection tells how the Little People protect certain Cherokee Elders, such as when the narrator's mother spoke of how a small helper lived in her house, for whom the mother left food out. The mother told how "[w]hen you would feed them, you would never see them eat, but you would know that they would eat the food" (*Stories of the Yunwi Tsunsdi* n.p.).[5] One day, a friend of the mother came to visit, but the mother was not at home, so the friend waited out on the porch. While sitting on the porch, the woman had wood chips thrown at her but couldn't see anyone or anything nearby and had no idea where the wood chips were coming from. She waited a while and decided to leave, and even as she walked to her car, wood chips hit the ground behind her. The next day, the friend called the mother and told her of the experience, who, in turn, told the friend it was just the Little People who watch over her house (*Stories of the Yunwi Tsunsdi* n.p.). There are countless other stories, many of which I have heard personally or experienced myself, but far too many to write down.

Besides the terms *Yunwi Tsunsdi* and Little People, some modern Cherokees refer to the small beings—usually the "meaner" ones, who would be the Rock People—as "Brownies" (*Stories of the Yunwi Tsunsdi* n.p.), which seems to be a cultural borrowing from the Gaelic immigrants who settled within Cherokee territory. These Gaels brought their own stories of the "Brownies, dwarves, elves, leprechauns, goblins, gremlins, pixies, and the like" who, no doubt, bore striking similarities to the Yunwi Tsunsdi of Cherokee country (*Stories of the Yunwi Tsunsdi*). The knowledge and awareness of small people who mainly live in the woods and waters is only one of numerous parallels between Indigenous cultures of Turtle Island and that of the Gaelic-speaking, clan-focused cultures of Ireland, Scotland, Wales, and the Isle of Man; however, time does not allow for an accurate or comprehensive discussion of these parallels so we will only briefly focus on the matter of the Little People. It would seem that the usage of the term "Brownie" is the only borrowing that a few of the Cherokees have done from the Gaels in this regard. James Mooney, who grew up hearing his Irish immigrant mother tell the old stories of the wee folk in her homeland, makes a strong attempt at drawing comparisons between the two sets of cultural beliefs. When he relates stories he has been informed of about Little People, he frequently calls the Cherokee Yunwi Tsunsdi by the names of "fairies" and "sprites" and uses those terms interchangeably (*Myths of the Cherokee* 331, 334, 476–77), which is clearly an attempt to define this "race of spirit people who lived in the highlands of the old Cherokee country" (330) as something palatable for his non-Cherokee colleagues at the U.S. Bureau of Ethnology who would be familiar with the Irish leprechauns, etc. A few decades later, John Witthoft and Wendell Hadlock take a cue from Mooney in their 1946 paper entitled "Cherokee-Iroquois Little People" when they refer to "[t]he prominence of dwarfs in Cherokee mythology" and the "dwarf lore of the Six Nations" (413). Indeed, even Jeannie Reed begins her introduction to the student-written collection of Little People stories with the above-mentioned quote in her very first sentence despite the inaccuracy of it. She also mentions "Rumpelstiltskin," "Snow White and the Seven

Dwarves," and even "Rip Van Winkle" before asking the pertinent question: "Regardless of our familiarity with the subject matter of small folk, do, or can, we accept them as more than literary creations?" (*Stories of the Yunwi Tsunsdi*). I am not convinced this sort of comparison is helpful or productive, and I suggest it may actually detract from immersing oneself in the cultural vibrancy that is prominent in the modern tellings of encounters and family stories concerning the Yunwi Tsunsdi among the Eastern Cherokees. It is understandable to draw comparisons for those non-Cherokee readers of such a collection; however, it is quite inaccurate to do so without recognizing that the Little People have existed in Cherokee land since the beginning of the Earth and that they are visibly, culturally, and socially Cherokee.

Witthoft and Hadlock seem to concur, as they point out that even though these dwarves of "American Indian pantheons" (413) often "closely resemble European folk figures and might be considered a borrowing from European tradition" (413), they find no hard evidence of such cross-cultural sharing. The pair also points out that "[s]uch Little People are so widespread in America . . . and often so isolated from a suitable European tradition, that a foreign origin seems improbable as a general explanation for their existence" (413). In regard to the Yunwi Tsunsdi, Witthoft and Hadlock argue that "Cherokee tradition is rather conservative and has borrowed relatively little of White folk-belief in many of its aspects, as judged by public collections and our own observations among the Cherokee. The Cherokee Little People give one the impression that they are an integral part of a highly elaborated tradition in which European motifs are rare, although it may well be that important modifications of this tradition have taken place" (413). Historian Raymond Fogelson agrees when he points out that numerous American Indian cultures across the continent hold a belief in Little People and that, among the Cherokee, this belief is "deeply imbedded" so that "their existence cannot easily be explained away as a simple product of European diffusion" (96).[6] He adds that there is no ethnographic or historical mention of biological dwarfism within the Cherokee communities or any other tribe in the Southeast. None of the aforementioned non-Cherokee scholars admit to accepting the idea that Little People exist, at least within the traditional Cherokee homeland, yet most do acknowledge that the belief is strong among ancient and modern members of the community and that the Yunwi Tsunsdi are vital characters within this cultural landscape. After all, these small beings are clearly Native and are reported as speaking the

Tsalagi language, drumming and singing similar songs as the humans, and dressing and looking much like the Cherokees with long black or gray flowing hair, along with having always resided in the mountains. They do not have a pot of gold at the end of every rainbow, which is a big part of the stories about Irish leprechauns, as greed and selfish protection of individual material possessions is not a Yunwi Tsunsdi characteristic nor a Cherokee value. And unlike leprechauns with their gold, it is most certainly not desirable to catch a Little People to steal from them.

Finally, we know that many oral stories of the European tradition begin with "Once upon a time" and end with "and they all lived happily ever after," while Native stories do not follow that literary form of having a clear beginning and ending. Jeannie Reed notes that many of the Little People stories begin with sentences like "'When I was a little girl' or 'One time my cousin and I,'" which led her and the student group to realize they "were collecting neither myths nor legends, but actual stories—narratives retelling specific events," which she also posits is proof these stories are not of "mythical or legendary origins" (*Stories of the Yunwi Tsunsdi*). Reed seems to have accepted the belief that the Little People do indeed exist today and live among the Eastern Cherokees and offers the collection of narratives to help understand the connection between Yunwi Tsunsdi and mortal beings. It is important, too, to recognize that any bad or mischievous behavior by Little People is balanced by the good deeds that each may perform, in protecting a home or scaring away unwanted visitors or even invisibly guiding someone who is lost in the woods. Indeed, it can be thought their abduction of wandering toddlers and raising them as one of their own may be a positive and helpful action as well, for in doing so, the Little People are providing love and protection for a child who may have been harmed by a vicious animal or hurt by a brutal fall down a ravine. I have heard it said that when the Little People see a small child alone in the woods, their logic is that the parents do not or will not take good care of the baby—this serves as a warning to young parents to take heed and never let their child out of their sight. As Elder Al Lossiah tells us, there are always lessons to be learned from the Yunwi Tsunsdi, and they will forever be a part of the Eastern Cherokee world.

For thousands of years, before any Cherokee now living can personally remember, an Asgaya egwa (large or giant man) by the name of Tsutlakalv[7] lived in a very specific area of the Balsam Mountains called Tsunegvyi[8] but was known to wander all over what is now called the Appalachian Range. He was a powerful being and so large that he could step over mountains with one stride of his long legs. It is said that Tsutlakalv had a habit of throwing large boulders over the mountains, although no one seems to know if this was done in anger or in play. Perhaps he was simply cleaning up his living area. It could have been for any or all of these reasons because so little is known about this giant that we can only speculate today (Belt, Lecture). Those huge boulders can be seen throughout Tsalagi country—up and down the hills, some precariously perched high atop a mountainside, some partly embedded into the red clay of a hillside or out in a field, and others scattered throughout the many rivers and springs that run through the valleys. The Cherokees know that Tsutlakalv threw these rocks a very long time ago, because trees and bushes have grown up all around them, making the boulders look like they simply dropped from the sky into the middle of the woods or alone out in the middle of a flat grassy field. Visitors to the Eastern Cherokee reservation and to the Great Smoky Mountain National Park often remark on the massive, car-size boulders—some even as big as a small house—because they look quite out of place. Park rangers and geologists generally attribute it to ancient earthquakes and rockslides, but the Cherokees know better, especially as the ones resting out in a field are often far away from any hillside from which they could have slid down. Tsutlakalv is the only being from the ancient oral histories who had the strength to do this, and he is the best example of the two-sided meaning of the word *Usgaseti*—both wondrous and dreadful, for the Cherokees who met or saw him were frightened *and* amazed at his appearance, yet there are no reports of him ever harming anyone, unlike other Dusgaseti. In fact, it sounds like Tsutlakalv was usually misunderstood because he was so very different-looking than any other Cherokee. He kept to himself, avoiding contact with other Aniyvwi (humans) except for the Cherokee woman, whom he took as his wife, and their children.[9] The most detailed account is in Mooney's book.

TSUL'KALU', THE SLANT-EYED GIANT

A long time ago a widow lived with her one daughter at the old town of Kanuga on Pigeon river. The girl was of age to marry, and her mother used to talk with her a good deal, and tell her she must be sure to take no one but a good hunter for a husband, so that they would have some one to take care of them and would always have plenty of meat in the house. The girl said such a man was hard to find, but her mother advised her not to be in a hurry, and to wait until the right one came.

Now the mother slept in the house while the girl slept outside in the asi [hot-house]. One dark night a stranger came to the asi wanting to court the girl, but she told him her mother would let her marry no one but a good hunter. "Well," said the stranger, "I am a great hunter," so she let him come in, and he stayed all night. Just before day he said he must go back now to his own place, but that he had brought some meat for her mother, and she would find it outside. Then he went away and the girl had not seen him. When day came she went out and found there a deer, which she brought into the house to her mother, and told her it was a present from her new sweetheart. Her mother was pleased, and they had deersteaks for breakfast.

He came again the next night, but again went away before daylight, and this time he left two deer outside. The mother was more pleased this time, but said to her daughter, "I wish your sweetheart would bring us some wood." Now wherever he might be, the stranger knew their thoughts, so when he came the next time he said to the girl, "Tell your mother I have brought the wood"; and when she looked out in the morning there were several great trees lying in front of the door, roots and branches and all. The old woman was angry, and said, "He might have brought us some wood that we could use instead of whole trees that we can't split, to litter up the road with brush." The hunter knew what she said, and the next time he came he brought nothing, and when they looked out in the morning the trees were gone and there was no wood at all, so the old woman had to go after some herself.

Almost every night he came to see the girl, and each time he brought a deer or some other game, but still he always left before daylight. At last her mother said to her, "Your husband always leaves before daylight. Why don't he wait? I want to see what kind of a son-in-law I have." When the girl told this to her husband he said he could not let the old woman see him, because the sight would frighten her. "She wants to see you, anyhow," said the girl, and began to cry, until at last he had to consent, but warned her that her mother must not say that he looked frightful (usga'seti'yu).

The next morning he did not leave so early, but stayed in the asi, and when it was daylight the girl went out and told her mother. The old woman came and looked in, and there she saw a great giant, with long slanting eyes (tsul'kalu'), lying doubled up on the floor, with his head against the rafters in the left-hand corner at the back, and his toes scraping the roof in the right-hand corner by the door. She gave only one look and ran back to the house, crying, *Usga'seti'yu! Usga'seti'yu!*

Tsul'kalu' was terribly angry. He untwisted himself and came out of the asi, and said good-bye to the girl, telling her that he would never let her mother see him again, but would go back to his own country. Then he went off in the direction of Tsunegun'yi.

Soon after he left the girl had her monthly period. There was a very great flow of blood, and the mother threw it all into the river. One night after the girl had gone to bed in the asi her husband came again to the door and said to her, "It seems you are alone," and asked where was the child. She said there had been none. Then he asked where was the blood, and she said that her mother had thrown it into the river. She told just where the place was, and he went there and found a small worm in the water. He took it up and carried it back to the asi, and as he walked it took form and began to grow, until, when he reached the asi, it was a baby girl that he was carrying. He gave it to his wife and said, "Your mother does not like me and abuses our child, so come and let us go to my home." The girl wanted to be with her husband, so, after telling her mother good-bye, she took up the child and they went off together to Tsunegun'yi.

Now, the girl had an older brother, who lived with his own wife in another settlement, and when he heard that his sister was married he came to pay a visit to her and her new husband, but when he arrived at Kanuga his mother told him his sister had taken her child and gone away with her husband, nobody knew where. He was sorry to see his mother so lonely, so he said he would go after his sister and try to find her and bring her back. It was easy to follow the footprints of the giant, and the young man went along the trail until he came to a place where they had rested, and there were tracks on the ground where a child had been lying and other marks as if a baby had been born there. He went on along the trail and came to another place where they had rested, and there were tracks of a baby crawling about and another lying on the ground. He went on and came to where they had rested again, and there were tracks of a child walking and another crawling about. He went on until he came where they had rested again, and there were tracks of one child running and another walking. Still he followed the trail along the stream into the mountains, and came to the place where they had rested again, and this time there were footprints of two children running all about, and the footprints can still be seen in the rock at that place.

Twice again he found where they had rested, and then the trail led up the slope of Tsunegun'yi, and he heard the sound of a drum and voices, as if people were dancing inside the mountain. Soon he came to a cave like a doorway in the side of the mountain, but the rock was so steep and smooth that he could not climb up to it, but could only just look over the edge and see the heads and shoulders of a great many people dancing inside. He saw his sister dancing among them and called to her to come out. She turned when she heard his voice, and as soon as the drumming stopped for a while she came out to him, finding no trouble to climb down the rock, and leading her two little children by the hand. She was very glad to meet her brother and talked with him a long time, but did not ask him to come inside, and at last he went away without having seen her husband.

Several other times her brother came to the mountain, but always his sister met him outside, and he could never see her husband. After four years had passed she came one day to her mother's house and said her husband had been hunting in the woods near by, and they were getting ready to start home to-morrow, and if her mother and brother would come early in the morning they could see her husband. If they came too late for that, she said, they would find plenty of meat to take home. She went back into the woods, and the mother ran to tell her son. They came to the place early the next morning, but Tsul'kalu' and his family were already gone. On the drying poles they found the bodies of freshly killed deer hanging, as the girl promised, and there were so many that they went back and told all their friends to come for them, and there were enough for the whole settlement.

Still the brother wanted to see his sister and her husband, so he went again to the mountain, and she came out to meet him. He asked to see her husband, and this time she told him to come inside with her. They went in as through a doorway, and inside he found it like a great townhouse. They seemed to be alone, but his sister called aloud, "He wants to see you," and from the air came a voice, "You can not see me until you put on a new dress, and then you can see me." "I am willing," said the young man, speaking to the unseen spirit, and from the air came the voice again, "Go back, then, and tell your people that to see me they must go into the townhouse and fast seven days, and in all that time they must not come out from the townhouse or raise the war whoop, and on the seventh day I shall come with new dresses for you to put on so that you can all see."

The young man went back to Kanuga and told the people. They all wanted to see Tsul'kalu', who owned all the game in the mountains, so they went into the townhouse and began the fast. They fasted the first day and the second and every day until the seventh—all but one man from another settlement, who slipped out every night when it was dark to get something to eat and slipped in again when no one was watching. On the morning of the seventh day the sun was just coming up in the east when they heard a great noise like the thunder of rocks rolling down the side of Tsunegun'yi. They were frightened and drew near together in the townhouse, and no one whispered. Nearer and louder came the sound until it grew into an awful roar, and every one trembled and held his breath—all but one man, the stranger from the other settlement, who lost his sense from fear and ran out of the townhouse and shouted the war cry.

At once the roar stopped and for some time there was silence. Then they heard it again, but as if it were going farther away, and then farther and farther, until at last it died away in the direction of Tsunegun'yi, and then all was still again. The people came out from the townhouse, but there was silence, and they could see nothing but what had been seven days before. Still the brother was not disheartened, but came again to see his sister, and she brought him into the mountain. He asked why Tsul'kalu' had not brought the new dresses, as he had promised, and the voice from the air said, "I came with them, but you did not obey my word, but broke the fast and raised the war cry." The young man answered, "It was not done by our people, but by a stranger. If you will come again, we will surely do as you say." But the voice answered, "Now you can never see me." Then the young man could not say any more, and he went back to Kanuga. (337–41)

There is not just one story about Tsutlakalv the giant; rather, there are many stories, much like Uktena and the Yunwi Tsunsdi. This could be because Tsutlakalv did not die, like some of the other Dusgaseti from Cherokee orality, but he disappeared and is believed to be living with his family inside of a mountain—more about that shortly—or some say he went up into the sky and has never been seen since. Not only was Tsutlakalv an Asgaya egwa—a giant man—but his face looked different than other, smaller Cherokee men.[10] He usually stayed away from other people and did not like anyone to see him in the light of day because he had had many bad experiences of people either being afraid or laughing at him. His face was different in that he had eyes that slanted; this is why James Mooney calls him "the Slant-Eyed Giant" (337). The actual meaning of the name Tsutlakalv, according to Cherokee language instructor Tom Belt, is slightly different from Mooney's translation. Belt says to imagine a long stick that is propped up against something, so that it is slanting—that is called *tlakalv*, and when you add the plural possessive of *tsu*, it becomes the full name of Tsutlakalv, meaning that it is "like two sticks slanted, which he has"—a translation that does not specifically mention his eyes. Belt believes the giant's eyes probably looked like slits,[11] which may mean that people could not see his eyes very well, which would help to frighten some (Belt, Lecture).

Tsutlakalv seems to have been given particular responsibilities and is sometimes referred to by Mooney as the "great lord of the game" because he "owned all the game in the mountains" (*Myths of the Cherokee* 477, 340); Mooney also reports that the giant's name was often invoked within the hunting formulas or songs.[12] This title and description suggest a position of power or control, which is not quite accurate, according to Tom Belt, as it goes against the communal structure of equality and mutual respect or Duyvkta within which the Cherokees and nonhumans all lived. Rather, Belt says, Tsutlakalv was a "steward" who communicated well with the animals and the plant beings, and worked to negotiate and mediate whenever there were any problems (Interview #3). In this way, Tsutlakalv was practicing the concept of *Ulisgedi detsadayelvsesdi* as described in my introduction, in that he treated all the various beings in a sacred or important manner. In fact, it seems this giant was able to have good relationships with all the nonhumans, while it was the humans who could not seem to get over their fear of him; in this sense, the People forgot to practice kindness, harmony, and the Cherokee value of never giving offense. As a steward for the animals, Tsutlakalv was known to be a good hunter and provider for his family and impressed his wife-to-be and her mother with his skills—at one point bringing so many deer that it fed their entire village (Mooney, *Myths of the Cherokee* 338). Being a giant and able to peer over the mountaintops would have been an advantage for someone who kept track of where all the animals were, and it is easy to understand why Tsalagi hunters in olden times would have paid respect and spoken of Tsutlakalv in their hunting songs.

There are some cultural points to explain in the Mooney version of this story. Once Tsutlakalv has spent the night with the young Cherokee woman, he is referred to as her husband by the mother. Cherokee tradition considers a man and woman to be married when they start a life together. There was no formal wedding ceremony until the European introduced such a concept.

Perdue explains how the story of "the slant-eyed giant" violated the regular
marriage traditions of the man moving into his new wife's home with all of
her clan family. Since the "Cherokee regarded marriage as a family affair"
(*Cherokee Women* 43), the older females of the family often had influence on
the choosing of a new wife or new husband, but for the most part, the kin did
not force an unwanted partner on a relative. It was expected that the young
people would get the consent of their family, because the new husband was
to become a part of the wife's family and live in her village, yet the giant took
his new wife away to live in his home village. Perdue suggests that Tsutlakalv
and his young wife "refused to follow established practice," and because of
this "abnormal behavior" she was never allowed to see her family again (43).
Such "abnormal behavior" would most certainly go against Duyvkta and the
harmonious existence for which ancient Cherokees were expected to strive.
Another cultural point is that the young woman slept in an *asi* (*ah-see*) while
her mother slept in the house. An *asi* is a Cherokee hothouse, similar to what
other tribes would call a sweat lodge, but is a permanent structure made of
clay and wood. In the old days, the sick were doctored in one and slept there
while recuperating. During cold spells, the more vulnerable people, Elders
especially, often would sleep in one to stay warm in the dampness of the
mountains.

The version that Mooney presents is quite long and appears to be thorough,
yet there are many other things known about Tsutlakalv by today's Eastern
Cherokees. EBCI cultural preservation officer T. J. Holland points out that
Mooney does not explain just who the people are that are dancing and living
inside the mountain at Tsunegvyi—either because he does not know,[13] or he
chooses not to accept the Cherokee storytellers' explanation,[14] or felt it was
unimportant—but it would seem that the others dancing were Nunehi or
"the Immortals."[15] These are Spirit People, and Tsunegvyi was just one of the
places in Cherokee country in which they were known to dwell ("Cherokee
Cosmography"). It is not known if Tsutlakalv was an Immortal himself,
but we do know that his wife was Yvwi or human, and, for the most part,
Cherokees believe him to have simply been a giant man. No one really knows
why he was allowed to live among and spend his time with the Nunehi in
their sacred location, but this is clearly the blurring and blending of the
spiritual and physical worlds discussed in chapter 2. It does sound as if the
Cherokee wife and the children developed some of the special abilities that

Tsutlakalv had; this can be seen when the wife easily climbs over and down the steep, smooth rock face of their mountain home with the children in tow—a feat that her brother knew he could not do. There are also the tracks left in the stone by the family as they all travel to Tsunegvyi, which marks the path for the brother to follow. The spot where the footprints are embedded in rock is at the base of Datsunalasgunyi, which means "where their tracks are this way" (*Myths of the Cherokee* 480). That area is now called Shining Rock or Cold Mountain by the settlers.[16] Holland admits to having searched for the exact spot but has been unable to locate the tracks because of the dense woods and not knowing exactly where the embedded footprints lie ("Cherokee Cosmography"). Perhaps it is one of those more sacred things, which are not meant to be known today, or it may be known by someone who maintains the sacred knowledge.

Elder Tom Belt points out that no one knows what happened to Tsutlakalv. He may have gone back inside the mountain and the doorway closed permanently, yet there are other reports that suggest the giant simply disappeared into the sky. Belt says that many older Cherokees in all three communities believe that Tsutlakalv will come back one day and share his knowledge, once certain things happen, such as the Giduwah people coming back together (see chapter 5) and the language becoming revitalized, both of which are slowly happening. In other words, this will happen after the People have healed from the trauma of colonization and the forced removal, and everyone is participating in Duyvkta once again. Meanwhile, it is a mystery as to where Tsutlakalv is living. The lack of a clear-cut explanation for a final or current home for this interesting Usgaseti is in keeping with what Paul Zolbrod suggests as the function of such multilayered stories. "Orally transmitted verbal artifacts," he posits, "thereby combine to express a culture's full conception of the sacred by articulating the place of this world in a larger cosmic scheme; they define relationships among human groups; and they likewise define connections between human beings and other creatures, whether the animals who share the earth's products or the supernaturals who preside over them" (18). The accounting of Tsutlakalv going up into the Sky World ties in with the next story.

There is a large, flat soapstone boulder that sits out in the middle of a farmer's pasture just seven miles away from the present-day campus of Western Carolina University in the town of Cullowhee, about half an hour from the Qualla Boundary. The town's name is a corruption of Tsutlakalv-wi,[17] which means Judaculla's Place for the area in which the giant was thought to live at some point in time. This boulder is about twenty-two meters (or seventy-two feet) in size and is called, of course, Judaculla Rock.[18] It is covered with ancient drawings and symbols; archaeologists suggest these petroglyphs were created at least one thousand years ago, but no one knows for sure, just as no one knows what the meanings are behind any of the drawings. Some of the markings dug into the soft soapstone look like massive partial footprints,[19] and the stories say that when Tsutlakalv stepped down from the nearest mountaintop, which is now called Judaculla's Old Fields, he would step onto this boulder on his way to the nearby Tuckasegee River.[20] These footprints show seven toes, and the giant was said to have seven toes on each foot and seven fingers. Still other stories suggest that the vast array of symbols is actually a map, either of the surrounding countryside or even of the night sky and the thousands of stars and constellations (Belt, Lecture, and Holland, "Cherokee Cosmography"). Another possibility, according to Tom Belt, is that this was "our first written text" (Lecture) as the carvings may be an ancient writing system that has become lost to the Cherokee descendants of those Yvwi who first devised it. Both Belt and Holland point out that Sequoyah spent a great deal of time at Judaculla Rock during the thirteen years in which the literary genius worked on his syllabary, which brought full literacy to the entire Cherokee Nation just before the Removal; Belt posits that "Sequoyah may have had a deep insight into the petroglyphs" (Lecture). Both these modern storytellers, along with several others, suggest it may just be a matter of time before someone deciphers the writing code and understands again how to use the system. When one looks at this rock, one can see how all of these theories could be possible. This belief in an important cultural purpose of the carvings contrasts sharply with the boulder's description given by James Mooney, who states that it is "covered with various rude carvings" (*Myths of the Cherokee* 479), a condescending remark from the same expert who also states that the giant's nearby mountaintop home at Tsunegvyi was believed by early settlers to be "the special abode of the Indian Satan!" (479), thus perpetrating the distortion of an important Cherokee oral story.[21] Holland is more understanding of the drastic corruption of the Tsutlakalv story by Euro-American settlers and their renaming of Tsunegvyi to Devil's Courthouse when he states, "There is no context for

Tsutlakalv, or no prototype in Christian beliefs, so the story got changed" ("Cherokee Cosmography"). This kind acceptance of the settler's mistaken belief is yet another example of the Tsalagi value of never giving offense to another, which Elder Bob Thomas describes. However, there is another explanation for this name overwriting, which my language adviser, Ben Frey, says comes from Elder speaker Tom Belt. Frey explains that "'asgina' was a way of talking about a spiritual being—referring to Judacullah—but it was also translated to 'Devil,' and, of course, Christians labeled any 'pagan' spiritual beings as 'devils,' so in essence, the 'devil' in 'Devil's Courthouse' refers to Judacullah. The 'courthouse' part was because Judacullah was the adjudicator—the judge, governor, teacher in that place, who knew how things were supposed to be arranged, and the word 'courthouse,' 'tsunilawisdiyi', was synonymous with both 'courthouse' and 'church.' It was like his *council house*—a place both political from a jurisprudence perspective and also spiritual" (Frey email, 3 Aug. 2018).

Tom Belt tells another story about Tsutlakalv and his many troubles as a being who inadvertently scared people while he simply wanted to be a normal part of Ani-Yunwiyah society. It seems that the giant would sometimes come into the townhouse of various Cherokee villages while council was being held to discuss matters which were important to that village, probably in order to just sit and listen or possibly to have that sense of belonging with other humans. It was the custom that anyone who wanted to speak on an issue would have the opportunity to say what was on their minds, regardless of age or gender—everyone had the right to speak up, even if it took days to debate and make a decision. Tsutlakalv would only enter during evening council and would sit in a far corner of the seven-sided townhouse where it was dark,[22] since the fire that burned in the center did not quite light up the back corners. One village woman had noticed the large man slip in all hunched over to avoid hitting his head on the ceiling and take a quick seat in the back. The woman was so anxious to see who the large man was and what he looked like that she grabbed a handful of wood shavings that were kept nearby to help start the fire, and she threw them quickly into the fire, causing it to flare up and brighten the large room. When she saw the slanting eyes of the giant, she screamed out that he was Usgaseti, which scared many of the Cherokee sitting there, causing them to run out of the townhouse in fear. This rude behavior angered Tsutlakalv, and he shouted at everyone that they would never again see his face, and that he would stay far away from them (Belt, Lecture). Belt notes that it was a shame that the People did not realize the wealth of knowledge that Tsutlakalv had in regard to the plants, especially, and of the animals because that knowledge became lost when the giant disappeared into the side of the mountain or up into the Sky World—wherever it was that he went. He also took with him the knowledge of the carvings in the Judaculla Rock, and thus the disharmonious behavior of so many Cherokees caused this great loss of cultural teachings and the great personal harm toward Tsutlakalv (Belt, Lecture). Clearly, there are many lessons to be learned from this ancient story.

In looking at these Usgaseti stories, we must resist the standard classification system that so many anthropologists and linguists have applied to many Native oral stories like Tsutlakalv when they refer to such characters as "heroes." Several of the scholars on oral literature that are pertinent to my research include in their published works a category of stories which include the "Trickster/transformer/culture-hero" type of being (Petrone 16); however, there are no "heroes" among the Cherokees. Perhaps this is why no one knows the names of those men who listened and learned from the dying Stonecoat. The idea of one human or creature as superior to everyone else simply does not fit into a Cherokee worldview, which employs equality, harmony, acceptance, respect, and interdependency as being the most important aspects when it comes to relationships. No one person or being is more important than another, and what is best or good for the entire community is what everyone should strive to achieve and maintain. That is why the chiefs or leaders of a Cherokee village were no richer in material goods than the rest of the people; that form of inequality is part of the European system of capitalism where the self-centered goal is to become rich yourself, often at the expense and hard labor of others less fortunate. In the Cherokee worldview and the system of Gadugi, everyone is expected to do as much as they can for the benefit of others,[23] a system that can almost be equated to charitable works.

Tsutlakalv is clearly a complicated character, and the various stories, of which only a few are told here, leave many unanswered questions. What kind of being is this misunderstood giant? Is he a tremendously large man, or is he a Spirit being? If he is a man, how is it that he took a human woman as a wife yet lived among and danced with the Nunehi, who are the "Spirit Beings" and "Spirit Warriors" or, more specifically, the "Immortals"? And how did his human wife—a Cherokee woman—and their children also dance and live with the Immortals? Does it really matter which he was? What exactly is/was his life purpose, if he never got the chance to share his knowledge with the Yvwi because they were all too frightened of him? Perhaps these questions seem far too academic, inquisitive, and even intrusive for many Cherokees, since their worldview holds that all beings were made by the Creator and exist in the form that he or she made for them, that every living creature has the right to live and contribute to the natural system on Earth, that all creatures do indeed have a purpose and role in that natural world, and that such things should not even be questioned. Why should any Cherokees—ancient or modern—question the appearance of Tsutlakalv when, for the most part, their values include simple acceptance of the way things are? Yet it would seem that the Ancestors who encountered Tsutlakalv did not uphold this kindhearted Cherokee acceptance value and instead allowed their human frailty and fear to overpower them and cause them to run away in fright, while the nonhumans had a good relationship with the giant man. Perhaps the Cherokee encounters with the giant were actually a series of misadventures and missed opportunities to learn from Tsutlakalv, who held a wealth of knowledge about the animals, plant medicines, and environment from which the Cherokee could have learned. Instead, this Asgayah egwa lives on as a "mysterious" figure in whom the Cherokee fully believe, yet still they wonder just what he was all about.[24] Stories about Tsutlakalv continue to be shared today, and modern Cherokees are aware of the various landmarks and sacred sites connected to the great giant, speaking of him in a way that shows their continuing belief that he will return one day, that he is not dead, but that he will come back and again walk his path in these ancient mountains of the Cherokee homeland.

Perhaps there is a realization in this day and age of dangerous climate change that much knowledge was lost when this Cherokee steward of the land, animals, and plant beings went away. The landscape and surrounding geography for the Eastern Band have been altered by the settlers and their descendants, and now may be the time when Tsutlakalv is needed more than ever before. When such a story is retold, it brings the Ancestors alive again by "evoking the emotions of the listeners, transcending past-present-future. . . . Time does not imprison the story" (Fixico 22). This cultural reality of the prominence of Cherokee orature, unfortunately, leads many non-Native academics to label such stories like Tsutlakalv as "myths" or "legends." As Penny Petrone argues, this is done in order for Western scholars to have some sort of familiar theoretical framework and force Indigenous stories into a European-based set of literary rules and categorization, which is part of the reason that Craig Womack insists tribal stories should be examined through a tribal lens. Terms such as "myths" and "legends" describe works of literature that are assumed to be fictional in nature, and most non-Natives will automatically view a Native oral narrative that has been labeled as such to be simply made up and imaginary; meanwhile, to a Native person, these oral narratives are anything but untrue because "[a]ll Indian traditions are valid guides to reality" (Petrone 12). Petrone quotes Saulteaux/Ojibway storyteller Alexander Wolfe, who posits that "because Indian oral tradition blends the material, spiritual and philosophical together into one historical entity, it would be a clear violation of the culture from which it is derived if well-meaning scholars were to try to demythologize it, in order to give it greater validity in the Western sense of historiography" (12). It is this writer's belief that there is no place for Cherokee oral stories within any Western-based literary genre, and since critical theory from that mind-set is inadequate, often biased, and nowhere near being even an "awkward fit," it should not be applied for it only leads to culturally insensitive and inaccurate interpretations. Indeed, many Native oral stories must be approached not only with respect but with recognition of the sacredness that surrounds particular beings and land sites to which they are connected in order to fully understand the teachings.

Those sites connected to Tsutlakalv such as Tsuwatelda (Pilot Knob), Tsunegvyi (Devil's Courthouse), and Datsunalasgunyi (Shining Rock or Cold Mountain) continue to be "places of unquestionable, inherent sacredness on this earth, sites that are holy in and of themselves" (Deloria 331). This is true even for the white settlers and their descendants who live in North Carolina, because they, too, recognize many of those specific places as spiritually and ecologically significant. The colonizer government has created its own sacred shrines to nature by turning these Cherokee holy sites into a state park (Pilot Knob) while the latter two have become protected spots within the Pisgah National Forest, under the legal domain of the U.S. National Park Service, much like what has been done to other sacred Native sites out west, such as Grand Canyon, Yellowstone Park, the Devil's Tower, and the Black Hills, where Mt. Rushmore was carved into one of the Six Grandfathers—the name that the indigenous Lakota have always called those peaks. Of course, appropriating Native sacred sites of power and turning them into American nationalistic monuments and "legally protected" natural preserves or parks is clearly intended to disavow the Aboriginal peoples of Turtle Island and instead overwrite the land as being the native home of modern-day Americans—no matter from where their family emigrated. Alan Lawson suggests this is part of the "tripled dream of the settler situation: effacement (of Indigenous authority) and appropriation (of Indigenous authenticity)" while emptying out the land for new settlement (26).

One of the most ironic parts of such so-called protective appropriation and legalization has been that no one is/was allowed to pick flowers or other wild plants in those areas—including Cherokees—since the Park Service began operations in 1916. There are many edible and medicinal plants in those mountainous parklands that the Cherokees had traditionally harvested for food or medicines and which, until recently, were simply left to rot, because the gatherers would be hit with steep monetary fines if they were to be caught by park officials picking anything.[25] That changed in the summer of 2016 for the Eastern Band; the Park Service proposed a change in regulations to allow enrolled EBCI members to gather particular plants in the spring of 2015 (McKie, "NPS Proposes"). This suggested change in policy finally came after nearly twenty years of frustration by the tribal council and several chiefs in dealing with a frequent change of administration within the National Park Service. The former director for NPS told Eastern Cherokees in 2010 that he recognized they should not have been subjected to these rules concerning gathering Indigenous plants. Jonathan B. Jarvis then said, "The proposed rule respects tribal sovereignty and the government-to-government relationship between the United States and the tribes. It also supports the mission of the National Park Service and the continuation of unique cultural traditions of American Indians" (McKie, "NPS Proposes"). So, it took a full one hundred years of NPS overseeing traditional Cherokee lands appropriated and renamed as the Great Smoky Mountains National Park and a ban on plant gathering for the Indigenous peoples of the area before this ban was lifted. There are eight different national park locations in the United States where regulations had already been changed to accommodate nearby Native tribes who are now allowed to conduct traditional plant gathering. This new exemption for the EBCI was long overdue; however, the strict park rules continue to prevent the

Cherokees from ever conducting ceremonies or dances at those sacred sites with which the People and Giduwah culture are so deeply connected; even Cherokees are forced to "play tourist" in order to visit any of those ancient holy places. Even then, tribal members must contend with the daily crowds of tourists at locations like the Mulberry Place (Clingman's Dome), which makes it nearly impossible to have any privacy for prayers or rituals. It is a shame that Tsutlakalv is not still with us.

In order to understand the sacred power of those places within the Cherokee world like Tsunegvyi, it made sense to make a trip up the mountainside to witness firsthand the grandeur and spectacular raw beauty of the ancient home of Tsutlakalv and the Nunehi. My partner and I picked a spring day that was forecast to be sunny and warm in the western Carolina mountains with temperatures in the high sixties; however, the Spirits did not allow meteorological forecasters to be accurate that day. Instead, it was cloudy, crisp, and very windy through the Balsam Mountains. We took the Blue Ridge Parkway (another federally created and protected monument that cuts through the Cherokee holy land) out of Waynesville up to the area known as the "Devil's Courthouse." We passed right by it the first time because, surprisingly for us, there are no special signs for this powerfully sacred site, nothing to stop us or the thousands of tourists who drive in that area each year. There is merely a pull-off parking lot to drive into off the main two-lane road, get out, stretch the legs, and take photos of the mountainous splendor and awe-inspiring vista. A large wooden sign at the far side of the lot proclaims "VIEW DEVIL'S COURTHOUSE. ELEV. 5,720. ELEV. HERE 5,462. 20 min walk to pedestrian overview." Twenty minutes sounded like a nice hike, and so we walked over to the base of the trail and saw that it was a very steep climb, so steep that we both had to stop every twenty feet or so and catch our breath since the air is thinner that high up. Several times the thought flitted through my head that we were not going to make it, despite the fact that we were in decent physical shape, but we were determined—even when the blacktop-paved trail ended and the path became a muddy, rock-filled one with deep crevices in it. There was a rough wooden railing for part of the way up, but then that even came to an end—almost as if the park officials who laid out the trail did not believe anyone would make it up that far. My spirit began to doubt whether we should continue or not, and I wondered if perhaps we were not meant to walk upon the sacred peak; I even wondered if I was angering or insulting the Ancestors by bringing a

Kanienkehaka to a sacred Tsalagi location,[26] since our Ancestors were known to war with each other at times, despite being related through ancient ties of language and story. No matter; we continued huffing and puffing up the difficult trail to the rocky, rough summit and were rewarded with a physical blast of nature spirits. The actual clouds swirled around our bodies and the temperature dropped drastically. The winds picked up and buffeted us, whipping our clothes and eyeglasses around, roaring and whistling in our ears so that we could hardly hear each other speak—we simply grinned at each other because we knew we were in the presence of such powerful Spirits of the Sky World that we felt honored to have made it to the top. There is nothing more exhilarating than standing in the middle of a cloud as it swirls about you, caressing with an invisible touch and leaving damp goosebumps. Rather than a nice, smooth walk-around area for tourists to stroll about casually, like at other tourist overlooks in the mountains, the peak of Tsunegvyi was a series of boulders with a short, rough rock wall that offered little protection for anyone peeking over the edge. The view gave us a complete panorama of the four main Balsam summits in North and South Carolina and in Georgia. To say it was spectacular would be an understatement, and it was not just the view; we were physically and spiritually bombarded with a powerful display of the elements themselves. The cold clouds flowed all around us, covering us with mist and gooseflesh. We could see lower clouds blasting against the side of the mountain below and blowing up the sides all around us; my partner believed the foggy mist that ran straight up into the air looked more like smoke from a cooking fire—perhaps that of Tsutlakalv himself! We tried to listen for a hint of the singing, drumming, or dancing that may still go on inside of this mountain, but the Spirits would not allow that, as the wind blew and whistled in our ears. It was a tremendous feeling of cleansing and purification that neither of us will ever forget, and we felt so fortunate to have had the strength to climb to the top of Tsunegvyi that crisp spring day in mid-April as we made our offering of Tsola to the Spirits.[27] It is undoubtedly a good thing that the hike up is so strenuous, taking much more than twenty minutes, because only the hardiest visitors will take the trouble to climb it, and one would like to think that such people would indeed appreciate having their senses overwhelmed as they stand and look out from this sacred location over these ancient lands. It is sad to think that some modern-day Cherokees have grown up only knowing of the overwritten stories and place-names that the colonizer has imposed upon these sacred spots, yet even these culturally insensitive and sacrilegious actions have not diminished the natural spiritual power of these holy Earth connections. Lakota scholar Vine Deloria Jr. (enrolled member of the Standing Rock Sioux) points out that all world religions have their own powerful sacred spots where the "highest spirits dwell" (331). There is no doubt that Tsunegvyi is such a location and a fitting place for the Nunehi to have resided.

Much like Tsutlakalv, there are many stories within the oral tradition about the Spirit People, the Nunehi,[28] and they are just as elusive as the giant, as far as personal encounters go—unlike the Little People, of whom nearly everyone has a story. The Nunehi are also called the "Immortals," but the meaning of the word seems to literally be "the people who live anywhere" for they generally make their homes inside or underneath mountains or deep underwater, according to the storytellers who shared with Mooney (*Myths of the Cherokee* 330).[29] Contemporary Eastern Band storytellers confirm this, and we have two modern tellings of the Nunehi, with the first by Kathi Smith Littlejohn from her CD titled *Cherokee Legends* (vol. 1), which connects to the horrors that came to the People after settlers moved into the Homeland.

NUNNEHI, THE GENTLE PEOPLE
Kathi Smith Littlejohn

If you ever go out / into the woods / and you think / you hear / someone talking / maybe some music / and you know / there's no one else around you / there's a reason for that. / Out into the woods / there lives the Gentle People / and we call them / the Cherokee word / Nunnehi / which means gentle people. / The Nunnehi look a lot like / Cherokee people / only they live underground / in a special / special place. / One time / the Nunnehi came to the Cherokee people. / It was a very big surprise. / A Nunnehi man came to the head village / and said / you're going to have to come with us now. / All of you / pack up your belongings / and in seven days / you will have to come with me / and come to live / with the Nunnehi. / Well, you can imagine / what everyone was thinking. / Why!? / Where are we going to go? / Why do we have to go?! / I don't wanna go! / Well I want to go! / And they argued / back and forth / for days about / what was going to happen. / They asked him on the seventh day / where they were going / and why. / He said something terrible / is going to happen. / Something / worse than any flood / or any famine

/ that you have ever / known before. / Some dark and terrible day is coming / and you have to leave now / to save yourself. / Well, / when he said that / they decided to go with him. / So they packed up all their / belongings / and they followed him for miles / until they came to a / big stone / way deep / in the mountains / and as they watched / the stone rolled away. / They rushed to the entrance / to see what was beyond there / to see where they / were going / and it was the most / beautiful place / that they had ever seen. / The most beautiful place that they could / imagine. / The air just seemed to dance / with joy. / It was beautiful. / Without even looking back / many families / rushed ahead / and as they turned to close the door / forever / they saw a group / standing / way in the back. / The chief went over and asked them / Why aren't you coming in? / We're getting ready to close the door. / You have to come now. / And the old people in the group said / We were born here / and no matter what happens / we want to stay. / Young people said / We want our children to be born here / in the mountains / where our grandparents were born / and we decided / to stay. / He was torn between / going with this group and staying / and he decided that / he needed to stay / for whatever bad / was coming. / He needed to help lead his people. / The stone rolled over / and we've never seen / or heard from them / again. / The others remained / and these are the ones that / we're descended from. / The bad part / was the Trail of Tears / and the removal that forced thousands of people / to leave this area / and go to Oklahoma. / So if the Nunnehi ever / come again / we know something bad is / going to happen / and we'll have to decide / what to do then. / But remember that / as you're out in the woods / and you might hear something / you might hear some music / you might hear someone talking / that's the Nunnehi / and they're reminding / that they're always with us. (*Cherokee Legends*, vol. 1)

James Mooney has several stories about the Nunehi, including one about the way they assisted the Cherokee people before removal by "warning them of wars and misfortunes which the future held in store" (335). Similar to Littlejohn's story, Mooney's "The Removed Townhouses" explains how the Spirit Warriors helped lift and remove an entire Cherokee village in order to save them from the colonizers' invasion. Such stories act as a bridge of sorts that allow the ancient Nunehi to continue to be a part of modern Cherokee life and oral tradition. The following story from Mooney's collection gives personal accounts of encounters with the Nunehi and connects them closely with particular sites within the Cherokee homeland.

THE NUNNE'HI AND OTHER SPIRIT FOLK

The *Nunne'hi* or immortals, the "people who live anywhere," were a race of spirit people who lived in the highlands of the old Cherokee country and had a great many townhouses, especially in the bald mountains, the big breaks on which no timber ever grows. They had large townhouses in Pilot knob and under the old Nikwasi' mound in North Carolina, and another under Blood mountain, at the head of Nottely river, in Georgia. They were invisible excepting when they wanted to be seen, and then they looked and spoke just like other Indians. They were very fond of music and dancing, and hunters in the mountains would often hear the dance songs and the drum beating in some invisible townhouse, but when they went toward the sound it would shift about and they would hear it behind them or away in some other direction, so that they could never find the place where the dance was. They were a friendly people, too, and often brought back lost wanderers to their townhouses under the mountains and cared for them there until they were rested and then guided them back to their homes. More than once, also, when the Cherokee were hard pressed by the enemy, the Nunne'hi warriors have come out, as they did at old Nikwasi', and have saved them from defeat. Some people have thought that they are the same as the Yunwi Tsunsdi', the "Little People"; but these are fairies, no larger in size than children.

There was a man in Nottely town who had been with the Nunne'hi when he was a boy, and he told Wafford all about it. He was a truthful, hard-headed man, and Wafford had heard the story so often from other people that he asked this man to tell it. It was in this way: When he was about 10 or 12 years old he was playing one day near the river, shooting at a mark with his bow and arrows, until he became tired, and started to build a fish trap in the water. While he was piling up the stones in two long walls a man came and stood on the bank and asked him what he was doing. The boy told him, and the man said, "Well, that's pretty hard work and you ought to rest a while. Come and take a walk up the river." The boy said, "No"; that he was going home to dinner soon. "Come right up to my house," said the stranger, "and I'll give you a good dinner there and bring you home again in the morning." So the boy went with him up the river until they came to a house, when they went in, and the man's wife and the other people there were very glad to see him, and gave him a fine dinner, and were very kind to him. While they were eating a man that the boy knew very well came in and spoke to him, so that he felt quite at home.

After dinner he played with the other children and slept there that night, and in the morning, after breakfast, the man got ready to take him home. They went down a path that had a cornfield on one side and a peach orchard fenced in on the other, until they came to another trail, and the man said, "Go along this trail across that ridge and you will come to the river road that will bring you straight to your home, and now I'll go back to the house." So the man went back to the house and the boy went on along the trail, but when he had gone a little way he looked back, and there was no cornfield or orchard or fence or house; nothing but trees on the mountain side.

He thought it very queer, but somehow he was not frightened, and went on until he came to the river trail in sight of his home. There were a great many people standing about talking, and when they saw him they ran toward him shouting, "Here he is! He is not drowned or killed in the mountains!" They told him they had been hunting him ever since yesterday noon, and asked him where he had been. "A man took me over to his house just across the ridge, and I had a fine dinner and a good time with the children," said the boy, "I thought Udsi'skala here"—that was the name of the man he had seen at dinner—"would tell you where I was." But Udsi'skala said, "I haven't seen you. I was out all day in my canoe hunting you. It was one of the Nunne'hi that made himself look like me." Then his mother said, "You say you had dinner there?" "Yes, and I had plenty, too," said the boy; but his mother answered, "There is no house there—only trees and rocks—but we hear a drum sometimes in the big bald above. The people you saw were the Nunne'hi."

Once four Nunne'hi women came to a dance at Nottely town, and danced half the night with the young men there, and nobody knew that they were Nunne'hi, but thought them visitors from another settlement. About midnight they left to go home, and some men who had come out from the townhouse to cool off watched to see which way they went. They saw the women go down the trail to the river ford, but just as they came to the water they disappeared, although it was a plain trail, with no place where they could hide. Then the watchers knew they were Nunne'hi women. Several men saw this happen, and one of them was Wafford's father-in-law, who was known for an honest man. At another time a man named Burnt-tobacco was crossing over the ridge from Nottely to Hemptown in Georgia and heard a drum and the songs of dancers in the hills on one side of the trail. He rode over to see who could be dancing in such a place, but when he reached the spot the drum and the songs were behind him, and he was so frightened that he hurried back to the trail and rode all the way to Hemptown as hard as he could to tell the story. He was a truthful man, and they believed what he said. There must have been a good many of the Nunne'hi living in that neighborhood, because the drumming was often heard in the high balds almost up to the time of the Removal.

On a small upper branch of Nottely, running nearly due north from Blood mountain, there was also a hole, like a small well or chimney, in the ground, from which there came up a warm vapor that heated all the air around. People said that this was because the Nunne'hi had a townhouse and a fire under the mountain. Sometimes in cold weather hunters would stop there to warm themselves, but they were afraid to stay long. This was more than sixty years ago, but the hole is probably there yet.

Close to the old trading path from South Carolina up to the Cherokee Nation, somewhere near the head of Tugaloo, there was formerly a noted circular depression about the size of a townhouse, and waist deep. Inside it was always clean as though swept by unknown hands. Passing traders would throw logs and rocks into it, but would always, on the return, find them thrown far out from the hole. The Indians said it was a Nunne'hi townhouse, and never liked to go near the place or even to talk about it, until at last some logs thrown in by the traders were allowed to remain there, and then they concluded that the Nunne'hi, annoyed by the persecution of the white men, had abandoned their townhouse forever. (330–33)

There are many Eastern Cherokees, and, no doubt, their brethren in Oklahoma, who still feel the connection with the Nunehi when visiting or traveling within certain locations in the homeland, since these narratives are connected to very specific places within the original territory.

As the cultural resource officer for the Eastern Band, T. J. Holland carries much knowledge about the Spirit Warriors. He tells the story of one group of Nunehi who lived deep within the Tuckasegee River near Bryson City at a place called Tikwalitsi or Tuckalichee, and this particular group of Immortals are "like Cherokees in every way except that they eat people" ("Nunehi").[30] The oral tradition tells of a number of particular spots along several of the rivers in the original territory where these human-eating Dusgaseti beings were known to dwell, and at least one or two stories where a Cherokee who went below the water with one of these beings was allowed to return to his village, after being treated kindly. The stories name specific locations with

Cherokee place-names, thus giving more evidence of the intimate Indigenous connection to the homeland. There are a number of locations that were home to different communities of Nunehi, most of which were up in the highest reaches of the Bald Mountains where few trees grow because of the sheer rock faces;[31] however, there are at least two spots in the downtown area of the reservation where they also live/d. In his lectures on Cherokee cosmography, Holland describes one location that is actually a partial mound that sits along the Oconaluftee River behind the football field at the old Cherokee high school;[32] there is only half a mound there after some excavation work was done in the early 1900s. That digging was halted once the excavators learned of the burial there of Cherokees who had died of smallpox in the 1866 epidemic—the last time the sickness swept the community. This mound is called Nvnunyi or "Potato Place," which Holland explains is a newer name, since the Cherokees did not cultivate potatoes until the mid-1700s after the crop was brought from Europe; he has also been told by some language speakers that the original name of that mound was actually Nunehi-yi, which means "place of the Nunehi" ("Nunehi"). Another downtown home of Nunehi is inside of a ridge on the western side of the river behind what is now a Burger King restaurant. This ridge is called Nugatsani, which is an old Cherokee word to describe a high ridge with a long gradual slope. Holland says there are old stories of people hearing voices and singing or even seeing the Nunehi themselves in times past near these two downtown sites ("Nunehi"). It was interesting to hear an older Cherokee woman in the audience tell how her uncle used to own that land and that the story of the Nunehi living there was told within her family. Perhaps those sounds could still be heard today were it not for heavy car traffic streaming through the area.

Holland also speaks of the best-known story of the Immortals that is connected with the highly sacred mound called Nikwasi or "Star Place," which was the heart of the ancient town of Nikwasi or Nockasee—one of the Cherokee Middle Towns. The sacred Fire, which is the heart of all Cherokee life and rituals, was kept burning within that townhouse; family fires were restarted from this particular sacred Fire once a year at Green Corn time. Such a name suggests a deep and ancient connection to the Sky World, where all Earth beings originated and from where the original Fire came that the little Kananeski Ama'iyehi brought back in her tusti bowl. Nikwasi sat at the head of the Little Tennessee River and was the site of frequent ceremonies that friends and relatives from the other surrounding towns would attend.[33] Most importantly, the mound itself was home to a community of Immortals, and "Cherokee have long reported hearing drums and singing from the area of the mound and have always attributed the music to the Nunnehi,[34] who are known to love to sing and dance in the Underworld" (Mooney, qtd. in Muse, "Nikwasi"). Those particular Nunehi were Spirit Warriors (Owle refers to them as soldiers) and, in ancient times, had been seen streaming out of the eastern door of the earthen mound to come to the aid of the Cherokees during battles with any of their old enemies—be they Shawnees, Creeks, or Senecas.[35] There are too many such stories to relate here, but the one told most often is of the time when a band of Senecas came down from the north to attack the village while all the men were out hunting—except one old man.[36] He was chopping wood when he looked up and saw the enemy; he threw his hatchet at the nearest one and ran back to his house to grab his weapon. Upon returning, the man was "surprised to find a large body of strange warriors driving back the enemy" (Mooney, *Myths of the Cherokee* 337). He joined them, and the group of warriors fought hand-to-hand until the Seneca enemies were pushed back up the nearby creek until they finally broke rank and made a rapid retreat across the mountain. The old man turned to thank the other warriors but instead found himself alone as "they had disappeared as though the mountain had swallowed them. Then he knew that they were the Nunnehi, who had come to help their friends, the Cherokee" (337).

The various stories about the Spirit Warriors give a vivid description of these Immortals and how they rushed to the aid of the Nikwasi villagers in different times of danger. At one time, a powerful tribe from southeast of Cherokee country made war upon many of the Lower Town villages,[37] killing people and destroying their homes as they moved along before advancing up the mountains to the Middle Towns. Mooney's informants told him that "[t]he Nunnehi poured out by hundreds, armed and painted for the fight, and the most curious thing about it all was that they became invisible as soon as they were fairly outside of the settlement, so that although the enemy saw the glancing arrow or the rushing tomahawk, and felt the stroke, he could not see who sent it" (336–37). The story goes that when the enemy tried to hide behind rocks or trees, the arrows of the Nunehi would go right around and kill them, so there was no escaping. The slaughter was so fierce that soon there were only a handful of enemies remaining, and they threw themselves to the ground and cried out for mercy. This was at the head of the Tuckasegee River, and ever since then the Cherokees have called that particular spot Dayulsun-yi or the "place where they cried" (337). According to the ancient traditions of war, the Nunehi chief then told the remnant group to go back to their tribe and take news of their defeat and to never again attack a peaceful people. Once the strangers left, the Spirit Warriors went back inside Nikwasi mound,[38] and they are still there (Holland, "Nunehi"; Mooney, *Myths of the Cherokee*).

Not only do the Cherokees believe in their existence, but some of the Yuneg settlers hold this to be true.[39] It is hard to tell if this is simply another example of cultural appropriation or true belief, but there is a story—still told today—that during the American Civil War, the Nunehi even came to the aid of the non-Native residents of the new town of Franklin, which was built upon the land where the Cherokee village of Nikwasi had always stood. (The three-story-high mound remains intact and undisturbed in Franklin, and that land is owned by the town, which is, at times, a bone of contention for the EBCI.) Elder storyteller Freeman Owle shares the well-known story of the Nunehi and their role as Spirit Warriors, presented in Barbara Duncan's *Living Stories of the Cherokee*. Owle has a personal style that is welcoming and comfortable for non-Cherokee audiences because their Ancestors are often included in his tellings.

THE NIKWASI MOUND
Freeman Owle

> Nikwasi was down on the valley of the Tennessee,
>> and all of a sudden the Creeks began to come up and attack
>> and threaten to destroy the village of Nikwasi.
> The Cherokee people rallied,
>> they came to protect the village,
>> but over and over again the Creeks came in greater numbers,
>> and eventually the Cherokees were losing, very badly.
> And they'd almost given up,
>> when all of a sudden the mound of Nikwasi opened up,
>> and little soldiers began to march out of this mound by the thousands.
> And so they go out and they defeat the Creeks,

and like in biblical times
    they kill all of the Creeks except for one.
And he goes back and tells the other Creek brothers and sisters,
    "Never ever mess with the village of Nikwasi,
    because they have spirit people who protect it."
And never again
    was this village attacked by the Creeks.
It was during the Civil War time
    that the Yankee soldiers came down from the north,
    and they were camped out
    and ready to come down and to burn
    the little town of Franklin, North Carolina.
They sent scouts down to Franklin, North Carolina,
    and the scouts went back telling their commanding officer,
    "You can't attack Franklin, North Carolina.
    It is heavily guarded, there's soldiers on every corner."
And the soldiers went around,
    towards Atlanta, Georgia, and burned everything in the path.
But Franklin, North Carolina, was not touched.
And then the history and the reality was
    that every able fighting person left Franklin
    to fight in the Civil War.
There were no men here.
The old Cherokees say it was the Nunnehi, the Little People,
    that again protected
    Franklin, North Carolina. (201–2)

Even though Mooney gives this particular story just a brief, one-sentence mention, both Cherokee and non-Cherokee historians and storytellers enjoy sharing this longer version.

Holland offers more detail and explains that it was a troop of Federal (Union) soldiers who were on their way to meet up with General Sherman for his infamous march through Georgia, which was mainly burning homes and crops of southerners in hopes of starving them and ending the long-running Civil War. This group of blue-coat soldiers saw the town of Franklin from their vantage point up a nearby hill and waited for the cover of dark to send scouts down to take a look.[40] It seems that those scouts came back with reports of there being a soldier posted at each and every house and shop; in other words, Franklin was too well protected for these Union soldiers to make a foolish attack or raid to steal food, so they wisely continued on their journey down to Georgia. Meanwhile, the townspeople were completely unaware of the danger that had just passed them, and Holland explains that this story only came to light months later when some of those Federal soldiers happened to meet Confederate soldiers from Franklin who were imprisoned at a northern camp. It is important to note that the stories of the Nunehi of Nikwasi/Franklin were probably only known locally, and there is no logical reason that any Yankee soldiers could have been aware of this ancient Cherokee story in that particular location (Holland, "Nunehi"). So, Holland asks, who were those soldiers who stood guard that night in Franklin, preventing a surprise attack on the defenseless townsfolk—mainly women and children, whose men were gone off to fight in the Confederate army? Many Cherokees accept this as just one more story about the power of the Spirit Warriors and their responsibility to protect what was one of the most sacred mounds throughout this ancient homeland, which, ironically, could not be protected from the repeated attacks by the new Americans during the Revolutionary War, since the Cherokees were allied with the British at that time.[41] Some believe the Immortals knew the Americans would win and the feared removal would take place, so the belief is that the Nunehi are waiting inside the mound for the sacred Fire to return. This optimistic and deeply held belief is part of the ancient prophecies that predict the Cherokee people coming back together after the Fire returns from its home in the West, for it is then that the entire nation will walk the path of Duyvkta together. That healing is already under way with more and more cultural activities taking place between the three bands of Cherokees; my final chapter will discuss this prophecy at greater length.

There are also stories of the Nunehi inviting Cherokees in different villages to come and live with them in their protected places, and, in some stories, the people did exactly that. The Littlejohn and Owle versions are both hauntingly prophetic of the upcoming forced removal that separates the People. Both versions tell how in one village, while the people were gathered in the townhouse and holding council, the door hide lifted high enough for someone to enter, but no one did, yet there was no wind to lift the door. Owle describes how a green-colored light appeared in a corner,[42] and slowly an unfamiliar Cherokee man materialized from the light and began to speak to those gathered, saying, "'You, my brothers and sisters, must follow me. / For out of the east will come a group of people / who will destroy your homes. / And your villages will be burned, / and your children will be killed, / and your homeland will be taken away, / and never again will you be happy.' / And so the Cherokee said, / 'No, we can't leave, / because this land belonged to my mothers' mothers' mother'" (Owle, quoted in Duncan, *Living Stories* 240–41). In this version, similar to Smith Littlejohn's telling, half of the village's people decided to go with this stranger, who led them out of town and up to a sacred mountain where they could hear people laughing and singing inside.[43] The man touched the rock cliff, and it opened up to reveal a "stairwell leading up to a beautiful land / of springtime and summer" (241). Upon seeing the fruit trees and butterflies, the people decided to go in and live forever and be happy—all but one man, who had left family back in the village. He wanted to go get them and bring them to this wonderful place, but when he got back with his loved ones, the mountain had closed up. His family thought he was crazy and so left him at the mountain and went home. The man remained outside the rock cliff for seven days, and then began to hear singing from deep within the mountain. He went back to the village and told the people that if they listen quietly at any time, they would hear their people inside the mountain singing and happy (241–42). Holland tells another story of a village that also heard warnings of bad times ahead and were told to gather in their townhouse and fast for seven days and pray—just like Tsutlakalv had told his wife's village to do—and that the Nunehi would lift up the entire village and carry it to their home in the mountains. The people of Asgeya-yi (Men's Town) became frightened as their townhouse and mound were picked up in the air, and they cried out, so that the Nunehi were startled and let a part of it drop to the ground. That fallen part became a smaller mound known today as Setsi while the rest of it with the townhouse were placed upon Tsudayelunyi (Lone Peak) in Graham County, North Carolina, near the head of the Cheowa River where it was then changed to solid rock so that the new home is inside that mountain. Another townhouse was also removed and was placed at the mouth of Shooting Creek and is now underwater, buried inside of Dustiyalunyi or Lake Chatuge (Holland, "Nunehi"). All these stories tell that the Cherokees who went to live inside those mountains are alive and happy where they are.

The idea that a better life for humans who face hardship and suffering in the future can be had if they go to live in the Spirit World is one that is echoed in other world religions; however, for the Cherokees, this is not necessarily a totally separate realm or world than the physical one in which we all live. The Cherokee worldview holds that the Spirits are with us all the time and that the physical and Spirit World blend at different times, in different places, and in many ways. It seems natural that the Spirits of the Cherokee Ancestors would wish to protect them in any way they can, and Mooney points out that the stories of the townhouses and villages being relocated by the Nunehi took place well before the Trail of Tears and that perhaps the Immortals were forewarning the Cherokee people of that horrific event that would decimate the tribe (*Myths of the Cherokee* 335). There is no question among the Eastern Cherokees or their brethren in Oklahoma that those two particular villages with their townhouses full of people were taken away by the Nunehi because the locations where each was placed can be seen today and are familiar landmarks. Mooney also points out that one of the things that many Cherokees dreaded most about leaving the homeland was the fact they were "compelled to leave behind forever their relatives who had gone to the Nunnehi" (*Myths of the Cherokee* 336).

In his book with oral storytellers from the Cherokee Nation of Oklahoma, Chris Teuton presents their thoughts on "the way in which spirit and world interconnect within a Cherokee worldview" (*Cherokee Stories* 204), particularly through the Usgaseti stories of wonder. Elder Hastings Shade describes how Native people have long used the ability to change from human to animal forms—what many call shape-shifting—and explains that such experiences are part of the nearness of another world or realm when he says, "'We speak of parallel worlds. We're here, the parallel world is here,' Hastings said, and gestured to two sides. 'Within that step, just like the step here. The parallel world is a step here,' he said, and gestured again to the side. 'Within our path. That's how close we are to this spiritual world'" (204). Teuton notes that many experiences that merge the physical and metaphysical are strange or unbelievable to some people, but not to "those with deeper knowledge of Cherokee medicine and traditional beliefs" (204). It is part of the ancient Kituwah way of life to be concerned with the Spirit power that is all around us, what Paul Zolbrod attempts to define within the word "sacred" when he theorizes that all Native oral tradition is "sacred poetry" (12–13). He posits that "the sacred helps to define a community by linking it with something beyond itself in space, time, and natural limits, while simultaneously connecting it with what exists naturally and can be observed within spatial or temporal limits" (16). Karl Kroeber suggests that any non-Native studying such Indigenous oral tellings generally can't begin to grasp the power of such stories unless one understands that what seems strange or impossible isn't intended to be told that way just for listeners' amusement or for superficial effect. "Read as Indians heard them," he adds, "these stories are troubling (and exciting) because they make manifest the deepest psychological or sociological forces that determined the nature of the lives of tellers and audiences, forces which, except for the stories, would have remained unacknowledged and unexamined—and therefore potentially disruptive and destructive" (6). Kroeber notes that such tribal stories seem strange only because they are much more "culturally serious . . . and demand far more daring, adventurous, and ultimately responsible imagining" (6) than most people today are used to, living in a world of television and written literature that often already supplies the imaginary structures.

These Dusgaseti stories are indeed sacred because they are an effective cultural instrument that encapsulates the sense of wonderment and even dread, at times, of the Cherokee reality—both physical and spiritual, and without restrictions of time or space. The long-held knowledge of the spiritual beings who are intimately linked to particular spots within the ancient homeland give further evidence of not only the Cherokee's own indigeneity to the physical Earth sites but even to the spiritual realm that surrounds the hills, waters, valleys, and rock formations throughout this area. The stories demonstrate the relationships that the Giduwah people have had for thousands of years with the various Dusgaseti and continue to hold sacred. Despite the fact that some of these awesome and dreadful beings have created great fear among the Cherokee at different times, these wondrous creatures have also proven to be beneficial for Giduwah culture and spirituality. The next chapter will continue this examination of the Ancestors' stories that are still told today by and among the Eastern Cherokees—stories that not only keep the old ways alive but help buffer this Indigenous community from the daily onslaught of a foreign culture while helping to educate at least some of those foreigners. By teaching non-Cherokees about the culture in a friendly and neighborly fashion, the EBCI hope to help erase the misunderstandings and stereotypes that have existed for too long about the Cherokees and, indeed, for all Native people. Welcoming outsiders and tourists by inviting them to sit and listen to experienced storytellers share their knowledge of Tsalagi life and history is in keeping with Duyvkta by promoting harmony and kindness, while also fulfilling principles of Gadugi as the friendly education of outsiders is what is best for the entire Qualla Cherokee community. As my next chapter will demonstrate, the storytellers in this group are not only skilled in their word art but are able to captivate, entertain, and teach the crowds of non-Cherokee visitors in a way that promotes the friendly atmosphere of this Native community.

4

Nudele yvwi dideyohdi

◆ To teach other people, to make them strong ◆

Sharing Tsalagi Oral Teachings with Others

A crowd of about forty visitors of all ages gathered in the park near a large campfire on the banks of the Oconaluftee River near dusk on a mild September evening. The couples and families found seats on the rough-hewn wooden benches set up around the large stone-encircled firepit, while a few set up their lawn chairs. Their small children quickly ran down by the river, to gaze and perch precariously on the large river rocks on the shore's edge, bringing warnings and remonstrance from their parents sitting nearby. The audience was shaded by the many trees around the park area, and an end-of-summer breeze rustled the leaves. The noise of long lines of tourist traffic surrounded the group on two sides, while the gurgling of the mountain stream rapids in front of them offered a comforting contrast to the vehicular cacophony. Whispered excitement bubbled throughout the crowd as many of them looked all around for the Native storyteller to approach. The visitors anticipated a special treat that evening, as they awaited Cherokee's most popular and best-known storyteller. Several young Cherokee men, dressed in traditional 1700s-style clothing, stood under the small wooden shelter nearby, laughing and talking as their young children also ran around and chased one another throughout the hilly park, under the watchful eyes of their mothers, aunties, and grandmas. Occasionally, one of the men would call out to the children in the ancient Cherokee language with words that must have sounded foreign to the visitors seated nearby. A few of the tourists sipped coffee from Styrofoam cups, and several of them donned their jackets as the sun dipped behind a nearby mountaintop and the chill of the evening crept into the area. Finally, an older Cherokee gentleman, wearing a ribbon shirt and brown felt hat, walked over in front of the crowd and offered a friendly "*Siyo!* "[1]

It is Elder Lloyd Arneach,[2] the much-anticipated star of the show—a storyteller who has won awards throughout the state of North Carolina and the American Southeast, most recently from Western Carolina University,[3] for his easygoing, down-home-style oratory skills and expertise in sharing not only the ancient originary stories of the Cherokee people but also his personal life narratives, which are uniquely Cherokee and often typically Native American yet accessible in the way the tales make listeners of all cultures recognize some common life experiences we all share. Lloyd launches into the first of his vast repertoire of anecdotes and stories, and each telling and retelling brings about head nods, laughter, and sometimes looks of surprise from the non-Cherokee folks in the bonfire ring. Whether they realize it or not, this modern-day setting is a physical replication of the way many Cherokees would have heard the cultural stories over the thousands of years in which these original human beings have resided upon this sacred mountainous homeland. The way that the stories are now being shared with the descendants of the colonizers who first invaded and later stole the land from the Cherokees is an intentional, deliberate, and calculated method of rewriting and displacing the settler history, which is all too often the only history the visiting tourists have ever learned. The stories—whether originary, ancient, animal- or human-focused, romantic, humorous, modern, anecdotal, personal, or communal—are shared in a way that blends time and space, making what seems old feel new and what may be newer seem ancient. Arneach is one of many community orators, and the Eastern Band of Cherokees utilize them in the band's efforts to assert its sovereignty and Indigenous rights in an often-politicized county/state/federal arena, while still maintaining good relations with the non-Cherokees residing around and within the Qualla Boundary. It is a delicate balancing act but not that difficult for this Native group that has always held values which urge them to live harmoniously within the larger natural world and to work individually and collectively to coexist peacefully with all the other life-forms—this now includes settler descendants.

Storytelling permeates the cultural atmosphere of the Qualla Boundary, much like the kudzu vines engulf and envelope the hillsides, and the aroma of boiled peanuts, a local delicacy, fills the misty air throughout the community. These Eastern Cherokee storytellers are masters of the spoken word and breathe new life into the ancient stories, bringing cultural knowledge and teachings into modern existence through "the oral tradition which binds the successive states of Cherokee society through space and time" (Meredith and Meredith 7). Like many storytellers around the world, their job is to do more than just entertain the tourists; it is also to inform, educate, and, at times, persuade the visitors of the Cherokees' steadfastness and rightful continuing existence within the historically anti-Indian region of the southern United States and throughout their mountain homeland. Hopi scholar and filmmaker Victor Masayesva Jr. posits that "[o]ral traditions are the expression of a tribe's sovereignty in matters of culture and beliefs, encapsulating the totality of its understanding of life and living" (92). By drawing on the rich, continuing oral tradition, the Ani-Yunwiyah are ensuring the continuance of their own culture and community but also influencing thousands of non-Cherokees each year and imprinting upon their very psyche the vitality and uniqueness of Cherokee culture. These stories continue to be "one of the time-honoured ways in which societies . . . affirm their identity, establish their history, demonstrate the intellectual and emotional integrity of their critical and creative practices, and exhibit the character of their intellectual and emotional lives" (Chamberlin 73).

Stories and "legends"[4] have been an intricate component of the tourism industry in and around the Qualla Boundary since car traffic first made its way through the newly established Great Smoky Mountains National Park in the late 1930s, under the administration of President Franklin D. Roosevelt.[5] The Smoky Mountains are known for the breathtaking natural beauty of their Carolinian forests, cloudy peaks, and crisp mountain streams, and it is not surprising that one of America's new national parks should be established in the region.[6] It is also a well-known fact that the Eastern Cherokee reservation, located adjacent to the park, was viewed as an enticement for motoring tourists to make the region a destination spot, because the government expected that most Americans would want to "see the Indians."[7] The Qualla Cherokees had sold a large, thirty-three-thousand-acre tract called the "Love Speculation" in 1899, which was intended for the new park. Once the political wrangling over building roads through the mountains was completed, a number of Cherokee men became employed through special federal relief work programs during the Great Depression and completed the roadwork. Within the next decade, the Qualla Boundary began to see its share of tourists, and this led to the establishment of motels, restaurants, and Indian craft shops on the reservation—for the most part, owned by white businessmen who leased the land from the tribe (French 76–77). This practice continues even today, as the businesses now include nearly every major hotel and motel chain and fast-food restaurant common in the United States, along with a major casino that is owned by the EBCI and co-managed by Harrah's Casinos—all to entice the tourists to come and "experience Cherokee" (Visit Cherokee North Carolina).

As the Qualla community adapted to its new status as an "Anglo-American tourist attraction" (French 77), other culturally focused sites and events were conceived for the Eastern Cherokees, including a "living" village, a Cherokee museum, a Native artists cooperative, and an outdoor drama that would tell the story and history of the Cherokees—all of which continue today as main attractions for non-Cherokee visitors.[8] Each of these venues offers a cultural education that is, for the most part, controlled by the band and its tribal council and elected chief or, in the case of the museum, by a Native board of directors. Storytelling plays a major part throughout this cultural landscape, as there is a concentrated, tribally funded emphasis on education and cultural awareness for the settler/tourists who visit. This use of the oral tradition for educational purposes takes the form of the summer riverside bonfire storytelling already mentioned, along with historical plaques; public relations and tourism brochures for the tribe; community-wide events geared toward tourists (such as the annual Cherokee Voices Festival at the museum each June); CDs, DVDs, and VHS tapes of storytellers for sale; television commercials; and a plethora of other mass media. Daily storytelling and history-sharing occurs at the Museum of the Cherokee Indian, the Oconaluftee Village, the "Unto These Hills" outdoor drama in the summer, and in the Qualla Arts and Crafts Co-op. These many varied performances (some live, some recorded, and some impromptu) of the culture, history, and Cherokee-centric stories are in keeping with the modern continuance of the ancient oral tradition and are deeply embedded in the Cherokee psyche of today. The Qualla Cherokee community has always relied on its rich history of the spoken word for cultural endurance and persistence, and there has been no interruption or diminishing of this ancient art form, much like the basket-weaving, blowgun-making, and pottery-sculpting that local artists continue to produce. Pueblo scholar Simon Ortiz writes of the necessity of telling the stories, as "through the past five centuries the oral tradition has been the most reliable method by which Indian culture and community integrity have been maintained. And, certainly, it is within the tradition that authenticity is most apparent and evident" ("Towards a National Indian Literature" 9).

Not all Native/First Nations groups would feel comfortable putting their culture on display in the fashion that the Eastern Cherokees have done, but this sort of sharing in a friendly and harmonious fashion with the colonizer descendants is in keeping with what Cherokee anthropologist Robert K. Thomas discusses in his unpublished master's thesis, "Cherokee Values and World View." Thomas, an Oklahoma Cherokee who lived for a couple of years on the Qualla Boundary in the late 1950s (he wrote this thesis in 1958), does not differentiate between the Eastern Cherokees or their western siblings, except in a few details, but speaks of Cherokees in general. He suggests the core of the value system is that "[t]he Cherokee tries to maintain harmonious interpersonal relationships with his fellow Cherokee by avoiding giving offense, on the negative side, and by giving of himself to his fellow Cherokee in regard to his time and his material goods, on the positive side" (1). Thomas chooses to use the term "giving offense" rather than aggression because he feels being offensive is behavioral while aggression is psychological. To give offense would be "any situation in which the autonomy of the individual is interfered with. These situations, behavior-wise, would range from areas of over-zealous joking or unsolicited advice to open hostility" (2). However, he adds, if a person offends another, one should not then resort to acting aggressively toward the offender because such retaliatory behavior would further disrupt the harmony within the group. Oftentimes, the group or Cherokee society at large will pressure the offender to stop her or his bad behavior, and this pressure is usually enough to cause the offender to stop, "[b]ut open hostility between two people on the local level must not appear." Thomas notes that the use of gossip is a "means of social control in Cherokee society" (2), and if the gossip does not influence the offender to change her or his behavior, those around her or him will withdraw and leave the person isolated. The isolation is not meant as a punishment, because Cherokee society would much prefer the person stop their disharmonious and bad behavior rather than punish the offender, as "punishment simply compounds the disharmony" (4). So, in general, traditional-minded Cherokees will strive for harmony *at all times,* avoiding conflict or saying or doing anything that will hurt, embarrass, or offend another person because "[h]armonious relations are the norm—the minimum—rather than some goal to be reached" (4). I suggest that, given the situation with non-Cherokee tourists and visitors traveling through the community on a daily basis and often staying for several days, the Eastern Cherokees have extended this value system to include their behavior toward those outsiders and to welcome them, rather than ignoring or being rude to the non-Natives. Since the cultural attractions are a large part of the landscape of the reservation, it is an opportunity, then, for Cherokees involved in the tourism business to warmly welcome the visitors and offer Cherokee hospitality, which includes storytelling and sharing of history.

While living for three years on the Qualla Boundary, the first of my family in three generations to move back,[9] I oftentimes felt frustrated by what I sometimes viewed as passivity by other Cherokees I knew. Part of that, no doubt, was due to the fact that I had been raised in Detroit in a neighborhood that frequently saw violence, a lifestyle that encouraged me to become an aggressive person. Standing up for myself and sometimes fighting were simply my reality, though over the years of being away from that racially tense environment, along with becoming a parent, I have learned to use my words rather than my fists. I am no longer aggressive but am most certainly assertive when I feel the need, yet even my subdued assertiveness did not meld with the Cherokee worldview I encountered among my friends and kin, and I found I had to reign myself in. If I complained about the bumper-to-bumper tourist traffic to any friends or my adoptive family around Cherokee, I was gently reminded that the tourists drove slow because they were gawking at the sites and probably had never seen real Indians before, or perhaps they had never driven in the mountains and were being overcautious. If I scoffed at what seemed naïve questions and comments made by the tourist audience toward the Cherokee storytellers, those orators often would kindly and gently suggest to me that many of the visitors did not know about Cherokee lifeways and that it was up to us as Cherokees to teach them because the American history taught in schools did not include anything positive about Cherokees and other Native Americans. It became clear to me that Thomas's theory of nonaggression and "conscious avoidance of interpersonal conflict" (Purrington 253) plays out every day around the Boundary in most of the dealings that Cherokee people have with non-Native friends, coworkers, and visitors as the Ani-Yunwiyah readily accept the responsibility of sharing their culture and welcoming everyone. This hospitable atmosphere throughout the Eastern Cherokee homeland would most certainly influence the large numbers of tourists who visit the Great Smoky Mountains National Park—the highest numbers of any of the national parks in the United States, including Yellowstone and the Grand Canyon. The public relations theme of the year 2013–14 for Tourism Cherokee and the Chamber of Commerce reads, "How will Cherokee affect you?" and printed materials show a photo collage of both Cherokees and non-Cherokees enjoying the many attractions and events meant to show how visitors can feel at home in this Indigenous territory. A few years back, a special passport was given out to visitors who stopped at the tourism bureau, which let the non-Cherokees know they were entering a country other than the United States. Along with that, in the summer of 2012 the University of North Carolina offered a special six-week program called "Cherokee Study Abroad" that offered students a chance to study first on the EBCI reservation for two weeks and, after one week of retracing the Trail of Tears from the South out to Oklahoma, spend another three weeks within the Cherokee Nation in Tahlequah. Students could experience what it was like to "live in a nation within a nation" as they studied "abroad" in the two homelands of the Cherokee people. A part of that program included meeting the Cherokee historians and storytellers in both communities at particular cultural sites.[10]

Employing the ancient stories in a modern retelling and reshaping, along with the addition of newer, post-Removal stories of the Eastern Cherokees, functions in a number of ways to inform the colonizer descendants that the Cherokees in this area of the American South have always been there and will remain as Indigenous caretakers of this particular environment.[11] The oral tradition has evolved in a way that allows for the Real Human Beings to use their strong storytelling voice to resist the confinements of colonialism. The Qualla Cherokees utilize the stories in an external fashion—told within the community but for the outsiders whose culture and society exert great pressure upon all Native American groups to conform and assimilate. Simon Ortiz argues that "because of the insistence to keep telling and creating stories, Indian life continues even if it is a 'struggle for life' and for 'salvation and affirmation'" ("Towards a National Indian Literature" 11). In line with Thomas's "Cherokee worldview" (1), the stories as told publicly act in a subtly resistive manner to help decolonize the Cherokees while reminding and reaffirming the tribe's first-on-the-land status to the settler descendants and newcomers, in case they do not fully accept that America, as a country, came into existence after a series of political lies, broken treaties, unjust intrusions, and violent land grabs perpetrated by their European ancestors (the "founding fathers") and the subsequent colonial government upon a Native tribe who had been welcoming and willing to live harmoniously with the newcomers.

Let us examine the roles that the continuing oral tradition within the Eastern Cherokee territory now fulfills. First, we'll look at the externally focused use of storytelling, which is directed toward non-Native visitors and those who come to work or live on the Qualla Boundary, and then my fifth and final chapter will present internally focused oral narratives and usages of *Tsalagi gawonihisdi aksasdohdi* (to talk or we are talking Cherokee) that preserve and perpetuate the culture and lifeways.[12] The employment of oral tradition for external purposes or for the listeners from outside the tribe include:

- Affirmation of Cherokee people in this region by rewriting colonizer notions of all Indians being removed from the South;
- Resistance to ongoing encroachment and a reclaiming of particular land;
- Reinscribing the land by informing visitors of original place-names and connected stories;
- Asserting continuity of Cherokee sovereignty;
- Exhibiting the uniqueness of Cherokee culture and examples of settler appropriation of some of that culture;
- Legitimizing Cherokee adoption of particular settler values and inventions;
- Establishing harmony by noting similarities with non-Cherokee settler descendants; and
- Educating visitors about the need for environmental respect, sensitivity, and conservation.

The use of storytelling to educate and inform non-Cherokee visitors is comparable to Thomas King's notion of "associational literature" ("Godzilla vs. Post-Colonial" 245). King, who claims Cherokee heritage, posits that "[a]ssociational literature, most often, describes a Native community" (245) and thus locates story very much within the Native world and community, rather than the non-Native one—resisting the notion of Native literature being postcolonial, which ties the work to the colonizer more than the Indigenous group, something that both King and I are reluctant to do. Associational form gives preference to the Native culture and instead focuses "on the daily activities and intricacies of Native life and organizing the elements of plot along a rather flat narrative line that ignores the ubiquitous climaxes and resolutions" (245) that are such an important part of non-Native literature. King suggests that in Native literature (and thus, I suggest, in oral storytelling), the focus is on the group over the individual, and this allows for a story "that de-values heroes and villains in favour of the members of a community" (246) and avoids conclusions and judgments. Stories and teachings from the Cherokee oral tradition, as in other Native cultures, do not tidily sum matters up and do not make judgments (more on that in my next chapter with storyteller Kathi Littlejohn); rather, it is left up to the listener(s) to take whatever lesson is right for them from a story, and this varies from person to person. As we saw in the Dusgaseti stories of my second and third chapters, there are no individual heroes since every creature and being is important. In the case of Spearfinger or Stonecoat, the entire group worked together to rid the land of the horrors each being brought. According to King, associational literary form "helps to remind us (Natives) of the continuing values of our cultures," offers usable cultural information and history, and gives evidence of the "cultural tenacity and a viable future" of the group/community, which could be tied to an ongoing or future revitalization of that culture's language, spiritualism, and lifeways (246). Conversely, non-Native listeners on the Qualla Boundary will also gain insight into the value, vitality, and veracity of Cherokee culture and teachings. King suggests that associational literature presents for the non-Native a select yet limited access to the Native world, allowing the reader/listener "to associate with that world without being encouraged to feel a part of it" (246). In the case of Cherokee storytelling for tourists, the non-Cherokee visitors can witness, hear, and feel immersed in the culture and may certainly understand the cultural crossovers into southern

Appalachian lifeways yet know those crossovers originated within the Native culture of the area; this gives the visitor a sense of appreciation, along with the realization that he or she is simply visiting the Cherokee society and culture. The "associational" form of stories also differs greatly from another Native literary style, which King identifies as "polemical." The polemical is more of an assertive, "in-your-face" form that tends to point out the injustices and impositions perpetrated by non-Natives and focuses more on the clash between the two cultures (244). This form of resistance literature has become a powerful style of modern storytelling for many contemporary Indigenous writers from across North America and is at the heart of Native literature courses in numerous universities, including where I teach.

At first glance, the stories shared by Elder Lloyd Arneach seem welcoming and even comfortable for the visitors. His friendly and humorous approach tends to put everyone at ease, but his performance and spoken delivery work in ways that consistently talk back to the colonizer descendants and point to his firm belief in the strength of the Ani-Giduwah and their culture. While waiting to start one session, he jokingly tells his audience that if anyone needs a free haircut, they have come to the right place—a reference to the brutal practice of scalping, which was introduced by the early settlers, possibly the "French and English, who offered bounties for Indian heads but finally accepted scalps since heads were so bulky" (Wetmore 125). Arneach begins most of his performances with ancient stories—generally the Creation story or one of the many animal stories, which may or may not have human characters. By doing this, he establishes the primordiality of the Tsalagi culture and their attachment to this Earth and that his Ancestors, not theirs, are Indigenous to these mountains, and that the Creator caused this to be so. Arneach shares many of the animal stories, which present the agency of all nonhuman beings.

HOW THE DEER GOT HIS ANTLERS
Lloyd Arneach

Now / the Deer and the Rabbit / got into a tremendous argument. / And this was before Deer got his antlers / this story tells us / how the Deer got his antlers. / Well, / the Deer and the Rabbit would / argue about who was the / fastest animal of all. / The Deer said, "I could run and / leap a great distance / in a single bound!" / And Rabbit would say, / "While you're up in the air / I'll run underneath you / and I'll get there / before you come down." / And they argued / back and forth. / Oh / the other animals got / tired of listening to them / arguing all the time. / Finally one of the animals said, / "Why don't you have a race? / Whoever wins the race / we know is that fastest animal of all!" / Well, Deer immediately agreed. / Rabbit was a little slow. / He said, "Nope! / Got to be worth my time." / One of the animals came forward. / They'd carved a beautiful set of antlers / and they said, / "I will give this set of antlers / to whoever wins the race." / The Deer looked at the set of antlers / thought how'd they'd look on his head / he said, "Yes! / I will run for the antlers." / And Rabbit looked at the antlers / and thought how they'd look on / his head. / He said, "Yes! / Yes, I'll run for the antlers!" / And then Rabbit said, / "Where shall we run?" / One of the animals said, "Well. / Why don't you start here / and you can run through the thicket over there. / Well, once again / Deer immediately agreed. / Once again, / Rabbit was a little slow. / He said, "Well, / I'm new to this area. / Can I go in the thicket and look around?" / And the animals said, "Sure! / Go Ahead." / So Rabbit went into the thicket. / The animals waited and waited. / Rabbit didn't come back. / Finally they sent one of the / small animals into the thicket after him. / In a few minutes / the little one came back / and he said, / "Rabbit is cutting a shortcut through the thicket! / He's going to cheat!" / They couldn't believe / Rabbit would cheat about something / this important! / In a little while / Rabbit came back out of the thicket / he lined up / and said, "Okay Deer. / Ready to go. / Deer, better get over here. / If you don't get over here, / the antlers are gonna be mine!" / And one of the animals said, / "Rabbit, / one of us said / you're cutting a shortcut through the thicket." / Rabbit said, "No, no, no I'm not!" / And another animal said, / "Well Rabbit, / then one of you / is lying. / We will all go in the thicket / and see who's lying." / They saw / that Rabbit had been cutting a shortcut through the thicket. / He came back out of the thicket / Rabbit was quiet. / He'd been caught in his lie. / And then one of the animals said, / "Rabbit, / you would cheat / and you would lie / to win these antlers. / Whoever wears these antlers / must wear them with / honor and respect. / And Rabbit, / you couldn't wear them with / honor and respect. / So we'll give them instead to the Deer." / And they called the Deer forward / and then he sat down / and they put the antlers on his head. / And they grew into his head in an instant. / And they have grown there / from that day until this. / But the Deer always loses his antlers / once a year / to remind him / it was not always so. (*Cherokee Bonfire* DVD, 30 June 2013)

There are a number of *Tsisdu* (rabbit) stories in the Cherokee world, and she is often seen as mischievous and self-serving, willing to tell untruths in order to cheat others or even to protect herself. This is also true of *Tsula* (fox) in another story by Arneach.

HOW BEAR LOST HIS TAIL
Lloyd Arneach

Now / the animals came down[13] / and / there's several characteristics of the animals / but these stories tell us / how some of these things happened. / Now long ago / Bear had a long / bushy tail / and the bear woke up in / the middle of winter / and he wasn't supposed to do that. / He was supposed to sleep / all winter long / and of course / when he woke up / OH! / he was hungry! / And he came out of his den / and he started walking through the snow / looking for food / he was walking on the path through the forest / and ahead of him / he saw a fox / coming / along the path toward him / and Fox had a / stringer of fish over his shoulder. / Fox was walking along / with his head down / and he didn't look up. / And when he did look up / Bear was right in front of him. / And Fox knew he couldn't run away / with all these fish. / Bear could catch him / and he didn't want to tell Bear / he had stolen these fish / from the mink / while the mink was out in the river fishing / 'cause then Bear would take them / from him! / Well, Fox is a great storyteller / and he came up with this story. / He kept walking and / Bear got up to him and said / "Fox, uh / you got a lot of fish there / and I'm awfully hungry. / Can you give me / just one?" / And Fox knew he'd ask for another one / and another one / and he'd eat all the fish. / So Fox told him / "Well, Bear / let me tell you how I caught all these fish / and you can / go catch fish too! / And you can catch more than I've got." / Bear said, "Well, / how'd you do that?" / And Fox said / "I went down to the river / I took a big stone and I / knocked a hole in the ice / and I turned around / I stuck my tail down in that ice. / And after a while it started hurting / where the fish were biting. / Oh! It hurt so bad and / finally when I stood up / all of these fish were / hanging on the hairs of my tail. / And Bear! / You got a longer / bushier tail than I've got. / You'll catch more fish than I've got!" / Bear said / "Why, thank you, / I'll do that!" / And Bear went on down to the river / and he / got a big rock / and he / knocked a hole in the ice / he turned around / put his tail down in that ice. / Sure enough! / Just like Fox said / in a little while it started hurting / and Bear was thinking about / all the fish who were / biting the hairs on his tail. / And he couldn't stand the pain / any longer so / finally he / tried to stand up / and he couldn't stand up! / The ice had frozen around his tail / and he was stuck! / And he kept pulling and tugging / and tugging / and finally / BOOP! / He pulled loose / and when he did / he left his long bushy tail / frozen / there in the ice. / And all he had left was that / little stub of a tail that he has / till this very day. / And today, / whenever Fox sees Bear in the forest / Fox runs away / because Bear still remembers how / Fox cost him that / long, bushy tail. (*Cherokee Bonfire* DVD, 30 June 2013)

The Cherokee animal stories may seem humorous and entertaining to the non-Native audience, who may liken such stories to Aesop's *Fables*,[14] but, as in those ancient Greek stories, there are always lessons to be learned about bad behavior, trickery, and gullibility as well as information for the listeners of the agency and unique personalities of the animal persons involved.[15] James Mooney notes, "In Cherokee mythology . . . there is no essential difference between men and animals. In the primal genesis period, they seem to be completely undifferentiated, and we find all creatures alike living and working together in harmony and mutual helpfulness" (261). The animal stories shared by Arneach and the other storytellers inform the listener that the four-footed and winged creatures make conscious decisions about what kind of relations they will have with one another and what kind of things each will do; the stories show the consequences of any bad treatment of one another and point toward the way humans have mimicked their animal siblings. This is unlike non-Indigenous anthropological and scientific researchers who are often surprised by animal behavior, which "seems human" at times. Instead, as Davy Arch suggests, without learning from the animals, the Ani-Yunwiyah would not know what to do. In his storytelling, Arneach puts the animals front and center, which speaks against the Euro-western notion that man is the center of the world and that other creatures were inferior in comparison—an Indigenous ideology that may seem foreign for the newcomers to Cherokee country.

With another ancient story, Arneach shares the Cherokee belief in the spiritualism of the animals. As he explains, the Creator has even made for them their own sacred spots within Cherokee country—locations most humans are not aware of but that the animals continue to recognize.

THE HEALING LAKE
Lloyd Arneach

Now if you follow the Oconaluftee River here / to the headwaters in the Great Smoky Mountains / and then you travel three days west / from the headwaters / you'll come to a large grassy plain / on the far side you will see a huge cliff / but you will see nothing in that grassy plain. / You won't see anything on the cliff / on the sides, / but if you fast properly / you can come back to the site; / it won't be a large grassy plain / it will be a lake. / Coming out of the cliff / will be waterfalls / and swimming on the surface / will be ducks and geese and birds of all kinds / and fish will be swimming in its waters / and animals will be on the shore / around the lake / and sometimes you might see / a wounded bear / plunge into the lake / swim across / and when he comes out on the far side / he will be healed. / This is a magic lake of the animals / where they go to get healed / but very few people have ever seen this because / they don't know how to fast properly / to prepare themselves / to have this gift shared with them. (*Cherokee Bonfire* DVD, 29 June 2013)

In this telling, the Elder storyteller uses the word "magic," rather than the real name of Vdali Nvwoti (Medicine Lake) by which the Cherokees know it, quite possibly to help the non-Cherokees have some comprehension of the healing power of this unknown water location.[16] Arneach makes it known that only those humans who know the old ways and respect those ancient ways of their Cherokee Ancestors would receive the gift of witnessing this truly remarkable and sacred site, which is still present within the Cherokee homeland. Such a sacred location would not be visible to anyone there in the audience or, indeed, not to all Cherokees. By pointing up the mountain to where the national park begins, Arneach locates and centers the Kituwah people in relation to the colonizer invention known as a national park, which, for many Americans, is a sacred and spiritually powerful piece of land; however, this was Cherokee land long before the park was decreed, and the Cherokees knew and many still remember nearly every hill and vale. Yet the audience feels comfortable with his mention of the park, because they are familiar with it as Americans and believe it belongs to them, so in this way Arneach's story is nonconfrontational and harmonious.

He also invites the listeners to imagine what it must have been like for Native people before the coming of the white man in a riddle story he shares, telling folks, "Go back about four or five hundred years. You're a Native

American. You know the song of every bird in the forest. You know the sound
a fox makes when he hears mice in the tall grass. As you're going through the
forest, you hear a sound you've never heard before" (*Cherokee Bonfire* DVD,
29 June 2013). In this brief description, he points to the immense body of
traditional ecological knowledge that most Natives in that time period would
have possessed. He continues describing how an Indian would see a very tall
animal that separates and makes two different sounds that have never been
heard before on this continent, then comes back together and becomes tall
again. Arneach has not told them that it is a Sogwili (horse) and rider that
he is talking about, describing the first horse that the Spaniards brought
over to this land,[17] and asks the audience to guess what it is. Not only is the
horse's whinny an unknown sound, but so is the clang of metal-on-metal,
as the conquistador climbs down. Most cannot figure it out, and finally one
person guesses, but in the telling of this story, Arneach has defined the
strangeness of things that were brought by the Europeans and how the Native
peoples adopted certain things quickly and made them their own, as if horses
had always been here. He points out that it is the Plains Indians, not the
Cherokees, who became masters at horseback warfare—again busting the
stereotypical idea that *all* Indians rode horses on the plains and shot arrows
while galloping along.

Arneach takes the theme of Native adaptation and adoption of Euro-western culture and inventions further when he shares a personal story of how
he is often asked by some folks what it is like to live in a tipi. He laughs
and relays how he tells the person, "I don't know! I've never lived in one"
(*Cherokee Bonfire* DVD, 29 June 2013). This audience laughs with him, not
realizing the naïveté is symptomatic of the typical American when it comes
to knowledge of Indigenous peoples and groups. (Again, to maintain good
feelings, Arneach cleverly always refers to this "previous" audience and that
"particular" unnamed fellow who asks, so as not to offend the crowd in front
of him.) First, he points out that early Cherokees did not live in tipis but rather
in log homes, which the settlers chose to copy. So Arneach tells the crowd
that he always describes his own life, in a house with electricity and heat, a
television, microwave, two computers, and many modern conveniences. Then
he tells listeners that he also has one hundred horses. Amazed, the naïve
guest of the previous audience asked the storyteller where he keeps his horses.
Pointing over toward the road, Arneach says, "Right there, in the parking lot,

under the hood of my SUV" (*Cherokee Bonfire* DVD, 29 June 2013). This sort of appropriation within Native storytelling and literature is addressed by Craig Womack in his writings on Native-specific and tribal-specific literary theory. Opposed to the idea of giving colonialism so much authority that all Native life is defined in relation to it, Womack chooses to focus on how Native people incorporated new traditions into their culture. He posits the assumption that cultural contact between Natives and the colonizer can mean that "things European are Indianized rather than the anthropological assumption that things Indian are always swallowed up by European culture," rejecting "the Supremacist notion that assimilation can only go in one direction, that white culture always overpowers Indian culture, that white is inherently more powerful than red, that Indian resistance has never occurred in such a fashion that things European have been radically subverted by Indians" (*Red on Red* 12). That sort of Native subversion and appropriation plays out every day on the Qualla Boundary, as the Eastern Cherokees reap the revenue generated by their Indian casino as well as from the cultural offerings there are marketed to the outside public through all forms of mass media.

Daniel Heath Justice echoes Womack's perspective when he discusses the adaptive nature of the Cherokee people, in particular when modern Cherokee writers utilize the English language, rather than the Native tongue, for their fiction and poetry. In his book *Our Fire Survives the Storm,* he asserts: "Cherokee literature [written] in English is deeply rooted in Indigenousness, by the sheer act of Cherokees asserting their nationhood and cultural continuity through whatever means have been available at the time" (13). I suggest that the same holds true for the creative use of English today for Eastern Cherokee oral artists, since it is the main language spoken by the majority of EBCI band members and also must be employed for storytelling to non-Cherokee visitors. Rather than rejecting Euro-western ideas and technology, many Cherokees, Justice notes, have embraced much of white civilization and its ideas and woven those "good things" that settler culture offers into Cherokee culture, adapting and adopting and making it their own. Culture is ever-changing, and it is possible to utilize Western ideas, religion, goods, and technology in a strictly Indigenous fashion. Justice posits that "[c]ultures affect one another, and they intersect in unexpected and often complicated ways—this is a given and natural consequence of being alive in the world, whether the cultures are human, four-legged, winged, plant, stone, or otherwise defined.

Yet while influence is, to varying degrees, a reality of existence, so too is some measure of internal cultural coherence, the ability of cultures to define and recognize themselves in whatever way seems best to them" (213). This is how the Cherokee concept of gambling, such as with the ancient peach pit or the butter bean games or stickball contests, have come to include bingo and casino revenues for the tribe, or the way various dishes cooked with hog meat are incorporated into the contemporary form of traditional Cherokee foods, such as its use in greens, beans, and other vegetable dishes. (Hogs are not native to North America; the Spaniards brought them.) Another example is the way certain churches around the reservation still offer services in the Cherokee language or even how the Fourth of July holiday has been Indigenized with the involvement of the Steve Young Deer Post of the American Legion, which is made up of Cherokee veterans.

Justice's comments on cultural borrowing and exchange parallel the comments made by artist and storyteller Davy Arch, who expresses how the Cherokee clan system is based on the kinship of the various animal families and how they behave and treat each other. He says our Ancestors carefully watched the animals and birds and realized those creatures all worked together to live peacefully and cooperatively in order to have enough food and shelter, as is evidenced in several of the origin stories, such as "How the Animals Brought the Fire" or "How the Hummingbird Brought Back the Tobacco" (Personal interview). In both stories, the nonhumans worked together to help the humans, who seemed helpless, weaker, or incapable of fending for themselves.

Lloyd Arneach makes use of his skills of subverting and manipulating the English language within his oral performance. He gives yet another example of his personal appropriation of a white invention, which Cherokee people decided was a good thing to utilize, when he shares another story that again demonstrates how similar yet very different his upbringing as an Eastern Cherokee has been from that of his listeners.

I grew up on the reservation and / when I was young / most of the people I knew / didn't have electricity in their homes. / They heated with wood; / they cooked with wood. / We had lanterns / that we used for / light at night. / Well, my grandmother / was one of those / who didn't have / electricity. / I went in the service. / I learned about electricity / electronics / became an aircraft electrician. / And while I was in the service / my grandmother finally had / a power line run to her house. / Well, while I was in the service / I found out / we didn't call it an outhouse. / We called it a Latrine or a Head. / Permission to go to the head, sir? / Move, move, move! / So I came home. / When grandma got power to her house / I ran a power line / from the house out to the head. / I put a lightbulb out there / and thus, I became / the first person / to wire a head / for a reservation. (*Cherokee Bonfire* DVD, 30 June 2013)

Such a story always brings chuckles and applause for Arneach's clever play on words, as he transports his audience back to a simpler time and helps them see how Cherokees dealt with life's basic necessities—an experience many younger folks would never have known. Anishinaabe writer Basil Johnston suggests that many oral stories can best be understood if told in a humorous fashion and that laughter is an essential part of "Indian story-telling" (7). He says, "It is through stories that the knowledge and understanding of one generation are passed on to the next. Although the themes are far-ranging and often deep and serious, the story-tellers could always relate the stories with humour" (7). With this clever narrative about wiring his grandmother's outhouse, Arneach also shares the fact that he is a veteran of the American military, an important thing to note, for it means he is respected for that in the southern states—again promoting the feeling of harmony and mutual formative experiences between Cherokees and non-Natives. In each audience he encounters by the bonfire, there are always several veterans in the crowd, as their ball caps attest.

In another historical tale, Arneach explains how Cherokee homes didn't have a door; rather, a large deerskin was hung over the front opening, which was lifted when anyone wanted to go in or out, and there was no need for locks. He says, "You wouldn't steal from one another / you wouldn't / move the hide aside and go in the cabin / and take things when people weren't there. / You didn't steal from your own people. / This was *never* done" (*Cherokee Bonfire* DVD, 30 June 2013). In noting that theft from your own people was taboo, Arneach lays out the strong values and trust that Cherokees held for one another and the communal and familial fashion in which they lived. He then explains that today, his house has security lights, motion detectors, locks on his car and house doors, and then pauses before adding, "Now . . . we are civilized" (*Cherokee Bonfire* DVD, 30 June 2013). The audience laughs with his jibe at modern American society, quite possibly because they, too, live with such physical restraints and insecurities. Arneach's tongue-in-cheek personal narratives are evidence of why he has won so many awards for storytelling, a skill that he says he learned from two of his uncles while growing up.

Another Elder storyteller shows a completely different form and style when sharing the oral tradition—that of factually and firmly educating the non-Natives who come visiting, for he makes it clear to them that they are sitting within the sovereign homeland of the Tsalagi people and that the Cherokee have always been here. Freeman Owle,[18] a lifelong educator who has taught at both the elementary and the high school on the reservation as well as at a nearby Swain County school, takes his role as teacher seriously. Incorporating many Cherokee words within his stories, Owle moves smoothly from Dayunisi and the Creation to the Fire story to how the animals brought disease to the Cherokees for disrespecting them with overhunting.[19] He doesn't skip a beat as he describes the way the little water spider weaves her silk into a basket and pats mud onto it to hold the burning ember and thus teaches Cherokee women how to make their beautiful pottery, blurring time and history to show how vital such animal contributions still are to today's culture on the Qualla Boundary. He encourages the audience to go across the road to the museum and the arts and crafts shop to see the unique handmade pottery for themselves and to remember the water spider. He tells a story of a man who became sick and went looking for help at homes of each of the seven clans, yet all were afraid to let him into their house because they had children and knew nothing of his sickness. Owle describes how the man was finally welcomed by a woman of the Ani-Waya, the Wolf Clan, and the way the man taught her about the various plants and what each would cure. Swinging his arm all around him and pointing at the trees and plants, Owle tells the audience, "This is a pharmacy that never closes" (*Bonfire Storytelling* DVD, 6 June 2012). In so doing, the storyteller informs the guests of the power of the Earth and its bounty that is still vibrant there in the Smoky Mountain home of the Cherokees, and how that knowledge continues to be used and respected today. Owle doesn't suggest that this Indigenous knowledge is restricted to the Cherokees but rather that the original people there have it, use it, and respect the gifts from the Earth and the Creator.

The Elder educator works science into the medicine story, explaining how the bark from the willow is used today to make aspirin, and how the allspice plant can take the gamey taste out of deer meat. Blending his formal educational training in astronomy, geography, and earth science into the ancient stories, Owle asserts the idea that his Ancestors knew about many things long before modern scientists made discoveries. He warns about the modern lifestyle that has people stuck in traffic for hours in their commute home, only to get up the next day to do it all over again. Likening it to a Sogwili wearing blinders to keep from seeing anything else around him, Owle suggests that people—*all* people—look to Cherokee beliefs to make them healthy. He tells the audience:

We have to have balance / duyvkta / the Cherokee call it. / Duyvkta. / If you eat too little / you're gonna be sick. / If you eat too much / you're gonna be sick. / If you get too angry / you're gonna have problems. / If you're unable to get angry / then people are gonna mistreat you. / You have to have a balance / right in the middle. / Think about a seesaw / or a scale. / That's balance. / It's what we have to reach for. / Duyvkta. / We have to seek that. (*Bonfire Storytelling* DVD, 6 June 2012)

Owle encourages the audience to look for Duyvkta or harmony like the Cherokees do—by taking time in their busy lives to listen to nature and hear the symphony of sound, whether it is the song of birds first thing in the morning or the gurgle of a waterfall; he reminds them not to forget how to feel the warmth of the sun or witness the splendor of a colorful sunset. These acts of balance and good living are a part of the spirituality of the Cherokees. Owle notes that "many people thought that Native Americans were savages" (*Bonfire Storytelling* DVD, 6 June 2012) and then explains the ancient daily Tsalagi ceremony known as "going to water" where everyone, regardless of age, would start their days by going en masse down to the river for physical, spiritual, and emotional cleansing (as well as communal laughter, talking, and just socializing).[20] This is a prayer ritual that continues to be conducted by many Cherokees even today, and the People are encouraged to go to water for purification of spirit, mind, and body before taking part in any ceremonies, stomp dancing, stickball, other physical exercise such as competitive sports, and many social gatherings. Owle tells his listeners how the Tsalagi kneel by the river and place their hands in the water, then throw the water over their left shoulder seven times and have a personal talk with the Creator. He explains, "That is a very / spiritual thing to do / when you awaken in the morning" (*Bonfire Storytelling* DVD, 6 June 2012), and he brings it into modern terms when he describes how anyone who does not have access to a river like the one flowing behind him can simply turn on the water tap in their sink and "Touch it to your forehead / and say those prayers / just as the birds do / early in the morning. / They're giving thanks. / Have you ever really listened / to their voices? / They're jubilant / and happy. / Beautiful! / They're singing their best songs / in the morning / and I think we / as human beings / should sing those best songs also" (*Bonfire Storytelling* DVD, 6 June 2012). Many scholars who examine Cherokee history and culture prefer to liken this act to the Christian baptism, which is also connected to prayer and spiritual purification, a suggestion that the harmonious-minded Cherokees have accepted, particularly those who have adopted that religion. In sharing information about this ancient and continuing ritual, Owle is welcoming outsiders to the world of the Cherokees and, like other storytellers, creating friendly, harmonious relations—another example of King's notion of associational literature/orature.

The ancient story known as the "Origin of the Pleiades"—so named by James Mooney in *Myths of the Cherokee*—is another favorite of this orator, though Owle uses his own title.

THE SEVEN LAZY BOYS
Freeman Owle

One of the first games they invented / was named Chunkey / and the chunkey stone was round / and it's a stone that was rolled across these / flat river bottoms / and they would throw spears at it / before it fell over / and the one who got closest to the stone / before it fell over / was the winner of that part of the game. / And there were seven boys / who loved to play chunkey. / They loved to play this game so well / that they were up in the morning before daylight / they were out in these big flat fields / and they were rolling that stone / and throwing their spears / over and over and over again. / Grandmothers would come down and say, / "Hana tsutsa! / Come over here boys." / And they would say, / "Do yusdi tsaduliha? / What do you want?" / They said, "You need to come and help us / in the village. / You need to get some firewood / so we can cook!" / The boys said, "We would rather play chunkey." / Cherokee people were nonconfrontational. / They didn't say / things / that would hurt their children's / feelings / and development / for the rest of their lives. / They told them stories / like I'm telling you today. / Maybe talk about the possum / instead of talking about the child / which made an awful lot of difference / you know. / Those boys said, "No, grandmother / we'd rather play chunkey," / and Grandmother walked away. / The next day Grandmother was back. / Nisi, / Tsanisi, / your grandmother. / Oginisi, / our grandmothers. / They came back / and they said, "Boys. / You need to come and help / carry some water / to the village." / They said, "No! / We're gonna play chunkey!" / So they let them play chunkey. / They never missed breakfast / they never missed lunch / they never missed dinner. / They were always there. / And you think to yourselves, / what did Native Americans eat before / settlers came? / Plenty. / We had things here / that the settlers / never heard of. / They would go out / and they would gather the corn / and then potatoes / and all of these wonderful / wild plants / and the beans / and the squash / and they would put 'em in a bowl / and they would boil 'em / and they would put venison in there / with them. / Sounds pretty good, huh! / And so they boiled this stuff / and it smelled so good / these boys smelled it / and they came rushing in for dinner. / When they sat down at their places / at the floor / they would lift up those soapstone bowls / and the other children / who had been working had that / wonderful soup. / But those boys went over / and picked up their bowl / and as they looked inside / they saw a little chunkey stone / and water. / They were so angry and said, / "Grandmother, / how could you do this to us?" / And so, / Grandmother said, / simply, / "You love chunkey / so now you can eat chunkey soup." / You can find that in grocery stores today, right? / And so, those boys / went outside; / they began to dance. / They were dancing in a counterclockwise way. / And you ask yourself, why / did they dance / counterclockwise? / We have had hurricanes here this season / tornadoes / in the northern hemisphere / normally / usually / most of the time / unless there's another one close by / causing it to turn in the / opposite direction / tornadoes and hurricanes spin / in a counterclock / wise way. / And if you go home tonight / and fill up your sink / and pull the plug on it / that water is gonna spiral / counterclockwise / going out of the sink. / So the Cherokees dance / counterclockwise. / Those boys began to dance, / they began to dance so hard. / They were so hurt, / they were so angry / that they began to raise up / into the air / and go into the heavens. / And Grandmothers came rushing out / knowing that they were going up / into the heavens. / They tried to grab 'em / and bring 'em back down / but they missed. / Those boys continued to go / into the air. / About this time of the evening / and they continued. / The Grandmothers watched, / as it got dark, / they were still going. / After a long, long time / they stopped. / And they made a formation / in the heavens. / And if you look up there tonight / you're gonna see / those seven lazy boys. / Pleiades. / Some people call it / the Seven Sisters. / Cherokees call it / seven lazy boys. / It's in the perspective / that we look at things / as human beings / we look from a perspective / from which we came. / Many times we come / that we look at the moon / we say / "Oh, there's a man in the moon." / Maybe. / And many of the Native American people / see different things in the moon. / Many of them look up / and if you look up tonight— / I want you to look / I don't think the moon will be full / tonight. / But if you look at the moon when it's full / you'll see a bear / sitting there. / Blink your eyes one time / and look again / you'll not see the old man / but you'll see a bear / sitting there / facing the right / sitting on his haunches. / So Cherokee people look at things / from a different angle. / The most important things that / we do in life / are not those things / that are selfish / that we always do for ourselves. / And this is a teaching of this story. / We should not only think about the things / that we want to do / but we should think about the things / that will / best help all the people / gathered around us / beginning with our family / our children / our parents / our grandparents. / Cherokees / look up / to the elders / and it hasn't been long / that I've been called / one of those older ones. / And it's a great honor / to be old. / Because / other people / look to you for advice. / They look to you for the / wisdom that you lived through. / And it's not all on the internet / and it's not all / on the television. / It's not all in your peers. / But it's those many years / that we've gone through. (*Bonfire Storytelling* DVD, 6 June 2012)

Owle sprinkles in words from the Tsalagi language as he speaks so that the audience can understand that the Cherokee Ancestors were not only present when this seven-star constellation was formed but that those Ancestors participated in the actual cosmological event. He tells of the *tsutsa,* the seven "lazy" boys who spent their days playing the ancient game called *gatayusti,* or chunkey, and how their *dunilisi,* or grandmothers, would get annoyed with them for not doing what they were needed to do. But those Cherokee grandmothers wouldn't scold the boys and just let them go do what they wanted, which causes Owle to note, "Cherokee people were nonconfrontational. They didn't say things that would hurt their children's feelings or development for the rest of their lives. They told them stories, like I'm telling you today. . . . Maybe talk about the possum instead of talking about the child" (*Bonfire Storytelling* DVD, 6 June 2012).[21] For the visitors, this concept of a nonviolent teaching method is in direct contrast to the "spare the rod and spoil the child" belief of many southerners who are of the Southern Baptist faith,[22] as so many have grown up with physical discipline being advocated and employed by not only parents but educators and lawmakers as well. In saying this, Owle demonstrates the difference between Native and settlers' practices in this region.

The story progresses to the point where Owle notes that the boys dance counterclockwise, faster and faster. He asks the audience why they would dance counterclockwise, explaining how tornadoes and hurricanes normally spin in that direction, thereby making the connection between the elemental power of wind and water and the external power created by the dancing movements of the People. Owle mentions to the audience about how water swirls down the sink in that same counterclockwise fashion (which they'd be familiar with), probably to help those non-Natives make their own personal connection to the story. There are many ancient Cherokee stories like this one and those presented in my first chapter that explain the formation of the Earth and the Sky World and define the roles the animals and humans have fulfilled and continue to fulfill in a manner of both Gadugi and Duyvkta. By sharing the stories in the fashion that he uses, Owle employs Native science as defined by Cajete in *Native Science: Natural Laws of Interdependence*. In the foreword to the book, Blood/Blackfoot Confederacy scholar Leroy Little Bear explains how, in order to understand Native science, one must understand the cultural worldview or paradigm of Native peoples. That paradigm "is comprised of and includes ideas of constant motion and flux, existence consisting of energy waves, interrelationships, all things being animate, space/place, renewal, and all things being imbued with spirit" (x). That constant flux or movement includes the ongoing transformation, growth, and renewal that is the very essence of life on Earth and in the cosmos and operates in a network of relationships similar to a spiderweb. In the Native worldview, all of Creation and all life are interrelated. Little Bear points out that "[i]f human beings are animate and have spirit, then 'all my relations'[23] must also be animate and must also have spirit. What Native Americans refer to as 'spirit' and energy waves are the same thing. All of creation is a spirit. Everything in creation consists of a unique combination of energy waves" (x). Owle's retelling of the ancient story of the seven *tsutsa* who danced up and became the Pleiades constellation explains how the Tsalagi boys participated in this cosmic formation. These seven young men continue today to live in the sky as a group of star beings who have their own energy and life force; meanwhile, the Tsalagi today, many years after that Creation, recognize the origins and the connection their Ancestors have and that they, too, hold. With each telling and retelling of the story, the Cherokees are reminded that those stars are not distant, disconnected balls of fire that have nothing to do with their world but rather that the seven stars are their relations who used to be Cherokee boys who loved to play *gatayusti*.

Within the oral tradition of any culture, a story can mean something different to each and every listener, depending on their personal background, culture, religion, and life experiences. After telling the Seven Lazy Boys story, Owle notes that "it's in the perspective / that we look at things / we look from a perspective / from which we came" (*Bonfire Storytelling* DVD, 6 June 2012). He points out that many people look at the moon when it's at its fullest and believe they see a "man in the moon." To that, Owle says, "Maybe," adding that when many Cherokees and other Natives look at the full moon, they see a Bear,[24] facing to the right, sitting on its haunches. "So Cherokee people look at things / from a different angle," he tells the crowd, demonstrating the difference between the Euro-western perspective, which holds humans as most important, and a Native viewpoint, which allows for animals or nonhumans to figure prominently. Owle's straightforward method of intertwining scientific knowledge of the mutually dependent relationships between all creatures within the Cherokee environment through his stories demonstrates the complexity of beliefs and ecological knowledge held by his Cherokee Ancestors and passed down to him. This acknowledgment of the power of stories is echoed by Little Bear in speaking of Cajete's theories of Native science. In his foreword to that book, Little Bear addresses the importance and vitality of such Native storytelling, positing, "It is not just the words and the listening but the actual living of the story. The author [Cajete] does a beautiful holistic treatment of Native American science by giving it 'livingness' and spirit. The Native American paradigm comes to life as the author weaves through ecology, relational networks of plants, animals, the land, and the cosmos. It is a renewal ceremony of Native American knowledge, a storytelling of the discoveries of regular patterns manifesting themselves in the flux. In other words, Native American science is a search for reality, and this is 'science'" (xii).

This is not to say that Native science is better or more valid than Western science but rather that each carries a different way of viewing the world, much like what Owle tells his audience. Cajete notes how Indigenous cultures recognize that the Earth is populated with a wide variety of living entities and that humans should and do engage with other creatures through the senses of our bodies, creating holistic relationships and interdependence (27). This is why, according to Cherokee speaker Tom Belt, our language and other Native languages are action- or verb-based, as opposed to the English language, which is object- or noun-based (Lecture). Yet Western science does not generally engage with living creatures in their own environment but rather treats each being as an individual object to be studied in a laboratory through a microscope or by other methods of testing and experimentation—something that Native science would consider unrealistic. Instead of isolating living beings for study and analysis, Native science observes and learns from the connectedness of the surrounding ecology as a whole and the way in which creatures of all species interact with and relate to one another, including the role people hold. This sort of TEK (traditional ecological knowledge) or Native science is a large part of the oral narratives and stories of each and every Indigenous culture on Earth.

Unfortunately, as Cajete points out, Western science defines Indigenous relations to other Earth beings as "animism," a term that has become steeped in cultural bias, as Western thought tends to discredit Native beliefs for recognizing the life and agency of what others consider inanimate objects like mountains or rocks. He notes that "[a]long with words like 'primitive,' 'ancestor worship,' and 'supernatural,' animism continues to perpetuate a modern prejudice, a disdain, and a projection of inferiority toward the world-view of Indigenous peoples" (27). Yet if human perception occurs through participating with our surrounding environment, "then it can be said that 'animism' is a basic human trait common to both Indigenous and modern sensibilities. Indeed, all humans are animists" (27). This understanding is absent from most proponents of Western scientific thought, yet there are some who are more open. Little Bear refers to Jeremy Hayward, a British physicist, who suggests that the modern view of science overall is distorted and "leaves out the sacredness, the livingness, [and] the soul of the world" (ix). Little Bear agrees with that and posits that Native science, which is countless centuries old, can easily and admirably fill those gaps (xii).

Freeman Owle tries to fill in possible gaps in the knowledge of visitors about the natural beauty and abundance of the mountains and forests surrounding them as they sit by the bonfire. He challenges his listeners to take a step back in time, asking,

What were things like / when the settlers first came? / You ever thought about that? / This whole continent was almost / out to the plains / forested. / This was a place where / there were American chestnuts / that grew in the forests / and they were the largest trees / in the forest. / In the fall of the year / my father told me / that the chestnuts were a foot deep / in the forest. / They fed the animals and the people. / And you know he said / almost every step you took / walking through these beautiful mountain forests / you would find wildlife / jumping up and running away. / Wild turkey and deer / and the streams were filled with fish. / He said it was a beautiful time to live / in this part of the world. / People lived in harmony with the animals. / And then we had progress. (*Bonfire Storytelling* DVD, 6 June 2012)

The story from Owle's father is an intergenerational memory that Owle has embodied within his personal memory, and with his retelling, it becomes embodied within the communal collective memory and quite possibly in the psyche of many non-Native listeners.[25] Such stories, much like the ones that Lloyd Arneach learned as a child from his two uncles, "act as the vehicles of cultural transmission by linking one generation to the next" (McLeod 68). McLeod posits that such handed-down stories allow for a form of "coming home" for Native peoples, which functions as "an exercise in physical and spiritual cartography" (70); as such, it "involves the attempt to recover collective narrative memory and to reconnect to the territory of our ancestors" (71). This reconnection is vitally important for diasporic Cherokee people like me and countless others, who have grown up away from the homeland—and even for some home-raised Tsalagi because the Qualla Boundary is only a small portion of the original territory upon which our Ancestors lived. So many more stories are attached to areas now out of the hands of the People and belonging to non-Cherokees or their government. Hundreds of thousands of acres of the homeland were chiseled away by the British in the early days of colonization, through forced treaties, coercion, and lies.[26] Owle touches on this fact in this next narrative, when he notes that ancient agreements made between Cherokees and their tribal neighbors were always concluded by smoking Tsola or tobacco.

All of those treaties / lasted them a lifetime. / But when they started signing with a pen / every time there was a signature / the Cherokee people would lose / thousands of / square miles of territory / until they would find / thirty-three treaties that were signed / and thirty-four that were broken / and the Cherokees ended with zero.[27] / Nothing. / And you wonder / how in the world do you still / have this land / here today? / Well, we bought this land back / by working and putting it into / a fellow's name / by the name of Will Thomas[28] / who was a citizen / and Thomas / was an adopted grandson / of Drowning Bear, / Yonaguska / and that's why this is called / the Qualla Indian Boundary[29] / and not the Cherokee Indian reservation. / It was not reserved for us / by the federal government. / We bought it back. (*Bonfire Storytelling* DVD, 6 June 2012)

With the telling of this historical narrative, Owle dispels the long-held belief in the American South that *all* Indians had been removed from the region in the 1830s, reaffirming to the audience that the Eastern Cherokees have always lived in these mountains and will continue to live there *nigohila*—forever. This story of resistance and adaptation speaks back to the colonizer and quietly but firmly asserts that the Cherokees have not been "given" this land but have bought it legally through the hard work and savings of their diligent Ancestors,[30] who were truly thinking ahead seven generations. This act of calm, organized defiance—finding a way to buy their own land back when Indians were not considered legal beings with the right to own land—was planned and calculated as Wil-Usdi and his adopted people played the unfamiliar white man's game and did whatever they had to do to remain in the homeland. No doubt most Americans, and certainly most white southerners, do not know the true story of how this small band of Eastern Cherokees continue to reside in their ancient homeland, and storytellers like Freeman Owle quietly and firmly inform these settler descendants in a friendly manner, without pointing a finger of guilt in the direction of the audience but rather calmly offering testimony to the power of this culture and the tenacity of these people. His explanation about the treaties also clarifies that it was the Yunega or white man, not the Cherokees, who broke every single agreement and continue to whittle away the land base of this obviously peaceful tribe of Natives. Owle often precedes this narrative with the story of the "Hummingbird and the Tobacco" so that the audience can also understand the sacred and vital importance of Indigenous Cherokee tobacco, for it not only heals the sick but also prevents the person using it from lying and going back on their word—something that the white man's pen and paper tend to consistently do, regardless of the supposed permanency of the written word.

The Elder storyteller closes his performance in the Duyvkta manner by emphasizing balance and harmony to the audience. He tells them, "We know things have happened in the past; those things are not always good things. But we believe in being people of today and maintaining that balance. . . . We are responsible not for those things that happened in the past, but we are responsible for those things that we do for the future. So you are all our brothers and our sisters, and we walk hand in hand into tomorrow. *Sgi! Denadagohvya!*" (*Bonfire Storytelling* DVD, 6 June 2012).[31] These kind words demonstrate how Freeman Owle takes his responsibility as an educator, as an Ani-Yunwiyah, and as an Elder seriously and uses his oratory skills to educate outsiders and assert Cherokee sovereignty and nationhood, while still making those visitors feel welcome.

There is yet one more postsettler story to discuss, one that is often shared by the Eastern Band of Cherokees to educate their non-Native visitors and perhaps pull at their heartstrings, and that is the story of Tsali.[32] The Tsali story has been told during every performance of the *Unto These Hills*[33] drama at the outdoor amphitheater on the Qualla Boundary since the play first began in the summer of 1950.[34] The play "traces the Cherokee people through the ages, from the zenith of their power through the heartbreak of the Trail of Tears. It ends in the present day, where the Cherokee people continue to rewrite their place in the world" ("Unto These Hills"). I remember first hearing this tragic account when I was a preteen, and it is the type of story that can bring a tear to the eye of many a visitor and audience member for the obvious injustices and inhumanities suffered by a peaceful Native group at the hands of the powerful government of the United States and the genocidal policies of Andrew Jackson. The Tsali story is a narrative of an event that occurred just prior to the forced removal, but it is also a controversial story among the Eastern Cherokees as there are many different versions, and documented evidence suggests the way it is most often told is romanticized and far from the truth. This particular story has origins in 1838 and has morphed over the years; Wil Usdi, or Will Thomas, is said to have altered the story in order to gain sympathy for the thousand or so Cherokees who were still hiding out in the mountains from the U.S. military sent in to gather them for removal ("Tsali," DVD, 2005).

Tsali and his family were just one of many forced out of their home by armed soldiers and made to leave nearly everything behind but the clothes on their backs. They lived in the Snowbird community of what is now the Qualla Boundary.[35] This roundup was taking place across Cherokee territory, starting first with the Georgia state militia and spreading throughout the homeland in eastern Tennessee and western North Carolina; the Cherokees were marched on foot across the mountains to a number of stockade holding pens in Tennessee—much like the ones animals were herded into for containment[36]—before the march west to Indian Territory on the other side of the Mississippi River. (We will not deal with all the inhumane treatment of the Ani-Yunwiyah here, since there are many historical accounts of the *Nvno unitsoyilv*.)[37] It is said that the middle-aged Tsali, his wife, brother, sons, and grandchildren were pushed along at bayonet point by several soldiers who were being hostile and abusive toward the Cherokee family. One soldier reportedly prodded Tsali's wife, who had a hard time walking, to rush her along, which caused her to trip and fall down. The men were so upset by the treatment that, speaking in the language, they conversed and decided to fight back. They waited for their opportunity and finally attacked the soldiers. In the process, one of the soldiers was killed and the others ran away. Tsali and his family quickly fled high up into the mountains and found a cave in which to hide. It was not long before the surviving soldiers reported back to their superior officers and an unsuccessful search began.

When General Winfield Scott realized the futility of trying to find a group of Natives in the mountain recesses and peaks that they knew better than anyone, he sent word by one of the Cherokee leaders to find Tsali with a proposition: if Tsali and his sons gave themselves up to face the charge of murder, the army would stop trying to find the last of the Cherokees still hiding out in the mountains to avoid capture and instead would allow them to stay in their homeland. Tsali and his sons supposedly received a visit from Wil Usdi (Will Thomas), who happened to know exactly where they were hiding. They heard the proposition from him, and the men of the Tsali family decided to sacrifice their lives so that the rest of the Cherokees not yet captured could remain. The story says that Tsali and his three sons were taken into custody to be executed by a firing squad made up of all Cherokees; the youngest son's life was spared because of his young age. James Mooney recounts the ending in this way: "On hearing of the proposition, Charley voluntarily came in with his sons, offering himself as a sacrifice for his people. By command of General Scott, Charley, his brother, and the two elder sons were shot near the mouth of Tuckasegee, a detachment of Cherokee prisoners being compelled to do the shooting in order to impress upon the Indians the fact of their utter helplessness. From those fugitives thus permitted to remain originated the present eastern band of Cherokee" (*Myths of the Cherokee* 131).

Ever since the incident, Tsali has been hailed as a hero to his people, the Eastern Cherokee, and this story has been acted out thousands of times in the outdoor drama every year since the 1950s. Hundreds of thousands of non-Cherokee tourists and visitors to the reservation have heard this tragic story of a "common man's hero" who "join[ed] the Cherokee ranks of the 'Old, Beloved Men'" (Bedford x), and the story is retold by numerous tourism websites and in marketing materials. It is a poignant story of desperation that seems effective in bringing out colonizer guilt as well as empathy from the descendants of the settlers who brought about this human tragedy against a group of original Americans who clearly have persevered, endured, and come out stronger. Most people, upon hearing the story of Tsali, are deeply moved and can be described as rooting for the Cherokees while watching the drama, if one judges by the comments and discussion going on in the busy walkways and environment around the outdoor amphitheater on a summer evening, and even by the teary eyes visible among the audience. Denton R. Bedford,[38] who calls Tsali the reluctant hero, posits, "Surely this is a strong story of love for country, and a stirring message of patriotism,[39] one to touch the hearts of all mankind. Surely Tsali can stand shoulders high with any other national hero. To this day, he is not so recognized. He pricks the white man's conscience by reminding him of his perfidy. But that bright day of moral justice may still come. We live in that hope" (xi). Indeed, that moral justice seems to have already come about, as the oral story of Tsali has been relayed innumerable times for the visitors to Eastern Cherokee territory, and so many of them have walked away with a clearer understanding of what happened to the Tsalagi people in the genocidal upheaval of the late 1830s.

There is only one problem, according to EBCI cultural resource officer T. J. Holland, which is that the way the story is told about Tsali is not what actually happened. Holland, as a tribal historian, has relied on written documents and depositions, like that of Tsali's wife, given after she had arrived in Indian Territory (present-day Oklahoma) and army accounts of the event, along with oral stories handed down from some of the Cherokees involved in the actual capture of Tsali, through their descendants who still reside in the Snowbird community. The version that Holland first describes does not mention any harassment of Tsali's ailing wife but rather that a baby died because of the soldiers' physical brutality. Most of the versions told to visitors also do not tell of the fact that it was a family group of sixteen, or that two soldiers actually died from the attack by the Cherokee men. For many years, the stage version I remember seeing as a preteen presented the attack on the soldiers as a retaliatory reaction meant to protect the women. This is something that any man might do, not just Native men, because of the unnecessary bullying from a group of outsiders who clearly had the upper hand since they had the weapons and the Cherokee men were unarmed. As a diasporic Cherokee, not having grown up on the Qualla Boundary, I only knew the standard Tsali story that is publicly presented, and it was not until I began my research that I heard the more factual account.

Even the version told by direct descendants of Tsali is quite different from the public story. His great-great-granddaughter, Emaline Littlejohn Cucumber, grew up hearing the family account, which tells that it was really two young women who took Tsali's tomahawk as he and all the rest of a group of Cherokees slept out in the woods while the white soldiers who captured them were resting nearby; these two women are said to have actually committed the murder of the single soldier, according to the family narrative. Once the pair told Tsali what they had done, he decided to take the blame rather than the young women, knowing it meant death. This family version holds him as a hero to the People because before he agreed to be executed, Tsali asked that the remaining Cherokees hiding out in the mountains be allowed to stay in the homeland, and his request was granted ("Tsali," DVD, 2005). There are other Cherokees who are recorded on this DVD of oral histories of the Eastern Band who accept and recount the hero version of the story, and this may be a matter of the strict adherence to maintaining the friendly and harmonious relationships with all other members of the community and the desire to avoid giving offense to any descendants of Tsali who continue to reside in Snowbird; it may also be a matter of belief in the power and truth of oral stories.

Holland agrees that Wil Usdi did indeed go and talk to Utsala, who was one of the chiefs at the time in the Snowbird area. Yet the idea of gaining an agreement from General Scott, who was in charge of the forces gathering the Cherokees, had not come into play, so Holland says that notion of obtaining a promise of safety for remaining Cherokees did not serve as an incentive for other Cherokee men to go and find Tsali in order to bring him in to be punished for the murder. Those captors went to find Tsali and his relatives on their own accord so that things could be made as right as possible. There was a strong move underway for the Cherokees to take control of their destiny and conduct their own relocation with as little trouble as possible, and certainly with no violence. As Holland notes, this action was the only violence in the removal of sixteen thousand Cherokee people from their ancient home to new lands, albeit an unfamiliar and possibly undesirable home site because of enemy tribes and rough farming. Many Cherokees had voluntarily relocated early on to as far away as Arkansas and into what would become eastern Oklahoma,[40] and so many still in the homeland knew deep in their hearts that it was their destiny and simply a matter of time, particularly after the illegal signing of the Treaty of New Echota. As Holland points out, the act of murder was an affront to the ancient ways of the Principal People and posed a serious threat to the peaceful and organized removal that Principal Chief John Ross worked toward ("Tsali," DVD, 2005).[41] According to the old clan law, when a person murders another, restitution must be made through the killing of a member of the same clan as the offender;[42] although that specific clan rule may not have been utilized in this case, it simply comes down to the murderer(s) giving up their own life/lives.

One would hope that when James Mooney interviewed Wil Usdi in the insane asylum (*Oral Histories* DVD), he would have kept the man's mental health in mind and perhaps heard the adopted Cherokee give his story with a certain healthy amount of skepticism. It is clear that Mooney was not skeptical and, perhaps due to the romantic value of the Tsali legend and the way it could be utilized to garner sympathy for the Cherokee cause of that time—which was the move to establish a legal reservation and thus home in the late 1880s in the inhospitable South—Mooney includes Wil Usdi's exaggerated version of the Tsali story (*Myths of the Cherokee* 131). Many Eastern Cherokees do value the memory of and the contributions made by Little Will Thomas and would prefer not to harm his reputation by noting that he had lost his sanity by this point. Many of the Cherokee men in this North Carolina region fought under Thomas's command during the Civil War,[43] and the fact that he always pushed for the promised American citizenship for his adopted people cannot be contested.[44] As Elder storyteller Freeman Owle has already noted, Will Thomas collected and used the savings of his Cherokee brethren in order to purchase and cobble together enough parcels of land to create what would become the Qualla Boundary; he did this at a time when Indians in the South had no legal status as people and could not own land, so having Thomas invest their hard-earned dollars was the only way to legally reclaim their own home. This most certainly showed the trust and respect the Cherokees had for Yonaguska's adopted white son, and he did not let them down or steal their money, so many Cherokees even today will not utter a bad word about Wil Usdi. We must also keep in mind that James Mooney himself counted several Cherokee families among his friends and was known for bringing his wife and children with him years later for visits, so he most certainly was sympathetic to what Thomas tried to achieve. Yet it is clear that the romanticized version being perpetuated every summer night in the *Unto These Hills* performance does not exactly sit well with many members of the Eastern Cherokee community, so one wonders why they allow it to continue. Is it the fact that even though Cherokees know what that real story is, they allow for the overly romanticized version to continue to be told to outsiders, rather than stop its public telling altogether? It is one of the stories that non-Cherokees truly absorb and take away that leaves them with a deep sense of regret for what their government did in the past. It creates feelings of sympathy for the Cherokees as well as a desire to want to know more. I have heard this from people talking in the crowds in and around the amphitheater during and after the play. The Tsali story may not be entirely factual; no one seems to know for certain, but it is also a way of reclaiming history, which has too often been sugarcoated and told from the colonizers' view.[45] The Cherokee acceptance of allowing the Wil Usdi version to continue being performed/told is indeed an example of the community's constant effort at striving for harmonious and friendly sharing and, at the same time, acknowledging the contribution of the adopted son. No doubt some descendants of Tsali would be deeply hurt if the story as commonly told were to be stopped, and that simply is not the Cherokee way of avoiding harm or offending their own. This may also be why the storytellers do not choose to tell the Tsali story in their public performances.

The story of Tsali is a conflicted part of the modern-day Cherokee oral tradition and is indeed one that had to be included in this discussion as a popular and often-told oral story—one that so many white southerners are now familiar with which inclines them to sympathize with the folks on the Eastern Cherokee reservation. And while there is much of the oral tradition that is willingly shared by the Eastern Cherokees in their Gadugi manner of educating and welcoming people from outside the culture, there is also a great deal of the continuing oral tradition that is carefully held and shared within the seven communities of the Qualla Boundary. Not only storytellers but ordinary, everyday community members make use of their talents in telling oral narratives in order to hand down history and teachings to the upcoming generations so that there will always be a Cherokee presence in the mountains. These moms and dads, grandparents, cousins, older brothers and sisters, and other folks in these Qualla communities gladly do their part to contribute to the ongoing regeneration of their unique Cherokee culture. We will examine these communal oral stories and teachings in my final chapter.

5

Detsadatlanigohisdodidegesdi

◆ Strengthen one another with encouraging words in all that you do ◆

Tsalagi Stories Told for Tsalagi

This final chapter will turn our gaze internally within the small community of Tsalagi residing on the Qualla Boundary to witness and examine specific ways in which the oral tradition functions to promote Cherokee national-ism in the sacred homeland, self-governance among the Eastern Band, and sovereignty in the face of colonizer-imposed laws and regulations in a quiet, harmonious method of resistance and reclaiming of culture and land.[1] This vitally important way of using the oral histories and narratives that have been handed down may be the most powerful form of Gadugi in the way that stories build and support Cherokee culture and thus the community as a whole. Such stories nourish the spirit and the mind and remind everyone of who they are and why they exist. In order to move forward, a people must know where they come from, and "[n]arrative and oral tradition help to build an oral history for accounting for the past of a community" (Fixico 29). When a society is aware of and informed about their past, the people will be stronger together and be able to build a future that is for everyone's betterment living there, thus creating and producing new cultural narratives. The spoken word in the form of stories, songs, prayers, narratives, history lessons, and spiritual and traditional teachings allows for the following:

renewal and strengthening of Cherokee nationhood in an occupied homeland; justification for the reclamation of local mounds and sacred sites; embodying memories of removal and colonial injustices; instilling pride within the new generations and training community leaders by informing them of all things Cherokee; cultural and spiritual reinvigoration throughout each community on the Boundary; promoting the roles of Elders and language speakers; assisting in language education at New Kituwah Academy and in the Cherokee school system; continuance of healthy and harmonious intergenerational relationships; and a resurgence and regeneration of the physical and spiritual things that make Cherokee culture so unique. What I refer to as the internal usage of oral tradition is a way of rekindling that sacred Fire which has always burned for the Real People.

This final chapter examines the ways and forms in which the Eastern Cherokees living on the Qualla Boundary today continue to use the oral tradition in a near-daily fashion. Some of the time it is done within an organized event conducted for the purpose of teaching and learning the culture and history of the People, while at other times the spoken word is so ingrained into daily lives that one hardly recognizes that one is receiving a cultural teaching because the living oral tradition holds an intrinsic and powerful vitality. This may happen during tribal social events, fund-raising dinners and feasts, or when crossing paths with a community Elder who possesses the "gift of gab" and thus offers her or his lifelong knowledge of community memories sprinkled with a quick language lesson, or it may happen in the halls of a tribal office building or school—anywhere that Cherokees gather. There are so many instances when the power of the spoken word plays a key role in accomplishing many large and encompassing objectives of cultural retention and revitalization, but there is only so much room here to discuss this large body of oral usage.

In *Red on Red: Native American Literary Separatism,* Craig Womack offers readers what he calls his Red Path criticism, which calls for Native literatures—including the oral tradition, which he suggests has always been political—to be examined through a tribal lens from the inside out, creating "Native critical centers" (12). Referring to his own Creek people, Womack argues, "The oral tradition is a living literary tradition, the standard by which Creek stories, oral and written, are judged. Like any other literary tradition, it consists of a complex body of genres, characters, settings, plots, images, symbolic systems, structuring devices, as well as a relationship to larger Creek ceremony, society, politics, and government" (66–67). He notes that since literary theory is created relationally to literature, then Native oral tradition is instrumental to the development and defining of Native literary criticism, adding that "[o]ral tradition, then, becomes central to Native political analysis" (66–67). It's within this line of thinking that we'll examine the varied tribal-specific uses of Cherokee oral tradition and how it functions in its many forms to assert sovereignty and nationhood and to inspire nationalistic pride within the people of the Qualla Boundary.

The Eastern Cherokees employ the oral tradition in nearly every facet of community life, such as in the cultural and historical discussions held during the now-annual Kituwah celebration that unites all three bands of Cherokees at the original Mothertown; the sacred teachings that are shared before and during stomp dances;[2] the way particular local church services are conducted in the language; the monthly Cherokee Language Consortium,[3] which gathers language speakers to collectively devise new words (thus growing the Tsalagi language to include names for modern things like aluminum foil, penguins, pizza, overhead projector, and zebra); the Halloween hayrides at the Oconaluftee Village, which are often narrated by Davy Arch, who tells the scarier stories from around the Boundary; and the history and cultural mapping workshops presented by the tribe's cultural resources supervisor, T. J. Holland, to name just a few. In all these contexts, the spoken words of the continuing oral tradition are a vital and powerful expression of Cherokee nationalism, nationhood, sovereignty, resistance to the colonizer, persistence, and endurance. Holland poses his own questions on this, asking, "What makes a tribe or nation sovereign? Is it based on treaties? What caused these treaties to be written in the first place? I submit that the reason for tribal sovereignty is that each respective tribal nation has been viewed throughout history as a distinct social, cultural, and political group. This 'otherness' has led to removal, assimilation, and various other attacks on the culture, beliefs, and legal standing of tribal nations for hundreds of years. But in spite of assimilation efforts, Cherokee people have worked hard to maintain cultural identity, which I believe is the cornerstone of asserting sovereignty" (Holland, "Cultural Researcher"). One effective tool has been the oral tradition, as it is used as a frequent reminder of the foundation of Cherokee culture. Holland posits that the People are regaining control of the culture, knowledge, land,

and language after so many years of "outside influence," and it is helping them to reassert tribal sovereignty in a number of different areas. As he points out, the Eastern Cherokees have always retained their unique cultural identity, and this has helped them maintain their distinct nationhood throughout the years of oppression and genocidal tactics from the colonizer government. With his cultural knowledge, Holland is a storyteller himself.

In another example of how orality is used to define Cherokee nationalism, Eastern Band Beloved Woman Myrtle Driver, herself a fluent speaker, created a national anthem for the People—a powerful act of communitism. It was set to music by songwriter and musician Paula Maney Nelson, and the students at New Kituwah Academy have learned and performed it. Many of us heard it for the first time at the school's annual open house in 2012. The lyrics are as follows:

Na-sgi hi-go-wa-ti-ha-tsu (O say can you see)
Su-na-le ni-ga-li-sdi-sgv (When the morning comes)
No-le hi-tsa-tli-ni-gi-da ge-sv (That you are strong)
E-lo to-hi-ni-tsv-ne-lv (You have made the Earth peaceful)
No-le nv-do di-ka-lv-gv (And where the sun comes up)
To-hi ni-tsv ne-lv (You have made it peaceful)
I-go hi-da hi-tsa-tli-ni-gi-dah (You are always strong)
I-gv-sa Iga-tse-li ga-da-ti (We fly our own flag)
Ga-lv-la-di ga-da-ga-da-ti (Our flag flies high)
Ga-lv-la-di ga-da-ga-da-ti (Our flag flies high)
To-hi ge-se-sdi hi-de-hv (Let there be peace where we live)
U-na-tli-ni-gi-da a-ni-yo-sgi (Our warriors are strong).

The English translation does not do justice to the power and sense of Cherokeeness that is woven into the lyrics. It is a song of pride, independence, sovereignty, resistance, Cherokee nationhood—as is clear in calling it the "Cherokee Nations Anthem"—and a continuing insistence that the People are true warriors for holding fast to everything that makes them Giduwah and makes their mountain homeland sacred. The opening lines seem like an indigenized start to the "Star-Spangled Banner," a song that every schoolchild in America (myself included) learns and sings at appropriate events to promote patriotism and is a wonderful example of Indigenous appropriation of another settler item and an act of resistance as well. I personally view it as a way of saying to the colonizer government that their anthem is inadequate for this original culture and people, so it needs to be improved upon—but then, that is just my interpretation. Yet this anthem promotes Cherokee pride and insists on the validity of the tribal flags (all three bands of Cherokee have created and fly their own), along with asserting nationhood. The key theme and words used most in the refrain are *Tohi,* which means peace, and *U-na-tli-ni-gi-da,* which means strong. The term "warrior," as we have seen from Cherokee history, is not restricted to just men but includes women as well. The warriors of the Cherokee people now use other forms of weapons that are nonviolent but still protect the People and promote the culture. The most important of those tools of battle and resistance are the spoken words. It always comes back to that. Sara Snyder, the director of Cherokee language studies at Western Carolina University, wrote her PhD dissertation on the language, "Poetics, Performance, and Translation in Eastern Cherokee Language Revitalization." As a non-Cherokee, she took the WCU language courses under Tom Belt and became so fluent that she taught for four years at New Kituwah. Snyder posits that the anthem is "a vehicle for enacting and experiencing tribal sovereignty for students at New Kituwah Academy, the Eastern Cherokees' tribally controlled language immersion school," where the anthem is sung every morning. Students go outside and stand facing east (where the sun rises) while they sing a morning song and the Cherokee anthem (67).

It is for the children that Kathi Littlejohn continues to tell her stories. She enjoys seeing their young faces light up when she shares the ancient tales, which have so many lessons for young minds and hearts—no matter how old the listener. Littlejohn grew up away from the Qualla Boundary, living in several different states as both her parents were schoolteachers who taught in a number of districts, before returning to Cherokee when she and her siblings were teenagers. The responsibility of educating children by the old method of storytelling is not an art she was taught but rather one she fell into when taking a university course in education. Littlejohn laughs when she says that the first Native legends she learned were from the Northwest Coast tribes, and that was what she presented as her course project. The feedback was so positive that she decided to learn the old Cherokee stories that had shaped her own family's culture since time began. It all came together when her family returned to the Boundary and she took a job at Cherokee Elementary, where it did not take long for her to put her talent for storytelling to work within the classroom. This Elder from the Ani-Godagewi (Wild Potato Clan/ People) believes the young Cherokee children, indeed, *all* youngsters, are the most receptive, saying, "I just love telling a story and then later . . . I love to see the children pick it up and then tell it. I think that's why I continue to do it—just to pass it on" ("Tsalagi Storytellers Roundtable" CD, 17 October 2013).

Littlejohn and her gift for the spoken word are often called upon by the community, particularly for the many social and cultural events that go on across the reservation, such as the annual Cherokee Fall Fair, held every October.[4] The fact that the 2013 fall fair carried the theme of "Cherokee People: Our Legends, Our Tales" and had six storytellers (including Littlejohn) as the grand marshals of the opening-day parade speaks to the importance of and respect shown for these carriers of Cherokee culture and history. I was able to video-record Littlejohn when she was the first on stage for children's day at the 2013 fair to share the animal stories; the first full day of the fair is a day off from school for all children on the Qualla Boundary, as the community focuses on and celebrates the young generation and all their many accomplishments as well as what it means to be Tsalagi.[5] The grandstand was packed with families as Littlejohn first told about how the Daksi (turtle) broke its shell;[6] she asked everyone to imagine being afraid of the little box turtle, because in the old times he was one of the meanest animals around and very much a bully—one that all the bigger animals were frightened to be near. The story tells how the vicious Daksi makes demands for food from the Wayah (wolves) and then has the nerve to eat his food with a wolf-ear spoon. Littlejohn delights in describing how the nasty terrapene finally gets his comeuppance when a pack of Wayah give chase and Daksi falls a great distance onto large rocks,[7] busting his shell into thirteen pieces (the number corresponds to the thirteen moons that occur during the year). It is only through use of a medicine song that Daksi heals himself and brings all of the shell back together, forever after carrying the scars upon his back to remind him of his narrow escape. This incident changes Daksi and he loses the reputation of being a violent creature, although the turtle continues to possess its gift of medicine powers. The lessons and values to be learned from this story are numerous, and Littlejohn leaves it up to the children and parents in the crowd to decide what it means to them. The Cherokee approach to learning from the old stories contrasts with the way stories are utilized in modern school classrooms, according to Jerry Blanche in his

Native American Reader: Stories, Speeches and Poems—stories, he notes, that too often have happy endings with all problems resolved. He suggests that Native stories do not wrap up the ending and tell the listener what the moral to the story is; rather, the storyteller allows the individual listeners to take from it what they will, for each story can mean something different to everyone hearing it. Noting that stories of brave and kind-thinking people and animals may encourage children—and adults as well—to want to do what is right, Blanche posits that "Indian wisdom stories are not dogmatic, over-simplified, prescriptive teachings. They are highly individualistic learning experiences from which wisdom can be sought and self-discovery can be enhanced" (27).

When Littlejohn turns to the well-known story "How the Opossum Lost His Beautiful Tail," she calls for young participants to come down onto the stage in order to "make them animals."[8] A half-dozen children dash down the stone bleachers, clamoring excitedly to play the silly and vain *Siqua utsetsdi* (possum), the sneaky and vengeful *Tsisdu* (rabbit), or the mischievous *Taladu* (cricket).[9]

HOW THE OPOSSUM LOST HIS BEAUTIFUL TAIL
Kathi Smith Littlejohn

A long time ago / the possum had the most / beautiful tail / of all of the animals / he was very proud of this tail / and he always bragged / about it. / The other animals / especially those that had beautiful tails / got very tired of hearing his bragging / they would walk up to possum / and say / good morning possum / how are you? / and he would turn around / and shake his tail / and say / me and my tail are just fine / and they would say / possum / come and help me today / I could really use your help / and he'd say / Oh no / no / I / I can't help you today / I have to go and wash my tail / they decided that / they would teach the possum a lesson / and they came up with a trick / they knew that possum / had always wanted to be the / lead dancer / but they never asked him to / because they knew / he and his tail / would get in everyone's way / they sent word to him / and invited him / to be the lead dancer / he was so excited! / He ran over to the barber / Mr. Cricket / just like the animals knew that he would / and asked him to stop / doing what he was doing / and just work on his tail / Cricket started singing a / little / song / and / humming / and / combing out / that tail / in the warm sun / and possum fell fast asleep / as soon as he was asleep / Cricket cut off / every hair on that tail

/ and then to hide it / wrapped it up / with a ribbon / when possum woke up / he looked at his tail and said / Cricket / what / what have you done? / What is this? / and Cricket said / Ah / I have made / the most beautiful tail design / don't take the ribbon off / until you actually / step out and start dancing / or you'll mess up the design / Possum was so excited / he didn't even thank the Cricket / he ran off / and got first in line / and began yelling at / all the other animals / look at me! / I'm the lead dancer! / Get behind me / and my tail! / Come on, hurry up! / Get behind my tail! / The drums started and / possum stepped out / he remembered what Cricket said / and he / took off the ribbon / sure enough / everyone shouted / and pointed at his tail / with that he danced / all the harder! / He shook his tail / around and around / then everyone started laughing / and pointing at his tail! / He looked back over his shoulder / to see why they were laughing / and when he saw that naked / bony tail / he was so embarrassed / he rolled over and / played like he was dead / and even today / when you / surprise a possum out in the woods / he'll roll over / and play like he was dead / and that's how / the possum lost / his beautiful tail. (Littlejohn, "How the Opossum")

Littlejohn speaks the story and the Cherokee children act out their particular animal behavior, a transformative series of actions as they slip back and forth between animal and human behavior while allowing ancient times to meld with the present day. What may at first appear to be childs' play and a way to entertain the crowd is a powerful form of cultural expression and continuity, a strong oral thread that has been woven in and out, back and forth, since the Earth and all its inhabitants were created.[10] Much like in times past, allowing the young ones to role-play within the storytelling process helps them witness and participate in the kinship connectedness between the four-footeds and insects, and to recognize the similarities they, as Cherokee children, have with the animals and bugs while demonstrating how every creature's behavior influences and affects others. It is a way of instilling within the younger generation of Cherokees the uniqueness and beauty of the culture and empowers them to claim it as their own; in this way, the children become vessels to carry the ancient culture forward.

This method of animating age-old values and morals through the youngsters is in line with what Virginia Moore Carney suggests when she quotes Okanagan elder John Kruger, who says, "What [a] story does is speak in the present and bring the past forward, so we can have a future" (Carney xi), and the children playing as animals are a bright future indeed for the Eastern Cherokees. Such oral tellings not only teach the young or uninitiated but also reinforce this unique worldview and perspective that many older Cherokees have held for their entire lives; essentially, hearing and participating in the oral tradition teaches one how to be a good Yvwi, and when someone forgets how to live harmoniously, there's often someone else in this community who can use the power of words and stories to help that wayward person back to the proper, respectful, right path of life or Duyvkta. Donald Fixico notes how "Elders shared their knowledge via the oral tradition, passing down historical accounts of the people from one generation to the next. . . . Oral accounts contained parables and lessons, and the young people learned from them; morals of stories told by their elders enlightened them on virtues, values, and the importance of respecting taboos" (36).

There are many Elders and adult Cherokees who practice the oral tradition in an informal fashion—many, many people I met during my research were storytellers in their own right and often didn't recognize or acknowledge their talent, yet just a simple conversation with them brought out many teachings. Such a natural proclivity to share oral narratives and teachings connects with Neil McLeod's discussion of how embedded memories are carried by the Elders among his Cree people and indeed all Indigenous groups, and these are a form of counterpoint to the colonizer's narratives (18). He maintains that his culture's foundation "lies in the memories of" his grandparents and great-grandparents, who have retained and embodied varied narratives from their grandparents, with stories reaching back many generations and carrying the power of history so that today's young can be shaped by "the echo of generational experience" (7, 6). These intergenerational stories for the Cherokees are more than the ancient originary stories or personal narratives of encounters with Yvwi Tsunsdi (Little People), and they include the series of historical events and injustices perpetrated by the colonizer upon this Indigenous nation—stories of the Trail of Tears, for example, have a resounding and rippling effect on not only the families that made it to "Indian Territory" and their descendants in Oklahoma but also on the lives of the Eastern Cherokee families today. When this small band of Tsalagi living in the original homeland hear those family stories, it reminds them of the struggles their Ancestors endured in order to remain in the homeland created for them while the bulk of the nation's citizens were marched to

Oklahoma to build a new life, and that reminder itself encourages many of today's Cherokees to tenaciously hold onto their language, land, spiritual practices, and culture. Stories from the Removal still bring tears to the eyes of modern descendants and indeed to many outsiders who may get to hear those family narratives. Later in this chapter, I will examine the practical and daily uses of the oral tradition that shapes the internal communal sense of Cherokee-ness and national pride.

The New Kituwah Academy is the language-immersion school on the Qualla Boundary. Their curriculum and daily activities are based on the spoken word, as the students and teachers converse in Cherokee only during the school day. The oldest class to graduate is the sixth-graders, and these second-language children speak Tsalagi nearly as well as the Native speakers who work there, teaching them, counseling them, and sharing stories with them. Several Elders are on staff there so that the children have an intergenerational learning experience and, most often, one that is much like their home environment. Several of my friends are on the parent board of New Kituwah and are committed to a Cherokee language–based education for their child(ren). Those parents are also working hard themselves to become more fluent in spoken Cherokee and, in many cases, to learn to write in the Sequoyah syllabary as well. At last count, there are just over three hundred fluent speakers on the Qualla Boundary, and many of them are these children. Along with speaking Cherokee all day, the use of the oral tradition is paramount at New Kituwah Academy. It is here that I attended lunch-hour community language lessons once a week taught by lifelong speaker Gilliam Jackson, and we adult attendees often had the pleasure of seeing the children in the other large activity room there, learning old Cherokee dances with some of the guest Elders and hearing the origin and animal stories from those community members who are storytellers. As I found out firsthand, the older children are very familiar with the Dusgaseti-like Utlvta (Spearfinger), Nunyunuwi (Stonecoat), and Tsutlakalv (Judaculla) and talk about these beings in an accepting manner, much like many adults. One child said she wasn't afraid of Spearfinger, because her grandmother had told her the scary creature didn't live there in Cherokee but rather over in Tennessee. Having these children who speak the language learn those ancient stories as part of their school curriculum ensures the perpetuation of Cherokee culture because the youngsters know and can share the stories in both Cherokee and

English; after all, the stories are more powerful when told in the language because that is how they were originally spoken, and so many Cherokee words and phrases do not easily translate into English. This gives legitimacy to the power of orality and the uniqueness and strength of the old stories that are so deeply connected to place.

In order for a nation to rejuvenate itself and assert its nation status, it must have leaders who are steeped in the history, language, and culture of their people, and the EBCI has instituted an internal community training program that is designed to do just that. The Right Path Du-yu Dv-I Adult Leadership Program has operated since 2010 and utilizes a great deal of the Cherokee oral tradition in the work to "produce generations of selfless Cherokee leaders" and "support lifelong, culture-based leadership learning" ("Right Path Program Summary").[11] There are no books or manuals that can help to teach these young future leaders how to be a good Yvwi,[12] so the program relies on the traditional cultural knowledge and expertise of an array of local band members (and the occasional person from the Cherokee family out west) who come in to share their Indigenous knowledge by talking to the group, thus teaching in the time-honored form of orality. Right Path utilizes the Gadugi concept of community, which, again, is defined as "People coming together as one and helping one another."[13] Program director Juanita Wilson explains that Right Path allows for participants to learn to always consider how any action will affect the entire community; when one practices Gadugi in every aspect of one's life, there is no room for self-centeredness, selfishness, or greed—traits that too often are attached to outside politicians and leaders (Wilson, Phone interview). The practice of thinking first of others and offering kindness and help coincides with the values as laid out by Robert Thomas that encourage each Cherokee to be a good person "by giving of himself to his fellow Cherokee in regard to his time and his material goods" (Thomas 1). First and foremost, the Du-yu Dv-I program is designed to help the specially chosen community members delve deeper into their Cherokee culture and history in order to bring out their personal leadership competencies, which they can take back into their own community and develop projects that will benefit everyone around them, fulfilling the spirit of Gadugi. The group meets for two days every month for an entire year. Each month they learn about a different aspect of the culture, everything from the traditional foods that are gathered, harvested, and then prepared; to how local artists create their baskets, pottery, masks, or woodcarvings from local natural materials; to the history and significance behind many land sites such as the numerous village mounds; to the various ancient dances, songs, and ceremonies that are still in use today. The group of future leaders also learns to speak and write (in the Sequoyah syllabary) the Cherokee language throughout the course of the year with specialized instruction from several of the Native language speakers on the Boundary. The overall focus is on tribal identity, values, and history, yet there is also some training about other American Indian cultures so that participants can recognize the uniqueness of Cherokee culture and also gain a broader knowledge of other Native nations and the similarities ("Right Path Program Summary"). And even though the group meets for just two days each month, the learning within and from the community goes on nearly every day for these future leaders.

There is a strong emphasis on "experiential learning, with mentorship and internship components" ("Right Path Program Summary"), which allows for each member of the group to work closely with an Elder and a speaker while also sharing with the group what they have learned as individuals. Working along with an Elder who not only speaks the Tsalagi language but also knows and practices the teachings and life lessons that come from the oral stories integrates and reinforces the power of the oral tradition into the very being of the young leader—the integration is holistic because the power of the words become embedded into the spiritual, emotional, intellectual, and physical parts of each young Cherokee receiving this training. Other basic concepts include creating group projects that focus on "improving and restoring aspects of Cherokee culture and community," along with promoting "self-determination and assertions of tribal nation sovereignty at all levels of influence" ("Right Path Program Summary"). Du-yu Dv-I is not a college or university course, so participants do not receive a credit; rather, it is based on traditional Cherokee ideas about the lifelong process of learning and growing. The syllabus explains it this way: "Learning, formally and informally, has historically always been held in high regard by the Cherokee people. It is upon this principle of dedication to education by the Cherokee people [that] the Right Path Program is established." In addition to this principle, another important aspect the Cherokee people attach to education is that "One is responsible for their own learning." Put simply, one can only be exposed to learning; what one garners from that exposure is up to the "student."

Repetition is an important instrument used in Cherokee teaching ("Right Path Program Summary").

Placing the onus for learning on the individual allows for each person to work at their own pace, in their own way, in order to bring out their own unique potential. Participants are expected to have a deep interest in doing what they can do for their people, and each respective group over the years has the chance to nominate other band members who, they feel, would be good candidates for the Right Path in the next year. It is an honor to be nominated, and these young Cherokees recognize this honor and put forth their best effort; I say this because I have personally known several people who have gone through the program, and, as Juanita Wilson points out, Right Path has changed their lives, and many have stepped up as community leaders in their own fashion. As director, she has witnessed how learning the Du-yu Dv-I way has brought out the best in each individual and helped build their confidence so they will try things they never would have considered before. For some, it has brought them out of their shells, so to speak, and they have learned that they truly matter within their home communities and can make a difference in others' lives by adopting and using old tried-and-true Cherokee values and perspectives. Then, later, many of these alumni participants come back and speak to the newest group, again employing orality as these alumni share with the new students what they as participants have learned and how they have used that new knowledge in a respectful, selfless way to help the People in their own community or across the Qualla Boundary (Wilson, Phone interview). In this way, the oral tradition continues and the Gadugi concept flourishes.

I was fortunate enough to sit in on one Right Path session that was held at the Kituwah site in June 2013 when a brother Cherokee from Oklahoma came to talk. Ryan Mackey, or Wahde, is one of a group of young Cherokees who has rekindled the Fire at the Squirrel Ridge stomp grounds near Locust Grove, Oklahoma. He speaks the language, is a leader (singer) there, and has a wealth of cultural knowledge; his position with the Cherokee Nation is as their history and cultural specialist, and he helps train tribal employees of the Nation. Wahde shares with the group what the diasporic Tsalagi people out west have done to hold tightly to their heritage and also speaks about some of the sacred sites and stories there in the eastern homeland, reminding everyone what a blessing it is to be at the Mothertown. He mentions how Kituwah is not only the name of the Mothertown but how the word has become attached to what is known as the Kituwah Society. We are told that these are the Cherokees who keep the old ways alive. Wahde describes how that designation came about after the Civil War, which many Cherokees fought in, and how it was a complicated time for the People.[14] Giduwah became a concept and way of life out in the new territory and actually created a national identity for the full-blooded Cherokees, in particular, at that time. He explains the concept: "Leadership and idealism of how we treat one another, role expectations, certain behavioral patterns that were expected in how we treat each other, how we have self-respect. It was a value system that became tied to that word *Giduwah*. . . . If we're treating each other in the right way, at the same time we're helping ourselves . . . that if you're walking the way God wants you to walk, you're walking those footsteps . . . then you're Kituwah. It's almost like you're protected . . . so by living in the way that we're supposed to live and being good people and treating each other right, at the same time it's like asking for God's protection, and you're asking for God's grace and for his blessing" (Mackey).[15]

Wahde tells the Right Path group that in order to be a Real Human Being, you are to follow these Giduwah teachings or goals or laws. This is just one small portion of the oral history and teachings that were shared that day, and a great deal of it was in the language, with Wahde breaking down the Cherokee words into English so that the meanings behind the ancient words would be understandable for all. This young leader from the Cherokee Nation out west spoke for well over an hour and then invited everyone to dance around the firepit there by the Tuckasegee River, a short walk from the Kituwah Mound. Stomp dances are held after dark and are generally spiritual, but since it was daytime and no fire had been struck, this dancing was considered more social. A number of us who attend stomp regularly had been invited out to help Wahde demonstrate the dances to the Du-yu Dv-I folks.[16] By combining the oral transmission of history and teachings with the physical activity of dancing on the same Earth as the Ancestors alongside the ancient Equoni in which they all would have bathed and drunk helped solidify the strong feelings of walking in balance and sharing harmonious times with fellow Giduwah people with the Ancestors watching over that day.[17] It was an instance of embedding these stories and words into the spirit of everyone there—a lesson no written book could have offered to these future Eastern Band of

Cherokee community leaders. Historian William G. McLoughlin defines this Kituwah spirit as "loyalty to each other, concern for the spiritual power in their way of life, and their insistence upon the fundamental importance of tribal unity and harmony." He goes on to say, "No one can study the Cherokees without coming away with deep respect for their dignity, their familial commitment, their intelligence, and their profound generosity of spirit" (xv). It is the Giduwah spirit that defines the Cherokees, bringing them through many hard times and making the People and culture stronger.

The Snowbird community on the far western side of the Eastern Cherokee territory is considered the most traditional of all the communities because of the continued and enduring language usage there as well as the living traditions of orature and craft-making. Snowbird is about fifty miles, or a sixty-minute car drive, from downtown Cherokee through the Nantahala Gorge and is somewhat isolated, even though it sits near the small town of Robbinsville, North Carolina. It is made up of a number of land tracts that are not connected but rather "intermingled with white-owned land" (Neely 14). The community boasts a wealth of artisans who still make the baskets, pottery, blowguns, and wood and stone carvings as well as those who still gather the medicines and wild plants for home use. Oral storytelling here is not done so much on a public basis because this area does not capitalize on the tourist trade the way that the main Qualla Boundary does;[18] still, plenty of stories are shared within the Snowbird community among the Cherokee families. Stories of the Yunwi Tsunsdi abound here, since there are particular areas around the deep valleys and crisp, fast-moving streams in which the Little People are known to live, and some of those areas are best not crossed on foot. After all, not all Yunwi Tsunsdi are friendly, and particular Little People communities may even trick and torment any wayward human who comes along. Some of those stories show up in a collection of interviews conducted with Elders of Snowbird in an Eastern Band oral history project of 1989 known as the "Fading Voices" project. One special issue of the *Journal of Cherokee Studies*[19] was dedicated to publishing many of the interview transcripts (in English) and photos of each particular Elder or couple. This entire collection is part of the archives of the Museum of the Cherokee Indian and is there for public use, particularly to teach the younger generation of Cherokees about what life is like in Snowbird and about many of the crafts, food preparation, singing, and spiritual ways—both Cherokee and Christian. These personal narratives are powerful; readers and listeners can get an idea of the historical struggles and the survivance techniques used by Snowbird families through the Great Depression, boarding school, sicknesses, food shortages, and many of the other hardships endured over the early to mid-1900s. It is hard not to admire the physical and cultural endurance of this tight-knit community, which never for a moment put aside their language or heritage despite the obstacles. Many of these interviews were conducted in the Cherokee language by fieldworkers who speak it,[20] and the "recorded interviews [are] on cassettes with transcriptions in both English and the Cherokee syllabary, memorabilia, slides, videos, and photos of the participants" ("Fading Voices"). The Elders who shared at that time ranged in age from fifty-seven to ninety-four years old, and obviously many of them are gone to the Spirit World now. Some of their particular arts included gathering and using medicine plants, making hominy, churning butter, basket-making, beadwork, blowgun-making and shooting, hand-styled coffin-making, soap-making, quilting, singing gospel songs in Cherokee, and storytelling. Project director Lois Calonehuskie writes that she was honored to have the chance to interview this group of Elders who knew her growing up in Snowbird. "I sat with the elders in the evenings," she says, "listening to their colorful words as I followed them through their early years of tilling the soil, building roads, making baskets, cooking food, going off to school, and telling generation legends. The memories were both happy and sad" ("Fading Voices").

Those memories of Cherokees who had been born in the late 1800s to early 1900s offer a fascinating glimpse into a way of life that is rapidly disappearing, even in this most-traditional Cherokee community. Most grew up knowing and using what is commonly referred to as Indian doctors for when they were sick or injured,[21] and many of these Snowbird Elders know a fair bit about plant medicine themselves; this knowledge comes across clearly in the transcribed interviews. Life was hard and people were poor during these Elders' younger years; several talk about going to work in the fields and helping with planting, harvesting, and hoeing corn as young as ten years old, while others did all sorts of manual labor to earn a wage—sometimes far from home—such as building roads, logging, or cooking for logging camps. It is clear that these Snowbird Cherokees have always been very industrious and accepted the idea of working hard, something that seems to be a strong value among many Cherokee families wherever they come from. Many Elders came from large families and saw not only their fathers go out to work, but their mothers as well often had some sort of job—either at home or elsewhere—where they also made money for the family. Most families relied on their own gardens and picked wild greens. Some had chickens and/or pigs that could be butchered for meat; they also dried a lot of their produce on tin roofs to preserve it for the winter months. Several Elders spoke of helping their mothers gather oak splits and prepare the splits to make baskets, including dying them with natural colors from bloodroot, black walnut, and yellowroot, and later continuing the family craft with their own children. Much of their clothing was hand-made by the women, and the common way to wash clothes was to boil them and scrub them on a large rock with homemade soap, which they also made themselves. The most important crop—Selu—was ground into cornmeal or cooked in lye over large outdoor fires to make hominy for use in many dishes ("Fading Voices"). A great deal of what the Elders speak of includes the unique parts of Cherokee culture that have existed since Creation.

Their stories tell how even though all Cherokee children were expected to go to school, not many went on a regular basis to the school that was in their area of Snowbird, so it eventually had to close for lack of students. For some, it was a long journey on foot over the mountainous terrain, and one woman recounts how they never got new books; instead, year after year the same textbook was used so many simply stopped going because they weren't learning anything new. As an early example of institutionalized racism and segregation, one female interviewee pointed to a nearby building to her home and explained that it was the school for white children from the town, but Cherokee children were not allowed to attend there; it was only for whites, and they got the new textbooks. Eventually, most school-aged Cherokee children were removed from Snowbird and transported to the boarding school on the Qualla Boundary, where they lived for the entire school year. It took a full day of travel by train, bus, and then by pickup truck to go the fifty miles to the main part of the Boundary and the boarding school. Almost all the Elders told of not being allowed to speak the language, being punished for doing so, and so often running away. Some were caught and brought back, while some never did return to the boarding school. One or two of the Elders said they learned a lot while at the school. Half the school day—four hours—was spent in studies, and the other half doing all the manual labor required of them such as fieldwork and tending livestock for the boys and cooking, scrubbing floors, washing dishes, and sewing clothes for the girls—heavy work, and they earned no wages at all ("Fading Voices"). This child labor is essentially what kept the institution functioning on a daily basis—a common story at other Indian boarding schools across the country.

One of the Snowbird men talked about stickball or *anetsodi* (to wrestle) and the medicine ceremonies connected to preparations for playing the ancient game that has long been used for settling disputes; it is known as *danawa usdi* (the little brother to war). So much of the ballplay preparations involved the oral tradition, as a medicine man issued instructions, helped with purification, and prayed and scratched the players' skin in order to put medicine on them to make them strong and fast.[22] One Elder offered information about the Cherokee dances throughout the early 1900s, such as where dances were held and how everyone brought their offering of dirt to build a mound in a certain spot—a ritual practice relevant to the rebuilding of the Kituwah mound to be discussed later in this chapter. It is not surprising that there always were a few carpenters in the community who could make coffins when someone died, and some of the Elders talk about how the deceased's body was washed and cared for, along with ancient Cherokee beliefs about the spirit and afterlife. Some told stories in this collection, mainly animal stories that show what is considered the human behavior of many of the four-leggeds. Going to church was a big part of everyone's life around Snowbird, and many met their life partners at church functions. For the most part, sermons back then were given in the language and the hymns sung in the language; those who could read and write in the syllabary often had hymn books and Bibles written in it ("Fading Voices").[23] The act of translating Christian stories, songs, and sermons and bringing it all into the Cherokee oral tradition is an example of the harmonious adaptation and adoption of the "new" ways and religion brought by the colonizers.

In her anthropological study of the Snowbird community, Sharlotte Neely notes that acceptance of Christianity and subsequent church attendance has allowed the Snowbird Cherokees to have an amiable relationship with the white families in the area (3–5). Neely describes the "Trail of Tears Singings," one more form of the oral tradition for which this community is known (113–33). These three-day events (Friday, Saturday, and Sunday) take place in the coolness of June near the flowing mountain waters of Snowbird Creek and Cornsilk Branch in Graham County. As Neely points out, it's like a reunion of Eastern and Western Cherokees, and for a few days each year, the Nation seems as one in this highly significant and spiritual event, which began in Oklahoma in the 1950s and was brought to this traditional Eastern community in the late 1960s. The singing is of gospel hymns generally in the Cherokee language, but many non-Cherokees from the area also attend and the songs are then sung in English. The songs are the same ones the People who walked the Trail of Tears sang at that time (1838–39), and they represent a Cherokee adoption of settler religious customs that have been made uniquely Cherokee through the living language. Traditional foods are served, and those attending and participating sit in lawn chairs, wooden pews brought out of a church, or upon quilts thrown on the ground; it is reminiscent of the outdoor preaching and revivals for which many Southern Baptist congregations are known. Neely notes that this event is joyous and even thrilling for those taking part (113), and busloads of Oklahoma Cherokees often arrive on Saturday, along with white singing groups from nearby states, filling the grounds to capacity (117). It is empowering for these Cherokees to reclaim this horrific, genocidal trauma that decimated a quarter of the Nation and turn it into a positive and healing event that utilizes the language and the oral tradition while bringing together members of the diasporic bands, along with welcoming and incorporating non-Cherokees from the area.

The *Nvno unitsoyilv* or "path/trail where they cried" has its own set of stories, most of which are historical family/community narratives that are highly political and nationalistic, to say the least. They tend to be deeply heart-wrenching, since this is about the trauma and upheaval that physically and spiritually tore Cherokee society apart, leaving a small handful behind, quietly hiding in the southern mountains, while a larger group walked on foot to the new "Indian Territory" in the *wudaligv* (west). You may recall that the Darkening Land or the Spirit World is to the west, and no doubt many of the People thought they were walking westward to a certain death, ripped from their homes and the land that held the bones of the Ancestors. Clearly, knowledge of this genocidal forced trek of misery, starvation, and deprivation with death for a full one-quarter of the Cherokee nation is deeply embedded in the bodies and memories of most every Cherokee on the Boundary. In talking about racialized memory, Jace Weaver quotes Laguna Pueblo poet Paula Gunn Allen, who noted that "[t]he workings of racial memory are truly mysterious. No Cherokee can forget the Trail of Tears," while Weaver, who is of

Cherokee descent himself, reflects that "[t]he Cherokee *can* never forget . . . not because of some genetic determinism but because its importance to heritage and identity are passed down through story from generation to generation" (7). Those stories of an "incident [that] is germane to our history" (Strickland 8), whether shared among the Cherokee people in Oklahoma or told within the Qualla community, help strengthen the Cherokee identity and reinforce shared cultural identifiers, for no matter where Cherokee people live, such narratives remind them of their origins and their Ancestors' fight to stay in that homeland. Their nation's battle to survive was waged in the U.S. court system by the tribe's educated leaders of the time, and it was an honorable battle by an Indigenous nation who had always tried to maintain peace and harmony against the overwhelming encroachment, intimidation, lies, and treaty violations by the much larger and more vengeful invader government. That well-documented part of history can be found in many books and is considered a dark chapter in American history,[24] but the handed-down stories told by descendants of those Cherokee families directly involved are emotional, matter-of-fact, and, quite rightly, difficult to listen to. Yet these narratives are a bloody thread woven within the Cherokee life tapestry—much like the colored yarns that are used for the finger-woven sashes many Tsalagi still create today—and must be told time and time again.[25] The stories speak of the hardships the Ancestors had to endure and the ways many found to resist the injustices. Craig Womack notes that such generational narrative "shapes communal consciousness: through imagination and storytelling, people in oral cultures re-experience history. This concept of ancestral memory relates to nationalism in that sovereignty is an intersection of the political, imaginary, and literary. To exist as a nation, the community needs a perception of nationhood, that is, stories that help them imagine who they are as a people, how they came to be, and what cultural values they wish to preserve" (*Red on Red* 26).

The Tsalagi have found ways to take those narratives and personal stories of a time and event that could have destroyed their society entirely and to utilize this oral tradition in a manner that helps today's Cherokee reexperience their Ancestors' upheaval and trauma and thus strengthen the connection between the generations. In listening to these stories of suffering and defiance, it is hard not to shed tears and feel deep, biting anger for what the People endured. The oral tales of the Removal describe how those Ancestors defied all odds and made conscious choices that would ensure the continuation of the lifeways and cultural knowledge, along with the People themselves. Simon Ortiz notes that the incorporation of traumatic events within a people's oral tradition instills the stories in the minds of the community, and there will be no forgetting. He believes such stories tell the Native view of the colonizer, which contrasts sharply with history books and accounts written by the Euro-Americans ("Towards a National Indian Literature" 9).

The story that Freeman Owle tells of his great-grandparents' escape from the forced march is one of defiance and determination. His family story is deeply personal and, through his telling, connects this past trauma directly to the present-day community and brings it to life for anyone who hears Owle's intergenerational recounting.

THE TRAIL OF TEARS
Freeman Owle

I found that out as I was growing up,
and my parents began to tell me this story of the Trail of Tears.
And you look at me and you say,
    "Well, he's probably as much Scots-Irish as I am."
Yes, I am.
But I am Uguku tsikayi Tsalagi ashkaya.
My name is Owle, I live in Birdtown,
    and I happened to grow up on the reservation.
Sort of like a little story that Marsha was reading to our daughter
        last night
about the zebra.
Says, "Are you white with black stripes or black with white
    stripes?"
Are you Scots-Irish with Indian, or Indian with Scots-Irish?
I don't know, I really don't.
All I know is I'm different from anyone who's ever lived,
    And different than anyone who ever will.
And my fingerprints are different, so I must be special.
They told me that
    my family was, in 1838, in a log cabin near Murphy, North
        Carolina.

And all of a sudden,
    Someone was banging on the door
    early that morning.
And they opened up the door and they looked out,
    and fifty Georgia soldiers were standing in the yard.
They said,
    Come out of the cabin."
And when my great-grandfather—
    I'll just call him grandfather—
    did,
    they burned the cabin to the ground.
He and his wife and small baby were taken to Murphy, North
      Carolina,
    put into a stockade,
    stayed there for six weeks.
There was no roof, only a line of poles
    encircling the stockade.
They say that
    the mud was deep,
    there wasn't much food,
    no one had anything to cover themselves with,
    but the baby survived because the mother was feeding it.
Early one morning,
    on that October morning
    when the frost was heavy
    and the ground was frozen hard enough for wagons to travel,
    General Winfield Scott began to march the people out of this fort.
So he marched them across the frozen ground
    and across the Santeetlah Mountains
    into Tennessee.
There was a woman by the name of Martha Ross,
    Scots-Irish and Cherokee.
She had a beautiful coat,
    and she began to look, late that night,
    and the rain was coming down, and it was cold,
    and she heard a baby crying.

She went to the sound of the baby and found the child
    very cold
    and wet—
    it had pneumonia.
She covered the child with her coat,
    and two days later she died of pneumonia herself.
It is people like this
    who have made contributions to the Cherokee society.
It is people like the people of North Carolina
    who allowed those people living in North Carolina to remain
        there.
The history is written,
    the history says
    that North Carolina did not remove its Cherokees.
They were called the Oconaluftee Cherokee.
And you go see *Unto These Hills*, it doesn't mention this.
But they didn't make them leave.
The other fifteen thousand began to march on toward Oklahoma.
When they got to the Mississippi, they asked my grandfather
    if he would count the Cherokees who crossed the river.
And he said,
    "Yes, I will."
But he told his wife in Cherokee,
    "Go hide in the cane brake and take the baby with you.
    And I will tell them you're here.
    And we'll go back home."
So he counted the Cherokees as they crossed the flatboat across the
        Mississippi,
    and he told the soldiers,
    "All the Cherokees are accounted for."
And they said,
    "Are you sure?
    Go back to the river and check again."
And this was what he wanted,
    and he goes back to the river,
    and he look into the bushes and the brush,

and all of a sudden he leaps into the water.
They come running behind, and they shoot many times into the
    water.
They look into the black swirling waters of the Mississippi,
    and this Cherokee does not surface.
So—for a long time.
And they give him up as being dead.
He's breathing through a reed all this time.
And after he gives the soldiers time enough to go away,
    he comes up and he swims back
    across the Mississippi.
He looks for his wife on the other side,
    and—she heard the gunshots.
She ran
    with the baby in her arms,
    she would run all night long,
    and then find a briar patch to sleep in the daytime,
    or a farmer's haystack.
Took her several weeks to get back home,
    but she came on back to the old burned-out cabin site
    because that's all she knew as home.
She waited there week after week,
    and her husband didn't return.
She went down to the village,
    to the Scots-Irish settlers,
    and they gladly gave her food.
And they were feeding those Cherokees
    that were hiding in the mountains.
If the North Carolina people had been caught by the Georgia guard
    handing out food to the Cherokees,
    they too would have lost their land and been put in prison
    as Cherokee sympathizers.
But the Scots-Irish people were feeding her
    one morning, a year later,
    when she heard a noise up on the hill,
    and she looked and there was someone coming.

And so she ran and hid with the baby.
And after a while it was her husband
   coming out of the woods.
They were reunited,
   and we still live
   in a little place where they came and rebought with their own
   money
   called Birdtown.
And the reason they were able to rebuy it was:
   there was a wagon train coming through here,
   and it had a little baby on it—
   a little white child
   who was very sick.
And the parents were smart enough to say,
   "If we go on with this child, it's going to die."
And they said—
   have you ever heard the term, "Give it to the Indians"?
   They gave the child to the Indians.
Chief Yonaguska made the child better.
His name was William Holland Thomas.
Will Thomas was already a citizen of the United States,
   and the Cherokees could go and buy up land
   and put it in this child's name
   by the thousands of acres,
   and we are still here.
But in the early 1920s
   my grandfather, Solomon Owle,
   was living in this little place called Birdtown
   and paying his taxes to Swain County,
   and I think he was a good citizen.
The federal government looked down and said,
   "This can't be.
   This bunch of savages are not supposed to be able to take care of
     themselves."
And they came down and took the deeds away from these people
   and set up what they called the Qualla Indian Boundary.

They couldn't call it a reservation
    because a reservation is land that is given to the Indians,
    and the Indians are forced upon it.
This land was bought back
    under Will Thomas's name—
    see, it's not a reservation
    it's a little different.
You know, I came here tonight to tell you
    that the Cherokee people don't really hold any hatred
    or animosity in their heart
    for those things that happened in the past.
We can take our hats off to the past,
    but as one great gentleman said,
    "We should take our shirts off to the future."
The reason the Cherokee people survived
    is because they loved their neighbors
    and were good neighbors.
The Cherokees of today
    still welcome even all the visitors in the '41 Chevys
    and the '40 Ford coupes
    and the bears and everything—
    they were glad to see the tourists come.
And we're glad to see the tourists come, even today. (Duncan, *Living Stories*
    221–26)

What a remarkable story from his great-grandparents! We, today, can't begin to imagine the physical dangers that couple put themselves through. Owle's story speaks to the tenacity of the Cherokee people of the past and their will to remain in the homeland that the Creator made especially for them. It starts in much the same way that other stories of the Removal begin—with the sudden appearance of dozens, perhaps hundreds of Georgia militia (even in nearby western North Carolina) who showed up with guns and bayonets at the log cabin homes of the Cherokees scattered throughout the mountains. Some folks were sitting down to eat, others were out in their gardens working, but they all were just going about the business of living in the way they always had. The talk of being forced to leave had persisted for several years, but the physical attack upon the People still came as a surprise. Defying the U.S. Supreme Court ruling in favor of the Cherokees, the Georgia government moved ahead with its plan to round up the Cherokees for removal.[26] In some cases, once the soldiers had ordered the Cherokees to grab what they could or to leave it all behind, a family of settlers was waiting nearby to move right into the home. In other cases, the Cherokee families watched as the soldiers put a torch to their home and burned it down before ordering the captives to begin their long, arduous walk to the forts that had been set up to house them.[27] Owle speaks of his great-grandparents' return journey home in a matter-of-fact tone that demonstrates his knowledge of history and the veracity of the handed-down family story, which most every Cherokee adult and many of the children on the Qualla Boundary have heard, and there are other such family stories about relatives who escaped and returned home, such as with the Wachacha family in Snowbird ("Tsali," DVD, 2005).[28] It is quite easy for people listening to Owle's story—Cherokee or not—to look about them in this lush, mountainous land and imagine the fear of those Ancestors being forced at bayonet point to simply walk away from their homes and the only life they ever knew to face the unknown in the West and possible death. Such retelling of Cherokee history establishes the Indigenous truth of the worst results of British and American colonization and, in essence, allows for the slow and vitally necessary process of decolonization to continue for this group. It also reinforces Cherokee nationalism. There is tremendous pride in knowing your Ancestors were defiant and fought back, in court and in other ways, to stay in the home territory. When they were made to leave it only by force from a stronger enemy, somehow they endured the long miserable walk, buried their dead babies and elders, and worked hard to build a new life or managed to elude their captors and find their way home to the southern mountains as Owle's ancestors and the Wachacha family did.

Many Eastern Cherokees and their siblings from Oklahoma are now retracing the routes taken by the Ancestors on the *Nvno unitsoyilv* in a number of ways, in order to experience the strenuous trek mile by mile and hear the historical narratives about each of the memorial sites along the way. This sensory experience is something that reading an engraved government-provided plaque or marker cannot equal.[29] The Remember the Removal bicycle ride takes three weeks and runs the 950-mile northern route of the Trail of Tears[30]—a route that took the Ancestors weeks and weeks to make.[31] The

Cherokee Nation of Oklahoma initiated this project and in 2011 invited their Eastern Band family to pick five enrolled members to join the western riders in this grueling bicycle ride; each year since then a group of mostly young Cherokees (though there have been a few in their fifties and sixties who also did it) has taken up the honor and trained for the long journey in June. EBCI participants receive history and cultural lessons from experts at the Museum of the Cherokee Indian as part of their training and hear of the many campaigns conducted prior to Removal by tribal leadership to sway the American public, such as "speaking tours by young educated Cherokee men throughout the northeast" and editorials at that time in the nation's bilingual newspaper, the *Cherokee Phoenix*, which, ironically, was published in Georgia (McKie, "Remember the Removal"). These oral history lessons prepare the minds and spirits of these bike riders so that when their group stops at each important site along the way, they will understand how hard the Ancestors fought to remain and how devastating this forced march was for them. The modern Cherokees may be using bicycles for their nearly thousand-mile trip, though such a ride is difficult in itself, but they can get a taste of what the People endured along the way and the tremendous hardships and danger because of the winter weather, ice on the rivers and creeks, lack of adequate warm clothing and footwear, and the near-constant hunger and thirst. After all, the bulk of the Cherokee people made the trip in the winter of 1838–39, and most were on foot.[32]

The removal riders gather at the Mothertown in early June for prayers and speeches; it is a chance for the community to gather and express their support for and pride in these citizens of their nation for re-creating the journey of sadness and tears. The removal ride actually begins at New Echota, Georgia, which was the capital of the Cherokee Nation up until the time of the trail and, as described in my introduction, is now a state historical site;[33] the riders then travel up to Red Clay, Tennessee, formerly Red Clay Council Grounds and the site of the last full council of the tribe that was held prior to Removal.[34] Tribal historians, cultural experts, and language speakers from both the Eastern Band and the Cherokee Nation of Oklahoma talk and share their knowledge with the group at these sites. There is tremendous irony in the fact that these two states, Georgia and Tennessee—which were involved in the forced removal—have appropriated these two historically significant sites for the Cherokee people and turned them into state-owned historical sites, capitalizing even today on the injustices and land theft that took place. That being said, the Tsalagi people have, in typical Cherokee fashion, accepted the situation and been actively involved in re-indigenizing these sites by holding tribally sponsored events that have reunited the Eastern Band with their Western family members. In fact, the first-ever reunion of the Eastern and Western bands took place at Red Clay Council Grounds in 1984;[35] my parents drove down from Detroit to be a part of this exciting and emotional reunion, which had the chiefs and full councils in attendance along with many Elders and language speakers. In May 2013 New Echota was the site for the 175th commemoration of the 1838 Trail of Tears, which featured speakers and storytellers from both groups of Cherokees; many non-Natives from the area also took part in the remembrance event. I was fortunate to attend with my husband and share with him the things I know about life at New Echota in those old days, because I had visited there so many times as a child and teenager, as my father had been born and raised a few miles up the highway from the site, in a place called Sugar Hollow.[36] It is an empowering experience to be able to use the printing press at the *Cherokee Phoenix* building and print off the first page of that first edition, which came off the presses in 1828 and was typeset in both Cherokee and English.

Other re-creation journeys have been made of the Trail of Tears, such as in 2012 when the Cherokee Healing and Wellness Coalition on the Qualla Boundary offered a bus trip that traced one of the routes in reverse from Oklahoma for the participants to use the knowledge gained from oral storytellers and historians along the way for their own personal healing. This "Journey to Forgiveness and Healing" took Eastern Band members out to Tahlequah to meet up with members from the two bands there who also wished to travel to the various sites along the route, hear the stories, shed tears, hug one another, conduct ceremonies—and then work toward understanding what had happened to their Ancestors so that they can forgive, heal their hearts and spirits, and become better Giduwah people ("Journey to Forgiveness"). When the group returned to the Boundary, an event was held at the Mothertown so that they could share the stories of the trials and tribulations they had learned about with community members who came out to listen. A mother and daughter whom I know offered some of what they had learned on the journey, and the tears were flowing from us all.[37] After learning from storytellers along the way, these two women became storytellers themselves as they told us of heartbreaking accounts of women whose babies were frozen to death when the mothers woke in the morning, and stories of how many of the People perished in trying to cross the ice-filled waterways. This Deer clan Elder and her daughter also heard oral narratives of how so many of the older Cherokees knew they could not walk the great distance in the cold and, growing fatigued, simply laid down and died on the spot, knowing that their slow, plodding footsteps were slowing down the rest of their family. In other situations, adults gave up their blankets and warm clothing for the young children and babies; this is the true account of what happened with the wife of Chief John Ross, who died of pneumonia after giving up her blanket—which was part of Freeman Owle's story just recounted. There's something extremely powerful and haunting when one listens to such oral narratives and then witnesses how the trip affected those individuals who made the journey. It is hard to forgive those who caused such suffering and to let that deep-running anger go, but the stories are meant to help. This large part of the modern oral tradition keeps the Trail of Tears alive in the minds of the descendants, because we must always remember those who fell on the way and are buried throughout the miles of foreign territory—their bones and even unmarked graves have left a memory and an imprint on the land of that trail of destruction. These stories belong only to the Cherokee people, and that shared trauma and memory helps unite the three bands and strengthens feelings of nationhood. Events like the 175th commemoration and retracing the routes of the *Nvno unitsoyilv* are indeed empowering and healing for the People and heightens their feelings of Cherokee nationalism and pride. The reliving and reimagining through spoken stories of a physical and spiritual trauma perpetrated upon a racialized group by an invader government and citizenry help create and define Cherokee nationhood and cultural uniqueness.

As Cherokees, we are told that our Ancestors, the original Real Human Beings, all came from the Mothertown known as Kituwah and the village surrounding this sacred site. We are all descended from the first Ani-Yunwiyah who lived there. Language instructor Tom Belt speaks of Kituwah Mound in his classes at Western Carolina University,[38] and he directs students—both Native and non-Native—in the Cherokee Studies program to visit the site. He says, "This is the place where the people we call Cherokee began. . . . They were directed by God to come here, and the very first fire was given to the people here. . . . This place wasn't just a town—this was like the Vatican. This was the holiest of holies" ("Kituwah Mound"). Archaeologists estimate the site had been inhabited for close to ten thousand years, and as many as two hundred Cherokee lived there at any given time ("Kituwah Mound"). Oral history tells how the sacred Fire held within the townhouse atop the mound was used to rekindle the community fires in many of the other villages,[39] as Cherokees came from miles around the mountain territory and brought back the Kituwah Fire to their own village. Most often, those people would bring a scoop of dirt and/or ashes from their homes and add it to the Kituwah mound, making that physical, spiritual, and personal connection to the Mothertown. That most sacred piece of the Cherokee homeland was lost in 1823 when they were evicted, and this crucial 309-acre field on the banks of the Tuckasegee River near the small towns of Ela and Whittier was auctioned off and turned into farmland. In a distressingly disrespectful and destructive action, the high mound built over the centuries by the Cherokee was plowed and mown down as corn crops were planted and harvested, and at other times cattle grazed on the field. What started as a twelve-foot-high earthen mound thousands of years ago that housed a large village council house on top now only stands about five feet tall and 170 feet in diameter today;[40] in fact, the rise in the earth is barely noticeable to motorists traveling by on U.S. Highway 19. Yet this unremarkable-looking piece of pristine farmland that sits just nine miles from the Qualla Boundary is quite remarkable and quite inspirational for not only the Eastern Cherokees but also for members of both the United Keetoowah Band and the Cherokee Nation of Oklahoma.[41] For well over 170 years, the Cherokee could only watch as this sacred site was farmed and mown down and, even more recently, desecrated as an airstrip for remote-controlled model planes. Although the Cherokees will not fault the family that did this, it is common knowledge around the non-Native communities near Cherokee that this was the site of a sacred mound and village, because so much of the oral tradition concerning the Mothertown has been shared throughout western North Carolina with the settler descendants.

Then in 1996 an old prophecy was fulfilled, and the Kituwah Mound came back to the People. This prophecy, like several others, is only contained within the oral tradition and cannot be found written down anywhere. The first female chief of the Eastern Band, Principal Chief Joyce Dugan, struck a deal with the matriarch of the Ferguson family who had farmed that land for all those years to buy back the Mothertown. Some say that this was part of the ancient prophecy as well—that the land would be returned to a woman from a woman—significant in that it is the women in Cherokee culture who control or own the land and family homes (Perdue 24). The Eastern Cherokee purchase of what was essentially their own land cost the small band $3.2 million—a political and cultural decision that nearly broke the tribal coffers and was controversial at the time for the huge price tag—has since become a source of pride and a symbol of Cherokee nationalism and spiritual revitalization, a true rekindling of the sacred Fire.[42] It is clear that Chief Dugan and her council performed an act of Gadugi by buying back Kituwah, whether it was a popular decision at the time or not. Someone was certainly thinking ahead seven generations.

Chief Joyce Dugan is a storyteller in her own right; many of the eloquent speeches she gave while chief have been recorded and later transcribed for historic purposes.[43] She says that most everyone from the Qualla Boundary had heard the stories and knew that Ferguson Field was actually Cherokee land, even though they didn't fully know the meaning of it at that time. She exhibits the calm Cherokee acceptance of how things were when she says, "We'd always just known that was the Mound, and it never seemed to bother us that it wasn't ours, or that we couldn't see it, or visit it, or get on it or get around it. It was just there, and it belonged to someone else, and it was inaccessible. And we were never taught the significance. There were people that knew, but never really taught it." The chief was surprised by a phone call one day from a woman named Dottie Ferguson Parton, who asked Dugan to come and visit because she wanted to discuss selling the land back to the tribe. At the time, Mrs. Parton was living in a brick house across the road (Highway 19) from the Kituwah field, and Dugan says that it wasn't until she sat on that porch and looked across the road to the ancient lands and mound that she realized how beautiful and expansive it was.[44] Mrs. Parton explained that the family had received a purchase offer of $5 million for the land, which her brothers were prepared to take, but she felt strongly that the tribe needed it back because it belongs to them. Dugan says that as she sat there, looking across the road at the beautiful, lushly green, riverbank land, it dawned on her that, indeed, the tribe did need it back, "because it was so peaceful, and there was a sense that something came over me and I thought, You know what? We need this back." But the chief knew that there was no way the Eastern Band could match the offer that the Fergusons had received—the tribe had only just recently begun making money from the new casino, and there were so many needs within the community, such as housing, roads, and infrastructure. She had no idea just how her council would receive such an idea of buying back their own land (Dugan, Personal interview).

Dugan first went to a couple of tribal councillors who, she knew, were culturally knowledgeable and might support the move to buy the Kituwah lands. Then a lawyer was brought in who managed to get the Ferguson family to drop the price to $3.2 million. The chief drafted a resolution for tribal council, even though she was anxious about how the group would feel, yet she says she felt so strongly about getting Kituwah back by then that she had to proceed. Reflecting back more than twenty years, she says,

> I remember the day I took it in my legs were shaking because . . . I just wanted it so bad but was afraid they weren't gonna pass it, and then what? We're gonna just lose it. Well, there was very little discussion; there was a move to buy it. Actually, one council member said, "Why are we buying a graveyard?" And, if I remember right, I said that's all the more reason we should have it because that's our people. Anyway, I don't recall the vote, but it passed, and that was the beginning. And all of a sudden, all the history started coming forward about that place that had just been kept underground by most, and people started recognizing the importance of it all of a sudden. And I say to this day that I think that brought on a cultural revolution, in a sense, because it was the first time that tribal government said "our culture is important." We didn't have the money before that to do anything; it was just hand-to-mouth then, before the casino . . . depending on government funds, which were hit-and-miss, plus what few funds we got from tourism, taxes and so forth. (Dugan, Personal interview)

Dugan admits there was resistance from some in the community who felt the money should have been spent on other more pressing matters. But eventually, she says, things settled down and people began going down to Kituwah and hearing the history of the Mound, especially when teachers brought the children from Cherokee Elementary and New Kituwah Academy there. People seemed to develop an appreciation for the cultural and historical significance of this most ancient center of Cherokeeness. She credits UKB elder Tom Belt for sharing his knowledge of the Mothertown with everybody when they visited, pointing out that Belt had learned all about Kituwah while growing up in Oklahoma. Meanwhile, Dugan believes that the story of the Mothertown had been "hidden" within her own community simply because nobody thought for a minute that the land would ever come back to them and had accepted the loss from so many years ago.

Cultural preservation was something that Dugan had emphasized in her election campaign platform,[45] noting that "in order to preserve our culture and to teach our culture, the government had to take a primary stand, because the school was having to do it, but it was meaningless unless the head of the government didn't say, 'This is important'" (Dugan, Personal interview). This slowly moved front and center for the Eastern Cherokee community, and many other projects were created and flourished after the Kituwah acquisition, such as the Cherokee Preservation Foundation, which awards grants to tribal members and businesses who develop projects of cultural preservation and reinvigoration. This new cultural renaissance clearly has its roots in the reclamation of the Mothertown.

The decision had been made not to excavate at Kituwah because there were most certainly Ancestors buried on the grounds, and the People did not want them disturbed. Dr. Brett Riggs, an archaeologist from Western Carolina University, was called in to survey the site without digging.[46] He and his archaeological crew measured differential magnetism within the soil by using an electromagnetic pulse that is reflected back to them. The tests were run on top of the small mound that remains, and it showed there had been a council house that measured sixty-five feet in diameter and was octagonal with rounded corners. "In this case, you could see, very well represented, the outlines of the walls, the door, the orientation of the door and position, the hearth and position of the hearth relative to that door, so you could see what the main access was out through that town, but most importantly, the fact that the hearth is there" (Riggs, Personal interview). He notes that the door faced the Tuckasegee River in a southeasterly direction, and this is key in understanding how important the east-southeast access to the river was in terms of ceremonies and going to water. "We have a letter from 1882, before it had been plowed down in 1914, that showed it had been about twelve feet tall" (Riggs, Personal interview). Riggs says he met the man who'd been hired as a boy to plow down the mound back in 1914, and it had taken a week of plowing in circles to take it down to the point that the farmers could cultivate on top of it. Fortunately, the soil from the mound was not removed—a common practice by archaeological companies—but is instead distributed all across the acreage there. That means the Mothertown earth remains all around the' area, so in that sense, nothing has been lost.

After the tribal council approved the purchase of Kituwah, public hearings were held at the council house so that the reclaiming of the land could be discussed—much like in the old days when whole villages went to council—and all the people on the Qualla Boundary could become better educated about this particular parcel of land. Those who had the knowledge gave testimony of the stories they had heard. Riggs notes that it was truly interesting to hear when the Elders got up and spoke about what they knew from what they'd been told by their parents and grandparents. Not everyone knew the importance and significance of the Kituwah area, he says. But there were some who did know, and there were certainly Elders who knew about it. "People, . . . for a very long time, had not felt empowered to speak about these things, or judged that it was not proper to speak about those things at that time" (Riggs, Personal interview). Riggs said that even with the testimony from local tribal members who had always known about the historic and cultural significance of the Kituwah lands, there was a limit to the knowledge. Instead, he explains, "explicit descriptions about this place, and the way it figures into Cherokee traditions, came from Oklahoma," and he believes this is possibly because those diasporic Oklahoma Cherokees may have felt more empowered to speak about it, which goes hand-in-hand with Chief Dugan's thoughts on how the knowledge had been hidden away within the Qualla community. Yet the knowledge was out there, and the stories still lived, as Riggs notes, "in terms of what that was, in really ancient terms . . . the way that it figured into the whole cycle of prophecy associated with that place—I only heard that from people from the West" (Riggs, Personal interview); he refers to Tom Belt and his role as a knowledge holder. This demonstrates how certain oral stories have not been written down anywhere but continue to flourish and live in the original verbal manner—albeit in English rather than Cherokee. Riggs recognized the value of this usage of the oral tradition, saying, "These aren't just stories about this. . . . All these stories you've heard about, here's the physical evidence that goes with that, that you can't see by casual inspection, but it's here. Know that your stories are true. Quite apart from my professional role, I had quite a strong personal interest in this, in seeing the preservation of that place. Because it was very clear to me what a unique situation that was" (Riggs, Personal interview).

Riggs notes that even after the 1838 removal, there were still settlements nearby with Cherokee people living in them that were within sight of Kituwah Mound, up Galbreath Creek and Deep Creek, so the nearness of the People has been continuous. "We do know that people met and made conscious decisions about how they were gonna stay there," adding that the records show that as far back as 1818, Cherokees were working out strategies for communities to remain in these places. These Cherokee communities were isolated like islands, surrounded by Anglo settlers, and Riggs notes that this must have been very uncomfortable, but this was how the Cherokee people worked out how some would remain there in the homeland. He explains that there are documents which give evidence of these discussions of how to maintain a Cherokee presence, but nothing was written down as to *why;* often, even if discussions were recorded in the syllabary, these documents could and were at risk of being intercepted by outsiders bent on forcing all the Cherokee out. This danger reminded me of visiting, as a child, the log cabin childhood home of Chief John Ross from before the Removal in Rossville, Georgia—which is now a Georgia historic site—and climbing up into the secret attic with a shortened ceiling of about four feet high (you couldn't stand and had to sit on the floor).[47] This was where Ross met with other leaders to discuss the latest word about the political push from Washington to remove the Cherokees, and needless to say, these meetings were secretive since the men could have been arrested.

Since the tribe forbade actual excavation at the Kituwah site, the evidence of burials came about in an interesting way. Tribal members can have garden plots on the Kituwah grounds, and many have planted year after year since Kituwah was returned. Jerry Dugan, Chief Dugan's ex-husband, went out in the spring of the year 2000 to till his garden, and according to Riggs, "He saw a mound of raw dirt that looked like someone had been digging, so he was afraid that someone had been out there digging something up. When he walked up and saw the dirt, there were human remains on it. There was a part of a skull, there was a mandible, there were limb bones and ribs on this dirt pile. Then it was really clear that it had been kicked out of a groundhog hole. So, an investigation ensued; the first thing they wanted to ascertain was that it wasn't a recent skeleton. They contacted the police and the police office said, 'No, it's not'" (Riggs, Personal interview).

The tribal preservation officer at the time contacted Riggs and told him the tribe needed him to find a grave. Riggs was surprised, because he estimates "there are from hundreds to thousands of graves at this site, because people lived at Kituwah for hundreds and hundreds of years. Most people who lived there died there. And they died here, they're buried here" (Riggs, Personal interview). It was common practice in ancient times to bury the dead just outside of the house, or even inside the house in order to keep the family together. The tribe wanted Riggs to determine where the original grave of this person was, in order to return her/him to where that person belongs. He drove up to find a crowd there, and the site was cordoned off like a crime scene. He traced to where the groundhog burrow had run, and they laid an excavation right over that to dig down to undisturbed soil. By the end of the day, using his archaeological knowledge of the soil structure, he was able to determine exactly where the original grave had been. "Actually finding the grave had two purposes," Riggs explains. "One purpose was to show that there *was* a grave, and the other purpose was to put these remains back where they belong. . . . It was an adult female, obviously a Native person, obviously ancient" (Riggs, Personal interview). Riggs quoted Elder Tom Belt, who had said at the time, "When the grandmothers have to raise themselves up out of the ground to tell us, we need to listen." Riggs adds, "You realize what this place represents to a people. You can stand at the point and say that—what's three feet below our feet—not just represents, it *is* what makes the Cherokee people Ani-Giduwagi. This is it" (Riggs, Personal interview).

As Chief Dugan noted, not long after the Mothertown came back into the hands of the Eastern Band, people began visiting the mound for prayers and ceremonies, for the most part quietly and privately, but then, more recently, larger groups of Cherokees have reinstituted spiritual rituals at the site, and communal gardening has also become part of the landscape—much like the ancient times. An annual celebration is held in late June to inform and educate the community about the significance of the site, and more recently to bring together all three bands of Cherokees—a sort of homecoming for citizens of the two Oklahoma bands and a reunion for all.[48] Many today "see the site as a reminder of the unity of the Cherokee before their removal and dispersion" ("Kituwah Mound"). The annual Kituwah Celebration day is not only a time for the three bands of Cherokees to gather for socializing and feasting on traditional foods, but also an opportunity for communal discussion and sharing of cultural history and teachings through oral narratives presented by those most knowledgeable of particular aspects of the culture and history of the homeland.[49] As Riggs notes, "The place needs to remember the people. The place needs to know that the people are there and remember it, and that there will always be Cherokee people living within sight of that place" (Riggs, Personal interview). Since all three bands are separate political entities that must deal with outside control from the American government, there are restrictions on any joint economic or political ventures; however, the annual event is a chance for the three chiefs, vice chiefs, and band councils to hold a joint meeting and discuss cultural matters that affect all Cherokees, and certain projects have been implemented, such as the joint Remember the Removal bicycle journey. At each of these gatherings or reunions for all Cherokee people, the prophecies about the Fire are often spoken of, and there is a growing sense of a common ancestry, no matter in what part of the land now called the United States these modern-day Cherokees now live. Riggs offers his ideas about the enduring power of these prophecies:

> We have a magnetic image that says the hearth is here. If we can see that hearth, that means it's intact. If it's intact, we know the way these hearths are constructed—that means the ashes are still there. The charcoal is still there. That means the Fire is still there, means the Fire is only asleep. And through time, as people have shared things with me, and I understand better how this works . . . you know, one of those coals, one of those pieces of charcoal can be taken, put into a fire, and it's the same fire, which means, in some sense, the Mother Fire has never left there, but always and in every sense, it means this Fire can live again. It can be awake again. (Riggs, Personal interview)

This matches the prophecies that say the Fire is simply sleeping, and Riggs notes that even with a railroad track nearby and a road, this ancient Fire can still exist despite all these new entrapments of progress. People have driven by this living mound for decades and not realized what exactly was there, but Riggs has observed how more and more Eastern Band people are also awakening to the significance of the mound and its continuing vitality and power.

Many Eastern Cherokees who had never even set foot on the Kituwah acreage until the purchase facilitated by Chief Dugan are doing what they can to make the Mothertown their own, bringing their handfuls and scoopfuls of earth from their yards and adding it onto the mound to rebuild it. This rebuilding of the mound, one scoop of earth at a time, started with a ceremony with a group of Cherokee schoolchildren in 1998 under the guidance of Tom Belt, who reflected: "You're talking about kids who can't speak Cherokee, who watch TV all the time. All of a sudden, they reach back in time and say that's part of who we are. The very first rebuilding of the mound, it was the children who did it. Our ancestors are buried here. That's what they needed to see. When we begin to do these things again, who we are begins to mean something again" ("Kituwah Mound").

At first, this mound rebuilding was done informally, and, as mentioned, some people still just do it on their own, but there is now a concerted effort to encourage more and more Cherokees to visit and bring along with them a handful of dirt—most often wrapped in a red cloth or brought in a turtle shell scoop.[50] Leaders like Tom Belt, who is from the UKB and married to an Eastern Cherokee woman, take the time to conduct the proper ceremonies and speak particular words to show respect for the Spirits of the Ancestors who are buried all over the area; several of the younger Eastern Cherokee men are now learning those rituals, stories, and the proper words to say. A crowd of Giduwah people gathers around what remains of the original Kituwah mound and listens to the teachings and prayers, each holding their offering of Gadv before being invited to the top of the mound to pour their dirt onto the hill. It is a serious yet joyful undertaking and brings a great sense of reconnection with the Ancestors as it is the action taken, along with the orality used by the spiritual leaders, that infuses the event with Gadugi power. As discussed in my introduction, this collective ritual is similar to what Jace Weaver speaks of when he presents his theory of communitism and how vital this action is for Indigenous people who are part of "communities that have too often been fractured and rendered dysfunctional by the effects of more than 500 years of colonialism, [because] to promote communitist values means to participate in the healing of the grief and sense of exile felt by Native communities and the pained individuals in them" (xiii). Gadugi or Cherokee-style communitism is at the center of such a multilayered event that physically, spiritually, emotionally, and culturally binds the Cherokee participants to the Earth of their origins and to the memory of their Ancestors within this modern setting. It is deeply moving to stop and think of how we are walking or dancing with the Ancestors all around us, watching us continue the traditions that they started. Entire families stand in the long line, awaiting their turn with Gadv in hand, and all ages are involved; many people express how wonderful it feels to be there, and often there are tears in the eyes of the Elders especially.[51] Spoken stories have been handed down within families and within the seven communities on the Boundary, as well as among Oklahoma Cherokee kin, of the great loss when the Mothertown was ripped from their hands, but not from the hearts of the Ani-Giduwah. This mound rebuilding is a powerful communitist form of healing for the People, for the Earth herself, for the Equoni (river), and for all the other beings living there at the Mothertown.

Chief Dugan recognizes that once Kituwah came back to the tribe, things just started happening, as the People gained a new appreciation and pride in all things Cherokee. She notes that when she left office, she had no worries because people were stepping forward in regard to protecting Kituwah, such as in 2010 when Duke Energy started work on building a large electric sub-station a mere two hundred yards from the sacred Kituwah lands. In fact, the power company had already begun bulldozing part of a nearby mountainside to create flat land for construction—all without informing the EBCI tribal council—and caused a large outcry from numerous tribal members. Elder Tom Belt had gone to tribal council to urge them to take immediate action to stop Duke Energy, likening the action to "putting a McDonald's sign near the pulpit of a church" (ShelHarrell). Along with that, the assistant attorney general for the reservation, Hannah Smith, argued that "erecting this unattractive industrial-looking 'eyesore' so close in proximity to our ancient and sacred Mothertown was like putting up a power substation next door to a great cathedral (like St. Peter's Basilica in Rome)" (Sturgis). There was also a Facebook page called "Save the Kituwah Mound" that informed and organized concerned people (Sturgis), and the United Keetoowah Band of Cherokees denounced the Duke Energy plan in an official statement (ShelHarrell). After all, the Kituwah Mound and lands are listed on the National Register of Historic Sites (Chavez, "Eastern Band"), and tribal members pointed out that an environmental assessment had never been carried out on the land that Duke Energy purchased in 2008 for a new substation; however, because of the lower wattage that this facility would transmit, neither an environmental nor an archaeological study was required by the state's utility commission (Chavez, "Eastern Band"). This battle to stop such a desecration of the Cherokee Mothertown was eventually successful, and no electric substation has been built nearby. Dugan points out that people have become very protective of this land, and there haven't been any problems with the non-Cherokee citizens who live in Swain County or the surrounding area, so she feels that Kituwah is finally being respected and revered as it always should have been (Dugan, Personal interview).

In the years following the return of the Kituwah site, debate went on in the Qualla Boundary about how best to utilize the site,[52] with some wanting to do more than just leave it idle, considering the monetary cost to the tribe. Many EBCI members wanted to protect the sacredness and sanctity of the valley land and not allow anything to be done there that would desecrate the land—particularly since fifteen burial sites had been identified by archaeologists from the University of North Carolina, with speculation that another thousand probably exist ("Kituwah Mound"). After years of community discussion—much like the old days when every Cherokee would come to the village council house and everyone would get to speak their heart—the tribal council made their decision, based on an impassioned presentation along with legislation authored by the manager of the New Kituwah Academy, Renissa McLaughlin. She and others wanted to prevent any development from ever happening there, and the new "sacred site" designation ensures that. Chief Dugan points out, "There's someone who will always step up to protect that place" (Dugan, Personal interview). The *Cherokee One Feather* newspaper of the EBCI offers this from McLaughlin's presentation: "Kituwah is the original Mother Town of the Anikituwagi or Cherokee people. This is the place where our grandparents received the Laws of the Seven Clans and the Sacred Fire, both given to us by the Creator. This means that Kituwah was given to us by God. . . . Kituwah Mound was built with the Sacred Fire in its center. It is scientific fact that the ashes of the original fire are still present. The sacredness of Kituwah extends not only to the mound itself, but the associated village that occupied the entire valley" (McKie, "Kituwah to Be Protected").[53]

The council's decision was unanimous. The chiefs of the two Oklahoma bands of Cherokees support the EBCI's move to protect the site and recognize it "as a sacred area embodying 'not only the remains of our ancient ancestors, but the sacredness of all that existed in our past, as well as all that it embodies for future generations'" (Chavez, "EBCI Council").[54] The reclamation and repatriation of Kituwah Mound, along with designating it as a sacred site, make a strong statement of nationalism by the Eastern Band of Cherokee, and again, buying their own land with their money demonstrates their sovereignty and resistance to colonizer land theft and desecration, along with practicing the ancient Cherokee value of harmonious relations with every being in the area—including colonizer descendants who also now call the old Cherokee lands their home. Eastern Cherokee officials had worked for many decades within the colonizer system and were well aware of the futility of making demands for a return of sacred land, so they simply decided to once again use their own funds to buy back their land, in the same fashion that their Ancestors had pooled their hard-earned pay and trusted Will Usdi to buy enough land for the small band to again have a home. Most certainly, there is irony in a Native group buying land that the Creator had made for them, that they had always lived upon, and that the white man had stolen by force—however, such actions of both Gadugi and Duyvkta ensured the Cherokees could continue to live peacefully among their non-Cherokee friends and neighbors without hard feelings on either side.

Another ancient village site, the Cowee Mound, has also been repatriated by the tribe, and this, too, is a powerful statement of nationhood because of the particular history of the Cowee village.[55] The town was the diplomatic and political hub of the nation, and "what Washington D.C. is to the United States, Cowee was to the Cherokee people. Cowee was the centerpiece to diplomatic, commercial, and agricultural usage, and it was home to some of the smartest, wisest, and bravest" ("Why Is the Cowee Mound"). Much like Kituwah and many other ancient Cherokee village sites, the Cowee Mound passed out of Cherokee hands early in the nineteenth century as the territory was overrun by settlers and land theft occurred. Mooney's informants tell that it was one of the oldest and largest of the villages, with at least one hundred houses, and was rebuilt after being burned by the Americans in 1776, and so continued to be occupied until the 1819 land cession (*Myths of the Cherokee* 377–78). Cowee overlooks the adjoining Hall Mountain Tract about six miles outside of Franklin, where the Nikwasi Mound is located; Nikwasi was the home of the Nunehi Spirit People, as described in chapter 3. When a proposed development threatened the Cowee historic site and its natural beauty, the conservancy group Land Trust for the Little Tennessee (River), or LTLT, moved quickly to buy up the land through a special grant from a national group, Community Forest and Open Space Conservation Program, through the U.S. National Forest Service. That $300,000 of funding was then matched by the EBCI, which allowed the tribe, once again, to buy back their own land. These deliberate political actions by the tribal government are vital, because as Brett Riggs points out, "The acquisition of these places (mounds) is all about asserting sovereignty" (Riggs, Personal interview). In this case, an act of Indigenous sovereignty is also benefitting the settler-descendant neighbors of the Qualla Cherokees.

On May 31, 2013, a signing and celebration took place that saw the tract signed back over to the Eastern Band (Jones). After discussions within the Qualla community, the tribe has created plans for "a network of walking and biking trails as well as interpretive signage, a pavilion, and perhaps a small camping area. 'The goal is to emphasize the natural and cultural significance of the area,' said Tommy Cabe, forest resource specialist with the tribe" (Kasper). This plan coincides well with what the local conservation groups had hoped for when this process began, and it will allow for a large area of protected forest as well as open space for anyone—Cherokees and non-Natives alike—to enjoy the natural beauty of the Tsalagi homeland.[56] Returning the land to the tribe is significant because Cowee was a thriving center of Cherokee civilization and diplomacy, and a commercial center for trade that drew Natives from all over the southeast and as far as the Atlantic Ocean. It was reported by botanist William Bartram in 1776 that the council house atop the Cowee Mound was so large that it could accommodate several hundred people, and the village itself had around one hundred houses (Chavez, "Eastern Band"). Mooney tells how a white man named Wafford, who was married to a Cherokee woman, described for Mooney a trip he made to Cowee as a child: "He found the trail leading to it worn so deep in places that, although on horseback, he could touch the ground with his feet on each side" (*Myths of the Cherokee* 378). It is deeply significant that this land, this important site of Cherokee civilization, has been returned. As former Principal Chief Michell Hicks noted during the 2013 signing and celebration, "When we put our people to rest, it's perpetual. . . . We have to make things right and that's why we're here today" (Kasper).

In his role as Sequoyah Distinguished Professor of Cherokee Studies, Brett Riggs also has a story about the Cowee Mound as well. He worked there in the early 1980s while still a graduate student at the University of Tennessee, looking for the old house of Euchala, who had a reserve there in 1819—this was during the time that the federal government would award plots of a few acres to enrolled Cherokees, and these plots were known as reserves. Riggs shared his knowledge about the Cowee mound and how a settler had laid claim to the land. Euchala filed suit against the man, and it went to the North Carolina Supreme Court, with Euchala winning. Thus, the state had to negotiate contracts with all the Cherokees who had their reserve land taken by squatters in the area. Riggs met and learned about this history from a settler family who owned the land that had the actual mound on it. The grandfather of the female owner, Catherine Hall Porter, had built the family house there in the 1820s, which she still lived in in 1984; this is why it's called the Hall Tract. Hall Porter told Riggs that her grandfather's uncle had preached a sermon there on top of the Cowee Mound to Griffith Rutherford's army in 1776—which is ironic, considering it was Rutherford's army that burned over twenty Cherokee villages to the ground. She also said her aunts could speak Cherokee, which wasn't unusual for the time, as many white settlers learned the language in order to do business with the local Cherokees. Riggs notes that this shows how these communities of Natives and white settlers were interwoven. He says he likes the continuity and how this particular land base, which had been an old Cherokee village, had been in the hands of a single family since it had left Cherokee hands, just like Kituwah. And the Cowee mound had never been excavated because this female owner wouldn't allow it. She also ran off potential poachers who were interested in digging into the mound, with the false assumption there were items of value buried by the Cherokees—as if it were an Egyptian pharaoh's tomb. Hall Porter would have a shotgun in hand to scare strangers away (Riggs, Personal interview).

EBCI tribal member Jeremy Wilson has made it his personal project to educate the rest of his community and those non-Cherokees living in the area about the Cowee Mound and its historic importance, now that the 108-acre tract in what is now Macon County is back in the hands of the People. Wilson held an internship with the LTLT and created an educational project about the Cowee Mound and village that included talking with Cherokee Elders who shared their knowledge and stories about Cowee. Those oral narratives helped Wilson make that modern connection with the ancestral history. He asked language instructor and Elder Tom Belt to explain why Cowee was so important to today's Cherokee:

> Cowee is a gift, it was always a gift, ever since the inception of it, ever since they laid the first fire here, it was always a gift. Since the loss of Cowee through intrusions, violence, the burning, the time when it was taken away, and we were no longer allowed to live here, it is proportionate to how much we have lost as a people. If we are in fact people who care about our history, our culture, and who we are, then we have to take care of these places. Cowee is the marker of who we are, these mountains all around us are who we are, this is our home. Reconnecting with Cowee is not an acquisition of property, an acquisition of real estate or anything like that, it is actually reconstructing the Cherokee nation, we are putting the tribe back together, and that is why it is important. We just haven't been allowed to do that in a very long time. ("Why Is the Cowee Mound")

It is clear that after reacquiring several village sites and mounds, along with other small land tracts, that the act of reconstruction of the nation is indeed going on, though Belt is the first I've heard put it into those terms. Elder storyteller and Beloved Man for the Eastern Band, Jerry Wolfe, echoes Belt's sentiments when he says that this land return was a historic milestone for the People;[57] he feels relieved to know that Cowee is now protected. Wolfe believes it is a great opportunity for young Cherokees to learn about their past and to see how the site would have looked in its natural state. He notes that "the mound is a very historical site—it's there for the reason of permanent keeps" (Kasper).

Meanwhile, Jeremy Wilson, a band councillor for the Wolftown community, has found modern ways of teaching Cherokee youth about this powerful history. His project includes creation of a site on social media to educate others; that Facebook page, from which the above Belt quote is taken, is called "Project Cowee Reconnection." Wilson has also utilized his skills as a public speaker to share historical and cultural information about not only Cowee but also all of the remaining mounds that were the centerpiece of dozens of Cherokee villages in ancient times. At the Kituwah Celebration in 2011, Wilson shared his knowledge with the attending Cherokees from the three bands; I was fortunate to be there and hear the history and the arguments as to how important these various mounds and ancient village sites are, and how the tribe needs to reclaim as many as possible. Wilson's oral narratives brought to life a picture of how our Ancestors had lived, as we all sat there at the Mothertown and within a stone's throw of the original Kituwah Mound with her sacred Fire still burning deep in the Earth. His words inspired a sense of unity and Cherokee nationalism among the crowd, helping rekindle the Fire that we are told must be kept alive so that our culture may live and prosper. Such "oral tradition and listening to stories allows people to 'feel' and become a part of the past and sharing a sense of time and place with the people" (Fixico 29). This kind of oral discussion of the land creates an atmosphere of kinship and belonging for those diasporic Cherokees, myself included, who are not fortunate enough to live in the homeland.

The day after Cowee was returned, former chief Hicks spoke to the bicycle riders from the Eastern Band who were taking part in the Remember the Removal ride of 2013 and had gathered at the Kituwah Mound for the community to see them off. Hicks talked about the repatriation of Cowee, noting what a great day it had been for the tribe. Referring to another sacred Cherokee village, he said: "There's a mound in Franklin named Nikwasi. It needs to be back in the hands of the Cherokee" (Jones). This may have set the stage for a complicated territorial battle with the town of Franklin, since the town's citizens pooled their monies years ago to buy the mound, which sits in the middle of town and is a tourist attraction of sorts. Franklin citizens are proud of their stories that tell how even the young schoolchildren saved their allowance and brought in their nickels and dimes to put in the community pot to save the Nikwasi mound from a business development in the 1950s. For many years after, it was a revered green spot in the downtown of this quaint, art-minded town and was cared for. However, the Qualla Cherokee community has been critical of maintenance workers in Franklin who sprayed herbicide all over the ancient home of the Nunehi Spirit Warriors, killing the green growth and leaving the mound covered in dead, brown grass in the spring of 2012. Eastern Band officials did not like that the tribe had not been consulted before the deadly herbicide was applied on the lush green hill, and the Department of Agriculture fined the town for the action. Several town officials apologized for what had happened, but many Cherokees were so upset that a poll was conducted by the *Cherokee One Feather* newspaper that asked whether the tribe should be "given the option to take over the care and upkeep of the Nikwasi Mound" ("*One Feather* Poll Result"). A large majority of respondents said yes.

Then, in March 2014, Chief Hicks appeared before the Franklin Town Council to discuss Nikwasi; he shared his "belief that the protection of the mound should be the responsibility of the tribe" and offered to work with the town to find a way for this to happen ("Chief Hicks Speaks"). Maintenance of the grounds around the mound and of the high two-story mound itself has proven to be costly and time-consuming for the small town. Before the chief presented, Elder Tom Belt and young community member Mathew Tooni (a Right Path alumnus and up-and-coming storyteller) spoke to the council about the history and cultural importance of Nikwasi—again using the oral tradition to share with outsiders the Cherokee worldview ("Chief Hicks Speaks"). This harmonious and friendly approach acknowledges the town and its people for caring for this sacred site for so many years, yet firmly offers an alternative for the town that will bring the sacred responsibility of taking care of Nikwasi back to the Ani-Yunwiyah—and is a first step toward reclamation of this significant piece of earth and piece of Cherokee culture and tribal history. In his essay "Sacred Places and Moral Responsibility," Lakota scholar Vine Deloria notes that "[e]very society needs these kinds of sacred places because they help to instill a sense of social cohesion in the people and remind them of the passage of generations that have brought them to the present. A society that cannot remember and honor its past is in peril of losing its soul" (328). Such repatriation of mounds, village sites, and sacred pieces of land that are so deeply attached to Cherokee people and their culture are vital to the process of decolonization and clearly inspire a stronger sense of nationalism and nationhood, as these reacquisitions and reclamations declare to the colonizer government and surrounding non-Cherokee communities that the Eastern Band is a distinct and sovereign Indigenous nation that has always been there and is not going to go away.

A recent development reflects the tribe's concern over the perceived neglect by the town of Franklin of the Nikwasi mound and the way the damage of grass and earth has occurred. On September 4, 2014, the EBCI tribal council unanimously passed a resolution regarding the tribe's concern and desire for the deed for the Nikwasi mound to be returned to the Eastern Cherokees. Resolution 341-2014 notes the "disregard for the upkeep" and the repeated offers of maintenance assistance from the EBCI; it authorizes the tribe's legal department to seek the return of this ancient sacred site to the tribe (*Cherokee One Feather* Facebook page). The tribal council gave its unanimous approval when all rose to their feet. Chief Hicks told the audience that "it breaks my heart that we are in this position," adding, "[t]here is power in the statement that we are making today" (*Cherokee One Feather* Facebook page). The entire community audience in attendance rose to their feet and applauded. In launching such a united, concerted effort to bring this most sacred of all the village mounds back into the hands of the Eastern Band, there is no doubt Nikwasi Mound will come full circle and become part of the sacred homeland of the Anigiduwah once again.

Conclusion

Uninetsv oni ◆ Last Words

There remains so much to learn and to share of the Eastern Cherokee oral tradition, because this project barely scratches the surface. It is heartening to see how the stories and wealth of knowledge still retained by the people on the Qualla Boundary are being used today to present Cherokee perspective and history, along with the constant, daily regeneration of all things Cherokee in what could suitably be called a renaissance here in the twenty-first century. The continuance of the oral tradition among the Qualla residents includes many narratives—personal, familial, and communal—along with anecdotal stories. No doubt there was plenty of what we might call anecdotal or everyday orature in ancient times as well, but those types of spoken narratives were not recorded or necessarily known widely through the Cherokee villages, as these stories would have been more personal in nature. But many of today's band members on the Boundary are storytellers in their own right, without practicing the art in public—confining it to their family and friends instead—and although these are modern narratives, they reflect the ancient beings and demonstrate how "oral stories are contextualized within everyday conversations" (Teuton, "Interpreting" 548).

My second summer living there, I was reminded of the prevalence of every-day, anecdotal storytelling during a visit by my adopted sister, Bear Taylor.[1] I had planted a tiny garden on the rocky hillside behind our home in Tsisqua-hi (Birdtown) and was proud when a few plants struggled to existence in the "sugar dirt" of the red clay hill,[2] which were beginning to offer the occasional squash, pepper, or small bundle of collard greens. A torrential rain fell one day, so hard that the pelting, heavy downpour and strong winds knocked over the few cornstalks that had grown to a height of about four feet tall. Bear and I stood surveying the damage when she told me that I just had to tell those corn plants to stand up. I looked at her quizzically, not knowing what she really meant and thinking she was joking around. She informed me that that was exactly what her mother always did, anytime the weather had knocked over the corn. "You just gotta tell that corn to stand up. That's what Momma always did. She'd just holler at them corn plants and tell them to get back up. We needed them to grow and have ears of corn for us to eat, so they better stand right back up and get to growing. It'll work," Bear told me in all seriousness. I had known her mother, Miss Emma Taylor, for a few years before she passed away from complications from her diabetes, and with her passing, the community had lost one of the finest basket-makers around.[3] It was not hard for me to imagine Miss Emma, standing out in her garden with her scarf tied around her head the way those old Cherokee women wore them, hands on her hips and scolding her Selu plants for laying down on the job and ordering them to get back up and get to the business of growing some corn. Bear was quietly adamant that it was all I needed to do, because it had always worked when her mother told the corn to stand up again. I have always talked to my plants, especially when each was a tiny green sprout, so her advice made sense to me. The very next morning, I did exactly that. I may not have hollered at the poor, pitiful, falling-down cornstalks because I felt so sorry for them and was afraid of scaring them too much, but I did give them a stern talking-to and informed them that they had to stand up and grow right. It worked. Within a few days, my cornstalks were upright and healthy once again. It was easy to accept then how talking to the young corn plants reminded each of the stalks of their particular responsibility upon the Earth and of their purpose in helping to feed the Cherokees, in just the way that Selu, the Corn Mother, provided food for her family. Human beings, even today, continue to communicate with the plant beings, just like Davy Arch tells us in his narratives and as we hear in the story called "The Origin of Disease and Medicine," both from chapter 1. Thus, in talking with and listening to the green plant beings, humans can help them fulfill their important role, which is so intricately connected with the rest of life around them, since other creatures enjoy the tasty ears of corn, including the *Koga* (crow), *Tsisdetsi* (field mice), *Gvli* (raccoon), and the variety of *Tsvsgoyi* (insects) that are partial to this taste. I am told that this is why most Cherokees do not have scarecrows in their garden, since it is understood that those creatures also enjoy the offerings of plants and we should not discourage any of them in partaking of food.

I often heard such stories concerning the foods growing in gardens and the wild plant foods that I learned from my adopted sisters how to gather and cook—be it sochan,[4] poke salad, or ramps—or even learning how to prepare some of the other traditional foods, such as bean bread, chestnut bread, lye dumplings, greasy beans, and the many other various beans, squash, and mushrooms native to the mountain lands. This type of storytelling, though brief in nature, allows for the passing-on of traditional knowledge of Cherokee foodstuffs and its uniqueness, since food is one of the many intricate components of an Indigenous culture rooted firmly in the natural world and homeland in which the People reside.[5] Modern Cherokee stories and narratives are often "sprinkled throughout conversation, embedded in the flow of events and casual talk. They make a point or teach a lesson relevant to the events or the conversation in progress" (Duncan, *Living Stories* 15). This form of often brief anecdotal narratives included in "everyday conversation is, for Cherokees, an important social event. Depending on what kind of story is told and in what context, it can serve numerous purposes: a story-teller may display his humor, wit, knowledge, or rudeness; a listener may be entertained, gratified, reassured, or shamed" (Teuton, "Interpreting" 547). I always found it quite amazing how much history I learned in the aisles of the local grocery store in Cherokee or at the post office, just from stopping to gab with folks I knew. There are many, many storytellers and carriers of cultural knowledge of all ages.

All one needs to do is listen to the stories and drive or hike through any part of the sacred homeland to see the boulders thrown randomly by Tsutlakalv or the many dark coves where a few Yunwi Tsunsdi might hide, waiting to be mischievous. If one stands atop one of the many overlooks throughout the Smoky Mountains, it will not take long to imagine Suli egwa, the "father of all the buzzards we see now," soaring over the muddy Earth, lifting his wings in creation of the soft blue mountains and valleys (Mooney, *Myths of the Cherokee* 239). Drive over to the Mothertown at Kituwah Mound and you will find gardens filled with Selu to remind us all of the beauty of the Corn Mother's gift of herself to the People, so that there will always be food for the Cherokees. Then go for a walk upon the shortened mound there, take off your shoes and let your feet feel the earth, and know that the ancient Fire is still burning deep within that ancient earth, as the Ancestors watch from all around you. You may catch a glimpse of a fast-footed Ahwi and think of the story "How the Deer Got His Antlers" that Elder Lloyd Arneach tells so well, or there may be a Daksi or two on a log in the river that brings to mind how the turtle broke his shell because of his meanness and then used medicine to put it back together. If a fast-moving storm rumbles through the mountains, it will be the Anisgaya Tsunsdi who are sharing the gifts of thunder and lightning. Most anyone who does this will feel and understand how deeply Cherokee culture is embedded in and drawn from the red clay earth and woven into the trees and plants growing thickly throughout the land. Know that these stories will continue as long as Giduwah people live in the homeland.

There are countless other ways the ancient oral tradition is utilized in a manner of cultural continuance for the Eastern Cherokee people, such as new songs for stomp dances in the language, lyrics in both English and Cherokee created and performed by songwriter/singer Paula Maney Nelson, curriculum and activities for the Cherokee Central Schools, plays and skits for the annual fall fair, and so on. There is not enough space within this book to examine them all. It has also been a complicated challenge in this endeavor to present, analyze, and discuss spoken-word art and to do so on the written page; so much is lost without the reader of this project being able to see, hear, and witness the oral performances by the talented storytellers. My readers most certainly are missing out on exciting, powerful, and moving orature that, heard and felt in live performance, could conceivably change their lives in minute or large ways. The oral tradition continues to be the foundation of Eastern Cherokee culture and life. Its enduring vitality cannot be denied. Colonization may have drastically altered Cherokee lifeways and societal structure both for good and for bad, as the People adopted the helpful things the white man offered while resisting what was not deemed as good or compatible, but at all times they remained uniquely Cherokee. The oral teachings and history that have been passed down by each generation have allowed for Tsalagi to stay firmly attached to their land base and lifeways as they continue to utilize their Indigenous ecological knowledge to remind them of who they are and how to live properly in a harmonious fashion with all of Earth's creatures. Today's Eastern Cherokees may no longer live entirely off the land, but they still enjoy a close enough relation to their mountain environment and offerings from the natural world that many of the ways and foods of their Ancestors continue to be a large part of Cherokee life now. It is also interesting to note how so much of white Appalachian culture is merely appropriated from the Cherokees, such as many foods (indigenous to this geographical area) and their unique preparation as well as art forms like gourd art,[6] white oak and willow basket-making, red clay pottery, corn-husk doll-making, and a host of others.

Normally, a project like this would have a conclusion, but there is no end or finale to this formal discussion and analysis because the stories and songs will continue for the next generation of Eastern Cherokees and their children and grandchildren after that. The discussion, quite rightly, should continue, as I also hope my research will go on. We simply cannot cover all things Cherokee that are perpetuated by the oral tradition because it is a living being unto itself; it grows and lives on and hopefully never comes to an end—for the sharing of oral teachings, histories, and narratives will only end the day the Fire that lives in the hearts and spirits of Tsalagi people is extinguished. Researching and learning about the many facets of orature within this community where my Ancestors grew up has been a spiritual and educational journey for me personally, because until I finally got the chance to live on the Qualla Boundary, I did not really know *how* to be a good Giduwagi ageyah. Much of what I learned over three years of research (and decades of typical life learning while visiting in Cherokee) came directly through the oral tradition and the narratives and teachings that so many kind and patient people shared with me. This book is my humble way of giving back to the community and the Eastern Cherokee people who mean so very much to me. I only hope that at some point in the future, this work can continue in the same enduring fashion that Cherokee culture has and that these written words may help perpetuate the beauty of the Anigiduwahgi. *Hvwa!*

Appendix

The First Fire

James Mooney

In the beginning there was no fire, and the world was cold, until the Thunders (Ani-Hyuntikwala'ski), who lived up in Galun'lati, sent their lightning and put fire into the bottom of a hollow sycamore tree which grew on an island. The animals knew it was there, they could see the smoke coming out at the top, but they could not get to it on account of the water, so they held a council to decide what to do. It was a long time ago.

Every animal that could fly or swim was anxious to go after the fire. The Raven offered, and because he was so large and strong they thought he could surely do the work, so he was sent first. He flew high and far across the water and alighted on the sycamore tree, but while he was wondering what to do next, the heat had scorched all his feathers black, and he was frightened and came back without the fire. The little Screech-owl (*Wahuhu'*) volunteered to go, and reached the place safely, but while he was looking down into the hollow tree a blast of hot air came up and nearly burned out his eyes. He managed to fly home as best he could, but it was a long time before he could see well, and his eyes are red to this day. Then the Hooting Owl (*U'guku'*) and the Horned Owl (*Tskili*) went, but by the time they got to the hollow tree the fire was burning so fiercely that the smoke nearly blinded them, and the ashes carried up by the wind made white rings about their eyes. They had to come home again without the fire, but with all their rubbing they were never able to get rid of the white rings.

Now no more of the birds would venture, and so the little Uksu'hi snake, the black racer, said he would go through the water and bring back some fire. He swam across to the island and crawled through the grass to the tree, and went in by a small hole at the bottom. The heat and smoke were too much for him, too, and after dodging about blindly over the hot ashes until he was almost on fire himself he managed by good luck to get out again at the same hole, but his body had been scorched black, and he has ever since had the habit of darting and doubling on his track as if trying to escape from close quarters. He came back, and the great blacksnake, Gule'gi, "Climber," offered to go for fire. He swam over to the island and climbed up the tree on the outside, as the blacksnake always does, but when he put his head down into the hole the smoke choked him so that he fell into the burning stump, and before he could climb out again he was as black as Uksu'hi.

Now they held another council, for still there was no fire, and the world was cold, but birds, snakes, and four-footed animals, all had some excuse for not going, because they were all afraid to venture near the burning sycamore, until at last Kanane'ski Amai'yehi (the Water Spider) said she would go. This is not the water spider that looks like a mosquito, but the other one, with black downy hair and red stripes on her body. She can run on top of the water or dive to the bottom, so there would be no trouble to get over to the island, but the question was, How could she bring back the fire? "I'll manage that," said the Water Spider; so she spun a thread from her body and wove it into a *tusti* bowl, which she fastened on her back. Then she crossed over to the island and through the grass to where the fire was still burning. She put one little coal of fire into her bowl, and came back with it, and ever since we have had fire, and the Water Spider still keeps her tusti bowl. (*Myths of the Cherokee* 240–42)

Notes

Introduction

1. Cherokee is the name that other tribes used for the People known as Kituwah/Giduwah. There are no *r*'s in the Kituwah language, so in Cherokee it is pronounced *tsa-la-gi;* the use of the name Cherokee is today the common one for the People. Kituwah or Giduwah is the real name in the language, and in this manuscript I will use the two spellings interchangeably because that is the common practice. It is a sound that is best presented as either the *k* or the *g*, so both spellings are correct. I have confirmed this with Cherokee-language instructor Tom Belt, who teaches at Western Carolina University.

2. My grandfather was Sydney J. Sellers, and he left behind a few of his siblings, whose descendants are still on the rolls of the Cherokee Nation out west. We know little of my grandfather's family, other than that he grew up in Locust Grove, Oklahoma, about ten miles north of the capital of the Cherokee Nation in Tahlequah. He was born in 1882, well before Oklahoma's 1907 statehood, and seems to have left before so much Cherokee land was grabbed up for the new state. This government grab of more land, supposedly set out for Indians, decimated the huge tracts that had been awarded to the Cherokees upon removal from the South and their arrival in this new land. My grandmother was Willie Stokes, who died when my mom was just two, so we really know very little about her other than she was a mixed-blood Cherokee.

3. It was common practice for mixed-bloods in the South before and following Removal to keep it very quiet that they were of Native blood. There was the long-held generational fear that if the authorities found out, their entire family would be shipped out to Indian Territory/Oklahoma and their lands and homes would be auctioned off. This suppressed fear, surprisingly, continued for decades, so many families either kept quiet about their lineage or denied it when questioned. My father said that was the case in his family; he and his siblings were told to not say anything, and he was born in 1920 in north Georgia, about eighty years after Removal.

4. The official name for the North Carolina group is the Eastern Band of Cherokee Indians or EBCI.

5. This was the location of the government of the Cherokee Nation prior to the 1838 forced removal. New Echota is now a Georgia state-owned historical site and gives a glimpse into what life was like for the tribe at the time. It includes the original printing press for the *Cherokee Phoenix;* more on that in chapter 5.

6. This is the home of Joseph Vann, a wealthy mixed-blood who owned slaves that worked his plantation. It stands as an example of how many Cherokees, particularly mixed-bloods, accepted Euro-American values and emulated them, quite possibly in hopes of being allowed to remain in the homeland as settlers pushed for Indian removal in the South.

7. This is the location of the last full Cherokee council held before some Cherokees began to relocate to Indian Territory by their own choice. I will have more about this in chapter 4.

8. Again, the *k* and *g* spelling are both correct, and I will use them interchangeably, as most Cherokee do. Another term Kituwah people call themselves is Ani-Yunwiyah, which means the Original People or the Principal People, a term for all Indigenous people.

9. Whenever I write about any of the clans of the Cherokee, it will be capitalized as a proper noun, whether it is Bird clan, Wild Potato clan, or any of the others.

10. Deer clan people were also used as messengers, because their young folks were considered the fastest runners when there was news that had to be carried quickly to the many villages.

11. An enrolled member of the United Keetoowah Band in Oklahoma, Robert J. Conley was the Sequoyah Distinguished Professor of Cherokee Studies at Western Carolina University during the time that I was taking my Cherokee language lessons there. He is the most prolific Cherokee writer of all time, with over eighty books and numerous other publications. I am deeply honored to have spent time with him and that he read some of my creative work. My husband and I enjoyed his keen and dry wit and his humility. Robert passed away in February 2014, and the world of Indigenous literature lost a giant.

12. Unlike the Eastern Cherokees who continue to live in the ancestral territory, the Oklahoma family has had to adapt to living around and among other tribes

who were also relocated to "Indian Territory." In the early days, this sometimes meant trouble, but over the years, there has been much cultural sharing as happens with any diasporic peoples. However, like other diasporic groups, the two bands of Cherokees out west have held tightly to and maintained many of the old ways and the language. The Eastern Band, meanwhile, are far removed from any other Native groups and so have had less influence from others upon the traditional culture.

13. For convenience's sake, it is conversationally referred to as a reservation, and I will also refer to it as that.

14. The term "Boundary" is an old one, originating in the period when boundary lines were created by treaty between Indian land and white man's land. There is an historic sign on Asheville Highway (Highway 23) in nearby Sylva that denotes it as the "Indian Boundary Line" between 1802 and 1819. That road is now far removed from the actual boundary line of the present-day reservation, which shows how much Cherokee land has been taken from them.

15. Such things are conducted through songs, prayers, spoken phrases, or speaking words of encouragement—all forms of the oral tradition.

16. Quoted from Margaret Astrov, *The Winged Serpent*, 19.

17. This is the formal name of the first semester of the one-year Cherokee language course offered through Western Carolina University's Cherokee Studies program. The second term is the "Cherokee Speaking World."

18. Gustav Freytag was a nineteenth-century German novelist who created a pyramid diagram that shows common patterns in the plotlines of most written stories. He notes things like scene setting, inciting events, rising action to a climax and then falling, and resolution.

19. Cherokee sashes are generally made in this fashion.

20. Each of these storytellers and historians will be named throughout the following chapters as their personal and unique ways of sharing orally the many facets of Cherokee culture must be looked at individually.

21. I do have hopes of sharing this archive with the community in Cherokee, North Carolina, as my way of showing my gratitude and respect for all the many kind people who touched my life during my three years living there.

22. These latter media were kindly shared by the museum director and EBCI cultural officer, T. J. Holland, whom I also refer to in my fourth and fifth chapters for his oral accounts of local Cherokee history. Unfortunately, the Junaluska Museum no longer exists because of structural problems; it is hoped that a new one can be built.

23. As Chief Wilma Mankiller points out in her autobiography, there are some oral history accounts that say there was a written language for the Cherokee further back in time. This possibility is suggested in my third chapter in regard to Judaculla Rock and the carvings made there. Western Carolina University Cherokee-language instructor Tom Belt also asserts the existence of an ancient

writing system, but as Mankiller points out, "even if there was an ancient written Cherokee language, it was lost to the Cherokees until Sequoyah developed the syllabary" (81).

24. There are many good books about Sequoyah, too many to list, though I would recommend *Sequoyah: A Novel of the Real People* from Robert J. Conley's "Real People" series.

25. Other writing systems for Native languages, such as the Inuit's system known as Inuktitut, were a collaborative project based on other writing systems introduced by missionaries. The Inuktitut system is a modern contrivance, partly based on syllabics, which uses the roman alphabet but is written according to syllables ("Writing the Inuit Language"). The Mi'kmaq had ancient hieroglyphs that functioned as a memory aid and thus a writing system of sorts for telling stories; later, a logographic system was developed from those hieroglyphics and petroglyphs (Schmidt and Marshall). Two linguists, Dr. Bernie Francis, who is Mi'kmaq, and Dr. Doug Smith of the University of Toronto, identified a clear alphabet and created an orthography that is considered the official written language of the Mi'kmaq and still used today ("Bernie Francis"). Sequoyah's system is based on Cherokee syllables, but he created his own eighty-five symbols for each syllable.

26. Many of the young adults I know from my participation in stomp dances and events at the Kituwah dance circle are parents of children at the New Kituwah academy and are learning the language along with their young children in order to speak it at home.

27. The Cherokee-language course that I took at Western Carolina University offered writing in the language for the second year of the course.

28. The site is commemorated by NAJA, the Native American Journalists Association, as the birthplace of Native journalism, and a plaque welcomes visitors into the museum building.

29. The *One Feather* first issue was printed on December 17, 1965 (Jumper email).

30. This is not to say that there is no problem with illiteracy; Southwestern Community College has a small campus on the reservation and offers adult GED courses. While living there, I was offered a job as an English instructor.

31. This truly is an old pun that I have heard most of my life.

32. For many, this sort of editorial control is such a political matter that a project like this has no space for a thorough examination of the matter. I will merely note that the Native American Journalists Association, of which I am a former member, has held many discussions of this issue during their annual conferences.

33. Clapsaddle, a teacher who writes mainly children's books, was a finalist for the 2014 PEN/Bellwether Prize for Socially Engaged Fiction (Breedlove), a national literary prize, and she also won the 2012 Morning Star Award for Creative Fiction from the Native American Literature Symposium and the Charles Redd Center for Western Studies ("Clapsaddle Receives Literary Award").

34. A note on capitalization of the term Real Human Beings: this is the best-known translation to English of the Cherokee name for themselves and for all Native people, as explained above, of Ani-Yunwiyah. The term *Yvwi* is the word for all people.

35. Duyvkta is pronounced *duh-yugk-tah*.

36. I first discovered a bound version of the manuscript held in the Purdy/Kresge Library on the campus of Wayne State University in Detroit, Michigan, in 1980. It was a reference document that could only be viewed within the library and was not available for circulation outside the premises. In my great excitement at finding such a valuable document, I spent a great deal of time poring through the pages as if mining a treasure trove of sacred words and stories. For the most part, only Cherokees or scholars who studied the Cherokees were aware of the precious collection at that time.

37. This first edition was a joint effort with the Qualla Arts and Crafts Mutual and booksellers Charles and Randy Elder and published through Cherokee Heritage Books. The second edition from the museum is produced by Cherokee Publications. I feel fortunate to have my own copy of each edition, the first having been bought at the New Echota Museum in Georgia on a family visit there shortly after my father's death in 1985, as the staff there knew my father, John Muse, quite well. My father was born in a small cabin just a short distance away in 1920.

38. Mooney was born in 1861 in Richmond, Indiana, which had a large Irish community. His father, who died when young James was just a year old, had been an itinerant scholar in Ireland, teaching the Gaelic language and Irish history when it was illegal under English rule to do so (Duncan, "Introduction" 2).

39. Duncan notes that the bureau's founder, John Wesley Powell, would have preferred the agency to be given the label Bureau of Anthropology, as it was a broader field and one that was very much up and coming, along with ethnography. At this point, there was no formal university training or degrees offered in either of these two new disciplines.

40. The bureau was created to work on American Indian linguistic projects, hoping to document and classify the languages of the various tribes across the United States (Duncan, "Introduction" 3).

41. The two collections by Mooney are together in the one book, with *Myths of the Cherokee* first and the *Sacred Formulas* second. Each collection has its own separate page numbering, thus the need to stipulate which is which.

42. This is the name that I was honored with by Walker Calhoun, the community chief of the Raven Rock Stomp Grounds, where my son and I began attending Green Corn ceremonies and stomp dances in 1997. Ayosta was his grandmother and an accomplished basket maker; some of her baskets are in the Smithsonian Institute. Grandpa Walker told me that when she was a small girl, Ayosta used to get into her family's craftwork, messing it up, so she was named Spoiler or

"she spoils it." When asked why he should call me that, he craftily said, "Because you look like you could." I can share this story because it happened outside of the stomp grounds as we were standing outside of his house with his grown children around us.

43. Long was an uncle of Walker Calhoun's (his mother's brother), and Grandpa Walker learned his many songs and dances from this uncle.

44. Members of the Native American Church use peyote in their religious ceremonies, and Mooney defended the practice. He testified to the U.S. Congress that peyote use did not lead to addiction or social ills but rather "inspired its followers to lead better lives" (Duncan, "Introduction" 8).

45. The ancient honor and responsibility of being a Beloved Woman or a Beloved Man was given to both men and women who have gone to war and been recognized for specific acts of bravery. This will be explained more in-depth in my fifth and final chapter.

46. I am indebted to several language speakers in the Qualla community who helped me many times with translation and interpretation—Tom Belt, Gilliam Jackson, Louise Goings, Kevin Jackson, and Mike Thompson. I truly appreciate their patience with me, as a diasporic Cherokee descendant. Sgi/Wado nigada.

47. In their manuscript entitled "Chronicles of Wolftown," Ana and Jack Kilpatrick write of "[t]hat favorite Cherokee word *duyu: gh(o)dv*" as meaning "'right,' 'just'" for the way that it "binds the documents together with a living thread" in their discussion of civic records from the Wolftown community (10).

48. The seven communities are Birdtown, Yellowhill, Soco, Wolftown, Paintown, Big Cove, and Snowbird.

49. My father, John Muse, and Bob Thomas were friends when Dr. Thomas taught anthropology at Wayne State University in Detroit. I remember as a teenager when Bob visited at our home and the two men would discuss issues around Cherokeeness. My father organized many of the powwows in the Detroit area, and Bob would often perform sunrise ceremonies there. He always had his cowboy hat and smoked his pipe.

Chapter 1

1. I have written down all these stories in a form known as "oral poetics," a method used by many ethnographers and folklorists who record and transcribe oral stories and narratives, most notably by Dell Hymes when he worked with Native American stories. Each solidus (slash mark) represents the end of a spoken line, which I distinguished as a pause by the storyteller. Normally this story would be written out in a longer form, with each spoken line taking up one typed line; however, to save space here I have used the solidus, similar to how poetry is shortened in paragraph form. See Dell Hymes's "Ethnopoetics, Oral-Formulaic Theory, and Editing Texts" and also Barbara Duncan's *Living Stories of the Cherokee*, 22–24.

2. I video-recorded Arch at his workplace at the Oconaluftee Village on the Qualla Boundary on June 19, 2012. He is one of a number of storytellers who share their oral art in public settings, and he tells stories within nearly every casual conversation he has. The words of narrative and story simply roll out of his mouth and memory in an informative, friendly, and welcoming manner.

3. Cajete notes that most Native languages do not have a generic or group name for animals but rather refer to each creature by a specific name. He suggests that "[t]he fact that there are no specific generic words for animals underlines the extent to which animals were considered to interpenetrate with human life" (152). This may be why I find it difficult to lump the nonhumans together with a single, simple word or phrase.

4. A tourism TV commercial ran during the 2011 summer that showed two Cherokee men (one being Bo Taylor of the Museum of the Cherokee Indian) standing above a gushing waterfall. They spoke in the language to each other, with English subtitles. The one man asked Bo how old the waterfall was, and after a thoughtful pause, Bo answered that he didn't know, but that it wasn't as old as Cherokee culture.

5. Since much of the land surrounding the Qualla Boundary is owned by the National Park Service, the Cherokees have always been forbidden from gathering any wild foods or medicines; however, the NPS first proposed new regulations in April 2015 (McKie, "NPS Proposes") and finalized a new plan in June 2016 (McKie, "NPS to Allow") that would allow enrolled Eastern Band members to legally pick and gather particular plants, such as ramps, in the surrounding lands now called the Great Smoky Mountains National Park as their Ancestors had always done. It took a February 2016 meeting between President Barack Obama and former EBCI Principal Chief Patrick Lambert to move the plan forward.

6. This spring ceremony was appropriated by early settlers in the Southeast, and ramp festivals have popped up all over the mountain states and communities as ramps are now attributed by historians to an intricate part of Appalachian lifestyle and folklore, with little thought or credit given to the Native groups who introduced the pungent plant to the newcomers.

7. Thirty miles of mountain streams are stocked with mainly trout, while fishing tournaments throughout the summer are a big part of the tourism industry on the Qualla Boundary. Fishing regulations are enforced through the EBCI Fish and Game Department of the tribe (www.fishcherokee.com).

8. *Sgi* to Paint Clan elder (Auntie) Joanna Meyers for the kind gift of Geniusz's book.

9. For example, the Hopi of the Southwest desert, in their epic Creation story, believe they "came into being when the people emerged from the Lower World through an opening in the earth" (Courlander 9). The emergence form of Creation is a common theme in a number of Southwest tribes.

10. Arch gives the example of how when he is looking for medicine plants, upon finding the kind he needs, he will pass up the first six plants until he comes upon the seventh one. Then he will step back and watch that seventh plant for it to give him a sign that it is willing to give up its life to him. Usually, he says, it will be a leaf moving or a part of the plant that is growing in a different direction than the rest that will be an identifier for him. In this way, the medicine plant is communicating with the human—but only if they're prepared to listen and watch.

11. Once a month, on the Eastern Cherokee territory, a group of language speakers gather at the New Kituwah Immersion Academy for purposes of speaking in the language, teaching others, sharing new developments in language promotion, and to discuss the need and methods to create "new" words for the language to give names to things that did not exist within Cherokee culture of old. Also, once every three months, a Cherokee language consortium group of speakers from all three bands of Cherokees meet either in Oklahoma or North Carolina to work on the creation of new words.

12. Mooney refers to this story, rightly so, as "The First Fire," which is an accurate and appropriate title. In another book called *Native American Legends*, editor George Lankford tells the story almost word-for-word from the Mooney book; however, he labels it "The Theft of Fire" (Lankford 66), a name that makes the brave actions by the birds, reptiles, and animals sound like a crime. The title makes no sense and is somewhat insulting and demeaning when one considers the selfless courage of the nonhumans in their efforts to help all creatures. It suggests an attempt to sensationalize an important and sacred origin story. After all, how can fire be "stolen" when it's meant for everyone?

13. The little water spider is held in such high esteem by modern Cherokees that its likeness adorns many personal articles such as tattoos, T-shirts, beadwork, and other crafts, and is seen as the main image on the logo for the Museum of the Cherokee Indian. This Fire story is also presented over the speaker system at the museum during daily visits by tourists and again shows how even the smallest of creatures is necessary in the circle of life.

14. Ana was Cherokee from Oklahoma and worked with her husband on several manuscripts of Cherokee stories from her band, including their 1961 *Friends of Thunder: Folktales of the Oklahoma Cherokee*.

15. Many thanks to Cherokee elder and WCU language instructor Tom Belt for his help in translation. He suggests that this name may be linked with the giant hero, Tsutlakalv, who was so large that he could step over mountains and may have swung on the grapevines that grow throughout Cherokee country. There will be more about this important figure in chapter 3.

16. The most famous example of usurping an Indigenous sacred site is Mt. Rushmore, with the profiles of four American presidents dominating and desecrating

the sacred Black Hills of the Lakota people, who were systematically rounded up during the violent genocidal attacks known as the Plains Indian Wars.

17. This is the same pronunciation as Kanati. Mooney's variant is Kana'ti.
18. For further reading, see Theda Perdue's *Cherokee Women* and Sara Gwyneth Parker's PhD dissertation, "The Transformation of Cherokee Appalachia."
19. Generally, the person who committed murder was either offered up by their own clan for the victim's clan to do with as they wished; that person could either be killed or banished and sent to a white or peace town.
20. Also known as a townhouse. This term comes into play in other oral stories, such as when the bears held council in their townhouse in "The Origin of Disease and Medicine," to be discussed in this chapter.
21. My son, Sgigi (Dalton), and I began attending Green Corn ceremonies in 1997 (and later on my Haudenosaunee husband) held in Big Cove at the Raven Rock grounds. My husband and I had our wedding ceremony there in 2008. I will only address what is shared by others in written text, as we are told at the stomp grounds that what goes on there stays there and is not to be recorded in any form. I respect those responsibilities.
22. This is similar to the Haudenosaunee story of Sky Woman's daughter, who died in childbirth delivering her twin sons. When Sky Woman buried her daughter, she laid the plants she had saved from the Sky World from which she fell onto her daughter's grave. After her burial, certain plants began to grow in the ground above the daughter—corn, beans, and squash grew above her head, tobacco grew from her heart, and the strawberry plant grew from where her feet were. We see again how a woman's body offered the main staples that provide so much food and medicine. The story can be found on pages 3–4 of the Creation story in *Words That Come before All Else: Environmental Philosophies of the Haudenosaunee*.
23. In his Jungian analysis, G. Keith Parker suggests that Selu's death may have been a "symbolic death" that allows for something new to be resurrected—much as in dreams and in the way Carl Jung would have interpreted such an event (75). It is an understandable interpretation; however, Selu's giving of her own life was not simply symbolic, much like the death of Jesus Christ was not simply symbolic.
24. A beautiful statue of Selu as a young woman with a basket of corn graces the front entrance of Cherokee Harrah's Casino on the Qualla Boundary to greet the mainly non-Cherokee visitors. The statue, created by the talented artist Jenean Hornbuckle, an EBCI enrolled member, is quite beautiful as it is bronze and gleams in the frequent North Carolina sunshine. Many young Cherokee women carry the name of the Corn Mother as well.
25. Carney's book is entitled *Eastern Band Cherokee Women: Cultural Persistence in Their Letters and Speeches* and takes a look at the way women of the EBCI went

away to boarding schools like Carlisle and Haskell to learn a trade (like nursing) but never forgot their heritage and found strength in being Cherokee while adapting new lifestyles and teachings. Many of these women brought their new skills back to the reservation and accomplished great things for their people.

26. This fact may be one reason why today's Eastern Band storytellers choose not to tell the full story; this is part of the friendly harmonious way that Cherokees engage with their visitors—more on this area of the Cherokee worldview will be offered in chapter 4.

27. For more on this, see Rowena McClinton's essay "Cherokee and Christian Expressions of Spirituality through First Parents: Eve and Selu" in the 2017 book *The Native South: New Histories and Enduring Legacies*.

28. I must note here that Mooney uses the term "man" in his version, which reveals that his Euro-western perspective is clearly exclusionary of women. I choose to use humans.

29. Mooney notes that since the Yona found no way to stop the People in killing the Bear people that the hunter does not ask the pardon of a bear when it is killed for food. I would challenge that claim based on the present-day conduct of the Eastern Cherokees who hunt. They have been taught to always pray over the body of any animal they've killed, and Mooney's claim does not reflect the specific ways that hunters conduct prayer rituals for the various animals who give up their life. In fact, some will not hunt nor eat bear meat because of the ancient story that tells how an entire village of Cherokees were willingly turned into bears; in other words, it is strongly believed that bears were once people.

30. Kuwahi or Clingman's Dome, which is between Swain County, North Carolina, and Sevier County, Tennessee, has an elevation of 6,643 feet and is the second highest peak east of the Mississippi River, after Mt. Mitchell in North Carolina, which is 6,684 feet (www.clingmansdome.com).

31. This is a sacred story that is shared orally and never written down, and I respect that sacredness.

32. In fact, prayer before each meal was part of ancient spirituality, as we are told today that the first bite taken of a meal should be chewed a bit and spit on the ground, giving an offering and thanks back to Earth Mother.

33. *Kawi* is the plural form of *Ahwi*, or a single deer. Kawi is also the origin of Cowee, which is the name of the old village and mound, Cowee, that I discuss in chapter 5.

34. This is very important, as the mountains are home to poisonous snakes like the copperhead, cottonmouth, and the eastern diamond, timber, and pygmy rattlesnakes ("Amphibians and Reptiles of North Carolina").

35. My father was a self-taught pipe maker, and I am the caretaker of several pipes. The first one he made for me when I was sixteen is a small woman's pipe with a rattlesnake design wrapped around the stem. My youngest brother, Chuck Muse, also took up the art, and I have one of his pipes, as does my son.

36. Blowguns are made of long river cane, and contests are still held during the Fall Festival each year for Cherokees of all ages to compete for prizes.
37. For some medicines, it is only necessary to take some of the leaves or bark and leave the plant intact and alive. In other cases, it is the root that is vital, and taking that part, of course, kills a part of or the entire plant. Root medicine is often the strongest for that reason and the most potent in curative value—sometimes too strong.
38. This is the world the Cherokee hope to climb to, which is another step of life where we will all be happy and healthy. Therefore, existence on Earth is not the only place where life goes on, and it can be viewed as simply the early stage of our entire life's journey.
39. The Tsalagi word for the Creator is *Unelanvhi*, pronounced *ooh-nay-lah-nuh-hee*.
40. Mooney does not define who the Little Men are, but they could be either the Thunder Boys, who are referred to as the Little Men in the previous story of Kanati and Selu's two sons, or they could be some of the Little People, who will be discussed in chapter 3. These Little Men are clearly the medicine people or healers.
41. Today's environmental issues of climate change and the dangers presented by the depletion of the ozone layer and the connection of ultraviolet rays from the sun causing skin cancer should be viewed as a serious imbalance and disharmony upon the Earth and within the Sky World.
42. This is a complicated term for frightening yet marvelous creatures who should be avoided. More explanation is offered in the next two chapters.

Chapter 2

Note about the chapter title: Dusgaseti is the plural form of the word *Usgaseti*, pronounced *ooh-shka-say-tee*. There are several definitions of this word—one may seem more negative and another more positive in its connotation. Even creatures who are "dreadful" can also be "wondrous," leaving us to truly marvel at them; again, this multivalence shows the complicated balance of things within the Cherokee world.

The word *Tskili* means both witch and, as noted in Mooney's story of "The First Fire," it's also the name for the horned owl. Human witches are rumored to be able to turn into a horned owl, which makes a terrifying sound.

1. *Aniyvwi* is often used to refer to all types of Native people, much like *Onkwehonwe* in the Haudenosaunee languages or *Anishinaabe* in the Ojibway language.
2. Mooney spells his name as Tsul'kalu', while UKB elder and language instructor Tom Belt offers a spelling that is more correct.
3. Uktena is pronounced *ook-tain* or *ook-tain-uh* and in some dialects *yook-tain-uh*.
4. I must note that I'll use the masculine pronoun "he" for consistency since Owle and Mooney refer to it as "he," although there are, no doubt, female Uktena.
5. Parker's best-known work is *Seneca Myths and Folktales*, which was published in 1923, just about thirty years after Mooney's manuscript was registered with the Smithsonian Institute.

6. Mooney notes that *akta* is the word for eye but can also mean strong looker or keen-eyed because anything within the Uktena's range of vision is always seen and cannot escape being discovered (459). The *Dictionary of the Cherokee Language* spells it *a-gi-ta* for eye with the *i* being silent, thus *agta* (55).

7. The most recent retelling of this story that I heard while living on the Boundary from 2010 to 2013 was from Cherokee historian and EBCI cultural resource officer, T. J. Holland, who is director of the Junaluska Museum in the Snowbird community of the reservation, during a storytelling event February 27, 2013, at the New Kituwah Academy. He even had a slide of a very old newspaper article from Tennessee that showed a non-Native man who had pulled a horned serpent from a river there; however, I am unable to obtain any accurate source from which the news article came.

8. The state's name comes from the original name of an ancient Cherokee village Tanasi, pronounced *Tah-nah-see*.

9. For more reading on the Cherokee's direct involvement as Confederate soldiers in the Civil War, see *Storm in the Mountains: Thomas' Confederate Legion of Cherokee Indians and Mountaineers*, by Vernon H. Crow. In my family, both of my father's great-grandfathers died fighting for the southern army at the Battle of Vicksburg, Mississippi. We don't know if they were part of Thomas's Legion.

10. I have personal experience with this modern danger, as my son, who was eight years old at the time, was warned not to go swimming and tubing in the Oconaluftee one particular August afternoon, but some friends insisted on going. He fell violently ill that evening with a high fever and chills and remained sick for several days; he fully believed, as do I, that the Uktena made him sick that hot summer day, as he hadn't been exposed to anyone who was sick.

11. Other creatures may have benefited from the Uktena's healing powers, but the stories only speak of human interaction.

12. It is not unusual to find such small crystals on a normal walk through the woods, which I personally have done on my aunt's farm in Tellico Plains, Tennessee. It is also interesting to note that several other religions, particularly those known as "New Age," practice healing rituals with crystals, and we are all familiar with the use of crystal balls to foretell the future from other cultures around the world such as the Roma (previously called gypsies).

13. I must note that even though the word "Eskimo" is commonly used in the United States, it is considered a grave insult for Inuit people as it is a derogatory term. Thanks to Diane Obed from Hopedale Nunatsiavut, an Innu friend with her MA in Atlantic Canada studies, for this explanation. I'd also like to note that it is a shame that the name and identity of this Inuit knowledge holder is not given in the Swann text because I would like to list his name.

14. Mooney refers to him as Stone Man, but Cherokees call him Stonecoat, so I choose to use this term.

15. In the course of three years listening to many storytellers and orators around the Qualla Boundary, I found that Stonecoat is spoken of with great regard and even respect for the medicine formulas and knowledge as well as the hunting songs he shared with the People before he died. His gift is spoken of more than his tendency to kill and eat humans.

16. I overheard a group of young children, under the age of eight, talking about Spearfinger while preparing for an outdoor event at the Kituwah Mound, which is surrounded by wooded areas—the type of place she may have frequented. One older child assured the others that Spearfinger was nowhere near them but lived instead in Tennessee.

17. It helps to consider that Mooney was not writing down the stories for the Cherokees but rather for his colleagues within the Bureau of Ethnology and no doubt felt he needed to find comparisons within Euro-American culture to help them begin to understand Cherokee culture. For a Tsalagi audience today, of course, some of these terms such as "ogress" seem an uncomfortable translation.

18. I must point out here that it is/was not only women who were Tskilis, as many are/were men as well. For more Tskili stories, see the Mooney book or Robert J. Conley's *Witch of Goingsnake,* or *Friends of Thunder: Folktales of the Oklahoma Cherokees,* by Ana and Jack Kilpatrick.

19. In ancient times, there were prayers and formulas to keep Tskili away; no one knows how many formulas there may have been, and Mooney certainly does not have any recorded among the sacred songs and formulas in his book. There is a story by Robert Bushyhead in Duncan's *Living Stories of the Cherokee* entitled "Formula against Screech Owls and Tskilis" (176–78). In this story, Bushyhead gives a formula that is clearly a postcolonizer one, as he mentions swords.

20. The use of modern Western-based health services and hospitals, which often keep the Native patient there until their death, upsets the traditional practice of allowing the dying to pass on to the Spirit World from their own bed and home. Many older Cherokees still believe a Tskili could be lurking nearby, waiting to suck out their life.

21. I had the honor and privilege of visiting with Robert J. Conley in his office at Western Carolina University. I asked him about my favorite book of his, *The Witch of Goingsnake,* and whether the stories in it had actually come from oral stories. He chuckled and asked me how I was able to tell that, and I told him each story begged to be read out loud—and since I've worked as a radio journalist, I recognized the same style of writing for the ear. Robert confirmed that he had heard all the stories in the collection while he was growing up and decided to write them down. Since Robert has crossed over to the Spirit world, I greatly treasure my copy with his autograph inside.

Chapter 3

1. I'm grateful to my sister, Bear Taylor, for gifting me with her copy of this rare book.
2. Snowbird is reservation land but is located about forty miles away (near the town of Robbinsville) from the main land mass known as the Qualla Boundary. Since it's far removed from the heavy tourism trade, community members have maintained more of the traditions and language than "downtown" Cherokee. There will be more discussion about the Snowbird Cherokees in chapter 4.
3. I must note that I have never heard anyone use the singular form of the word, Little Person. Even if there is thought to be only one, he or she is referred to as *a* Little People.
4. Some community members whom I visited with, such as Elders Walter and Teresa Rattler, have shared their personal stories of frightful encounters, but as these are more personal in nature, I will not include details of those narratives.
5. I've been told that if a Little People in your house is being too mischievous and causing too many problems, it's time to leave a plate of food out for them, because there's a chance they are upset with you for not taking care of them. This simply involves making an extra plate of the family supper and setting it out overnight. They'll eat what they want, and their preference is for traditional foods.
6. Not only do the closely related cousins of the Cherokees, the Haudenosaunee (Iroquois) in the Northeast, have many varied yet similar stories of their own Little People, but Little People are also a part of the Indigenous cultures of the Northwest Coast area of Turtle Island; for example, see Eden Robinson's award-winning novel *Monkey Beach*, borne out of her own Haisla/Heiltsuk cultures in British Columbia.
7. Tsutlakalv is pronounced *Zhoo-tlah-kah-luh* or, more recently, spelled Judaculla and pronounced *Joo-duh-kuh-lah*. Judaculla is the modern form with which even non-Cherokees in the area are familiar and have appropriated to some extent.
8. The name means "where the Nunehi live," one of many such places (Belt, "Lecture"). White settlers called the stark, rugged mountaintop the "Devil's Courthouse" and started a "legend" that claims a cave inside is where the devil holds court. Despite the fact there is no devil or supreme evil being within the Cherokee belief system, the name has stuck and a sacred place now has a sinister label through colonizer overwriting.
9. There seems to be no memory or record of her name or clan.
10. I will not use the term "normal" because it is believed that every being looks exactly the way they are supposed to look; calling something normal or abnormal is completely inaccurate, and no such words exist in this Native language.
11. The Tsalagi use many masks, such as clan masks and masks for the Booger dance. There is one particular Booger mask with slanted eyes that looks somewhat like Inuit or Asian faces. It could be Tsutlakalv.

12. As explained in my first chapter, we should remember that Kanati, the Great Hunter, originally kept the animal beings in a cave, and they were prevented from escaping by the large boulder he placed there and rolled back when he wanted to shoot one for dinner. His two sons moved the huge rock and let the creatures escape; they have been free to roam the woods and hills ever since. Mooney has several hunting "formulas" or songs in his book, and some mention Kanati; Tsutlakalv is not spoken of, but Mooney only has a few songs, when in reality there were hundreds and perhaps thousands of hunting songs and prayers.

13. It is a well-known fact among Eastern Cherokees that the Elders who shared their stories with Mooney, such as Swimmer, Ayosta, and John Ax, did not tell Mooney many things because he was not a Cherokee and did not need to know the more sacred and spiritual details. Meanwhile, Mooney suggests that the storytellers' memories were not that good at times and they were frail. Holland disputes this and argues that those Elders knew their stories well and simply chose not to share certain things with the Yunega ethnographer and so withheld such information. This is in keeping with the Cherokee value of not giving offense.

14. In fact, Mooney used a number of white settlers whom he met and recorded their versions of some of the Cherokee stories; for example, see page 474, note 77, where Mooney states he got the great leech story from Swimmer and Chief Smith, and confirmed it with Wafford, a white man married to a Cherokee woman. These differing versions are included in his notes section (pages 428–505), which follows the translated stories.

15. Holland notes that Mooney spells this Nunnehi, which has become the accepted spelling in the area but is not proper according to some Cherokee speakers; there are no double consonant sounds in the language. Here I choose to spell it the proper way, which was suggested by the speakers with whom Holland talked.

16. *Cold Mountain* is the name of a 1997 novel by Charles Frazier that was turned into a Hollywood movie about the American Civil War; sadly, no mention is made of the Cherokee story of this sacred site.

17. Wi is pronounced *wee* and (along with *hi* and *gi*) simply means place, town, or village. Town residents of Cullowhee often have a sticker on their car that says WHEE and do not know that it means nothing more than place or town in the Tsalagi language. Cherokee speakers chuckle at this.

18. Recognizing the tremendous value of the artifact, the farmer (Parker family) who owns the field in which Judaculla Rock sits protected and cared for it for many years—a true act of Gadugi by non-Cherokees—until Jackson County took over the responsibility and created a small park for it. A bilingual sign is set nearby, explaining in both Tsalagi and English its designation as a "Cherokee Cultural Heritage Site." There is now an elevated wooden walkway around it where visitors can view it from above and marvel at the "pictographs" drawn

by the ancients. I must mention that a long black snake also seems to be the caretaker there; he/she followed my husband and me closely until we finally walked away and left the area.

19. According to Davy Arch, there are many soapstone deposits throughout the mountains, if one knows where to look for them, that have always provided the soft rock used for some pottery, pipe bowls, and other carving. Arch says there are many colors or types of the soapstone available and explains how small bowls of the stone were used by medicine people and healers to carry hot coals with them for purposes of healing and purification of warriors before going into battle. These bowls would have been wrapped in leather for carrying (Personal interview).

20. This sounds like a Cherokee word but is instead a settler corruption of the Tsalagi name for the river—*daksi-gi* or "place of the turtles," pronounced *dok-shee-gee.*

21. Most likely another example of how Mooney simply did not understand the cultural truths of what he was being told in his early days among the Eastern Cherokees; again, his views changed considerably the more time he spent on the Qualla Boundary.

22. There is a replica of the seven-sided council house at the Oconaluftee Indian Village in Cherokee, N.C.

23. On the Qualla Boundary, there is a group called the Cherokee Free Labor Company, which provides house improvements, repairs, lawn care, etc. for needy or disabled enrolled members all year around. These volunteers even help with things like digging graves for families who cannot afford to pay. This is in addition to the annual Gadugi "Day of Sharing" in the late spring already mentioned in my introduction.

24. There is no Cherokee word for mysterious. *Usgaseti* would be the closest word to describe that English notion.

25. American ginseng is one example of a powerful medicinal plant that many Cherokees still gather within reservation lands for personal use or to sell, and it is quite limited and hard to find. A great deal of the ginseng grows in the parkland, and park officials spray the plants with a dye that stays with the plant, and if anyone is caught having picked the dyed plant, they face steep fines— including Cherokees. So, these valuable plants stay in the ground, and many see this as a tremendous waste of a rare and powerful medicine. However, many non-Cherokees in the South make a living from picking and selling American ginseng, and it is evidently a cut-throat competition as the profits are high, as is the risk of getting caught and fined for poaching and trespassing on private property. The History Channel carries a show that glorifies the exploits of some of the men who illegally harvest ginseng in the South (*Appalachian Outlaws*).

26. Kanienkehaka is a Mohawk. This is the word they call themselves, pronounced *guh-yun-gah-hah-gah.*

27. *Tsola* is Cherokee for tobacco.

28. Nunehi is pronounced *noo-nay-hee*.

29. The Nunehi look just like any other Cherokees and are the same size as humans, unlike the Little People who are said to be around two feet high or around the height of adult knees.

30. I have had the exact spot pointed out for me by Louise Goings as we drove by on our way to Kituwah Mound. It is understood that you do not go swimming there.

31. This is the geographical name given by the U.S. Park Service to that group of mountains that border the Great Smoky Mountains and the Blue Ridge Mountains, so named for their treeless, rocky peaks.

32. As mentioned earlier, Cherokee villages were built with a mound and townhouse on top as the center of the community. Non-Cherokee settlers have often dug up such mounds in hopes of finding relics or skeletal remains, in this particular case using Cherokee workers who needed a job. The mounds were *not* used as burial sites in ancient times.

33. Besides the main thirteen ceremonies that coincided with the thirteen moons of the year, there were other, smaller rituals that took place, such as coming-of-age and possibly naming ceremonies.

34. This is the spelling Mooney uses, which T. J. Holland notes modern speakers say is incorrect.

35. No doubt this is in connection with the sun rising in the east and with the Cherokees and all others beings coming from the Sky Island in the eastern sky.

36. Seneca territory is what is now called western New York State. There are stories that say their young men could make the trip from their Allegheny foothills down to Cherokee territory on foot in just about a week's time.

37. So-called for their geographical locations. Lower towns were down in the southernmost valleys and always near rivers; the middle towns were up in the mountains and were also based close to water sources. The overhill towns were on the other side of the mountain range and into what is now Tennessee and Georgia.

38. Fortunately, the Nikwasi Mound has never been excavated by archaeologists and remains untouched in the center of the town of Franklin, North Carolina, unlike so many other Cherokee village mounds that have been desecrated in one way or another.

39. Shortened version of y*unega* or *yonega*, which simply means white or English people/language.

40. As opposed to the gray coats worn by Confederate soldiers of the South.

41. Indeed, the village of Nikwasi, like twenty-plus other middle towns including the Mothertown of Kituwah, had been burned to the ground twice—once in 1761 by the British during the French and Indian War and the second time in 1776 during the Revolutionary War by American general Griffith Rutherford whose campaign decimated a large portion of the tribe's residential land and

forced the Cherokees to sign yet another treaty, giving away even more homeland. There will be more information in chapter 5.

42. Glowing orbs of light have been seen throughout the Cherokee homeland over the centuries, often in particular areas, such as near where the old boarding school used to stand on the Qualla Boundary and around the area near where the old Cherokee hospital once stood. These orbs hover above the ground, and many Cherokees believe they are Spirits, according to Davy Arch, who tells stories when he conducts the autumn "haunted hayrides" for the Oconaluftee Village.

43. Owle does not name the mountain, but from his description, it sounds like Tsunegvyi.

Chapter 4

Note about the chapter title: I am extremely grateful to my WCU language instructor and elder Tom Belt for his help in arriving at the best title for this chapter. It took a long-distance phone call and a good discussion about the goals of my book before we hammered it out.

1. Pronounced *shee-yoh*, *Siyo* means hello in the language. Oklahoma Cherokees use the older version *Osiyo.*

2. For more information, go to Lloyd Arneach's personal webpage at www.arneach .com.

3. Lloyd was presented with the Mountain Heritage Award in September 2011. For further information, see the Digital Heritage site at http://digitalheritage .org/2012/11/lloyd-arneach-2011.

4. This term is too often used for Native origin stories. Much like the word "myth," it has a somewhat negative connotation, as it is defined as "a story, handed down from the past, which lacks accurate historical evidence but has been, and may still be, popularly accepted as true" (*New Webster's Dictionary* 565). I posit that this term belittles Indigenous oral stories and places them in the realm of fantasy. However, I have found that even Native people use the word sometimes, just because it is familiar for an audience.

5. A description and history of the Great Smoky Mountains National Park can be found on the park's website at www.nps.gov/grsm/index.htm. In addition, see the "Cherokees" webpage at this same website.

6. It took seventeen years to build the roadways and turn the wilderness into the park, which was dedicated in 1940. For further details, see www.gsmnp.com /great-smoky-mountains-national-park/history.

7. For more information about the political situation the Cherokees were forced into by the government at the time, with the threat of land allotment and tribal termination, read chapter 3, "The History of the Qualla Cherokee," in *The Qualla Cherokee: Surviving in Two Worlds,* by Laurence French. Also see chapter 5, "A New Park and a New Deal," in *Cherokee Americans: The Eastern Band of Cherokees in the Twentieth Century,* by John Finger.

8. More information can be found at the various websites for the Eastern Cherokee attractions, such as the museum at www.cherokeemuseum.org and the tourism website for the EBCI at http://visitcherokeenc.com.

9. Once my paternal grandmother's family (Gaston) left the Qualla Boundary, our family has lived entirely off the reservation. My grandmother, Maggie Gaston, grew up with her parents and siblings outside Chattanooga, Tennessee, on a farm her Scottish American father (Thomas L. Gaston) had bought with land settlement money from the Guion-Miller rolls. (*Sgi* to Robin Swayney at the Qualla Library for finding this on microfiche.) Then Grandma married and moved to Sugar Valley, Georgia, which is down the road from New Echota, the old Cherokee capital. My dad (he was the oldest) and his six siblings grew up in Dalton, Georgia; he eventually married my mother and they relocated to Detroit in 1949. The U.S. Census for 1940 for Whitfield County, Georgia, lists my grandfather, Lester Muse, and his children all as "Indian." My grandmother was already deceased, and my father, as eldest, was no longer living at home, so neither is on that 1940 household census. It is shocking to me, given the racism and leftover fear from the Removal, that my grandfather was brave enough to write that down on a federal document.

10. This information was available on a flyer from the American Indian Studies department at UNC Chapel Hill in 2012.

11. Much like Tsutlakalv with his responsibilities within the natural world, as discussed in chapter 3.

12. I've been told there are different ways of spelling this last word—*aksasdohdi*. The spelling I've taken is directly from lesson sheets from language instructor Tom Belt, from the second term of his Cherokee-language course at WCU.

13. It's assumed that he means when the animals came down from the Sky Island during Creation.

14. Paul Zolbrod argues that Native American oral poetry is so powerful that even in comparison to that of ancient Greece, "we [will] find that with or without an alphabetical technology tribal North America is as much a wellspring of poetry as Europe has been" (34).

15. One of the biggest differences between such fables and Indigenous stories is that a moral was always offered at the end by Aesop, while audience members are allowed to determine what a Native story means for them personally.

16. The word "magic," as I discussed earlier in chapter 1, has a number of negative connotations but also several positive connotations, and I believe Lloyd is using the word in a positive vein—given his personality. It may seem like a suitable word to help non-Natives understand the concept of powerful, spiritual Indian medicine that can heal the sick and wounded simply by immersing them in it. Again, any Christians in the audience can easily relate this to the power of baptismal waters or holy water in the Catholic Church. There is also the notion of the "magical" way that oral storytelling can transport the listener to another

place, another time, and allow them to participate in the story by using their imagination, and that is part of the power of "listening" and "feeling" the story. There are many possible reasons he chose to say "magic."

17. There are old stories among the Cherokees that tell of strangers with shiny hats and hair all over their faces—stories that coincide with the brief forays by Spaniards into the mountains of Cherokee territory. Their gold- and fortune-seeking murderous rampages took place more to the south and into the west as they massacred many Native peoples on their quest for the infamous City of Gold. It is believed they were not interested in the Cherokees, for, at that time, there were no reports of the yellow rock in their area.

18. I remember first meeting Freeman when I was just a teenager, as my father considered him a friend and someone he liked to visit and talk with whenever my family visited Cherokee.

19. Dayunisi is the water beetle, or earth diver, from chapter 1.

20. This daily act and close spiritual connection to mountain waters—be they rivers, streams, creeks, or ponds—is so important in Cherokee culture that there is actually a plaque set along the nearby river trail that runs along part of the Oconaluftee River and within the national park land that explains the importance of "going to water." This plaque is part of the historical series that the National Park Service has located along this trail which connects one of their large visitor centers to the reservation. Tourists can walk this natural winding pathway, enjoy the river, and read the plaques that give cultural lessons about the Cherokees from the ancient stories.

21. Owle is referring to one of the most popular animal stories, about how the possum lost his beautiful tail due to his vanity and self-centeredness.

22. Like many Cherokees, my parents and grandparents grew up as Southern Baptists and firmly believed in whippings with a switch or a leather belt to punish children for wrongdoings and to prevent them from further bad behavior; although many Cherokees now have indeed converted to Christianity and some, no doubt, do use corporal punishment, a large majority still favor the ancient, nonaggressive method of raising children.

23. *Mitakuye Oyasin* is a well-known prayer phrase usually spoken in the Lakota language, which translates to "I am related to all that is" (Battiste and Henderson 50). Vine Deloria Jr., a Lakota himself, points out that speaking this phrase is not simply religious but "also has a secular purpose, which is to remind us of our responsibility to respect life and to fulfill our covenantal duties" (52).

24. There is no Bear clan among the Cherokees; however, one of the ancient stories tells how an entire village of Cherokees became bears by choice, so the bear is generally thought of as being a brother or sister human, as evidenced by bear's ability to walk on two feet.

25. I know that in hearing Freeman's story myself, I was able to envision what those thousands of chestnut trees must have looked like and also to relate it to

learning how to make traditional Cherokee chestnut bread with some of the other women from the stomp ground, thus embodying his story in my spirit. Many *sgi* to Amy Grant Walker for teaching a bunch of us women how to make chestnut bread.

26. There's not space enough here for a full discussion of the numerous treaties that the Cherokees were forced to sign and that were subsequently broken, first by the British and then by the new American government. For a more detailed accounting of the treaties and subsequent land loss, see *The Cherokee Indian Nation*, by Duane H. King; *The Cherokee People*, by Thomas E. Mails; and *The Eastern Band of Cherokees, 1819–1900* and *Cherokee Americans: The Eastern Band of Cherokees in the Twentieth Century*, by John Finger.

27. The thirty-fourth treaty (1835) was the illegal one known as the Treaty of New Echota, which was signed by a small group of Cherokee men who desired removal to Indian Territory because they were the wealthier mixed-bloods who owned slaves and also felt that removal was inevitable. These men were not authorized to sign anything because they did not speak for the People. Because of their violation of the laws of the Cherokees, they were subsequently put to death after they arrived in what became Oklahoma. That illegal treaty essentially signed away all remaining Cherokee lands in the Southeast for $5 million, a tract of land in the West, and some other concessions (Finger, *Eastern Band* 16).

28. Will Thomas, or Wil-Usdi (little Will for his short height), was a young white boy who was being raised by his widowed mother in the nearby town of Waynesville, North Carolina, and had gone to work in a store in Cherokee territory. Yonaguska was impressed by the hard-working young man and chose to adopt him into the band, thus making him a Cherokee citizen. Since Indians could not own land after the Removal, the remnant Cherokees worked hard and gave their money to the trusted Wil-Usdi, who bought tracts of land and put it all into his name, in the plan to amass enough tracts to create a land base for the remaining Cherokees (Finger, *Eastern Band* 13). For more information and history, see the books previously listed in footnote 26.

29. Qualla was the name of the nearest ancient village to what is now downtown Cherokee or the business and political hub of the Boundary. "Boundary" is an older term that denotes how boundary lines were drawn to separate Indian-owned land and white-owned lands. Various historical signs around the Boundary and nearby towns show this term.

30. We will also see this philosophy of buying back their own land in the final chapter, as the EBCI work toward legally reclaiming several sacred sites.

31. *Sgi* means thank you, and *Denadagohvya* translates to something like "until our paths cross again" or "until we see each other again."

32. This is the Cherokee form of the English name Charley. Since there are no *r*'s in the Tsalagi language, it is pronounced something like *zha-lee*.

33. The title of the play is taken from the Bible verse Psalm 121:1, which reads, "I will lift up mine eyes unto the hills, from whence cometh my help" (King James Version).

34. The outdoor drama, simply referred to as "the drama" by most Eastern Cherokees, runs Monday through Saturdays during the tourist season from May 1 to mid-August, when school resumes and the children in the cast must return to classes.

35. This is a remote and fairly traditional community that is part of the Qualla Boundary, which is about a forty-mile car drive from downtown Cherokee, where the main business hub is with all the tourist attractions, council house and chief's office, hospital, casino, etc. Snowbird is closer to the Nantahala Mountains, another range in the Appalachians.

36. These stockades were nothing more than open-air, fenced-in pens, which offered no protection from the elements and no place for outhouse facilities. Vermin and rats ran rampant. Approximately four thousand Cherokees died from starvation, dehydration, dysentery, and contagious sicknesses even before the actual march to the west began. There are many excellent books about the trail; for a full historical accounting see any of the following: *The Cherokee Indian Nation: A Troubled History*, by Duane H King; *After the Trail of Tears*, by William G. McLoughlin; *The Cherokee Nation*, by Robert J. Conley; *The Cherokee Trail of Tears*, by David G. Fitzgerald and Duane H. King; *Trail of Tears: The Rise and Fall of the Cherokee Nation*, by John Ehle; and *The Cherokee Removal: A Brief History with Documents* and *The Cherokee Nation and the Trail of Tears*, by Theda Perdue and Michael D. Green, to name a few.

37. The Cherokees called this removal the "path/road where they cried," which became more commonly known as the Trail of Tears. Many *sgi* to my adopted brother Michael Thompson (Deer Clan) and his language teacher Garfield Long.

38. Jeanette Henry, the editor of the Indian Historian Press, which published Bedford's book in 1972, acknowledges Bedford as a Minsee Indian; however, my research does not show any such tribe/First Nation, and this could possibly be a typo and should read Munsee (Delaware or Lenni-Lenape) instead.

39. I must note here the problems with a term like "patriotism," which Bedford too deeply connects to American patriotism in his efforts to appeal to non-Cherokee readers and position Tsali as an American hero. I would not use the term, and I have not found its usage in the writings of any other Native scholar in addressing Native nationalism.

40. These early removers were historically referred to as the "Old Settlers"; for further information, see *The Cherokee Nation and the Trail of Tears*, by Theda Perdue and Michael Green, 146–48.

41. This is one of the translations of *Ani-Yunwiyah*, as is the Original or Real Human Beings.

42. For more on clan laws and responsibilities, see Theda Perdue's *Cherokee Women*, 142–43.

43. For more information on the Eastern Cherokee role in the Civil War, see *Storm in the Mountains: Thomas' Confederate Legion of Cherokee Indians and Mountaineers,* by Vernon H. Crow.

44. The sentiment at the time of Removal was that if the Cherokees became legal American citizens, they could not be dispossessed of their homes and lands; however, it took many years of vigorous campaigning by Wil Usdi to finally get citizenship for the remaining Cherokees. See John R. Finger's work *The Eastern Band of Cherokees, 1819–1900.* Native Americans overall did not receive American citizenship and the right to vote until 1924, three years after American women won voting rights.

45. While traveling to New Echota, Georgia, for the 175th commemoration of the Trail of Tears, I came across an historical plaque in the town of Ellijay that referred to the "evacuation" of the Cherokees having begun in that area. One of the stockades that held the captured people had stood there in Gilmer County. I felt incensed at this misleading word usage, since "evacuation" actually means "to remove someone from a dangerous place" according to the *Merriam-Webster Dictionary* website (www.m-w.com). The plaque gave the impression the Georgia Militia had done the Cherokees a favor ("Garden Club of Ellijay").

Chapter 5

1. There are over thirteen thousand enrolled EBCI members, with about 60 percent of them living on the Qualla Boundary, according to the Cherokee Chamber of Commerce website.

2. I mention these because they are so important for sharing the ancient spiritual teachings and ceremonies, but I will not be discussing them, for those words are only meant for Giduwah people and any visitors to the grounds.

3. The Eastern Cherokee speakers meet monthly, and every three months a gathering is held of speakers from all three bands of Cherokees, and the location switches back and forth between North Carolina and Oklahoma.

4. This is one of the oldest continuous such fairs held on a Native American reservation. October 2012 saw the Eastern Cherokee celebrate the 100th Fall Fair, which I was fortunate to attend and participate in. The five-day autumn event began as a way to celebrate the harvest, much like many fall fairs across the United States, but along with prize ribbons for the best vegetables and fruit grown, awards are given out for such traditional Cherokee arts and crafts as pottery, basket-making, beadwork, sewing, finger-weaving, and wood-carving, along with the more modern Native arts styles. There are also categories in the arts for the young folks, based on age. Ancient games like blowgun shooting, archery, and stickball are also featured. It is a time when Cherokee culture and heritage is put on display and honored. Many feel the fair takes the place of the ancient harvest or Green Corn ceremonies that were held in each village. The traditional Green Corn ceremony was lost for many decades before being revived

by Walker Calhoun in the early 1990s at the Raven Rock stomp grounds in Big Cove.

5. There are many events centered around young Cherokees, such as the Growing Ones Youth Powwow held during the Memorial Day weekend as well as a special awards day for the end of the school year, which sees the top achievers recognized by the chief and tribal council, to name two.

6. This is the eastern woodland box turtle, which lives in Carolinian woods. Cherokee women use its shell as leg shakers for stomp dancing, thereby distributing the powerful medicine that Turtle possesses.

7. James Mooney recorded and translated other endings to the Daksi story, which can be found in *Cherokee History, Myths and Sacred Formulas,* 278–79. Littlejohn's version is the better-known one today.

8. This is one of the more familiar stories told in the community and is included in the James Mooney book. This is Littlejohn's version taken from her storytelling collection *Cherokee Legends* on cassette tapes; because the stage version consisted of a fair bit of physical movement by the children and stage directions given to them, it made more sense to use in this book a transcribed version that Littlejohn had told before.

9. Many who have written about Native oral stories make a great deal about the trickster character within each Indigenous culture, and some would say that for the Cherokee, it is often the rabbit or fox. Anyone familiar with Joel Chandler Harris's slave stories of Br'er Rabbit and Br'er Fox in his *The Complete Tales of Uncle Remus* will recognize many of the Cherokee origins in those tales; indeed, some of those Cherokee stories were published in the late 1820s in the bilingual newspaper, the *Cherokee Phoenix,* while Harris published his collection in 1880. I feel the trickster has been overblown, and some non-Native theorists often look for a trickster where none exists. In the Cherokee worldview, we are all capable of being mischievous, just as any animal, bird, fish, or plant can also behave in that way while simultaneously holding the more positive traits. In his *Cree Narrative Memory,* Neil McLeod notes that the English word "trickster" means something that is not truthful. He posits that "[t]he term trickster is part of this same trickery, making Indigenous narratives conceptually empty and potentially devoid of truth" (97).

10. Indeed, there are such wonderful lessons to be learned from this popular Cherokee story about the possum's vanity that Gregory Cajete refers to it in his chapter "Animals in Native Myth and Reality," noting that it is a story about human frailties (165–66).

11. This is one of the many ways of spelling the word *Duyvkta* of which we have been speaking. The written English version of any Cherokee word is spelled out phonetically, and spellings vary by individual, according to their dialect.

12. I must note that most of the participants are young; however, there are occasionally folks over forty who have been nominated to take this leadership training,

and it is the program's graduates who nominate others whom they deem to have the right mind-set and values to learn how to be a good community leader.

13. Many *sgi* to Kevin Jackson for this interpretation—one of many community members who have helped me with the language.

14. The Cherokees, both in the East and the West, were pulled into the Civil War, even though leaders tried to make it known the Nation was neutral. Some of the members of what became the Eastern Band served in the regiment named for Wil Usdi, or Will Thomas (the Thomas Regiment), while the Oklahoma Cherokees became involved in a number of ways as soldiers. Again, for more information, see Vernon Crow's *Storm in the Mountains: Thomas' Confederate Legion of Cherokee Indians and Mountaineers.*

15. Most of the spots where I have used ellipses are the places where Wahde switched over into speaking in the language, as he would say the Cherokee words that explained more fully the ancient concepts behind the teachings. Although my personal knowledge of the language is rudimentary and I could certainly grasp the meanings that day, I cannot begin to transcribe the words in the language here. It is remarkable to hear the language portions because one can hear and see the deeply profound concepts and values attached to the long phrases in the language and how difficult it is to translate them. In addition, my recording of his talk was of poor quality because it was a very windy day at the Mothertown. *Sgi* to Michael Thompson for his help with the audio recording.

16. There is a great photo of this particular dance demonstration on the cover of the "ga-du-gi 2014" annual report for the Cherokee Preservation Foundation. Even though we danced in the hot sunshine that day, the picture was Photoshopped to give the appearance of a nighttime stomp, complete with the moon up in the sky. Again, stomps are always held after dark. This photo can be seen at the CPF website at http://cherokeepreservation.org/news-pubs/2014-ga-du-gi -annual-community-report.

17. Recall in chapter 4 Freeman Owle's explanation of the daily ritual of going to water, which started the day for all Cherokees in the two dozen or so villages throughout the land. We are frequently reminded of the power of going to water for our prayers.

18. However, that may be changing, as another Cherokee-owned casino opened in the fall of 2015 in Murphy, North Carolina, which is the largest town close to the Snowbird community and offers employment to enrolled members as well as other local people.

19. This excellent journal began publication in the summer of 1976 and is sponsored by the museum. It is a tremendous source for research into all things Cherokee, with most of the contributions written by scholars and other experts, both Cherokee and non-Cherokee, who have studied the history and culture for many years.

20. Lois Calonehuskie and Gil Jackson (one of my language teachers) were the fieldworkers, and both are from the Snowbird community.

21. Some Cherokees still refer to such doctors as conjurers because they don't only use the plants and herbs but also say prayers, sing songs, and use other items to help with the efficiency of their ministrations and healing.

22. Cherokees of North Carolina and Oklahoma continue to play stickball and often do exhibition games at various events within the community and even for outside events in non-Cherokee towns. For more information on this ancient game, see "Stick Ball" on the website www.cherokee.org/About-The-Nation /Culture/General/Stickball-a-ne-jo-di or the video entitled *"Anetsodi"* produced by stickball expert J. P. Johnson (Gvdutsi doka) of the Cherokee Nation of Oklahoma, which contains old photos and rare footage of the game (www.youtube.com /watch?v=9iXQ_boUiTQ).

23. Although my father could not speak, read, or write Cherokee, he did own a New Testament in the language that he had been gifted. I have inherited that, along with his *Dictionary of the Cherokee Language*, by J. T. Alexander, a book that has proven invaluable in writing this project. To my collection of language books, I have added the *Cherokee-English Dictionary*, by Durbin Feeling from the Cherokee Nation of Oklahoma.

24. It is one of the only times in American history when a sitting president, Andrew Jackson, openly defied a U.S. Supreme Court ruling and refused to put a stop to removal. When Chief John Ross took the legal fight all the way to the top court, Justice John Marshall ruled in favor of the Cherokee Nation. In modern times, there was a social movement afoot throughout what is called Indian Country to petition the White House to have Jackson removed from the twenty-dollar bill. Even the *Washington Post* has run editorial columns advocating for the removal of Jackson (irony noted). President Obama had announced in 2016 that Jackson would be replaced by former slave-turned-abolitionist Harriet Tubman, but in April 2018 the Trump White House postponed the move until 2020.

25. This ancient art is one of many exhibited at the Oconaluftee Indian Village in Cherokee, N.C. Traditional clothing, whether for men or women, often used a woven sash as a belt.

26. There has long been speculation by historians that Andrew Jackson secretly sent word to the Georgia governor of the time, George R. Gilmer, to quickly move forward and order state militia to remove the Cherokees, since the state had already removed the Creek Nation, in defiance of the Supreme Court decision against the Indian Removal Act. For more information, see the *New Georgia Encyclopedia* (www.georgiaencyclopedia.org/articles/history-archaeology/cherokee -removal).

27. There is no need here to describe fully the filth, the mud, the lack of food or the moldy, bug-infested food, the miserable weather conditions, or even the lack of bathroom facilities of any kind. Needless to say, dysentery, dehydration, starvation, and disease took many Cherokees before the actual walk to the west could even

begin. For more reading, turn to John Ehle's *Trail of Tears;* John Finger's *The Eastern Band of Cherokees 1819–1900;* Theda Perdue's *The Cherokee Removal: A Brief History with Documents* and *The Cherokee Nations and the Trail of Tears*—to name a few. For a documented factual account by a soldier involved in this travesty, see "The Diary of Lt. John Phelps" in the *Journal of Cherokee Studies* 21 (2000), or Private John G. Burnett's writings at www.cherokee.org/AboutTheNation /History/TrailofTears/JohnBurnettsStoryoftheTrailofTears.aspx.

28. Wachacha and his brother Junaluska led a group of about fifty Cherokees who all broke away from the march and made their way back from Oklahoma to the mountains; Junaluska years earlier had saved the life of Andrew Jackson when the Cherokees helped the U.S. military defeat the Creeks at the Battle of Horseshoe Bend.

29. These government-sanctioned plaques or markers too often reflect the colonizer version of history. Evidently there are hundreds of markers now throughout the states that the Cherokee Removal traveled through, and it does seem to be generating more interest and learning about the Trail of Tears. There is a website called *Historical Markers Project* that documents all kinds of such markers throughout the United States, but the ones for the Trail of Tears are somewhat mixed in with others, so it is impossible to gauge just how many markers there actually are.

30. This ride takes place in early to mid-June, and the 2018 journey had just taken place as I revised this chapter.

31. There were three particular routes taken by the fifteen thousand Cherokees, who had been divided up into groups with chosen Cherokee men who were trusted to do their best to lead their group. The most dangerous part of the trip clearly was crossing the fast-running Mississippi River.

32. There are a number of famous paintings by American artists of the Trail of Tears, such as a series by Max D. Standley (www.maxdstandley.com/trail_of _tears_series/the_trail_of_tears.html) or one by Robert Lindneux, which can be viewed at www.pbs.org/wgbh/aia/part4/4h1567.html. Of course, there are many works of art by Cherokee artists that render their version of how this travesty unfolded.

33. The Eastern Band is still quite involved with this now-state-owned site that houses the printing press for the *Cherokee Phoenix* newspaper—printed in the Sequoyah syllabary—the nation's courthouse and council house, and a museum. For more information, see http://gastateparks.org/NewEchota.

34. For more information on events held at the Red Clay site, see http://tnstateparks .com/parks/about/red-clay.

35. "Western" is a colloquialism; many folks on the Qualla Boundary used to refer to the Oklahoma Cherokees as the Western Band. I remember hearing it a lot when I was a young teen.

36. My dad used to point out the area "down in the holler" where his family's home had stood, in a very rough and wild valley. There was never really a town or anything, so it was just referred to as Sugar Holler. This is near the Chatsworth Highway, and there are now lavish houses worth a quarter million and more.

37. I'm honored to have spent time with Deer Clan elder Miss Amy Walker, who knew my father, and her daughter Becky Walker. These two women are a source of inspiration for many Tsalagi people.

38. I learned a great deal from Belt's storytelling and oral narratives that went hand-in-hand with learning the language. Many stories, some that I had heard before—along with the unfamiliar ones—became clearer when language was attached and cultural references and landmarks were given specificity and clarity through the language, which is a vital part of the oral tradition.

39. Fire was also taken from the Nikwasi Mound, since it was a holy or sacred site as well, as described in chapter 3. Again, this was the home of the Nunehi Spirit People, or Immortals, so some Cherokees may have preferred to go to Nikwasi, especially if they lived closer to it than the Mothertown.

40. This statistical information is taken from the website for Harvard University's Pluralism Project in their research report entitled "Kituwah Mound, NC" under the category Native Religion. This report is the most concentrated archaeological examination of the sacred site and its history I have found through my research.

41. While living on the Boundary, my husband and I resided in Birdtown, the Qualla community closest to Kituwah. I often took the short drive there to sit and study and enjoy the peace and quiet and the strong spiritual feelings of being around the Ancestors.

42. The money came from the small revenues of the first tribal casino; a newer, larger one has been built since then, and the monies generated from that large casino have led to a great deal more economic growth not only for the Eastern Band but for surrounding communities. This revenue has also led to an upsurge of projects within the Qualla Boundary, enriching the lives of enrolled citizens and allowing for greater independence and self-governance.

43. EBCI communications officer B. Lynne Harlan—who is a poet herself—compiled these speeches for an archive.

44. The Parton house was part of the purchase and now houses the Ernestine Walkingstick women's shelter for the EBCI community.

45. Dugan was the twenty-ninth principal chief from 1995 to 1999. To date, she is the only female EBCI chief.

46. Dr. Riggs became the Sequoyah Distinguished Professor of Cherokee Studies at WCU in 2015. When he spoke at the Kituwah Mound in May 2016 at the twenty-year celebration of the return of the Mothertown (titled "We are Becoming One") with an audience made up of Cherokees from all three bands, it was clear how well respected and loved Riggs is. The fact that he was asked to speak first,

before Chief Dugan, then Vice-Chief Richie Sneed, and others, shows how important his role and his storytelling about Kituwah is to the People.

47. For more information, visit the website for the Georgia Historical Society at https://georgiahistory.com/ghmi_marker_updated/john-ross-home.

48. Each year's celebration has a particular theme; the one for 2012 was "A Prophecy Fulfilled," referring to the return of Kituwah mound and the reunion of the People at the town of origins and to the ancient oral teachings that included a forewarning about the coming of the Yunega or Europeans upon the eastern shores; the loss of the homeland—including the Mothertown—and the forced removal of most of the Giduwah people to the Darkening Land or the West; a near-smothering of the sacred Fire that burns in the center of the stomp grounds; and a return from the West of that Fire, which had been kept burning by certain chosen Cherokee men and women in anticipation of its return to the East so that those sacred Fires could be rekindled. The theme for 2014 was "Let's All Face East" and can be connected to several things—the prophecy of the Fire returning to the East, the origin story that tells how we all came from an island in the eastern sky, and the way we pray to the four directions beginning with the East where the sun rises. The 2015 theme was "Return to the Mothertown."

49. My husband and I were fortunate to attend three of the annual celebrations—one each of the years that we lived on the Qualla Boundary. It was a wonderful experience to hear the stories, share a meal of traditional Cherokee foods, dance some of the animal dances that have been with the People for hundreds of thousands of years, and participate in every way in the regeneration of the culture, including the ceremony for rebuilding the mound.

50. There are spiritual signifiers here, as the red cloth allows for prayers to hold more power, and the Daksi shell carries medicine within it, as evidenced in the story of the Daksi healing itself when its shell was cracked (see chapter 4); this is why the women wear Daksi shells at the stomp grounds. Bringing your own personal offering of dirt to add to the growing Kituwah mound makes each one of us a part of that sacred earth that holds the bones of the Ancestors.

51. My Mohawk husband and I took part in one of these ceremonies, and he chose to offer dirt that he had brought from his family's home at the Six Nations of the Grand River—a fitting symbolic gesture considering the shared origins of the Haudenosaunee and the Giduwah peoples, the hundreds of years of sharing between the two cultures, and the fact that the Tsalagi language is an Iroquoian one.

52. Chief Joyce Dugan does believe that a small area of Kituwah would be a fitting location for a larger language-immersion school—one that would bring entire families together to live and learn for a year or two. She also suggests that an archival facility could be set in a corner of the Mothertown site that was once the dairy portion of the Ferguson farm operations, simply because there are

archives of Cherokee materials all over and these items and documents should be brought back there to create a Cherokee-owned archive collection.

53. Mooney describes how the "everlasting fire" was built in the center of both Kituwah and Nikwasi mounds in a section entitled "The Mounds and the Constant Fire: The Old Sacred Things" (395–97).

54. This quote is taken from McLaughlin's presentation and is included in the news story in the *Cherokee Phoenix* newspaper from Oklahoma.

55. Mooney says that the name Cowee' cannot be translated but suggests it "may possibly mean 'the place of the Deer clan' (Ani'-Kawi')" (377). It is interesting to note that the Cherokee word for "coffee" is spelled *kowi* and also pronounced *kow-ee*. However, that is a newer Cherokee word because coffee was introduced by the Europeans. There is no *f* or "eff" sound in the language, so the People pronounced "coffee" as *kowi*.

56. For more information about the EBCI plans for the Cowee land tract, see Cherokee Preservation Foundation, "Cowee Cultural Corridor Development Project with LTLT," 2014.

57. The title and position of Beloved Man and Beloved Woman are ancient honors that had fallen by the wayside following colonization and the attack upon and burning of so many of the Cherokee villages in the 1760s–70s. This ancient way of showing respect and honor for the men and women who often had been warriors and late in life became peacemakers was reinstituted by the Eastern Band over the last twenty years or so. In particular, certain remarkable women like Maggie Wachacha and Louise Maney were given their title posthumously. Then, more recently, under former chief Michell Hicks, language speakers Ellen Wachacha Bird and Myrtle Driver were each given the honored position of Beloved Woman and Elder, while World War II veteran Jerry Wolfe was named Beloved Man for the Eastern Band, the first one in roughly two centuries. For more information, see "Jerry Wolfe Named Beloved Man" in the *Cherokee One Feather* of April 12, 2013, and "Ellen Bird Named EBCI Beloved Woman" in the *Cherokee One Feather* of November 12, 2013. Sadly, Jerry passed over on March 12, 2018.

Conclusion

1. Bear's real name is Ramona, but nobody calls her that.

2. So called for its grainy subsistence, sugar dirt requires a lot of mixing with manure and good store-bought topsoil; otherwise it is only suitable for a particular few vegetable plants.

3. I feel so fortunate that I have one of her purse-baskets, which I carry to stomp dances. It is one of my most prized possessions because she made it for me. She had already lost parts of each leg due to severe diabetes and was in a wheelchair when she wove that beautiful basket.

4. The Cherokee word for wild greens is *so-tsv-na*, which I suspect is pronounced

sochan in an abbreviated form by dropping the final *a* or *uh* sound, like many other words spoken in certain dialects.

5. There are a number of cookbooks written by various Cherokee women from the Qualla Boundary, and I have seen a couple of these well-known cooks featured on regional cooking programs on television.

6. Gourds are native plants that are not edible but can be fashioned into water dippers, kitchen scoops, or birdhouses and painted on the outside to create beautiful and natural works of art. Each year on the Qualla Boundary a gourd celebration is held and Native and non-Native artists from all over bring their crafts to sell.

Works Cited

Alexander, J. T. *Dictionary of the Cherokee Indian Language.* Sperry, Okla.: n.p., 1971.
"Amphibians and Reptiles of North Carolina." Herps of North Carolina. http://
    herpsofnc.org/snakes. Accessed 28 May 2015.
Appalachian Outlaws. History Channel. www.history.com/shows/appalachian
    -outlaws. Accessed 10 June 2015.
Arch, Davy. Personal interview. Recorded by author, 19 June 2012. DVD.
Arneach, Lloyd. *Cherokee Bonfire.* Recorded by author, 29 June 2013. DVD.
———. *Cherokee Bonfire.* Recorded by author, 30 June 2013. DVD.
———. *Lloyd Arneach, Cherokee Storyteller.* www.arneach.com. Accessed 7 February
    2014.
Astrov, Margot, ed. "Introduction." In *The Winged Serpent: An Anthology of American
    Indian Prose and Poetry,* 15–27. New York: John Day, 1972.
Battiste, Marie, and James (Sa'ke'j) Youngblood Henderson. *Protecting Indigenous
    Knowledge and Heritage: A Global Challenge.* Saskatoon: Purich, 2000.
Bedford, Denton R. *Tsali.* San Francisco: Indian Historian Press, 1972.
Belt, Tom. Lecture. 5 October 2011. Western Carolina University, Cullowhee Campus.
———. Personal interview #1. Recorded by author, 11 January 2012. Western Carolina
    University, Cullowhee Campus.
———. Personal interview #2. Recorded by author, 15 October 2012. Western Carolina
    University, Cullowhee Campus.

———. Personal interview #3. Recorded by author, 16 March 2013. Kituwah Mound, Cherokee, N.C.

"Bernie Francis." Cape Breton University Press. http://cbup.ca/author/bfrancis. Accessed 2 November 2018.

Blaeser, Kimberly. "Intersections with the Oral Tradition." In *Gerald Vizenor: Writing in the Oral Tradition*, 15–37. Norman: University of Oklahoma Press, 1996.

Blanche, Jerry. *Native American Reader: Stories, Speeches, and Poems*. Juneau: Denali Press, 1990.

Breedlove, Nick. "Local Writer among Finalists for $25,000 Literary Prize." *Sylva (N.C.) Herald*, 10 June 2014.

Bruchac, Joseph, and Michael J. Caduto. *The Native Stories from Keepers of the Earth: Told by Joseph Bruchac*. Saskatoon: Fifth House, 1990.

Burnett, Private John G. "John Burnett's Story of the Trail of Tears." Assumption College. www1.assumption.edu/users/McClymer/his260/JohnBurnettTrail.html. Accessed 4 July 2015.

Cajete, Gregory. *Native Science: Natural Laws of Interdependence*. Santa Fe: Clear Light, 2000.

Carney, Virginia Moore. *Eastern Band Cherokee Women: Cultural Persistence in Their Letters and Speeches*. Knoxville: University of Tennessee Press, 2005.

Chamberlin, J. Edward. "Doing Things with Words: Putting Performance on the Page." In *Talking on the Page: Editing Aboriginal Oral Texts*, edited by Laura J. Murray and Keren Rice, 69–90. Toronto: University of Toronto Press, 1999.

Chavez, Will. "Eastern Band of Cherokees Opposes Energy Substation Near Kituwah." *Cherokee Phoenix*, 9 February 2010. www.cherokeephoenix.org/Article/index/3632. Accessed 5 June 2017.

———. "EBCI Council Designates Kituwah Mound 'Sacred Site.'" *Cherokee Phoenix*, 17 December 2013. www.cherokeephoenix.org/Article/Index/7842. Accessed 31 May 2014.

"Cherokee." Great Smoky Mountains National Park. National Park Service. www.nps.gov/grsm/index.htm. Accessed 6 February 2014.

Cherokee Historical Association. www.cherokeehistorical.org. Accessed 30 April 2014.

Cherokee One Feather Facebook Page. www.facebook.com/tsalaginews. Accessed 4 September 2014.

"Cherokee Removal." *New Georgia Encyclopedia*. www.georgiaencyclopedia.org/articles/history-archaeology/cherokee-removal. Accessed 18 July 2014.

"Cherokee Reservation Cooperative Extension." Cherokee Preservation Foundation. http://cherokeepreservation.org. Accessed 28 May 2015.

"Cherokee Smokies—About Cherokee." Cherokee Chamber of Commerce. www.cherokeesmokies.com/about_cherokee.html. Accessed 18 June 2015.

"Chief Hicks Speaks to Franklin Town Board about Nikwasi Mound." *Cherokee (N.C.) One Feather*, 4 March 2014. https://theonefeather.com/2014/03/chief-hicks-speaks-to-franklin-town-board-about-nikwasi-mound. Accessed 17 June 2014.

"Clapsaddle Receives Literary Award." *Cherokee (N.C.) One Feather*, 3 April 2012. https://theonefeather.com/2012/04/clapsaddle-receives-literary-award. Accessed 3 April 2012.

"Clingman's Dome." Great Smoky Mountains National Park. National Park Service. www.nps.gov/grsm/planyourvisit/clingmansdome.htm. Accessed 6 June 2015.

Cohen, David William. "The Undefining of Oral Tradition." *Ethnohistory* 36, no. 1 (Winter 1989): 9–18.

Conley, Robert J. *Cherokee Medicine Man: The Life and Work of a Modern-Day Healer.* Norman: University of Oklahoma Press, 2011.

———. *Sequoyah: A Novel of the Real People.* New York: St. Martin's Press, 2002.

———. *The Witch of Goingsnake and Other Stories.* Norman: University of Oklahoma Press, 1988.

Courlander, Harold. *The Fourth World of the Hopis: The Epic Story of the Hopi Indians as Preserved in Their Legends and Traditions.* Albuquerque: University of New Mexico Press, 1971.

Cherokee Preservation Foundation. "Cowee Cultural Corridor Development Project with LTLT." *Cherokee Preservation Foundation Ga-du-gi 2014*, 6–7. Cherokee, N.C.: Cherokee Preservation Foundation, 2014. http://cherokeepreservation.org/wp-content/uploads/2014/05/Ga-du-gi-2014FINALWEB.pdf.

Crow, Vernon H. *Storm in the Mountains: Thomas' Confederate Legion of Cherokee Indians and Mountaineers.* Cherokee, N.C.: Press of the Museum of the Cherokee Indian, 1982.

Deloria, Vine, Jr. "Sacred Places and Moral Responsibility." In *Spirit and Reason: The Vine Deloria Jr. Reader*, edited by Barbara Deloria, Kristen Foehner, and Samuel Scinta, 323–38. Golden, Colo.: Fulcrum, 1999.

"The Diary of Lt. John Phelps." *Journal of Cherokee Studies* 21 (2000). Special issue edited by Sarah Hill.

Digital Heritage: Connecting Appalachian Culture and Traditions with the World. http://digitalheritage.org/2012/11/lloyd-arneach-2011. Accessed 7 February 2014.

Duncan, Barbara. "Introduction." In *Myths of the Cherokee and Sacred Formulas of the Cherokees*, 1–21. Cherokee, N.C.: Cherokee Publications, 2006.

———. *Living Stories of the Cherokee.* Chapel Hill: University of North Carolina Press, 1998.

Dugan, Joyce. Personal interview. Recorded by author, 19 July 2016. DVD.

"Eastern Band Buys Cowee Mound." *Cherokee Phoenix*, 8 January 2007. www.cherokeephoenix.org/Article/index/1793. Accessed 16 June 2014.

Ehle, John. *Trail of Tears: The Rise and Fall of the Cherokee Nation.* New York: Doubleday, 1988.

"Ellen Bird Named EBCI Beloved Woman." *Cherokee (N.C.) One Feather*, 12 November 2013. https://theonefeather.com/2013/11/ellen-bird-named-ebci-beloved-woman. Accessed 12 November 2013.

Evans, Lawton B. "Gold in North Georgia: Lesson 62—Removal of the Cherokees." *First Lessons in Georgia History*. New York: American Book Company, 1929.

"Fading Voices." *Journal of Cherokee Studies* 14 (1989).

Feeling, Durbin. *Cherokee-English Dictionary*. Tahlequah, Okla.: Heritage, 1975.

Finger, John R. *Cherokee Americans: The Eastern Band of Cherokees in the Twentieth Century*. Lincoln: University of Nebraska Press, 1991.

———. *The Eastern Band of Cherokees, 1819–1900*. Knoxville: University of Tennessee Press, 1984.

"Fish Cherokee." Visit Cherokee North Carolina. http://visitcherokeenc.com/blog /entry/ready-to-fish-cherokee-heres-everything-you-need-to-know. Accessed 6 June 2015.

Fixico, Donald L. *The American Indian Mind in a Linear World: American Indian Studies and Traditional Knowledge*. New York: Routledge, 2009.

Fogelson, Raymond D. "Cherokee Little People Reconsidered." *Journal of Cherokee Studies* 7, no. 2 (Fall 1982): 92–98.

French, Laurence A. *The Qualla Cherokee: Surviving in Two Worlds*. Lewiston, N.Y.: Edwin Mellen Press, 1998.

"Ga-du-gi 2014." Cherokee Preservation Foundation. http://cherokeepreservation .org/tag/publication. Accessed 25 June 2015.

"Garden Club of Ellijay's Trail of Tears Memorial Project." Garden Club of Georgia. https://gardenclub.uga.edu/tearsmarker.html. Accessed 17 June 2015.

Geniusz, Wendy Makoons. *Our Knowledge Is Not Primitive: Decolonizing Botanical Anishinaabe Teachings*. Syracuse, N.Y.: Syracuse University Press, 2009.

"Gold Rush." *New Georgia Encyclopedia*. www.georgiaencyclopedia.org/articles /history-archaeology/gold-rush. Accessed 8 May 2014.

"Great Smoky Mountains National Park." National Park Service. www.nps.gov/grsm /index.htm. Accessed 28 April 2014.

Harris, Joel Chandler. *The Complete Tales of Uncle Remus*. Boston: Houghton-Mifflin, 1983.

Hill Witt, Shirley, and Stan Steiner, eds. *The Way: An Anthology of American Indian Literature*. New York: Vintage Books, 1972.

"Historical Marker Project: Trail of Tears." Historical Marker Project. www .historicalmarkerproject.com/markers/HM1TJ_trail-of-tears_Spencer-TN.html. Accessed 4 July 2015.

"History and Culture." Great Smoky Mountains National Park. National Park Service. www.nps.gov/grsm/learn/historyculture/index.htm. Accessed 2 May 2017.

Holland, T. J. "Cherokee Cosmography." Lecture at New Kituwah Academy, Cherokee, N.C., 27 February 2013.

———. "Cultural Researcher." In *Portraits of the Boundary: Cherokee Stories about Language, Culture and Tribal Sovereignty*. http://cherokeeportraits.ryancomfor tmedia.com/?s=T.+J.+Holland. Accessed 10 October 2014.

———. "Nunehi, Spirit Warriors." Lecture at New Kituwah Academy, Cherokee, N.C., 21 March 2013.

Holmes, Ruth Bradley, and Betty Sharp Smith. *Beginning Cherokee*. 2nd ed. Norman: University of Oklahoma Press, 1979.

Hudson, Charles. *The Southeastern Indians*. Knoxville: University of Tennessee Press, 1976.

———. "Uktena: A Cherokee Anomalous Monster." *Journal of Cherokee Studies* 3, no 2 (Spring 1978): 62–75.

Hulan, Renee, and Renate Eigenbrod, eds. *Aboriginal Oral Traditions: Theory, Practice, Ethics*. Halifax: Fernwood, 2008.

Hymes, Dell. "Ethnopoetics, Oral-Formulaic Theory, and Editing Texts." *Oral Tradition* 9, no. 2 (1994): 330–70.

Jackson, Gilliam. "Cultural Identity for the Modern Cherokees." *Appalachian Journal* 2, no. 4. (Summer 1975): 280–83.

"Jerry Wolfe Named Beloved Man." *Cherokee (N.C.) One Feather*, 12 April 2013. https://theonefeather.com/2013/04/jerry-wolfe-named-beloved-man. Accessed 12 April 2013.

"John Ross Home." Georgia Historical Society. https://georgiahistory.com/ghmi _marker_updated/john-ross-home. Accessed 21 June 2018.

Johnson, J. P. (Gvdusti doka). "Anetsodi." YouTube. www.youtube.com/watch?v=9iXQ _boUiTQ. Accessed 27 July 2014.

Johnston, Basil. *Tales the Elders Told: Ojibway Legends*. Toronto: Royal Ontario Museum, 1981.

Jones, Jean. "Hall Mountain Ownership Returns to EBCI." *Cherokee (N.C.) One Feather*, 4 June 2013. https://theonefeather.com/2013/06/hall-mountain-ownership -returns-to-ebci. Accessed 20 June 2014.

"Journey to Forgiveness and Healing to Begin May 18." *Cherokee (N.C.) One Feather*, 16 April 2012. https://theonefeather.com/2012/04/journey-to-forgiveness-and -healing-to-begin-may-18. Accessed 17 July 2014.

Jumper, Robert. "Re: Question on history of One Feather." December 2014. Email.

Justice, Daniel Heath. *Our Fire Survives the Storm: A Cherokee Literary History*. Minneapolis: University of Minnesota Press, 2006.

Kasper, Andrew. "Site Near Cowee Mound Saved from Development, Turned Over to Tribe." *Smoky Mountain News (Waynesville, N.C.)*, 5 June 2013. www .smokymountainnews.com/archives/item/10467-site-near-cowee-mound-saved-from-development-turned-over-to-tribe. Accessed 17 June 2014.

Kilpatrick, Anna G., and Jack F. Kilpatrick. "Chronicles of Wolftown: Social Documents of the North Carolina Cherokees, 1850–1862." *Bureau of American Ethnology, Bulletin 196*. Anthropological Papers, No. 75. Washington, D.C.: Smithsonian Institution, 1966.

———. "Eastern Cherokee Folktales: Reconstructed from the Field Notes of Frans M. Olbrechts." *Bureau of American Ethnology, Bulletin 196*. Anthropological Papers, No. 80. Washington, D.C.: Smithsonian Institution, 1966.

———. *Friends of Thunder: Folktales of the Oklahoma Cherokees*. Norman: University of Oklahoma Press, 1994.

King, Duane H. *The Cherokee Indian Nation: A Troubled History*. Knoxville: University of Tennessee Press, 1979.

———. "James Mooney, Ethnologist." *Journal of Cherokee Studies* 7, no. 1 (Spring 1982): 4–9.

King, Duane H., and David Fitzgerald. *The Cherokee Trail of Tears*. Portland: Graphic Arts Books, 2008.

King, Thomas. "Godzilla vs. Post-Colonial." *New Concepts of Canadian Criticism*. Peterborough, Ont.: Broadview Press, 1997.

———. *The Truth about Stories: A Native Narrative*. Toronto: House of Anansi Press, 2003.

"Kituwah Mound, NC (Eastern Cherokee) (2004) Research Report." The Pluralism Project, Harvard University. http://archive.li/Golx. Originally accessed 31 May 2014.

Kroeber, Karl. "An Introduction to the Art of Traditional American Indian Narration." In *Traditional Literatures of the American Indian*, 1–24. Lincoln: University of Nebraska Press, 1981.

———. *Native American Storytelling: A Reader of Myths and Legends*. Malden, Mass.: Blackwell, 2004.

Lankford, George E., ed. *Native American Legends: Southeastern Legends: Tales from the Natchez, Caddo, Biloxi, Chickasaw, and Other Nations*. Little Rock: August House, 1987.

Lawson, Alan. "Postcolonial Theory and the Settler Subject." *Essays on Canadian Writing* 56 (1995): 20–36.

Lincoln, Kenneth. "Native American Literatures." In *Smoothing the Ground: Essays on Native American Oral Literature*, 3–28. Berkeley: University of California Press, 1983.

Little Bear, Leroy. "Foreword." In *Native Science: Natural Laws of Interdependence*, by Gregory Cajete, ix–xii. Santa Fe: Clear Light, 2000.

Littlejohn, Kathi Smith. *Cherokee 2013 Fall Fair—Storytellers*. 9 October 2013. DVD.

———. "How the Opossum Lost His Beautiful Tail." *Cherokee Legends*. Vol. 3. 1990. CD.

———. "Nunnehi, the Gentle People." *Cherokee Legends*. Vol. 1. 1990. CD.

Lossiah, Bo. "Re: Lyrics for Cherokee National Anthem." Email message to author. 3 September 2014.

Mackey, Ryan. "Wahdi. Wednesday 12 June 2012." *Duyvkta*. Recorded by Mike Thompson. 2012. CD.

Mails, Thomas E. *The Cherokee People: The Story of the Cherokees from Earliest Origins to Contemporary Times*. New York: Marlowe, 1996.

Mankiller, Wilma, and Michael Wallis. *Mankiller: A Chief and Her People*. New York: St. Martin's Griffin, 2000.

Masayesva, Victor, Jr. "It shall not end anywhere: Transforming Oral Traditions." In *Talking on the Page: Editing Aboriginal Oral Texts*, edited by Laura J. Murray and Keren Rice, 91–95. Toronto: University of Toronto Press, 1999.

McClinton, Rowena. "Cherokee and Christian Expressions of Spirituality through First Parents: Eve and Selu." In *The Native South: New Histories and Enduring Legacies*, edited by Tim Alan Garrison and Greg O'Brien, 70–83. Lincoln: University of Nebraska Press, 2017.

McGowan, Kay. "Seven Clans of the Cherokee." *Indian World News (Detroit, Mich.)*, January 1996.

McGregor, Deborah. "Coming Full Circle: Indigenous Knowledge, Environment, and Our Future." *American Indian Quarterly* 28, nos. 3–4 (Summer/Fall 2004): 385–410.

McKie, Scott. "Author: Cherokee Little People Are Real." *Cherokee (N.C.) One Feather*, 18 July 2014. https://theonefeather.com/2014/07/author-cherokee-little-people-are-real. Accessed 23 July 2014.

———. "Kituwah to Be Protected 'in Perpetuity.'" *Cherokee (N.C.) One Feather*, 16 December 2013. https://theonefeather.com/2013/12/kituwah-to-be-protected-in-perpetuity. Accessed 9 June 2014.

———. "NPS Proposes Tribal Exemption for Plant Gathering." *Cherokee (N.C.) One Feather*, 4 May 2015. https://theonefeather.com/2015/05/nps-proposes-tribal-exemption-for-plant-gathering. Accessed 24 May 2015.

———. "NPS to Allow Traditional Gathering in Parks." *Cherokee (N.C.) One Feather*, 11 July 2016. https://theonefeather.com/2016/07/nps-to-allow-traditional-gathering-in-parks. Accessed 19 April 2017.

———. "Remember the Removal Riders Embark on Their Journey." *Cherokee (N.C.) One Feather*, 30 May 2014. https://theonefeather.com/2014/05/remember-the-removal-riders-embark-on-their-journey. Accessed 6 July 2014.

———. "Tribal Members Training for Remember the Removal Ride." *Cherokee (N.C.) One Feather*, 25 March 2011. https://theonefeather.com/2011/03/tribal-members-training-for-remember-the-removal-ride. Accessed 18 July 2014.

McLeod, Neal. *Cree Narrative Memory: From Treaties to Contemporary Times*. Saskatoon: Purich, 2007.

McLoughlin, William G. *After the Trail of Tears: The Cherokees' Struggle for Sovereignty, 1839–1880*. Chapel Hill: University of North Carolina Press, 1993.

Meredith, Howard, and Mary Ellen Meredith. *Reflection on Cherokee Literary Expression*. Native American Studies, Vol. 12. Lewiston, N.Y.: Edwin Mellen Press, 2003.

Mooney, James. "Cherokee Theory and Practice of Medicine." *Journal of American Folklore* 3, no. 8 (January–March 1890): 44–50.

———. *Cherokee History, Myths and Sacred Formulas*. Cherokee, N.C.: Cherokee Publications, 2006.

———. "Myths of the Cherokee." *Journal of American Folklore* 1, no. 2 (July–September 1888): 97–108.

———. *Myths of the Cherokee; and, Sacred Formulas of the Cherokees*. From 19th and 7th Annual Reports, Bureau of American Ethnology. 1891, 1900. Reprint, Nashville: Charles and Randy Elder–Booksellers Publishers, 1982.

Murphy, Jami. "Cherokee Language Available on iPhone and iPod Touch." *Cherokee Phoenix*, 24 September 2010. www.cherokeephoenix.org/Article/index/4000. Accessed 15 April 2017.

Muse, Sandra. "The Nikwasi Sacred Mound: Celtic Overwriting of a Cherokee Village." Celts in the Americas Conference. St. Francis Xavier University, Cape Breton, Nova Scotia, 29 June–2 July 2011.

———. "North America's Oldest 'Monsters': The Beasts That Haunt the Forests and Hills of Tsalagi Country." Ghost Stories: Hauntings and Echoes in Literature and Culture Conference. McGill University, Montreal, 27 January 2012.

Neely, Sharlotte. *Snowbird Cherokees: People of Persistence*. Athens: University of Georgia Press, 1991.

"New Echota Historic Site." Georgia State Parks and Historic Sites. http://explore .gastateparks.org/info/106. Accessed 19 July 2014.

"One Feather Poll Result: Should the EBCI Be Given the Option to Take Over the Care and Upkeep of the Nikwasi Mound?" *Cherokee (N.C.) One Feather*, 11 July 2012. https://theonefeather.com/2012/07/one-feather-poll-result-should-the-ebci-be -given-the-option-to-take-over-the-care-and-upkeep-of-the-nikwasi-mound. Accessed 20 June 2014.

Ong, Walter. *Orality and Literacy: The Technologizing of the Word*. New York: Routledge, 1991.

Oral Histories of the Indian Removal "Trail of Tears" as Told by Members of the Eastern Band of Cherokee Indians. Qualla Boundary, N.C.: Cherokee Culture and Language Program, 2005. DVD.

Ortiz, Simon. "Introduction." In *Speaking for the Generations: Native Writers on Writing*. Tucson: University of Arizona Press, 1998.

———. "Towards a National Indian Literature: Cultural Authenticity in Nationalism." *Melus* 8, no. 2 (Summer 1982): 7–12.

Owle, Freeman. *Bonfire Storytelling*. Recorded by author, 6 June 2012. DVD.

Parker, G. Keith. *Seven Cherokee Myths: Creation, Fire, the Primordial Parents, the Nature of Evil, the Family, Universal Suffering, and Communal Obligation*. Jefferson, N.C.: McFarland, 2006.

Parker, Sara Gwyneth. "The Transformation of Cherokee Appalachia." PhD diss., University of California, Berkeley, 1991.

Perdue, Theda. *Cherokee Women: Gender and Culture Change, 1700–1835*. Lincoln: University of Nebraska Press, 1998.

Perdue, Theda, and Michael Green. *The Cherokee Removal: A Brief History with Documents*. Boston: Bedford/St. Martin's, 2005.

Petrone, Penny. *Native Literature in Canada: From the Oral Tradition to the Present*. Toronto: Oxford University Press, 1990.

"Pilot Mountain State Park." North Carolina State Parks. www.ncparks.gov/pilot -mountain-state-park. Accessed June 21, 2012.

Purrington, Burton L. "Reassessing Cherokee Studies." *Appalachian Journal* 2, no. 4 (Summer 1975): 252–57.

"Red Clay State Park." Tennessee State Parks. https://tnstateparks.com/parks/red-clay. Accessed 19 July 2014.

Reed, Jeannie, ed. *Stories of the Yunwi Tsunsdi: The Cherokee Little People.* English 102 Class Project, Western Carolina University, March 1991.

"Remember the Removal Cyclists Study Cherokee History at Museum of the Cherokee Indian." *Cherokee (N.C.) One Feather,* 8 March 2014. https://theonefeather .com/2014/03/remember-the-removal-cyclists-study-cherokee-history-at-muse-um-of-the-cherokee-indian. Accessed 19 July 2014.

Riggs, Brett. Personal interview. Recorded by author, 12 July 2016. DVD.

"Right Path Leadership Program Syllabus." Right Path "Du-yu dv-i," Adult Leadership Program. Email from Juanita Wilson. 27 June 2014.

"Right Path Program Summary." Right Path "Du-yu dv-i," Adult Leadership Program. Email from Juanita Wilson. 27 June 2014.

Roemer, Kenneth M. "Native American Oral Narratives: Context and Continuity." In *Smoothing the Ground: Essays on Native American Oral Literature,* edited by Brian Swann, 39–54. Berkeley: University of California Press, 1983.

Ruoff, A. LaVonne Brown. "American Indian Oral Literatures." *American Quarterly* 33, no. 3 (1981): 327–38.

Schmidt, David L., and Murdena Marshall. "A Brief History of the Hieroglyphs." In *Mi'kmaq Hieroglyphics Prayers: Readings in North America's First Indigenous Script,* 4–15. Halifax: Nimbus, 2006.

ShelHarrell. "Duke Energy Project Threatens Sacred Kituwah Site." *Western Carolinian,* 20 April 2010. www.westerncarolinian.com/news/view.php/417774 /Duke-Energy-project-threatens-sacred-Kit. Accessed 5 June 2017.

Snyder, Sara L. "Poetics, Performance, and Translation in Eastern Cherokee Language Revitalization." PhD diss., Columbia University, 2016.

Standley, Max D. *The Trail of Tears* Series. www.maxdstandley.com/trail_of_tears_series /tot_series.html. Accessed 18 June 2015.

"Stick Ball." Cherokee Heritage Center, Tahlequah, Oklahoma. www.cherokeeheritage .org/attractions/stick-ball. Accessed 27 July 2014.

"Storytelling—Cherokee Fall Fair." *Fall Fair 2013.* 2 October 2013. DVD.

Strickland, Rennard. *Fire and the Spirits: Cherokee Law from Clan to Court.* Norman: University of Oklahoma Press, 1982.

Sturgis, Sue. "Cherokees Fight Duke Energy Substation near Sacred Site in North Carolina." *Facing South,* 9 February 2010. www.facingsouth.org/2010/02/cherokees -fight-duke-energy-substation-near-sacred-site-in-north-carolina.html. Accessed 5 June 2017.

Swann, Brian. "Introduction." In *Smoothing the Ground: Essays on Native American Oral Literature,* xi–xix. Berkeley: University of California Press, 1983.

Teuton, Christopher B. "Applying Oral Concepts to Written Traditions." In *Reasoning Together: The Native Critics Collective*, edited by Craig S. Womack, Daniel Heath Justice, and Christopher B. Teuton, 193–215. Norman: University of Oklahoma Press, 2008.

———. *Cherokee Stories of the Turtle Island Liars' Club*. Chapel Hill: University of North Carolina Press, 2012.

———. "Interpreting Our World: Authority and the Written Word in Robert J. Conley's Real People Series." *Modern Fiction Studies* 53, no. 3 (2007): 544–68.

Thomas, Robert K. "Cherokee Values and World View." Master's thesis, University of North Carolina at Chapel Hill, 1958.

"Tsali." *Oral Histories of the Indian Removal "Trail of Tears" as Told by Members of the Eastern Band of Cherokee Indians*. Cherokee Culture and Language Program. 2005. DVD.

"Tsalagi Storytellers Roundtable." *Eastern Cherokee Storytellers Meeting at Oconaluftee Indian Village*. Recorded by author. 17 October 2013. CD.

Tuhiwai Smith, Linda. *Decolonizing Methodologies: Research and Indigenous Peoples*. London: Zed Books, 1999.

"'Unto These Hills' Outdoor Drama." Visit Cherokee North Carolina. http://visit cherokeenc.com/play/attractions/unto-these-hills-outdoor-drama. Accessed 30 April 2014.

Vest, Jay Hansford C. *Native American Oralcy: Interpretations of Indigenous Thought*. Vernon, B.C.: Charlton, 2014.

Visit Cherokee North Carolina. 2014. http://visitcherokeenc.com/#home. Accessed 8 February 2014.

Vizenor, Gerald. *Manifest Manners: Narratives on Postindian Survivance*. Lincoln: University of Nebraska Press, 1999.

Wahinkpe Topa (Four Arrows) [Don Trent Jacobs]. "Introduction." In *Unlearning the Language of Conquest: Scholars Expose Anti-Indianism in America*, 19–20. Austin: University of Texas Press, 2006.

Weaver, Jace. *That the People Might Live: Native American Literatures and Native American Community*. New York: Oxford University Press, 1997.

Weaver, Jace, Craig S. Womack, and Robert Warrior. *American Indian Literary Nationalism*. Albuquerque: University of New Mexico Press, 2006.

Wetmore, Ruth Y. *First on the Land: The North Carolina Indians*. Winston-Salem, N.C.: Blair, 1975.

Wheeler, Kip. "Freytag's Pyramid." Carson-Newman University. https://web.cn.edu /kwheeler/freytag.html. Accessed 23 November 2014.

"Why Is the Cowee Mound So Important to the Cherokee People?" Project Cowee Reconnection. 3 August 2010. www.facebook.com/Project-Cowee-Reconnection -125544504151432. Accessed 16 June 2014.

Williams, Samuel Cole, ed. *Lieut. Henry Timberlake's Memoirs: 1756–1765*. Signal Mountain, Tenn.: Signal Mountain Press, 2001.

Wilson, Juanita. Phone interview. 23 June 2014.

Witthoft, John, and Wendell S. Hadlock. "Cherokee-Iroquois Little People." *Journal of American Folklore* 59, no. 234 (October–December 1946): 413–22.

Womack, Craig. *Red on Red: Native American Literary Separatism.* Minneapolis: University of Minnesota Press, 1999.

Womack, Craig, Daniel Heath Justice, and Christopher B. Teuton, eds. *Reasoning Together: The Native Critics Collective.* Norman: University of Oklahoma Press, 2008.

Words That Come before All Else: Environmental Philosophies of the Haudenosaunee. Haudenosaunee Environmental Task Force. Cornwall Island, Ontario: Native North American Travelling College, 1992.

"Writing the Inuit Language." Inuktut Tusaalanga. https://tusaalanga.ca/node/2505. Accessed 2 November 2018.

Zolbrod, Paul. *Reading the Voice: Native American Oral Poetry on the Page.* Salt Lake City: University of Utah Press, 1995.

Index

Haudenosaunee, 255n22, 257n1, 260n6, 275n51
Hayward, Jeremy, 182
"The Healing Lake" story (retold by Arneach), 169–70
Henderson, Sa'ke'j Youngblood, 42, 62
Henry, Jeanette, 268n38
Hicks, Michell, 20, 234, 237–38, 239, 276n57
holiday celebrations, 173. *See also* ceremonies; Fall Fair
Holland, T. J.: on Mooney's ethnographic work, 261n13; on Nunehi stories, 147–48, 151–52, 153; on Tsali story, 187–89; on Tsutlakalv story, 133, 135–36; Uktena story retold by, 258n7; on vitality of oral tradition, 194–95
homelands, 32–33, 37–38, 84, 147–49. *See also* land politics
Hopi, 159, 253n9
horned owl, 257n. *See also* Tskili
horned serpent. *See* Uktena
horses, 171
"How Bear Lost His Tail" story (retold by Arneach), 168–69
"How the Animals Got Fire" story (retold by Arneach), 45–46, 173, 254n12
"How the Deer Got His Antlers" story (retold by Arneach), 166–67, 243
"How the Hummingbird Brought Back the Tobacco" story, 173, 184–85
"How the Opossum Lost His Beautiful Tail" story (retold by Littlejohn), 198–99, 266n21, 270n8, 270n10
"How the World Was Made" story (retold by Mooney), 35–36
Hudson, Charles: *The Southeastern Indians*, 100; on Uktena, 94, 95, 97, 98

hunting: disease from overhunting, 175; as lifeway, 57–58; songs and rituals of, 68, 69, 102, 104, 132, 256n29, 259n15, 261n12

immersion school. *See* New Kituwah Immersion Academy
Immortals. *See* Nunehi
inadv, 68–69, 89, 94, 246, 256nn34–35, 262n18. *See also* Copperhead; Uktena; Utsonadi
interdependence of animals and humans, 39–44, 70, 86–87, 97, 98, 169, 173, 253n3. *See also* traditional ecological knowledge (TEK)
interpersonal conflict, 161–63
Inuit, 99, 250n25, 258n13
Irish heritage and oral tradition, 20, 124, 251n38
Itagunuhi, 22, 35, 95

Jackson, Andrew, 185, 272n24, 273n28
Jackson, Gilliam, 201, 272n20
Jarvis, Jonathan B., 140
Jessan, 22
Johnston, Basil, 40, 174
Journal of American Folklore, 23
Journal of Cherokee Studies, 206, 271n19
"Journey to Forgiveness and Healing" event, 220
Judacullah (spiritual being). *See* Tsutlakalv
Judaculla Rock, 134–35, 137, 249n23, 261n18
Judeo-Christian tradition: Adam and Eve story in, 63; of baptismal ritual, 177, 265n16; Cherokee conversions to, 82, 266n22; Cherokee translations of literary works in, 209, 272n23; on magic and supernatural, 60–61, 71; and Tsutlakalv story, 136; on women's bodies, 104. *See also* colonialism

Jumper, Bessie, 120
Junaluska (man), 273n28
Junaluska Museum, 16, 249n22,
258n7, 271n18. *See also* Snowbird
community
Justice, Daniel Heath, 25, 172–73

Kanane'ski Amai'yehi, 7, 46–49, 84,
111, 148, 175, 246, 254n13
Kanati, 49–64, 255nn23–24, 261n12
"Kana'ti and Selu: The Origin of
Game and Corn" story (retold by
Mooney), 49–56, 57, 60, 255n17
Kanienkehaka, 53, 64, 141–42, 175,
262n26
Kilpatrick, Anna Gritts, 8, 16, 48,
252n46, 254n14
Kilpatrick, Jack, 8, 16, 48, 252n46
King, Thomas, 165–66, 177
Kituwah (town). *See* Mothertown
Kituwah, as term, 204–5, 247n1,
248n8
Kituwah Celebrations, 194, 228–29,
236–37, 275nn48–49
Kituwah Mound, 209, 221–33,
274nn40–41, 275n50
Kituwah Society, 205
Kroeber, Karl, 63, 71, 100, 155
Kruger, John, 199
Kuwahi, 67–68, 256n30

Lakota, 139–40, 254n16, 266n23
land politics: government-appropriated
sacred places, 139–41, 219–20,
254n16; homeland treaties and
land loss, 164, 183–84, 189,
267nn26–28; plant gathering
regulations, 140, 253n5, 262n25; of
Qualla Boundary, 159–60, 249n14;
renaming of sacred places, 56–57,
68, 260n8; during Revolutionary

War, 263n41. *See also* homelands;
mounds, sacred; Removal
landscape, description of, 88–89
Land Trust for the Little Tennessee
(River), 234
language: digital adaptations of, 17;
education and instruction of, 201,
250n30, 250nn26–27; features
of, 182; greetings, 158, 264n1;
Inuktitut writing system, 250n25;
and Judaculla Rock carvings, 135,
249n23; and literacy, 16, 17–18,
250n30; Mi'kmaq writing system,
250n25; orality and nature-based
knowledge, 42–43; reference books
on, 272n23; syllabary writing
system, 16–17, 21–22, 135, 250n25;
translations and oral tradition,
11–12, 249n17; use of English for
modern Cherokee literature, 172;
vitality of, 44–45, 194, 254n11,
269n3. *See also* Cherokee nationalism; oral tradition
Laurel People, 122. *See also* Little
People
Lawson, Alan, 140
leadership program, 202–5, 270n12
leeches, 261n14
legend, as term, 10, 98–99, 126, 139,
264n4
"Legends of the Uk'tena" story (retold
by Arch), 91–92
leprechauns, 124, 126. *See also* Little
People
Lightning, 61, 62, 63
Lincoln, Kenneth, 81
Lindneux, Robert, 273n32
literary criticism, 24–27, 193–94
Little Bear, Leroy, 180, 181, 182
Little Deer, 65, 68, 71
Littlejohn, Kathi Smith: background
and orality of, 196–97; *Cherokee*

motherhood, role of, 59–60

Mothertown: annual Kituwah Celebration, 194, 228–29, 236–37, 275nn48–49; Fire story about, 48, 237; Kituwah Mound, 209, 221–33; name of, 204–5. *See also* Cherokee nationalism

mounds, sacred, 263n32; Cowee, 233–37, 256n33, 276n55; Etowah, 5; Kituwah, 209, 221–33, 274nn40–41, 275n50; Nikwasi, 148–52, 233, 237–39, 263n38, 263n41, 274n39

Mt. Rushmore, 139–40, 254n16

Mulberry Place, 67–68, 141, 256n30

Muse, John, 4–5, 220, 251n37, 252n49, 265n9

Muse, Lenora Sellers, 3–7, 265n9

Muse, Lester, 265n9

Museum of the Cherokee Indian, 20, 36, 160, 219

mystery, as term, 41–42, 262n24

myth, as term, 10, 98–99, 126, 139, 264n4

Myths of the Cherokee (Mooney), 8, 20, 177, 251n36, 251n41

national anthem, 195–96

nationalism. *See* Cherokee nationalism

national parks, 139–40, 170, 254n16. *See also* Great Smoky Mountains National Park

Native American Church, 24, 252n44

Native American Legends (ed. Lankford), 254n12

Native American Oralcy (Vest), 42

Native American Reader (Blanche), 9, 197–98

Native literary criticism, 24–27, 193–94

Native Literature in Canada (Petrone), 11

Native science, 30, 38–39, 44, 180–82. *See also* traditional ecological knowledge (TEK)

Native Science (Cajete), 29–30, 180, 182

The Native Stories from Keepers of the Earth (Bruchac and Caduto), 13

natural elements, 61–63, 80–82, 88–89, 142

Neely, Sharlotte, 209

Nelson, Paula Maney, 195, 243

New Echota, Georgia, 5, 219, 220, 248n5, 265n9, 273n33

New Kituwah Immersion Academy, 17, 196, 201, 250n26, 254n11

Nigaya'iso gadugi nitsvnesdi, 28

Nikwasi Mound, 148–52, 233, 237–39, 263n38, 263n41, 274n39

"The Nikwasi Mound" story (retold by Owle), 150–51

Nockasee, 148

nonaggression as social behavior, 161–63

normal, as term, 260n10

North Carolina Cherokees. *See* Eastern Band of Cherokee Indians (EBCI)

Nudele yvwi dideyohdi. *See* oral tradition

Nugatsani, 148

Nunehi, 133, 137–38, 143–54, 263n29

Nunehi, as term, 261n15, 263n28, 263n34

"Nunnehi, The Gentle People" story (retold by Littlejohn), 143–44, 152

"The Nunne'hi and Other Spirit Folk" story (retold by Mooney), 117–19, 145–47

"Nun'yunu'wi, The Stone Man" story (retold by Mooney), 101–2, 258n14

Nunyunuwi story, 101–6, 258n14, 259n15

Nvno unitsoyilv. *See* Trail of Tears

Nvnunyi, 148

Unlearning the Language of Conquest (Topa), 45
Unto These Hills outdoor drama, 160, 185, 187, 190, 268nn33–34
Usdi, Wil, 184, 185–91, 233, 267n28, 269n44, 271n14
Usgaseti, as term, 87, 127, 257n. *See also* Dusgaseti
"U'tlun'ta, the Spear-finger" story (retold by Mooney), 106–9
Utlvta, 106–12, 259n16
Utsonadi, 69, 73, 74, 77–78, 90–92

Vann, Joseph, 5, 248n6
Vizenor, Gerald, 10, 44

Wachacha, 218, 273n28
Wachacha, Maggie, 276n57
Wafford, James D., 22, 234, 261n14
Wahde, 204–5, 271n15
Wahuhu', 46, 245, 259n19
Walker, Amy, 274n37
Walker, Becky, 274n37
Walkingstick women's shelter, 274n44
Warrior, Robert, 9
water, ritual and spiritual connection to, 176–77, 265n16, 266n20, 271n17
Water Beetle, 34–35, 42, 266n19
Water Spider, 7, 46–49, 84, 111, 148, 175, 246, 254n13
The Way: An Anthology of American Indian Literature, 10
Weaver, Jace, 9, 26–27, 210–11
weaving: basket weaving, 14, 70–71, 161, 203, 251n42; finger-weaving, 14, 211, 249n19, 272n25
western Cherokee. *See* Cherokee Nation (CN); United Keetoowah Band (UKB)
Western science, 181–82
Wild Boy, 50–56, 57, 63

wild foods. *See* food gathering, as lifeway
Wild Potato clan, 197, 248n9
wild ramps, 39, 253nn5–6
Wilson, Jeremy, 235, 236–37
Wilson, Juanita, 202
wisdom stories, as term, 9–10
witches. *See* Dusgaseti stories (dreadful); Tskili
The Witch of Goingsnake and Other Stories (Conley), 8, 62, 100, 259n21
"The Witch of Goingsnake" story (retold by Conley), 110–11
Witt, Shirley Hill, 10
Witthoft, John, 124, 125
Wolf clan, 53, 64, 141–42, 175, 262n26
Wolfe, Alexander, 139
Wolfe, Jerry, 16, 236, 276n57
Wolftown community, 236, 252nn47–48
Womack, Craig, 9, 24–25, 172, 211; *Red on Red*, 24, 193–94
women: as Cherokee leaders, 60, 255n25; division of labor, 57–58; land control by, 222–23; moon-time power of, 104–6; self-sacrifice in creation stories by, 59–60, 255nn22–23; shelter for, 274n44
woodcarving, 203
word weaving, 249n19
wrestling, 209

Yona, 64–67, 256n29, 267n28
Yonaguska, Chief, 184, 190, 216, 267n28
Yunwi Tsunsdi, 114–26, 206
Yvwi, as term, 19, 28, 251n34
Yvwi Tsunsdi, 114–26, 206

Zolbrod, Paul: on oral poetics, 71, 93, 134, 265n14; on physical/spiritual life, 92, 96, 100; *Reading the Voice*, 37; on sacredness, 154–55